Japan was ruled by warriors for the better part of a millennium. From the twelfth to the nineteenth century its political history was dominated by the struggle of competing leagues of fighting men. This paperback volume, comprised of chapters selected from volumes 3 and 4 of *The Cambridge History of Japan,* traces the institutional development of warrior rule and dominance. Among the topics discussed are the gradual nature of the shift from court aristocrats to military hegemons, the epic battles between the Taira and the Minamoto in the 1180s, the development of a new system of justice, and the fall of Kamakura – which was related to the great invasions launched by the Mongol emperor of China in 1274 and 1281. In addition to discussing the transitions between various regimes, the book describes the proliferation of Akutō, or outlaw bands; the rising level of violence, treachery, and revolt among the military leaders and contenders; and the building of a Tokugawa order. By the eighteenth century, warrior rule had come full circle. Centuries of peace brought a transformation and bureaucratization of the samurai class. Warrior values remained central to the ethical code of modern Japan, however. After the Meiji government was secure, its leaders designed their education and codes to preserve the values of loyalty and fortitude on which their warrior ancestors had prided themselves.

Warrior rule in Japan

WARRIOR RULE IN JAPAN

Edited by
MARIUS B. JANSEN
Princeton University

Published by the Press Syndicate of the University of Cambridge
The Pitt Building, Trumpington Street, Cambridge CB2 1RP
40 West 20th Street, New York, NY 10011-4211, USA
10 Stamford Road, Oakleigh, Melbourne 3166, Australia

First published 1995

Printed in the United States of America

Library of Congress Cataloging-in-Publication Data
Warrior rule in Japan / edited by Marius B. Jansen.
p. cm.
Includes bibliographical references and index.
ISBN 0-521-48239-9. – ISBN 0-521-48404-9 (pbk.)
1. Japan – Politics and government – 1185–1600. 2. Japan – Politics and government – 1600–1868. 3. Samurai – History. 4. Feudalism – Japan. 5. Feudalism – Japan. I. Jansen, Marius B.
DS857.W27 1995
952′.02–DC20 94-43177
CIP

A catalog record for this book is available from the British Library.

ISBN 0-521-48239-9 Hardback
ISBN 0-521-48404-9 Paperback

CONTENTS

PREFACE

Japan was ruled by warriors for the better part of a millennium. From the twelfth to the nineteenth century its political history was dominated by the struggle of competing leagues of fighting men. These centuries left a lasting imprint on the country's values and society. *Bushi,* "fighting men," and *samurai,* "those who serve," developed a rhetoric with emphases of loyalty and courage and worked out a code that came to be known as "Bushidō," the Way of the Warrior. A stern and ruthless ethic had no tolerance for compromise or defeat. Honor to name and family counted for more than life, and failure permitted only one honorable exit, the grisly self-immolation of *seppuku* or, the more vulgar term, *hara-kiri*. Leaders attracted followings of "house men," *gokenin,* who became in time their vassals and were entrusted with land and followers. The title of *sei-i-tai-shōgun,* "Supreme Commander Against the Barbarians," which had been used as a temporary commission for frontier wars in northern Japan, became a hereditary term that signified the "head of the warrior houses," *buke no tōryō*. It was vested successively in three lines, the Minamoto (1192–1333), Ashikaga (1333–1572), and Tokugawa (1605–1868).

The essays that follow, taken from volumes 3 and 4 of *The Cambridge History of Japan,* trace the institutional development of warrior rule and dominance. It is convenient to begin with the typology proposed by John W. Hall, who described a "familial" structure of rule that interacted with a more "imperial-bureaucratic" strain. From the middle of the third century to the middle of the seventh, "government in Japan was exercised by a hierarchy of ruling families whose authority, though secured originally by military force, was ultimately rationalized on the basis of lineage and exerted along the lines of kin relationship."[1] Although its claims were recorded only in the eighth century and then probably in response to new challenges, the imperial line, which professed descent from the Sun Goddess, came to stand at the

1 *Government and Local Power in Japan 500 to 1700: A Study Based on Bizen Province* (Princeton, N.J.: Princeton University Press, 1966), p. 6.

apex of this system. This sacerdotal and lineal priority gave it immense prestige and unchallenged legitimacy in the contention for power, with the result that not even warrior rule seriously endangered its position and priority.

From the seventh through the tenth centuries the powerful model of the bureaucratic states of Korea and especially China served to supplement this familial pattern with one of centralization and officialdom. It did not so much replace as add to the presuppositions of family and hierarchy that had existed earlier. The moral claims of the Chinese ruler as Son of Heaven were now added to divine authority. Power to administer the provinces and to regulate and tax landholdings through bureaucratic appointments, as was the case in the continental model, however, was soon altered by special arrangements that were made for great families and temples. Public land was privatized in *shōen* or estates, and at the capital high offices became monopolized by the great Fujiwara clan, whose founders had been instrumental in cloaking the sovereign with his new authority as Chinese-style ruler. At Heiankyō, or "Capital of Tranquility and Peace," as Kyoto was called, an increasingly rigid hierarchy of aristocrats controlled the workings of government while the Fujiwara, through intermarriage with the imperial line, determined the course of official appointment and routine. This bred an aristocratic society that offered little opportunity or tolerance to those outside its inner circle, and one better qualified to cultivate the gracious life depicted in the *Tale of Genji* than to keep order in a country in which exile from the capital meant cultural dessication and social exile for aristocrats. Recent studies of the development of Japan's warrior caste, on the other hand, make clear that Nara and Heian Japan were far from achieving the centralization that central edicts of the time suggested, and that local strongmen were accommodated by naming them commanders of the newly established militia.[2]

Jeffrey Mass's essay on the Kamakura bakufu emphasizes the gradual nature of the shift from court aristocrats to military hegemons. The early warrior leaders, he points out, were "military nobles" who were

2 Two recent works, though they differ sharply on many specific points, agree that there were important continuities between the Nara-Heian and Kamakura military developments. See Karl E. Friday, *Hired Swords: The Rise of Private Warriors in Early Japan* (Stanford, Calif.: Stanford University Press, 1992), and William Wayne Farris, *Heavenly Warriors: The Evolution of Japan's Military, 500–1300* (Cambridge, Mass.: Harvard University Press, 1993). Reviews highlight their differences: See Farris on Friday in *The Journal of Japanese Studies* 19, No. 2 (Summer 1993):456–9, and Friday on Farris in *Monumenta Nipponica*, 48, No. 2 (Summer 1993):261–4.

allied with provincial interests that felt discriminated against by the central hierarchy, and sprang from junior lines of houses hardly less illustrious than those at court. In the mid-twelfth century they were called upon by the Kyoto aristocrats to settle disagreements and disturbances, but once conscious of their power they did not return to subordinate positions. Yet their goals were more often to substitute themselves for their superiors than to reform the entire system. Taira Kiyomori was able, and Minamoto Yoritomo wanted, to place a daughter as imperial consort the way the Fujiwara had. Yoritomo placed more value on the high rank he received from the court than he did on the title of shogun, which he received in 1192 and soon passed on to his young son. It was the function of the Hōjō, who came to dominate the Kamakura regime, in their "need of an object for a regency, to invest the title of shogun with both a future and a past."

The warfare between the Taira and the Minamoto in the 1180s led to a new order, one dominated by the military. The epic battles of the two hosts, each led by aristocratic warriors, became the subject of legend and romance. In the aftermath of war Yoritomo, having eliminated possible dangers from within his clan and from rivals in the north, established his own military headquarters, or *bakufu*, at the eastern coastal town of Kamakura. From there he consolidated his dominance over the Kyoto court by seeing to it that lines of authority led from Kamakura to the provinces. The central device in this development was to force from the court permission to appoint *jitō*, or stewards, to private estates or *shōen*. The office served both as reward for his followers and as a device to control the warriors. Next came the appointment of *shugo*, provincial-level figures who were expected to perform guard duty at Kyoto, survey local order and crimes, and serve as officials of the new system of justice that was established.

In 1219 the murder of Yoritomo's heir brought new changes. Fictive relatives continued to be appointed to the office of shogun, but the Hōjō line of regents now came to dominate the Kamakura regime. In all of this the wishes of the emperor, reigning or retired (as *in*, or "cloistered emperor," so called because he usually took Buddhist vows in a nominal withdrawal from active contention) counted for little. In 1221 the retired emperor Gotoba challenged Kamakura dominance by attempting to pass out rewards to military figures on his own, but the force he raised was speedily defeated and he himself exiled.

The shuffle of grants of land that followed this incident contributed to important developments in the dispensing of justice, as the aggrieved and newly appointed made their way to Kamakura to plead for justice. Recently appointed stewards needed policing. In a society that was, as Mass puts it, "lawless yet litigious, restive yet still respectful of higher authority," the bakufu's efforts to regularize procedures and guard against flagrant miscarriages of justice brought codes of procedure, new standards of evidence, and provision for face-to-face confrontation between litigants.

All Kamakura institutions coexisted with the Kyoto administrative structure, and the profusion of claims between estate managers, proprietors, *jitō*, and *shugo* guaranteed a complex structure of decision and appeal in which litigation could often go on for years. Most *shugo* resided in their original base or in Kamakura, so that opportunities for troublemakers in the provinces were plentiful.

In time Kyoto and Kamakura procedures came to resemble each other. Shadow shoguns dealt with shadow emperors. *Jitō* positions were hereditary, and Kyoto took on some of the devices of Kamakura in legal procedures and institutions. In Kamakura days the bakufu remained an overlay, albeit an increasingly powerful one, on the aristocratic pattern of earlier government. In future centuries it gradually became an alternative.[3]

Professor Ishii's essay treats the fall of Kamakura. He relates this to the great invasions launched by the Mongol emperor of China in 1274 and 1281. The defeat of those attempts, which were probably the largest amphibious operations in history up to that time, contributed to the mystique of Japan as a land whose valiant defenders were favored by the gods, who had sent the "divine wind" (*kamikaze*) to destroy the invading hosts.

The essay makes it clear that the fighting weakened the bakufu because the fact that it was waged against a foreign foe meant that there were no lands with which bakufu vassals could be rewarded for their valor. Loyalties were further weakened because the bakufu took the occasion of the emergency to try to increase its power over the southwestern island of Kyushu. These considerations pose interesting questions for the impact of Japan's isolation from continental politics on its failure to develop a stronger central government before modern times. Historians often credit the early development of nation-states in Europe to the emergencies created by foreign war, and it is interesting to see how, in this case, considerations of defense combined with power plays by the regime. Equally interesting, however, is the re-

3 For discussions of the *bakufu* model of government in each of the three shogunates, see Jeffrey P. Mass and William B. Hauser, eds., *The Bakufu in Japanese History* (Stanford, Calif.: Stanford University Press, 1985), 264 pp.

minder that the bakufu felt it needed authorization from Kyoto to establish a regional governmental center on Kyushu to strengthen its control.

With rising dissatisfaction over the inability of the Kamakura bakufu to reward its vassals came an increase in lawlessness. *Akutō,* or outlaw bands, proliferated. Professor Ishii's essay portrays the rising level of violence, treachery, and revolt among the military leaders and contenders. In response, the Hōjō regents arrogated more and more provincial governorships to themselves and their followers, alienating others by their increasingly autocratic and high-handed behavior. Familial interests were once again proving stronger than bureaucratic considerations.

The collegial harmony and cooperation that is often ascribed to Japanese society was not conspicuous in Japan's medieval era. In Kyoto a shadow emperor often chafed against the restrictions posed by his retired but more powerful predecessor. In Kamakura a shadow shogun was dominated by his regent, and sometimes overshadowed by his retired predecessor as well. The bakufu intervened at will in Kyoto to settle disputes, and ended by ordering that imperial succession alternate between two lines and that no sovereign's tenure should exceed ten years. This understandably alienated Emperor Godaigo, who was able to rally enough discontented warriors to bring the Kamakura bakufu to its final crisis.

John W. Hall's discussion of the Muromachi bakufu carries the story on to the second shogunate. The Ashikaga, who emerged victorious over both Emperor Godaigo and their rivals in the Kamakura camp, chose to establish their headquarters in the Muromachi section of the imperial capital of Kyoto. The office of shogun was now formally linked with the title of leader of the military houses (*buke no tōryō*). In theory the delegation of power by the emperor remained essential, but the growing weakness of the imperial court in the face of territorial and economic aggrandizement by the provincial *shugo* governors, many of whom were now only nominally responsive to the shogun, raised new questions about the legitimacy of warrior rule. After the defeat of Emperor Godaigo's revolt an alternate line of emperors had been placed in "power" in Kyoto, while Godaigo's erstwhile followers maintained a rival court in the mountainous area of Yoshino, a beautiful area rich in cultural and historical associations. The struggle between the "northern" and "southern" courts was resolved a half century later by a settlement calling for alternation between the two lines in the future, though it was not long maintained.

The fourteenth-century warfare, however, proved decisive in the weakening of aristocratic and clerical control over provincial estates, and as a result the real power of the military governors grew steadily. The era also came to assume critical importance in the future history of imperial loyalism. Apologists for the southern, or Yoshino, line became regarded as paragons of moral excellence and military valor; Kusunoki Masashige, who commanded southern forces at the battle of Minatogawa, and Kitabatake Chikafusa, the author of a celebrated tract that related the imperial cause to gods and heroes, became fixtures of the textbooks of imperial Japan. Early in the twentieth century a dispute grounded in imperial ideology was waged over the question of which line of emperors should be considered legitimate, and a leading student of the "Kemmu Restoration" of Emperor Godaigo, Professor Hiraizumi (whose name can be discerned in several footnote references), was an inspirational teacher of young army officers in the perfervid nationalism of the 1930s. Thus debates about the process described here were charged with meaning for modern Japan.

Professor Hall points out that even for Yoshimitsu, the third, longest ruling, and most powerful of the Muromachi shoguns, court titles were all-important. Yoshimitsu came ultimately to possess all the formal rights of rulership, and he even styled himself "King of Japan" in correspondence with the Ming dynasty emperor of China in his eagerness to acquire Chinese recognition and goods. For this he was predictably excoriated by twentieth-century nationalist historians.

Centered as they were in Kyoto, the Ashikaga shoguns became leading sponsors of the arts. Their era and patronage proved of immense importance for a revival of classical culture – Chinese-style ink painting, the tea ceremony, the Nō drama, and the splendid "Golden" and "Silver" pavilions they constructed all marked a high point in Japanese aesthetics. Kyoto was also the center of Japan's most developed economy, and currents of commercialization, urbanization, and commerce helped to make possible a scale of aristocratic life that Japan had not known before. In the provinces, however, warrior chiefs were taking more and more land and authority for themselves and treating taxes as their private right. In consequence there was an increasing gap between the periphery and the capital, where the shoguns ordered their *shugo* to take up residence.

The fifteenth century witnessed an alarming increase in unrest and rebellion. From 1467 onward most of Japan was embroiled in a war that began as a dispute about imperial and shogunal succession. The influence and prestige of the imperial court was now at a low ebb, but before long that of the Muromachi shogun was only marginally higher. In 1500 a new emperor, Gokashiwabara, had to wait twenty years for formal enthronement because funds were lacking. Not one of the Ashikaga shoguns of the sixteenth century served out his term without being driven from Kyoto at least once, and the only one to die in his capital was murdered there.[4] Real power was beginning to lie with regional commanders who were consolidating their holdings and followers while their more aristocratic predecessors fought themselves to a standstill at the center.

It was a century and a half before order was restored in Japan. The intermittent warfare of the sixteenth century was termed Sengoku, or Warring States, by Japanese who compared it with the violence that preceded the emergence of the unified empire in China two milleniums earlier. Yet beneath the smoke of war economic change, trade and piracy, and regional consolidation were changing the face of Japan. The Tokugawa shogunate that emerged in 1600 inherited the fruits of this social change.

There was first of all a marked rise in internal trade and commerce. Many local warrior chiefs, like their counterparts in Europe earlier, established toll stations to profit from this exchange. There was also a considerable amount of trade with the continent. A tide of piracy launched by bands based along the western coast of Japan had ravaged coastal cities of Korea and China as early as the fourteenth century; the Ashikaga shogun Yoshimitsu had secured trading privileges with the Ming dynasty as reward for controlling that brigandage. His fifteenth-century successors, however, partly from choice and partly from weakness, failed to maintain that control, and as a result the continent again knew the scourge of pirate bands. The disorder in western Japan made its ports an inviting base for such groups, but in makeup they included Korean and Chinese as well as Japanese buccaneers. After the Ming rulers banned Japanese ships from their shores, trade for Chinese goods continued through the network of trading stations established by Chinese merchants throughout Southeast Asia. European traders, first Portuguese and Spanish and, after 1600, Dutch and English, fitted into this trading pattern from their bases in Macao, Manila, Indonesia, and India, respectively, and participated in a vigorous competition. Enmities grounded in European wars intensified rivalry and

4 George Elison, "Introduction," in Elison and Bardwell L. Smith, eds., *Warlords, Artists, and Commoners: Japan in the Sixteenth Century* (Honolulu: The University Press of Hawaii, 1981), p. 1.

provided openings for Japanese choice, just as Japanese disunity offered opportunities for Westerners.

The Portuguese, who arrived in the 1540s, brought with them firearms and missionaries of the Society of Jesus. Both were welcome to Japanese local lords, many of whom were vexed by Buddhist sectarian rebellions and all of whom were eager for weapons and wealth to strengthen their position against their neighbors. In 1580 a local daimyo who had become a convert made a donation of the port town of Nagasaki to the Jesuits, and it quickly became the center of the Catholic effort in Japan. The Jesuits, a semimilitary order that included members from late-feudal origins in Iberia and Italy, soon learned to work among the Japanese samurai and daimyo. Firearms were more welcome still. In a remarkably short time they were being produced in quantity in central Japan, and their use revolutionized warfare. The aristocratic and splendidly armored samurai of earlier times proved no match for disciplined infantry in carefully selected positions who loaded and fired by ranks in sequence. By the 1580s, though the Ashikaga shoguns still clung to position and rank in Kyoto, the future lay with regional leaders who preferred to draw on the resources of substantial units of land to organize significant numbers of men armed with muskets.

Oda Nobunaga (1534–82), Toyotomi Hideyoshi (1536–98), and especially Tokugawa Ieyasu (1542–1616) were the three who understood and utilized these possibilities to unify Japan. Nobunaga, born the son of a Nagoya lord, had a shrewd sense of politics, a quick grasp of the possibilities of firearms, and such complete ruthlessness in the extirpation of enemies that it struck fear into his opponents. His base, a large rice-producing area in central Japan, was both strategic and productive. He separated his forces from the peasantry and relied on the use of the new military technology, including guns and armored ships. His land surveys gave him confidence in what he could demand from the countryside, and his abolition of toll barriers undermined the power of earlier authorities. He had none of the compunction his predecessors might have shown toward religion, and was utterly merciless in his extirpation of Buddhist opponents, massacring the entire community of monks and their defenders and dependents on Mt. Hiei outside Kyoto; he was equally unforgiving of rural sectarians who resisted his commands. In 1568 he entered Kyoto in pretended response to the pleas of the Ashikaga shogun, but once there he speedily brought him to heel with strict orders not to make independent overtures to other military leaders. In 1582, as he was about to set out on a campaign to add western Japan to his conquests, he was attacked by one of his vassals and took his own life.

Hideyoshi, after dealing with Nobunaga's enemies, continued his conquests and brought the rest of Japan under his governance. His rise, despite his obscure peasant origins, stamps him as one of the most remarkable individuals in a turbulent era. In contrast to Nobunaga's ruthless treatment of those he had defeated, Hideyoshi tended to draw his rivals into the circle of his allies, allowing them to redeem themselves by valor in his service. As Nobunaga's lieutenant he had absorbed his tactical and strategic techniques, but he was more thorough still in ordering the compilation of a national land survey, ordering that samurai leave the countryside to become standing armies at the castles of their lords, and disarming the commoners through edicts ordering them to surrender all swords. After 1590, with the unification of Japan achieved, Hideyoshi developed grandiloquent thoughts of continental conquest and demanded that Korea give free passage to his armies in an assault on China. On being rejected, he launched a massive invasion of Korea in 1592. Initially successful, his forces proved inadequately supplied by sea, and when Ming dynasty armies entered the war to defend China's tributary state of Korea the Japanese commanders were hard pressed to maintain their gains and tried to convince Hideyoshi that the Chinese had capitulated. Furious when he was undeceived, Hideyoshi launched a second, punitive attack in 1597. When he died the following year his vassals and allies rushed back to take part in the renewed conquest for power in Japan. Like Nobunaga, Hideyoshi never took the title of shogun. He preferred the distinction of a title in the old court hierarchy.

Hideyoshi's plans for the succession of his young son were quickly undone by his most important ally, Tokugawa Ieyasu, who led a coalition of lords from eastern Japan to victory at the great battle of Sekigahara in 1600 before taking Hideyoshi's castle of Osaka in 1615. With this came a consolidation of power that was to last until the Meiji Restoration of 1868.

The Tokugawa order is the subject of the essays by John W. Hall and Harold Bolitho that complete this volume. Ieyasu, building on the work of Nobunaga and Hideyoshi, built a system that was at once centralized and decentralized. Historians have long debated its characteristics, and the term *bakuhan* state reflects the compromises of a system that was feudal in its allocations of lands to vassals, but centralized in the impositions the shogun was able to demand from them. Daimyo could be, and were, moved by the shogun, though the great historic houses, "outside" (*tozama*) lords, possessed of larger domains on the periphery, were seldom challenged. "Hereditary" (*fudai*) daimyo vassals held lands that were smaller in income, but more strategically located. They were also more numerous, and could be called upon to staff the higher offices within the bakufu structure. All lords came to be required to maintain residences at the shogun's capital; they were expected to house their families and those of their chief retainers there, and their alternate years of residence served as a substitute for the military service that had been expected of them before the Tokugawa peace. The bakufu reserved for itself the most important lands and all metropolitan centers, and dispatched lesser vassals to govern as part of a bureaucracy that involved some seventeen thousand men in hundreds of positions.

In addition to its hold on the metropolitan centers of Nagasaki, Osaka, Kyoto, and Edo and the most important mines, the bakufu reserved to itself rights of coinage (through the silver and copper guilds, the *ginza* and *dōza*) and of violence, calling on its feudatories when action was required for the suppression of rebellion or coastal defense. Feudal lords' succession, and their matrimonial alliances, were monitored, and related houses and collaterals were honored by permission to use the Tokugawa (and Matsudaira, an earlier house name) appellations.

The bakufu also claimed all foreign relations as its province. Hideyoshi had issued, and the Tokugawa enforced and strengthened, prohibitions on Christianity, which had gained numbers of daimyo and several hundred thousand commoners as converts. Nagasaki, once the Jesuit base, had come into Hideyoshi's hands in 1587 and became a shogunal city to which all foreign trade was directed. In 1637 the outbreak of a rebellion that took on a Catholic cast was followed by a ruthless extirpation of missionaries and their converts. Spain and Portugal, as Catholic powers, were thereafter expelled and Western contact was restricted to the Protestant Dutch, who were ordered to take up residence in an area in Nagasaki that had been prepared for the Portuguese. Japanese trading missions to Southeast Asia, which had flourished in the early Tokugawa years, were ended; Japanese were forbidden to go abroad, and, once gone, denied reentry on pain of death. Private junks from maritime China were directed to Nagasaki, where their goods were exchanged for Japanese products and bullion through representatives of merchant guilds in the great Tokugawa cities. Additional access to Chinese goods, especially the silk thread that was in great demand throughout the seventeenth century, came via Ryūkyū

(Okinawa), a dependency of the southern domain of Satsuma, and through Korea, with which relations were restored and which permitted the daimyo of Tsushima to maintain a trading station at Pusan. The attenuated nature of these foreign contacts led in time to the term "seclusion system," although cultural, economic, and intellectual contacts of many sorts were possible.[5]

Harold Bolitho's discussion of the *han*, or daimyo domains, shows that the bakufu policies were in many ways mirrored in miniature in the 260-odd daimyo domains throughout the land. Daimyo too collected their principal vassals and collaterals in the castle towns that dotted the coastal routes throughout Japan; they were the lords of semiautonomous states with armies of samurai, now urbanized; the states had their own tax systems, and sometimes paper and copper currency that circulated inside their borders, and they had their own codes of procedure and law, though they were administered in patterns that resembled those at the center. The domains were subordinate to the bakufu, but they were not taxed, except as their metropolitan estates, guard duties, and contributions to shogunal projects depleted their resources.

Throughout all Japan the farmers remained disarmed. The village was almost a world apart, a self-contained community ruled by its land-holding farmers who selected local elders and met in councils to discuss common problems. Its contact with the samurai world came at the county magistrate's office, where tax assessments were levied on the village as a unit and allocated by the elders. Village headmen, whether hereditary, appointed, or elected, were the fulcrum of political power; they bargained with the samurai authorities at the county seat. They were likely to be held responsible for whatever happened in the village, and in case of emergency it was they who would present protests and lead protestors.

The economic role and needs of the castle towns, and especially of the metropolitan centers, brought decisive social change as the Tokugawa peace continued. A resourceful class of townsmen catered to the needs of urban samurai. They ranged from great concessionaires who managed the transport and sale of rice, transfer of coin, and production and sale of the ever growing needs of the cities to petty tradesmen who lived on the edge of poverty. A popular culture of prints, books, and theater developed, not only in the bakufu's great urban centers,

5 Marius B. Jansen, *China in the Tokugawa World* (Cambridge, Mass.: Harvard University Press, 1992).

but on smaller scale in the castle towns of the domains. In the eighteenth century daimyo schools for domain samurai began to dot the land; with them came private academies for commoners able to afford instruction, and parish schools for the sons, and often the daughters, of commoners.

Warrior rule had come full circle. Centuries of peace brought a transformation and bureaucratization of the samurai class, who began as full-time fighters and ended as an underemployed peacetime army of occupation. Overall, the samurai share of the national produce became relatively smaller, until many of the commoners, once scorned by Hideyoshi, seemed to match or surpass all but the senior ranks in confidence and education. Samurai moralists felt obliged to explain their special position in society by an emphasis on duty and morality. At upper levels military perquisites continued, and samurai contempt for "stupid commoners" (*gumin*), as the stock phrase had it, shielded awareness that they were dependent on their labor. In the nineteenth century a renewed sense of foreign danger helped rekindle warrior consciousness and samurai spirit, but once it was clear that Japan's structure of society and government was incapable of responding to the West the Meiji state disarmed the samurai and armed the commoners as conscripts for the imperial cause.

Warrior values, directed now toward the sovereign, remained central to the ethical code of modern Japan. For a decade samurai malcontents threatened the stability of the Meiji government, but once it was secure its leaders, most of them former samurai, designed their education and codes with an eye to diffusing among the people at large the values of loyalty and fortitude on which their ancestors had prided themselves.

CHAPTER 1

THE KAMAKURA BAKUFU

The establishment of Japan's first warrior government, the Kamakura bakufu, represented both a culmination and a beginning. Since the tenth century, an increasingly professionalized class of mounted fighting men had served in local areas as estate administrators and policemen and as officials attached to the organs of provincial governance. By the twelfth century, warriors had come to exercise a dominant share of the total volume of local government, but even after two hundred years they remained politically immature. The most exalted warriors were still only middle-level figures in hierarchies dominated by courtiers and religious institutions in and near the capital. The bakufu's founding in the 1180s thus represented an initial breakthrough to power on the part of elite fighting men, but the fledgling regime was scarcely in a position to assume unitary control over the entire country. What evolved was a system of government approximating a dyarchy. During the Kamakura period, Japan had two capitals and two interconnected loci of authority. The potential of warrior power was clear enough to those who cared to envision it, but the legacy of the past prevented more than a slow progress into the future.

Until quite recently, studies of Kamakura Japan have tended to overstate the warriors' achievement, by equating the creation of a new form of government with the simultaneous destruction of the old. As is now clear, not only was the Heian system of imperial-aristocratic rule still vigorous during the twelfth century, but also it remained the essential framework within which the bakufu, during its lifetime, was obliged to operate. In this sense, the Heian pattern of government survived into the fourteenth century – to be destroyed with the Kamakura bakufu rather than by it. The events of the 1180s were revolutionary insofar as they witnessed the emergence of Japan's first noncentral locus of authority and Japan's first government composed of men not of the most exalted social ranks. But the bakufu, as we shall see, was a military regime dedicated to keeping warriors away from the battlefield and also to finding judicial answers to the feuds and disputes that were plaguing society .

THE BACKGROUND TO THE GEMPEI WAR

Despite its aversion to fighting, the bakufu was created by war, the Gempei (Genji versus Heishi, or Minamoto versus Taira) conflict of 1180–5. This was a much more complex upheaveal than its name implies. Far from being a dispute between two great warrior clans, as it is so often depicted, the Gempei conflict was a national civil war involving substantial intraclan fighting and also pitting local against central interests.[1] Indeed, the character of the violence was responsible for the type of regime that was created. Likewise, the backdrop to the conflict was a product of society's tensions and is therefore integral to the history of the Kamakura bakufu.

To understand the limitations of both the warrior victory and the resulting government, we need to trace the rise of the warrior class in the Heian period as well as the ascendancy of the Taira in the years just before the Gempei War. The original blueprint for imperial government in Japan did not envision a military aristocracy as the mainstay of administration over the countryside. Yet as the courtiers in the capital became more confident of their superiority, they began to loosen their grip over the provinces, exchanging governance over a public realm for proprietorship over its component pieces. The country was divided into public and private estates (the provincial lands known as *kokugaryō*, and the estates known as *shōen*), under the authority of governors and estate holders, respectively, who themselves made up the courtier and religious elite. The owners of land at the topmost proprietary level were thus exclusively nobles and clerics. The purpose of this privatization of land was to secure a flow of revenue that exceeded what was provided by the holding of bureaucratic office. In turn, this permitted an increasingly extravagant life-style in the capital. The division of the country was predicated in this way on the desire of *shōen* owners to be absentee landlords. Yet it was equally dependent on those owners' ability to draft into service a class of willing and obedient administrators.

1 See Jeffrey P. Mass, "The Emergence of the Kamakura Bakufu," in John Whitney Hall and Jeffrey P. Mass, eds., *Medieval Japan: Essays in Institutional History* (New Haven, Conn.: Yale University Press, 1974) (hereafter cited as Mass, "The Emergence"). The older view, which underemphasizes the social implications of the war, is ably treated by Minoru Shinoda, *The Founding of the Kamakura Shogunate* (New York: Columbia University Press, 1960).

This loosening of control from above also loosened the cement that bound the provinces to the capital. A degree of local instability ensued, which caused the lower ranks to look to one another for mutual support and protection. Leadership fell to persons of distinction whose principal source of prestige was an ancestry traceable to the capital. Thus, unlike the invaders who promoted the feudalization of Europe, local leaders in Japan were men with long pedigrees. They also retained their central connections, which meant that the developing class of provincial administrators were less members of local war bands than members of groups that were forming to secure the peace. This did not preclude outbreaks of lawlessness. But courtiers could always brand such outbursts as rebellion and enroll others as their provincial agents. In this way, at any rate, local and central remained essentially joined for the duration of the Heian period.

The warriors who were becoming the true captains of local society were called *zaichōkanjin,* or resident officials attached to provincial government headquarters *(kokuga).* Although the governorships themselves continued to rotate among courtiers in Kyoto, positions within the *kokuga* became hereditary. Later, during the early stages of the Gempei War, the developing cleavage of interests here was exploited by the founder of the Kamakura bakufu, Minamoto Yoritomo. However, during the two centuries preceding 1180, patrons in the capital were able to channel the energies of provincial subordinates towards mutually beneficial ends. On the one hand, the locals were given extensive powers in the areas of tax collecting and policing. But on the other hand, these same locals were obliged to work through their superiors to secure new appointments or confirmations of old ones[2] or to secure justice in the frequent legal battles between kin and nonkin rivals. Neither the local chieftain nor the clan head (if this was a different person) was empowered to provide these services on his own authority; he too was dependent on the support of a central patron. The result was that ownership and administration, authority and power, became separable, with little risk to the capital-resident proprietor. So ingrained was the psychology of a hierarchy in which the center dominated the periphery that in the absence of some regionally based patronage source such as the bakufu, courtiers in the capital, no

2 Titles became hereditary and subject to disposition by testament. But wills, in order to be recognized, required probate by the governor. For details, see Jeffrey P. Mass, "Patterns of Provincial Inheritance in Late Heian Japan," *Journal of Japanese Studies* 9 (Winter 1983): 67–95.

matter how effete, could remain the superiors of warriors, no matter how powerful the latter were.[3]

But Kyoto protected its interests in other ways, too. One of the most ingenious was to promote a handful of men as career governors. These persons might then be moved from province to province, much as modern ambassadors are moved today. The origins of this practice have not been adequately studied, but by late in the eleventh century the use of such representatives, now called *zuryō*, had become interwoven with the competition between the Fujiwara and retired emperor patronage blocs in the capital. By this time, governorships had become, in a sense, commodities circulating among the elite. The proprietary province (*chigyōkoku*) system, as it was called, was designed to allow patronage groups to function on both sides of the local land ledger (*shōen* and *kokugaryō*), with the governor as the principal instrument of manipulation. What is important to us is the identity and character of the journeyman governors who now came to be employed by the ex-emperors and Fujiwara. They were from the Taira and Minamoto, particular scions of which were recognized as career troubleshooters for provinces possessed by their patrons. Thus, to cite one example, Taira Masamori received successive appointments to at least nine provinces, as did his son Tadamori after him. And the latter's son, the illustrious Kiyomori, was governor of three provinces before beginning his historic ascent in the capital.[4]

The leaders of the Taira and Minamoto need to be appreciated in this light. They were not, as they are usually depicted, regional chieftains chafing under courtier dominance. Rather, they were bridging figures – military nobles in the truest sense – between the great central aristocrats, who were their patrons, and the great provincial warriors, who were their followers. The leaders' dual character, born out of service to two constituencies, is essential to an understanding of the slow progress of warrior development in its initial phase. It is also basic to the incompleteness of the warrior revolution that was later spearheaded by the bakufu.

The prestige of the Taira and Minamoto names, and the restraining influence they came to exercise, are reflected in still another way. The warrior houses that dominated the provincial headquarters commonly

3 In Weberian terms, the system was maintained by a subjective feeling by subordinates that courtier dominance was natural and legitimate. See Max Weber, *The Theory of Social and Economic Organization* (New York: Free Press, 1964), pp. 124ff.

4 Iida Hisao, "Heishi to Kyūshū," in Takeuchi Rizō hakase kanreki kinenkai, ed., *Shōensei to buke shakai* (Tokyo: Yoshikawa kōbunkan, 1969), p. 50.

bore these two surnames, along with one other, Fujiwara. These were seen at the time as connoting an aristocratic ancestry and served to bind provincials to the capital while they also awed truly native families. Not until Kamakura times did houses such as the Chiba, Oyama, and Miura, among others, come to be known by the names with which they are remembered historically.[5]

Unfortunately, this profusion of Taira and Minamoto surnames has led to the view that the chieftains of these two clans were able to fashion ongoing combinations of vassals. The notion of evolving warrior leagues supported the further notion that the histories of the Taira and Minamoto were in fact the proper framework for tracing the rise of the warrior.[6] However, the records of the era tell a much more modest story, forcing us to conclude that what has passed for coherent history is little more than disparate images pulled taut. The chieftains of the two clans did, at times, add a layer of authority that might be effective. But their assignment to a succession of provinces (not to mention long stays in Kyoto) all but ensured that whatever ties they had formed would inevitably weaken. Thus, the unique but ephemeral success of the most famous warrior of the era, Minamoto Yoshiie, needs to be juxtaposed against the peripatetic movements of the succession of Taira chieftains and the mixed success of Yoshiie's own great-grandson, Minamoto Yoshitomo. Yoshitomo was rebuffed as often as he was accepted in the Minamoto's historic heartland region, the Kantō, and he was ultimately defeated in 1160 by an army consisting of only three hundred men.[7]

Even though the saga of the Taira and Minamoto may thus be a weak framework for charting the road to 1180, the histories of the great provincial houses place us on much firmer ground. Here the emphasis is on an expansion of power within the traditional system of rule, along with the lack of any means for circumventing that system. In other words, what was acceptable in the earlier stages of growth did not necessarily remain so, especially as warrior houses came to feel vulnerable to pressures from above. The Chiba, for instance, discovered that the patronage of the Ise Shrine could neither prevent a major confisca-

5 To cite but one example, the body of documents bearing on the late Heian Chiba house refers only to the Taira. See "Ichiki monjo," in *Ichikawa shishi, kodai-chūsei shiryō* (Ichikawa: Ichikawa shi, 1973), pp. 363–74.

6 For an illustration, see George B. Sansom, *A History of Japan to 1334* (Stanford, Calif.: Stanford University Press, 1958), chap. 12.

7 Yasuda Motohisa, *Nihon zenshi (chūsei 1)* (Tokyo: Tōkyō daigaku shuppankai, 1958), p. 14; and Jeffrey P. Mass, *Warrior Government in Early Medieval Japan* (New Haven, Conn.: Yale University Press, 1974), pp. 35–44 (hereafter cited as *WG*).

tion of their holdings by a new governor in the 1130s nor protect them from further seizures by the shrine itself a generation later.[8] To the extent that experiences of this kind led to feelings of resentment, the environment in the provinces was being readied for change.

As we know, it was not the Minamoto who came to experience national power first but, rather, the Taira under the leadership of Kiyomori. Recent historians have amended the traditional view of his ascendancy by emphasizing both its limited nature and duration. Kiyomori is now seen less as a warrior riding the crest of a wave of support from the provinces than as a military noble who attempted, unsuccessfully, to use the scaffolding of imperial offices to achieve his hegemony. Lacking large numbers of warrior followers and also the administrative organization of a central proprietor, Kiyomori failed, until very late, to establish an identifiable "regime." His legacy, as we shall see, was to demonstrate the vulnerability of Kyoto to coercion and to destabilize the countryside. For these reasons, the brief period of his ascendancy must be counted as a direct contributor to the outbreak of war in 1180.

The Taira episode is divisible into two subperiods. From 1160 to 1179, Kiyomori operated in the shadow of his patron, the retired emperor Goshirakawa. Though he himself climbed to the top of the imperial office hierarchy, becoming chancellor in 1167, he remined dependent on the spoils system of the ex-sovereign. Wearying, finally, of established Kyoto's unwavering opposition to his membership in the capital elite, Kiyomori staged a coup d'état in late 1179, which removed the ex-emperor from effective power. Yet this action succeeded also in destroying the basic collegiality of the courtier class, which had always competed according to accepted rules. The damage in Kyoto was further compounded by Kiyomori's seizure of numerous estate and provincial proprietorships. This not only reduced the portfolios of his noble and religious rivals; it also upset the status quo in the countryside. Early in 1180, Kiyomori's own infant grandson became emperor, an event that accelerated a growing sense of malaise everywhere.[9]

While all of this was taking place, the Minamoto leadership was languishing in exile. Twenty years earlier, at the time of the Heiji incident, the sons of Yoshitomo, who was himself killed, were scattered throughout Japan. The eldest, the thirteen-year-old Yoritomo, was placed in the custody of the eastern-based Hōjō, a minor branch of

8 *WG*, pp. 48–54. 9 For the Taira ascendancy, see *WG*, pp. 15–30, 54–56.

the Taira. We have little information on Yoritomo between 1160 and 1180, save for the fact of his marriage to Masako, the daughter of Hōjō Tokimasa, his guardian. From the perspective of subsequent events, Kiyomori's leniency in dealing with the offspring of his 1160 enemy seems impolitic. Yet there was no way the future could have been foreseen: The heir to the Minamoto name was powerless and had been absorbed into the Taira by way of marriage to a Taira collateral.

It is in part owing to this absence of any political activity by Yoritomo that historians have found it difficult to interpret the tumultuous events that lay just ahead. The impediment to understanding can be removed only by minimizing the importance of the Taira–Minamoto rivalry, a sentiment evidently shared by Kiyomori as well. Thus, when Yoritomo raised his banner of rebellion in the eighth month of 1180, the support he attracted was determined by issues other than memories of some idealized past. The background of the Gempei War can be traced to two sources – the perception of vulnerability at court and the condition of warrior houses locally.

THE GEMPEI WAR

Belying true motivations, wars in Japan are waged under strict categories of symbols, none more important than devotion to a higher cause. In 1180, rebellion was justified on the basis of a call to arms against the Taira by a prince left out of the imperial succession. Though the prince himself was dead within several weeks (5/26), his overture retained great significance. The forces of Yoritomo later cited it as a pretext for their uprising (8/19), and so did the bakufu's later history of itself (the *Azuma kagami*) in its opening paragraph.[10] The broader context encouraging widespread violence yielded in this way to an official explanation.

Yet just as rectification of the succession had little to do with the outbreak of war, the outburst also cannot be explained as a spontaneous rallying to the Minamoto. As Yoritomo himself discovered, loyalty proved a singularly noncombustible element. Before a challenge might be mounted, the warriors of the east required time to gauge their current situations. The Chiba, with their recent history of setbacks, joined early (6/17), even though they bore a Taira surname. But for

10 *Azuma kagami (AK)*, 1180/4/9. The most accessible edition of the *Azuma kagami* is that edited by Nagahara Keiji and Kishi Shōzō (Tokyo: Jimbutsu ōraisha, 1976–7), 6 vols. The *Azuma kagami* covers the period 1180 to 1266 and was prepared in the early fourteenth century. The later sections are considered to be more reliable.

many other houses the issues were more complex, normally centering on inter- and intrafamily relations within their own home provinces. As part of the process, houses segmented into new alignments and subunits, and the provinces themselves became the staging grounds for a series of incipient civil wars.[11] To prevent the east from disintegrating into internecine conflict, Yoritomo was obliged to seek some new common denominator that would bind rather than divide the families under his leadership. The program he evolved was made part of his war declaration on 8/19. Rather than organize a war party to defend the court by dislodging the Taira, Yoritomo designed policies to satisfy the most deep-seated desires of the warrior class in general. The Minamoto chieftain promised what had never before been contemplated: a regional security system that bypassed Kyoto and guaranteed the landed holdings of followers. The vision was revolutionary – and led ultimately to the creation of the Kamakura bakufu.

Though Yoritomo couched his program in procourt and anti-Taira language, the effect of his plan was to disengage the east from central control, by converting its public and private officers into his own vassals. Specifically, he authorized the men of the region to assume possession over the holdings long associated with them and to petition Yoritomo for confirmations. The temper of the program was set when the governor's agent (*mokudai*) of Izu Province, the site of Yoritomo's long exile, was attacked on 8/17 by forces of the Minamoto. Similar campaigns followed (for instance, that of the Chiba against the Shimōsa *mokudai* on 9/13), and this rapidly became a movement to eliminate all representatives of the central government. At the same time, the tide of support, which had been sporadic to this point, now became a ground swell. Resident officials from various provinces pledged themselves to Yoritomo, as did a number of estate-based personnel. The effect of this was to deliver into his hands the potential for rulership over vast areas. This in turn was bolstered by the chieftain's assumption of a protector's role over the region's leading temples and shrines. Yoritomo achieved this latter goal by issuing public directives to the provincial headquarters, in effect, an assumption of the authority – without the title – of the governor. The issuance of such documents began on the same day that he declared war.[12]

11 For details, see Mass, "The Emergence," pp. 134–43.

12 "Mishima jinja monjo," 1180/8/19 Minamoto Yoritomo kudashibumi, in Takeuchi Rizō, comp., *Heian ibun* (Tokyo: Tōkyōdō, 1947–80), 15 vols., 9:3782–83, doc. 4883. This is the earliest document bearing Yoritomo's name.

Yoritomo still had many problems to overcome. On 8/23, an army under his command was soundly defeated at the battle of Ishibashi in Sagami Province. His opponents were not forces recruited and sent out by the central Taira but typically were local houses that were opposing other local houses. They called themselves Taira for the same reason that Yoritomo's men from Sagami called themselves Minamoto. Rather quickly, however, the Taira label became obsolete. Owing to Yoritomo's presence in the region, the appeal of his program, and a general rallying to his side, families that had remained neutral or had taken initial positions against him now sought to reverse themselves. Although this necessitated a submergence of hostile sentiments on the part of traditional rivals, the alternative was probably extinction. For his part, Yoritomo showed great leniency in welcoming earlier enemies and showed great understanding by dividing and recognizing new families. By the end of 1180, only the tiniest residue of a "Gempei" War remained in the east, with the task now one of purging and purifying rather than facing an enemy. Kamakura, with historic ties to Yoritomo's forebears, was selected as the seat for his government.

A Taira policy approximating quarantine actually encouraged Yoritomo's preoccupation with the east. A by-product was to make the Chūbu and Hokuriku regions, which were closer to the capital, the next arenas for conflict. Already by 1181, provincial warriors in these areas were seeking to expel Kyoto's representatives by using the same pretext as their eastern counterparts did. They postured themselves as Minamoto engaged in a crusade against the Taira. That Yoritomo was probably ignorant of most of the activities of those invoking his name suggests that the battleground, now of its own momentum, was rapidly expanding in size. At this stage – and until 1183 – Yoritomo was content to limit his personal involvement strictly to the east. For regions beyond the east he delegated a loose authority to two relatives, his cousin Yoshinaka and his uncle Yukiie.

In the meantime, the chieftain in Kamakura was identifying a new enemy. These were the collateral lines of his own house who were refusing to recognize his authority. Even before the end of 1180, Yoritomo demonstrated his unconcern with the Taira by marching east against the Satake, relatives who a generation earlier had refused to submit to his father. The differences between father and son (in effect, between the 1150s and 1180s) are instructive. Whereas Yoshitomo the father had been unable to subordinate recalcitrant Minamoto branches, Yoritomo the son used superior military strength to force the issue. The Satake were destroyed in battle on 1180/11/5. Other lineages were more prudent. The Nitta, for instance, reversed their earlier intransigence (9/30) and submitted to Yoritomo without a fight (12/22). Yet the chieftain in Kamakura remained vigilant. When another collateral, the Shida, showed signs of vacillation, Yoritomo rejected their submission and moved to destroy them (1181/int. 2/20). As we shall see, enmity toward kinsmen continued to be a much stronger inducement to action than did the nonthreatening Taira.

Between 1180 and 1183, Yoritomo worked assiduously to mold the eastern region into a personal sphere of influence. He did this by converting the existing officialdom into a private vassalage, by attempting to make himself the source of all patronage in the area, and by transforming a simple village, Kamakura, into a great center of government. Now when he prohibited local outrages, authorized fiscal exemptions, assigned new lands, or issued orders to provincial officials, he was doing so from a stationary base that he could realistically call his capital. Yet the Minamoto movement could not continue indefinitely to develop in isolation, because the contagion of violence under the Minamoto banner was rapidly spreading. Yoritomo eventually saw this development as an opportunity to inflate his own chieftainship. But he also recognized the danger to his fledgling authority of inaction in the face of warrior outlawry. Though the Taira in Kyoto and the Minamoto in Kamakura were reluctant to confront each other, developments in the provinces eventually forced the issue. They also forced the country's two governmental centers to seek an accommodation.

The years 1183 to 1185 witnessed a convergence of events on several levels. The Gempei War, desultory from the beginning, heated up and reached a sudden climax. The Kamakura bakufu assumed its basic form. The imperial court, with Kamakura's help, began to revive itself. And the warrior class, by means of sustained violence, achieved unprecedented new goals.

The inertia of the war's second and third years was broken in mid-1183 when Yoritomo's Chūbu deputies, Yoshinaka and Yukiie, broke through the Taira defenses and occupied the capital. For their part, the Taira leaders, carrying the child emperor with them, fled westward in an attempt to regroup. Though after the outbreak of war the Taira had made certain modest efforts to establish closer ties with the provinces,[13] they now had to base themselves there for the first time in a generation. At least superficially, the Taira and the Minamoto became comparable, with each side seeking the support of local warriors. In the capital there was general rejoicing over the departure of the Taira and genuine optimism over the prospects of converting the Minamoto into time-honored guardians of the imperial state.

But two major obstacles blocked such hopes – and worked to prevent Japanese history from reassuming its traditional pre-Taira course. The first concerned the nature and level of the upheaval in the countryside, which will be dealt with shortly. The second centered on the condition of the Minamoto leadership. Soon after his arrival in Kyoto, Yoshinaka began to posture himself as the true leader of the Minamoto and to impose his own form of dictatorship on the capital city. Yoritomo, beside himself with rage, did not, however, do the "logical" thing. He refused to abandon his own capital to contest his cousin in the country's capital. Rather, he began negotiating an accord with agents of the retired emperor that would give permanent status to his own government. And he began planning a punitive expedition against Yoshinaka that would be led by his own brother, Yoshitsune.

The accord was eventually hammered out in the intercalated tenth month of 1183 and has been hailed by some scholars as marking the official birth of the Kamakura bakufu. The argument here is that a rebel movement was now being given imperial sanction; a portion of what Yoritomo had earlier seized was now lawfully released to him.[14] The trouble with this view is that it makes Kyoto ultimately responsible for the creation of the bakufu and argues as well for a circumscribed authority. In fact, Yoritomo was already the governing power in the east, and the accord acknowledged that fact even as it called for a restoration of traditional proprietorships in the region. More to the point, as a result of the agreement, the bakufu's range of operations now became countrywide. From this juncture, Kamakura established itself as Japan's preeminent peacemaker, a responsibility that began as a military policing authority but soon became overwhelmingly judicial in nature. As we shall see, the dispensing of justice emerged as the

13 These efforts centered on the new local titles of *sōkan* and *sōgesu;* see Ishimoda Shō, "Heishi seiken no sōkan shiki setchi," *Rekishi hyōron* 107 (1959): 7–14; Ishimoda Shō, "Kamakura bakufu ikkoku jitō shiki no seiritsu," in Satō Shin'ichi and Ishimoda Shō, eds., *Chūsei no hō to kokka* (Tokyo: Tōkyō daigaku shuppankai, 1960), pp. 36–45.

14 For a discussion, see *WG*, pp. 72–77; and Uwayokote Masataka, "Kamakura seiken seiritsu ki o meguru kingyō," *Hōseishi kenkyū* 11 (1960): 175–81.

essence of Kamakura's governance and as society's greatest need during the thirteenth century.

The proof for Kamakura's new role lies in the sudden appearance of a type of document hitherto unseen. These were cease-and-desist orders issued by Yoritomo in response to appeals for assistance from traditional estate holders.[15] The development was revolutionary for two reasons. First, for the first time in Japanese history a noncentral source of authority was providing patronage for central recipients; this was a reversal of age-old practice and anticipated a new era of warrior dominance. Second, the decrees themselves provided visual testimony that the bakufu was now active in central and western Japan. This countrywide scope became a permanent feature of Kamakura's authority. At the same time, the language of the edicts made clear that Yoritomo recognized the legitimacy of the traditional proprietors' retaining their positions atop the land system. In a real sense, the one-time rebel was going on record as a force now for law and order. Henceforth, the rights of warriors *and* courtiers would be equally protected, a position adopted as the only realistic way to return the country to stability.

The postures of both Kyoto and Kamakura were in fact a response, not to the exigencies of war, but rather to the unprecedented outpouring of local lawlessness that swept Japan in 1184. Surviving documents reveal Kyoto's attempts to quell these outbursts by threatening traditional sanctions, and the dawning awareness that only Kamakura had any chance to restore true peace.[16] One result is that after disposing of Yoshinaka, Yoshitsune was ordered by his brother to remain in the capital and to establish a Kamakura office there. He was to issue desist orders in response to petitions from proprietors.[17] The effect of this was to reinforce both Kamakura's independence and the interdependence of government in practice.

Now that he was involved in central and western Japan, Yoritomo recognized the need to make contact with as many people and places as possible. He dispatched several of his most trusted followers westward and ordered them to enroll as vassals any who would pledge loyalty. First priority was to be given to the same *zaichōkanjin* and other local

15 For translated examples of such documents, see Jeffrey P. Mass, *The Kamakura Bakufu: A Study in Documents* (Stanford, Calif.: Stanford University Press, 1976), docs. 1–6 (hereafter cited as *KB*).

16 This is most poignantly depicted in a retired emperor's edict of 1184, in *KB*, doc. 7.

17 For a list of the edicts issued by Yoshitsune, see Mass, "The Emergence," p. 148, n. 71. A general discussion appears in Tanaka Minoru, "Kamakura dono otsukai kō," *Shirin* 45 (1962): 1–23.

officials who dominated the east's provincial headquarters. These men were to be promised the same confirmations and preferments as their eastern counterparts, because they held the potential of delivering to the Minamoto large numbers of subordinates. In this way, sections of territory in hitherto unfamiliar areas could be made the basis of some permanent Kamakura interest in the west.[18] Yoritomo's policy of vassal recruitment could then be joined by his other method of gaining a foothold in public and private estates, providing redress for proprietors' complaints of lawlessness.

Each province and district was different. Some had great families dominating them, others did not. Still others became centers of Taira partisanship. The result was that Kamakura's approach to individual areas required a capacity for flexibility. Likewise, because success, by definition, was bound to be uneven, the potential for influence would forever be mixed. Eventually, Kamakura would need to find a mechanism by which to introduce symmetry into its patchwork presence in the west.

Though the war was an obvious rationale for Minamoto penetration of that region, it is significant that the main-force fighting that now began was largely incidental to Kamakura's efforts at aggrandizement. For example, the battle of Ichinotani in Settsu Province in 1184/2 constituted only the second encounter between what might be called the main Taira and Minamoto armies.[19] Yet the latter's victory did not lead to Settsu Province's becoming a major Minamoto stronghold. Evidently, the pursuit of the war and the contest for control of men and land were separate processes. This is one reason that defeating the Taira, though recognized as necessary, engendered so little enthusiasm. Eventually, however, command of the principal Minamoto armies was placed in the hands of Yoshitsune, and in a series of brilliant maneuvers he pursued the Taira leaders and destroyed them at Dannoura in 1185/3.[20] The Gempei War, from beginning to end more framework than reality, was now over. But the forces that it had unleashed – the real war – were still in development. For Kamakura to carve a permanent place in the authority structure of Japan, it would have to devise strategies both to restore real peace and to satisfy its men. This meant finding ways to restrain and license, confiscate

18 For this effort in the different provinces of the west, see *WG*, pp. 79–89.

19 The battle of Fujigawa, occurring early in the war (1180/10), was the first such encounter. Taking place in Suruga Province immediately to the west of the Kantō, it led to the "phony war" that ended only at Ichinotani.

20 For an account of the battles and strategy of the war, Shinoda, *The Founding of the Kamakura Shogunate*, is excellent.

and confer, punish and reward. The institution of *jitō* met each of these several requirements.

THE GEMPEI AFTERMATH: *JITŌ* AND *SHUGO*

The year 1185 is one of the most famous in Japanese history. Its reputation derives from the Minamoto victory over the Taira and from the supposed inauguration of the bakufu's twin officer networks in the field, those of military estate steward (*jitō*) and military governor (*shugo*). As we have just noted, the Gempei denouement was largely an anticlimax, though it did have an unexpected impact on conditions in the countryside. With the war officially over, warriors could no longer use the Gempei labels to justify their private lawlessness. Their aggression was thus more directly an attack on the courtier-dominated estate system. During the middle months of 1185, pressure mounted on Kamakura to quell this rising siege of outlawry.

The bakufu was at a loss as to what to do. Conditions were made even more complicated by a deterioration in the relationship between Yoritomo and Yoshitsune and by the retired emperor's decision to exploit this situation. Thus, not only was there a continuing crisis in the provinces (much of it spearheaded by victorious Minamoto), but there also was a developing rift within Kamakura and between it and Kyoto. The difficulties between the brothers were what eventually brought things to a head. As we have seen, Yoritomo reserved his greatest sensitivity throughout the war for threats that issued from within his own clan. Quite predictably, therefore, when Yoshitsune began to steer a course during the ninth month that was openly rebellious, the Minamoto chieftain determined to seek his destruction.[21] Yoshitsune, however, eluded capture and succeeded in persuading the ex-emperor, Goshirakawa, to brand Yoritomo a rebel and to appoint the hero of the war as *jitō* of Kyushu. The stage was now set for one of Japanese history's most momentous developments.

Yoritomo responded to the crisis by dispatching an armed force to Kyoto that laid before the court a series of demands. Unfortunately, neither the precise content of those demands nor the court's reply can be ascertained, and so we must rely on an account that is now considered suspect. According to the *Azuma kagami*, Yoritomo forced the ex-

21 More has been written on the Yoritomo–Yoshitsune relationship than on any other familial rivalry in Japanese history. See Shinoda, *The Founding of the Kamakura Shogunate*, pp. 121ff; The chapter on Yoshitsune in Ivan Morris, *The Nobility of Failure* (New York: Holt, Rinehart and Winston, 1975); and the relevant sections of Helen Craig McCullough, *Yoshitsune: A Fifteenth Century Japanese Chronicle* (Tokyo: University of Tokyo Press, 1966).

emperor to authorize Kamakura's appointment of countrywide networks of *jitō* and *shugo*.[22] The importance of this development for premodern observers is that Yoritomo's authority to make such assignments was seen as the basis for his government's ongoing presence. Modern historians go even further than that. The power to appoint *jitō* and *shugo* represented no less than a merging of the systems of vassalage and benefice. By virtue of his new authority, Yoritomo became a feudal chieftain, and Japan was thereby launched on its medieval phase. Japanese history was part of world history, with east and west exhibiting similar patterns.[23]

There are many problems (and not a few virtues) in this latter form of reasoning. One difficulty has been a tendency to conclude too much from the *Azuma kagami's* description. Not only were there no *shugo* at all until the early 1190s, but *jitō* countrywide was not the same as *jitō* everywhere. Moreover, on a different level of argument, a basis for Kamakura's existence was hardly tantamount to Kamakura's displacement of Kyoto. The bulk of governance in Japan remained in the hands of traditional proprietors and governors for the duration of the Kamakura period. On the other hand, the authorization in question was momentous, first, because it was never rescinded and, second, because it did mark something strikingly new. Yet even having said that, feudalism at the end of the twelfth century registered only modest beginnings: Yoritomo's reach remained strictly limited, and more importantly, the bequests he made were over lands neither owned nor controlled by him. At all events, the chieftain in Kamakura did come to exercise a type of authority that was new to Japan. Its precise limits and nature are bound up with the office of *jitō*, to which we now turn.

The term *jitō* originated in the ninth century but did not become a land officership until the middle of the twelfth. Though its genealogy and history during the Heian period are the subjects of heated controversy,[24] our concerns are restricted to what happened to the title during the Gempei War. In part owing to its relative newness, local persons found it an attractive cover by which to justify unlawful seizures of

22 *AK*, 1185/11/29. This is the most famous entry in that chronicle.

23 Perhaps the classic expression of this older view is by Edwin O. Reischauer, "Japanese Feudalism," in Rushton Coulborn, ed., *Feudalism in History* (Princeton, N.J.: Princeton University Press, 1956), pp. 31–2. For a more recent discussion of the feudal aspects of Kamakura's early rule, see Jeffrey P. Mass, "The Early Bakufu and Feudalism," in Jeffrey P. Mass, ed., *Court and Bakufu in Japan: Essays in Kamakura History* (New Haven, Conn.: Yale University Press, 1982), pp. 123–42 (hereafter cited as Mass, "Feudalism").

24 A useful survey of the several arguments is by Ōae Ryō, "Jitō shiki o meguru shomondai," *Hōkei gakkai zasshi* 13 (1964): 26–32; also *WG*, pp. 102–11.

rights and profits from centrally owned estates.[25] That is, they claimed to be both Minamoto and privately appointed *jitō*, a combination that was designed to immunize them from central control but that actually helped solidify a growing identification of *jitō* with Kamakura. Most of this development occurred during 1184 and 1185, at precisely the same time that the bakufu was assuming its overt stance against warrior lawlessness. It was also the period when Yoritomo was seriously seeking a common denominator on which to erect a full-scale reward–control system. The office of *jitō* was eventually used for this dual purpose. As Yoritomo undoubtedly rationalized it, the most effective means of ridding the countryside of self-styled *jitō* was for Kyoto to authorize a Kamakura monopoly of that post. The bakufu chieftain would then move concertedly against bogus *jitō* while appointing deserving vassals to lawful *jitō* titles whose rights packages had been confiscated from losers in the recent war. In this way, the continuity of services to estates and their proprietors would be ensured, as would managerial tenures for loyal, law-abiding Minamoto. The bakufu would make the actual *jitō* appointments and also guarantee their lawfulness and reliability. Stable conditions would be restored; Kamakura's presence through its *jitō* would be permanently established; and the men of the bakufu would enjoy both security and elite status.

How much of this conception can be credited to Yoritomo in advance of its implementation is difficult to determine. What is clear is that the year 1186 witnessed many appointments to *jitō* posts. At the same time, unauthorized *jitō* continued to be disciplined, as did lawfully appointed persons who exceeded their rights. In many cases, *jitō* were dismissed, whether for unusually serious crimes or owing to unjustified appointments in the first place.[26] One result of this attention to lawfulness and reliability was a network of provincial officers in perpetual motion. Kamakura did not establish its *jitō* corps to have it become static in size or fixed in place. A second result of Yoritomo's willingness to punish even his closest vassals was credibility – with those who served him and with the estate owners who depended on him. A major consequence was the quick appearance of Kamakura's period-long contribution to governance in Japan, its capacity to arbitrate between the local and central elites.

The *shugo* institution, despite being accorded a simultaneous birth

25 *WG*, pp. 111–19; *KB*, docs. 6–7.
26 For example, the 1186 cancellation of a *jitō* post in the central region's Tamba Province; *KB*, doc. 30. The loser of the title was none other than Yoritomo's own brother-in-law, Hōjō Yoshitoki.

with the *jitō* by the *Azuma kagami*, belongs in fact to a slightly later period. Though the bakufu did appoint provincial-level officers from early in the war, they were evidently not called *shugo* but, rather, *sōtsuibushi*, an older title.[27] This distinction is actually extremely important. Kamakura's wartime *sōtsuibushi* were all-purpose provincial commanders bearing little resemblance to the legally constricted *shugo* of the 1190s and beyond. Indeed, the contexts in which these two officer types flourished is entirely different. Whereas the *sōtsuibushi* belonged to a period of helter-skelter growth on the part of the emerging Kamakura bakufu, the *shugo* were products of a damping-down process by a government seeking greater control of itself. The connection between the two titles, then, is largely superficial. Though both exercised provincewide authority, they had utterly divergent functions. The *Azuma kagami's* assertion of an 1185 authorization to appoint *shugo* is a confusion with *jitō* and a later rationalization by chroniclers intent on creating matching antiquities.

During the later 1180s, the urge to establish a workable division of responsibility with Kyoto gained impetus. The *jitō* institution constituted an important beginning here. Yet the country's proprietors were continuing to deluge Kamakura with undifferentiated appeals for redress, whereas the bakufu, for its part, had little idea as to whom it ought to recognize as permanent vassals. Yoritomo, indeed, became increasingly aware that his government had overextended itself. He therefore began to turn away petitions for assistance of the type he had earlier accepted. He also exhorted Kyoto to assume responsibility for matters now deemed outside his purview.[28] One result was the beginning of a jurisdictional separation between *jitō* and an equivalent managerial title, that of *gesu*. The former were declared men of Kamakura, with bakufu authority over appointments, dismissals, and punishments. The latter, though their perquisites and duties were indistinguishable from those of *jitō*, were now announced to be the responsibility of estate owners. This cutting edge between *jitō* and *gesu* became a prominent feature of the Kyoto–Kamakura dual polity.[29]

The matter of Kamakura's vassalage was an equally thorny problem, though one that did not receive Yoritomo's full attention until after 1190. Until recently, scholars assumed that Yoritomo devised the term *gokenin* at the same time that he launched his drive to power in 1180. The *Azuma kagami* uses the word in its earliest entries, and the

27 The finest treatment of the *sōtsuibushi–shugo* problem is by Yasuda Motohisa, *Shugo to jitō* (Tokyo: Shibundō, 1964), pp. 22–42. 28 *WG*, pp. 125–7.

29 The implications of the *jitō–gesu* division are treated in *WG*, pp. 136–42.

currency of the term also made sense historically. Yoritomo was a feudal chieftain, *gokenin* being the insignia of vassalage appropriate to his warrior movement. But as we now know, the term was not contemporaneous with the Gempei War and was not even used in the later 1180s.[30] Our conclusion is that vassalage remained a highly amorphous concept during the bakufu's first decade. Loyalty itself was often a matter of the moment, and "joining the Minamoto" could literally be done in isolation. Thus, when the war ended, a determination was still in the future as to the composition of a permanent band. The first group to be acknowledged received the initial round of *jitō* appointments, and these mostly were easterners. But each province of the country had warriors claiming to be legitimate loyalists. It was left to Yoritomo to devise a means to test this avowal and to move in the direction of a less disparate following.

It is not surprising, therefore, that the later 1180s witnessed a consolidation drive that was scarcely completed by the end of the century. Apart from the Kantō, the area of first concern was the Chūbu, the bloc of provinces between the country's two capitals. But no region of the country was fully secure, for Kamakura's command structure had never been unified. Numerous warriors remained under traditional chiefs. Yoritomo's solution to these problems was to engage the country's fighting men in yet another military campaign, this time against the north. The north was the site of a major enclave of private governance that had remained aloof from the Gempei War and later had given refuge to Yoritomo's fugitive brother, Yoshitsune. The Kamakura chieftain thus had several reasons to attack the family that dominated the region, the Ōshū Fujiwara.

In preparation for his campaign, Yoritomo authorized selected easterners to initiate a massive recruitment drive in all parts of the country. Though we lack detailed information on most areas, it is clear that warriors answered the call from as far away as Kyushu but that the greatest response came from the Chūbu.[31] Because the campaign itself resulted in a victory for Kamakura in 1189, Yoritomo found himself able to destroy the Fujiwara bloc on his eastern flank and to destroy or subordinate the Chūbu group on his western side. Elsewhere, he rewarded warriors who fought loyally and punished or purged those who did not.[32] A major step was thus taken in the direction of a kind of

30 Yasuda Motohisa, "Gokenin-sei seiritsu ni kansuru ichi shiron," *Gakushūin daigaku bungaku bu kenkyū nempō* 16 (1969): 81–110. For a discussion, see Mass, "Feudalism," pp. 131–7.

31 Kasai Sachiko, "Ōshū heiran to tōgoku bushidan," *Rekishi kyōiku* 16 (1968): 27–40.

32 This is vividly depicted in a Kyushu investiture of 1192; see *KB*, doc. 37.

balance sheet on the country's fighting men. This was not yet a policy of identifying permanent vassals, calling them *gokenin,* and including their names on vassal registers. But these steps were not very far away.

What was needed to implement such a policy was a corps of deputies with regular authority and uniform local jurisdiction. Here, then, is the basis for the *shugo* institution, provincial commanders who might also function as constabulary officers. The actual process by which the *shugo* were first set into place has unfortunately been lost to us, though a common surmise is that Yoritomo, on the occasion of his first trip to Kyoto since childhood (1190), forced the court to appoint him *shugo*-in-chief for the entire country.[33] Although there is no record of such an arrangement, personnel identifiable as *shugo* do begin to appear around 1192. This was just at the point that the *gokenin* label also appears along with indications of the first vassals registers.[34] The connections here can hardly be overlooked: The primary responsibility for installing and overseeing the *gokenin* system was granted to the *shugo,* who were themselves created as extensions of Yoritomo's declared lordship over his new vassalage. Moreover, with the institutionalization of *gokenin* there also appeared a second legal category, *higokenin* (nonvassals), both of whom may earlier have been "Minamoto." At any rate, by the early 1190s the three basic local innovations of the Kamakura bakufu, *jitō, shugo,* and *gokenin,* had been established. At variance with traditional accounts, it is not the *jitō* and *shugo* whose origins should be closely linked but, rather, the *shugo* and *gokenin.* Neither of the latter had anything directly to do with the Gempei War.

It has long been assumed that the final pillar in Kamakura's system, the office of shogun, was likewise set into place in 1192. Because of that event, this year is almost as well known as 1185. In a sense, however, the fame here is misplaced. Although Yoritomo was appointed shogun in 1192, he did not understand its significance, which was established only after his death. Thus, the Kamakura chieftain resigned the office in 1195, never supposing that posterity would credit him with starting a tradition of shoguns. For Yoritomo, the title was important only insofar as it might impress Kyoto; he returned to a more prestigious office (that of *utaishō,* or commander of the inner palace guards) in 1195 for precisely that reason.[35] Conversely, in no

33 For a discussion, see Yasuda, *Shugo to jitō,* pp. 45ff.

34 See the list of registers in Tanaka Minoru, "Kamakura shoki no seiji katei–kenkyū nenkan o chūshin ni shite," *Rekishi kyōiku* 11 (1963): 23.

35 For Yoritomo and the title of shogun, see Ishii Ryosuke, "Sei-i tai shōgun to Minamoto Yoritomo," reprinted in Ishii Ryosuke, *Taika no kaishin to Kamakura bakufu no seiritsu* (Tokyo: Sōbunsha, 1958), pp. 87–94; and Mass, "Feudalism," pp. 126–8.

ways was the post of shogun a capstone to his system of vassalage. As we shall see, it was left to the Hōjō, in need of an object for a regency, to invest the title of shogun with both a future and a past. Yoritomo thus became the first of a line of shoguns only in the memories of those who followed him.

In the wake of the northern campaign, Yoritomo, as mentioned, traveled to Kyoto for his first visit since childhood. By all accounts it was a triumphant venture. The chieftain of Kamakura was feted everywhere, and he was granted the *utaishō* title to which he later returned after three years as shogun (1192–5). A further preferment allowed him to open a *mandokoro*, a chancellery on the model of those of the great central aristocrats. Hereafter, decrees by his government issued from that organ rather than from Yoritomo personally.[36] This was, in a sense, a concession to bureaucratization, arguably the only one of import that he ever made. More typically, Yoritomo stood firm against the formation of enclaves of private power and shifted men about from one governmental task to another. He also continued his policy of purging warriors whose loyalty he considered suspect. During the 1190s, Yoritomo rid himself of certain province-level vassals in the west and evolved a complementary policy of elevating undistinguished easterners to positions of authority in the same region. As his thinking must have run, men of this type would owe their prestige to the largesse of the chieftain. In ways such as this, Yoritomo's temperament inclined him toward patrimonialism, though the realities of warrior power obliged him to adopt feudal techniques of organization as well.

To conclude this section on the era of Yoritomo, we should note the fluctuations in his relationship with Kyoto. The period covering 1185 to 1200 can be divided into three subperiods. The years between 1185 and 1192 witnessed a contest of sorts between the ex-emperor, Goshirakawa, and Yoritomo. This hardly constituted open warfare. Committed as he was to resuscitating traditional authority, Yoritomo dealt respectfully with the retired emperor throughout. For his part, however, Goshirakawa had little to lose by exploiting this advantage and by attempting to embarrass the rival regime in Kamakura. At any rate, when Goshirakawa died in 1192, there was little sorrow felt in the eastern capital. To prevent further opposition from Kyoto, Yoritomo decided to assume a higher profile in the politics of the court.

In the early stage of this effort, the Kamakura chief worked closely with a ranking ally in Kyoto, Kujō Kanezane. A problem developed,

36 For early examples of such edicts, see *KB*, docs. 12, 16–17.

however, when Yoritomo determined that his daughter should occupy the same imperial consort's position held by Kanezane's daughter. Yoritomo's goal was no less than to become grandfather to an emperor, and to promote that cause he undertook a second trip to Kyoto. This occurred in 1195 and was the occasion of his abandonment of the title of shogun in deference to a higher-ranking post, the office of *utaishō*. By this time, however, there were forces in the capital who saw in Yoritomo's gambit an opportunity to rid themselves of both Kanezane's and Kamakura's meddling. The result was exactly as the opposition interests in Kyoto had hoped. With Yoritomo's assistance, Kanezane was removed from power, but the eastern chieftain's plans for his daughter, owing to her untimely death, failed to materialize. Yoritomo, disappointed and chastened, turned his attention back to Kamakura. The period between 1196 and 1199 thus became a time of minimal interaction between the two capitals. The bakufu continued to accept courtiers' complaints alleging lawlessness by *jitō*. But a new power bloc had emerged in Kyoto over which Yoritomo exercised little leverage. When the eastern chieftain died in 1199, he could count as his most conspicuous failure the lack of closer relations with Kyoto.

THE ROAD TO JŌKYŪ

The period 1200 to 1221 has always had a quality of inevitability about it. This is because the Jōkyū disturbance, pitting the two capitals against each other, seemed a logical denouement to the establishment of a warrior regime in a country with only one prior governmental center. In fact, the war was considerably more complex than merely a fated showdown between older and newer authority systems. The lineup of forces in 1221 revealed societies in conflict as much within themselves as against one another; and the outpouring of violence that accompanied and followed the war suggests that the Gempei settlement, embracing various compromises by Yoritomo, had only superficially satisfied many of the country's warriors. A major result of the multisided Jōkyū struggle was thus a shift, if not a restructuring, in the power alignments between and within the two capitals as well as within the warrior class as a whole. For these reasons, the Jōkyū disturbance, belying its brief duration, was the most momentous event of the thirteenth century, rivaled only by the Mongol invasions.[37]

37 This multidimensional view of the Jōkyū disturbance is presented in Jeffrey P. Mass, *The Development of Kamakura Rule, 1180–1250: A History with Documents* (Stanford, Calif.: Stanford University Press, 1979), chap. 1 (hereafter cited as *DKR*).

The dominant theme of progress in Kamakura in the generation before Jōkyū was the rise of the Hōjō as hegemons. This was not the relatively easy progress it is often made out to be. The period was punctuated by power struggles and rebellions, and the Hōjō's emergence out of this milieu was anything but certain.[38] The background of the competition was the gap at the political center occasioned by Yoritomo's death. His successors, his sons Yoriie (r. 1199–1203) and Sanetomo (r. 1203–19), were not of the same mettle as their father, which meant that actual leadership fell to a coalition of vassals, itself an unstable arrangement. During the years 1200 to 1203, two families, the Hiki and the Hōjō, presided over this group. The head of the former was the father-in-law of Yoriie, who was himself hostile to his mother's family, the Hōjō. A bloodletting eventually ensued, which resulted in the replacement of Yoriie by the more pliable Sanetomo, as well as the destruction of the Hiki by their rivals, the Hōjō. The way was thus open for the Hōjō scion, Tokimasa, to assume brief but direct command of the Kamakura bakufu.

It has long been assumed that Tokimasa capped this dramatic rise in 1203 by becoming *shikken,* or regent, to the new shogun Sanetomo. According to this tradition, a sequence of *shikken* henceforth paralleled a sequence of shoguns. In fact, there is reason to doubt this version of events, as the title of *shikken,* meaning director of a *mandokoro,* could hardly have been initiated when there was no *mandokoro*. During this period the shogun was of insufficiently high court rank to open a formal chancellery.[39] Nevertheless, Tokimasa did dominate the bakufu until 1205, a fact we know from the regime's edicts, all of which bear his signature alone.[40] In that year he was displaced by his son and daughter, who, because their father's rule had not been institutionalized, failed to inherit all his power. Tokimasa's successors were thus forced to share authority with others, and for a decade after 1209 the *mandokoro,* now open, became the chief decision-making body in Kamakura and the principal issuer of its edicts.[41]

In 1213, another bloodletting occurred in which an old-line *gokenin* family, the Wada, found itself maneuvered into a treasonous position,

38 The clearest account in English of the rise of the Hōjō is by H. Paul Varley, "The Hōjō Family and Succession to Power," in Mass, ed., *Court and Bakufu in Japan*, chap. 6.

39 The *shikken* post of Tokimasa is noted in *AK*, 1203/10/9; for a critique, see *DKR*, pp. 77–79.

40 For example, *DKR*, docs. 55–59; *KB*, docs. 20, 33–34, 48, 100, 113, 161, 163.

41 For the role of the *mandokoro* during this period, see *DKR*, pp. 75–80.

giving the Hōjō ample reason to lead a bakufu campaign against it. Yet even now the Hōjō's hold over the governmental apparatus did not become entirely secure; there were fluctuations in the membership of the *mandokoro*, and the Hōjō were not always its directors. All this changed, however, in 1219 when the shogun was assassinated. This development gave the Hōjō a pretext on which to declare an emergency situation, which was close to the truth, as no successor was immediately available. In the absence of a nominal lord, the *mandokoro* ceased its formal activities, and Hōjō Yoshitoki, like his father before him, began issuing Kamakura's edicts under his own name. This time the Hōjō's accession to power within the bakufu proved to be permanent.

While the Hōjō were succeeding, finally, in securing their hegemony, a parallel situation was developing in Kyoto under a new retired emperor. Gotoba was the ultimate beneficiary of Yoritomo's clumsy meddling in court politics during the middle 1190s. When he "retired" in 1198 at the age of eighteen, his immediate task was to neutralize the bloc of supporters that made up his own entourage; it was this group that had engineered the removal of the Kanezane faction and blocked Yoritomo's designs at court. By 1202, Gotoba had succeeded in becoming his own master – and was also well on his way to becoming master of the capital. He established that his chancellery – the *in-no-chō* – was the central decision-making body in Kyoto, and he actively pursued greater wealth, often at the expense of rival proprietors. The result was a growing feeling of restiveness in Kyoto that paralleled a like sentiment in Kamakura.

Gotoba, indeed, attempted to capitalize on the growing warrior unrest, by providing an alternative source of patronage for the country's fighting men. He did this by recruiting both *gokenin* and non-*gokenin* for his private guard units and by distributing to these retainers various rank and office preferments. Although Gotoba might not have been aware of it at first, he was creating, with this activity, the core of an army that would later challenge Kamakura. The members of his guards units were drawn from east and west, a development that the bakufu took little notice of, as relations between the capitals were peaceful, if not unusually warm. In an earlier era, Yoritomo had fought court rewards for Minamoto who failed to be nominated by the chieftain. But now the shogun himself was a conspicuous recipient of court honors, whereas Kamakura remained parsimonious in granting *jitō* awards to most western vassals. In time, relatively large numbers of fighting men came to realize that the bakufu's existence was doing little to benefit them personally. Integrated, as in times past, with the Kyoto-controlled estate system, warriors of this kind were receptive to Gotoba's call to arms against Kamakura in 1221.

The events that took place in 1219 are generally considered to have contributed to the decision to wage war. During the previous year, Hōjō Masako had traveled to Kyoto to negotiate with Gotoba over the naming of a shogun-designate. Had Sanetomo had an heir, the trip would not have been necessary. But the Hōjō, for whom the post of shogun was the basis for their regency, had already decided to seek a successor from within the imperial family. Such a choice would provide the bakufu (and themselves) with an unimpeachable legitimacy, whereas for Gotoba (whose infant son was the designee) there was the prospect of a bakufu "absorbed" into the imperial state. Early in 1219, however, Sanetomo's assassination prompted a change of heart on the part of the ex-emperor, and he contributed to the crisis in Kamakura by reneging on his earlier agreement. After a show of force in the capital, the bakufu secured a compromise choice – an infant Fujiwara – to be the next shogun. But when the child was brought to Kamakura, the ex-emperor resolved to withhold his formal appointment.

These developments poisoned relations between the two capitals, though, remarkably, the sources fall suddenly silent regarding actual movement toward war. There is no indication of overt steps taken on either side to prepare for any kind of showdown. This silence continued into the spring of 1221, when the ex-emperor had already decided on his course. The magnitude of his error only makes more regrettable our inability to trace events from mid-1219. At any rate, we can imagine a fevered effort, which contributed to the court's debacle, to assemble a fighting force that might acquit itself. In the end, Gotoba's army was a potpourri of warrior society. Drawn mostly from the central and western provinces, but with a number of eastern defectors, the forces of the court had little internal coherence.[42] Whereas fighting for the bakufu meant the prospect of new *jitō* titles, fighting for the court promised nothing in particular. Negative (or passive) feelings toward Kamakura could hardly make up for the absence of a rewards program.

Nor had Gotoba taken account of the fact that like the Hōjō, he had alienated much of his own natural constituency. Presumably, he be-

42 The nature of Gotoba's army is discussed in detail in *DKR*, pp. 16–29.

lieved that the central *shōen* proprietors shared his distaste for Kamakura to the point that they would rally to his cause. He must also have expected delivery of the warrior-managers and the mercenaries who served them. In any event, the aristocracy's response was almost as mixed as that of the country's fighting men. Neutrality was the stance adopted by many, whereas others were simply not in a position to guarantee compliance by those living on their estates. A united Kyoto thus proved to be as elusive for Gotoba as it had been for Kiyomori two generations earlier.

Before moving to the Jōkyū encounter itself, it remains to be pondered what the ex-emperor hoped to achieve by his challenge to Kamakura. In his war declaration, he singled out Hōjō Yoshitoki, who was the nearest thing he could find to a common enemy for potential warrior recruits. The Minamoto, whose rule had already ended, could be praised for their service to the court, whereas the Hōjō, with some accuracy, could be condemned as usurpers. Beyond that, Gotoba entreated the men of Kamakura to rely henceforth on the judicial authority of Kyoto, a subtle plea, as it aimed at compromising Kamakura's jurisdiction without threatening to dismantle the bakufu itself. To have sought the support of warriors in overthrowing the warrior government could only have weakened Gotoba's chances for success. Conversely, the *gokenin* who joined the court did not do so out of a desire to destroy the bakufu idea or to end their own elite status. What they must have looked forward to was a reorganized regime with a new warrior leadership and a new form of cooperation with Kyoto. But Gotoba, whatever his rhetoric, could hardly have shared such views; his ultimate aim must have been to end Japan's dual polity, perhaps by placing *shugo* and *jitō* under his own authority. As we know, this potential divergence of goals had no time to surface. The Jōkyū disturbance, if not the violence that it unleashed, was over in less than a month.

THE JŌKYŪ DISTURBANCE AND ITS AFTERMATH

If the *Azuma kagami* is to be believed, Kamakura had no advance warning that Gotoba was preparing for war. Not surprisingly, the bakufu leadership was uncertain at first as to how to respond. The propriety of engaging an imperial army was debated; yet scruples gave way, under urging by the Hōjō, to the threat that was unmistakably at hand. Gotoba's war declaration reached Kamakura on the nineteenth day of the fifth month of 1221. Within a week's time, according to the *Azuma kagami,* a bakufu counterforce of 190,000 men had been assembled.[43]

The recruitment policies devised by the Hōjō had a direct bearing on the outcome of the war and the settlement that followed. Only easterners were called to service, although as Kamakura's armies advanced westward, local vassals were actively recruited. The Kantō-led military campaign thus formed a wedge for greater penetration of the west and also offered a chance for further consolidation of the Chūbu. Unlike the beginning stages of the Gempei War, then, the leadership in Kamakura determined to take the fighting directly to the enemy. The strategy worked splendidly, and on the fifteenth day of the sixth month the victorious bakufu army entered the capital. Brushing aside Gotoba's pleas for mercy, Kamakura scattered into exile the ex-emperor and other members of his war party.

So rapidly had events taken place that at first the bakufu could hardly have appreciated the extent of its victory. The full composition of the ex-emperor's army was a matter to be determined, and probes had to be undertaken to judge degrees of war guilt. Similarly, the bakufu had to examine its own army – who had fought and with what degree of valor. What complicated all of this was a reign of terror that now gripped the countryside. Both vassals and nonvassals interpreted the court's defeat as a license to engage in lawlessness.[44] So savage was this outburst that whatever Kamakura's instinct for revenge against Kyoto, its leadership realized that the traditional authority system could not, without risk to the bakufu, be dismantled. In fact, it would have to be restored, and Kamakura therefore took steps in that direction. It retained most of the governmental apparatus of the court, and it set into place a new retired emperor. At the same time, it undertook to return the countryside to peace by responding to the complaints of violence lodged by the traditional proprietors.

But Kamakura was hardly prepared to oversee a total return to the status quo ante. It replaced its ineffective Kyoto *shugo*'s office with a bakufu branch in the capital, the so-called Rokuhara *tandai.* It also reserved for itself the right to interfere in high-level personnel decisions at court, including the naming of emperors. It further made clear that Kamakura and Kyoto would henceforth work in tandem;

43 Two translations by William McCullough present a narrative account of the war: "The *Azuma kagami* Account of the Shōkyū War," *Monumenta Nipponica* 23 (1968): 102–55; "Shōkyūki: An account of the Shōkyū War," *Monumenta Nipponica* 19 (1964): 163–215, and 21 (1966): 420–53.

44 For a sampling of the violence in 1221 and 1222, see *DKR*, docs. 21, 24–26; *KB*, docs. 95, 112, 116.

the dual polity was a permanent reality that might never be challenged again. To underscore this, the bakufu began issuing legislative pronouncements, demonstrating parity with Kyoto as a lawgiving authority. Finally, Kamakura responded to the desires of its men by flooding the central and western provinces with massive numbers of new *jitō* assignments. This latter development constituted no less than a colonization drive, for the recipients were almost exclusively easterners and the appointment areas were the confiscated holdings of dispossessed westerners. As a result, the demographics of warrior strength in Japan shifted dramatically in favor of elite fighting men from the Kantō.

The restoration of stability, so high on Kamakura's list of priorities, was actually undermined by the introduction of large numbers of new *jitō* into unfamiliar areas. But this was the price that had to be paid to institutionalize a presence countrywide and to satisfy the expectations of a core constituency. A major result was a substantial bolstering of what had long since become Kamakura's principal governmental role, the dispensing of justice. With bakufu men in possession of rights in all parts of the country, it was more important than ever that the policing of *jitō*, immune from the discipline of *shōen* proprietors, be handled with dispatch. At first, Kamakura was hard-pressed to keep up with the demand for judgments, and in fact, its commitment to fairness may have suffered a bit. But these lapses proved momentary, as the bakufu was willing to reverse any mistaken decisions.[45] At any rate, the era was one of adjustment and change in Japan after roughly two decades of equilibrium.

The changes referred to here have less to do with substance and structure than they do with scope and numbers. That is, the Jōkyū disturbance yielded no institutionally new figures comparable to those evolving out of the Gempei War and its aftermath. What occurred after 1221 was an expansion of existing officer networks and authority, not some radical departure into new conceptual space. True, Kamakura now began posing as a lawgiving authority alongside Kyoto, and this was certainly unprecedented. But the enactments themselves did not infringe on the imperial sanction, and in fact, they acknowledged and fortified it. Moreover, Kamakura's efforts as a lawgiver were decidedly modest at first, and the bakufu carved out for itself no new spheres of local or central jurisdiction. What was new after 1221 was

45 A classic example, which involved attempts to rectify errors on four separate occasions, was finally put right in 1232; see *DKR*, doc. 33.

the growth of Kamakura's involvement in dispute resolution and its accelerated placement of *jitō*. The number of such *jitō* is perhaps the critical question, and herein lies an interesting tale.

According to a famous datum of history cited in the *Azuma kagami*, Kamakura profited from the confiscation of fully three thousand *shōen* as part of the Jōkyū settlement. If taken literally, a shift of such magnitude would have significantly tilted the court–bakufu balance. Kyoto would have suffered a cataclysmic setback and faced severe revenue shortages followed by immediate decline. In fact, however, the three thousand figure implied far less than it seemed to. In the first place, nowhere near that number of transfers can be corroborated; the total (as with the size of Kamakura's army) is likely exaggerated. Second, even if the number were accurate, it probably implied the total of transfers at all levels of authority. That is, Kamakura and Kyoto shared in this new largesse. The bakufu declared its right to fashion *jitō* assignments from the managerial packages belonging to those warriors caught on the losing side. Likewise, the court, with Kamakura's blessing, shifted an unknown number of proprietary titles from one segment of the traditional aristocracy – Gotoba's war party – to another, those who had remained neutral or shown sympathy for Kamakura. It is in this sense, that the Jōkyū disturbance engendered shifts both within and between Japan's two great power blocs. Research on the "Kyoto settlement" has only just begun, with indications that the major religious institutions came out strongest.[46] By contrast, scholarship on Kamakura is well advanced and shows a small number of proprietorships, against numerous new *jitō* titles.[47] As reflected in the overall settlement, then, the bakufu could be assured that the basic ordering of society was not being impaired. Warriors, difficult to control in the best of circumstances, would remain middle-level land managers.

A final point on this subject is that the postwar era was not limited to a year or two; Jōkyū land transfers are known from as late as the 1240s, though most of the shifts in holdings obviously occurred earlier. By 1225 or 1226, Kamakura was prepared to make structural changes in its organization that pointed the way to a new, mature phase in bakufu operations.

46 Kōyasan, in particular, profited from the court's defeat, but so did the Tōdaiji and the shrines of Kamo, Ise, and Iwashimizu; see *DKR*, pp. 38–40.

47 Details on some 129 post-Jōkyū *jitō* appointments appear in Tanaka Minoru, "Jōkyū kyōgata bushi no ichi kōsatsu – rango no shin jitō buninchi o chūshin to shite," *Shigaku zasshi* 65 (1956): 21–48; Tanaka Minoru, "Jōkyū no rango no shin jitō buninchi," *Shigaku zasshi* 79 (1970): 38–53.

BAKUFU GOVERNANCE

In 1224, Hōjō Yoshitoki died and was followed in death by Masako a year later. The new leader of the bakufu was Yoshitoki's son, Yasutoki, by consensus the greatest of the Hōjō regents. Born after the founding of the bakufu and educated in classical Confucianism, Yasutoki left a stamp on the regime's operations that survived until the end of the period. It was under Yasutoki that the bakufu's capacity for mediating disputes achieved new heights and under him also that Kamakura's reputation for good government became a fixture of the historical memory.[48] Kamakura's golden age, which began now, owed much of its luster to the efforts of this extraordinary man.

Yasutoki was an innovator right from the start. Desirous of ending the postwar emergency, he took three steps to place the bakufu on a more regular footing. First, he established the cosigner *(rensho)* institution wherein a coregent, drawn from his own family, would become part of Kamakura's formal apparatus.[49] Second, he promoted the idea of collegiality by creating a board of councilors *(hyōjōshū)* to function as the bakufu's ranking governmental organ. Finally, he moved to formalize the elevation of the shogun-designate, a step that his predecessors, even after the Jōkyū victory, had not taken. In the first month of 1226, the eight-year-old Yoritsune became the fourth lord of Kamakura.

These were Yasutoki's public moves. He also moved behind the scenes to ensure that the *hyōjōshū* would be responsive to his own wishes and become the new high court of Kamakura. Although the council, like the *mandokoro* before it, was a mixture of old-line *gokenin* and ex-noble legal specialists, it differed from its predecessor in being the instrument of its founder's will. The *mandokoro,* which had been founded by the Minamoto and which played such an important role during the period to 1219, was inactive throughout the 1220s and was subsequently divested of its entire judicial authority. In 1232, the shogun was promoted to a court rank high enough to make him eligible to open a *mandokoro*. But by that time Yasutoki was its director and therefore oversaw the chancellery's principal task of investing and

48 Note, for example, the high opinion of Yasutoki's tenure held by Kitabatake Chikafusa, author of the fourteenth-century *Jinnō Shōtōki: A Chronicle of Gods and Sovereigns,* trans. H. Paul Varley (New York: Columbia University Press, 1980), pp. 228–30.

49 Credit for this innovation used to be given to Hōjō Masako, based on an erroneous entry in the *Azuma kagami*. The correct attribution was made by Uwayokote Masataka, "Renshosei no seiritsu," in *Kokushi ronshū,* vol. 2 (Kyoto: Dokushikai, 1959), pp. 625–40.

confirming *jitō* posts. In sum, whereas the *mandokoro* dated back to Heian times and had an existence tied to the court-sponsored rank of the shogun, the *hyōjōshū* was a bakufu invention and a vehicle of the regent. To argue, as many historians have done, that the *hyōjōshū* constituted the beginning of a new conciliar phase in Kamakura history is to overlook the organ's origins and to ignore its subsequent dominance by the Hōjō.[50]

Although the sources do not refer directly to this process, from its beginning the council became the arena for a rapidly modernizing system of justice. As mentioned earlier, the bakufu had been placed in the position of judicial arbiter, literally from the first days of the Minamoto movement. The earliest settlements were edicts issued by Yoritomo himself, but after formation of the *mandokoro*, he centered much of this authority there. With the chieftain's death, however, the Hōjō, under Tokimasa, came to dominate the process (1203–5), though in the decade before Jōkyū the *mandokoro*, as noted, experienced its resurgence. From 1219 to 1226 it was the Hōjō once again who controlled the regime's judgments.[51]

Belying these power shifts at the top level of the bakufu, the techniques of justice were rapidly becoming more sophisticated. Technique, indeed, was emphasized from the start. Because Kamakura had no written laws at first or any philosophical traditions and because the country's estates were accustomed to having individualized precedents (*senrei*) made the basis of judgments, it was natural for the bakufu to stress procedure over principle. On a period-long basis, identifying and confirming local precedents served as the foundation of Kamakura justice. Flowing from this came basic attitudes toward impartiality, modes of proof, due process, and the right of appeal. In its maturity, the system was thus closely calibrated to the needs of a society that was lawless yet litigious, restive yet still respectful of higher authority.

A case in 1187 demonstrates the enormous potential of a system of justice whose principal objective was equity for the litigants rather than aggrandizement by their judges. At stake was the possession of an area in distant Kyushu to which the disputants had conflicting claims. In the words of Yoritomo's settlement edict, "The relative merits of

50 See Andrew Goble, "The Hōjō and Consultative Government," in Mass, ed., *Court and Bakufu in Japan*, Chap. 7, for a rejection of the conciliar view made famous by Satō Shin'ichi.

51 Hōjō control was direct from 1219 to 1226; thereafter it was through the *hyōjōshū*. Either way, judgments between 1219 and 1333 bore Hōjō names exclusively. These have been collected by Seno Seiichirō, *Kamakura bakufu saikyojō shū* (Tokyo: Yoshikawa kōbunkan, 1970–1), 2 vols.

the two parties have been investigated and judged, and [the *jitō*'s] case has been found justified." To establish this, proof records (*shōmon*) had been placed in evidence, and the "false claim" (*hiron*) of the challenger was dismissed. Finally, a copy of the edict was sent to the government headquarters (*dazaifu*) in Kyushu, where an additional order executing the decision was handed down.[52]

During the era of Yoritomo, justice, it may be said, remained the prerogative of the chieftain. Though he assigned trusted followers to cases and allowed them some leeway, he did not have professional investigators, much less a class of judges. A "judiciary" in the sense of a separate organ did not appear until later.[53]

The two decades before Jōkyū saw a number of advances in the way that Kamakura handled suits. And these were indeed suits: The system was accusatorial, with litigation initiated by a plaintiff. Moreover, on a period-long basis, the bakufu itself was never a party to such actions and thereby strengthened its reputation as an arbiter and not an inquisitor. It is logical that an investigative agency, the *monchūjo*, should have become active after Yoritimo's death. After conducting inquiries, which now involved a more clearly defined exchange of accusation and rebuttal statements (*sojō* and *chinjō*), along with gathering and analyzing evidence, the *monchūjo* issued a report, which was normally the basis of the judgment. From the beginning, written proof was considered more reliable than witnesses' or litigants' claims, and before long, distinctions among types of documents were introduced. In turn, as verdicts came to rest on documents, the crimes of forging, pilfering, and extorting records correspondingly became a problem. As Kamakura quickly discovered, advances in judicial technique were often followed by attempts to abuse or thwart them.

Integral to the progress in Kamakura was the promotion of a local support system. Because some types of allegations could most effectively be verified locally, *shugo* became the principal agents of investigation in the provinces. As the traffic of directives and responses increased, this served to tighten the bakufu's overall control of its vassalage even as it was expediting the handling of suits. The same end was served by Kamakura's issuance of formal questionnaires (*toijō*) and summonses (*meshibumi*) either directly or indirectly to defendants. As for the suits themselves, these tended to fall into three categories.

52 *KB*, doc. 14.

53 The standard view, based on the *Azuma kagami*, posits a "board of inquiry" (*monchūjo*) from 1184. I take issue with this version of events; see Jeffrey P. Mass, "The Origins of Kamakura Justice," *Journal of Japanese Studies* 3 (1977): 307–10.

The most prominent during the early period were actions lodged by traditional proprietors against *jitō*. Some of these were already quite complex, involving multiple issues, the product of diversified programs of lawlessness by increasingly ambitious *jitō*.[54] The second type of suit, which became far more important later, dealt with intrafamily vassal disputes, generally over inheritances.[55] Finally, there were complaints by or against *gokenin* alleging interfamily infringement.[56] Kamakura's official position against accepting courtier or warrior suits that did not involve vassals was occasionally transgressed by the bakufu itself. Yet the policy of separate jurisdictions with Kyoto remained in force and served as the principal basis for the era's dual polity.

There were, however, certain defects in the system that became more pronounced in the years immediately following Jōkyū. As mentioned earlier, due process was compromised somewhat under the weight of litigation caused by the emergency. This led to a rise in the number of false or frivolous suits and an increasing awareness that Kamakura's judgments did not contain enough information either to prevent repetitions of the same problem or to provide the bakufu with an easy basis for resolving future difficulties. Specifically, the edicts tended not to contain full-enough histories of either troubled areas or families and did not present summaries of the oral and written testimony constituting the basis for the judgment. In addition, by the late 1220s there existed a number of problem estates for which the bakufu had adopted conflicting positions in the past. In order to set the records straight and to line up, as it were, the precedents, Yasutoki was disposed to having Kamakura's highest court, the *hyōjōshū*, rehear such cases. From a handful of settlement edicts surviving from 1227–8, we see that Kamakura justice had taken a major step forward.[57]

Central to the advances made at this time was a new commitment to impartiality, in the form of the *taiketsu*, or face-to-face trial confrontation, and to recording the facts and the reasoning behind a judgment as based on the oral and written testimony. In the past, plaintiff and defendant had been regularly summoned, but it is not certain whether they faced each other and their interrogators simultaneously. Even now, only a minority of cases reached this ultimate test; but the princi-

54 A case in 1216, for example, embraced some sixteen disputed issues; see *KB*, doc. 93.

55 For example, the long-running case involving Ojika Island in Kyushu's Hizen Province. Kamakura first heard the suit in 1196, again in 1204, and thereafter repeatedly until it was settled with some finality in 1228; see *KB*, docs. 19–20; *DKR*, pp. 95–101.

56 For example, cases in Kyushu from 1205 and 1212; see *DKR*, docs. 57, 65.

57 See, in particular, the Ojika Island settlement of 1228, referred to in n. 55. A judgment in 1227/3 is the earliest of the "new" type; see *KB*, doc. 46.

ple of access, so crucial, had been established. The bakufu also made clear that the most extraordinary measures would be used to ferret out the truth. Witnesses, if needed, would be sought from the most remote corners of the land,[58] and summonses would be issued ad nauseum if it was thought they might help.[59] Conversely, Kamakura inculcated the notion that each stage in the judicial process was capable of serving as the final stage; we see no slavish devotion to the full reach of Kamakura's own system. The rationale here was to avoid squandering valuable resources, whether the litigants' or the bakufu's, and to give the system maximum flexibility. Thus, there would be cases when merely the lodging of a suit would induce the defendant to settle "out of court." Or perhaps the same result might occur at the point of acceptance of a suit or the delivery of the charges or of a summons. Under the Kamakura system, justice might be rapid or drawn out; in many instances it was unending, as formal appeals became possible and new suits on old subjects were commonplace. Indeed, it was Kamakura's objective to bottle up potentially explosive situations in litigation; that elite warriors subjected themselves to long-running encounters on the legal field of battle rather than on military battlefields proved to be one of the bakufu's most enduring accomplishments.

Nor did Kamakura justice become static or excessively bureaucratized. Soon after introducing the procedures that would serve as the core of the system, Yasutoki became active as a legislator. Drawing on his Confucian training and his evaluation of current realities, he became the guiding force behind the *goseibai shikimoku*, a behavioral code for *gokenin* that was promulgated in 1232. This formulary was important for several reasons. As the first document of its kind by and for warriors, it gave further evidence of Kamakura's parity with Kyoto and indeed served as the inspiration and precedent for all future warrior codes. Nevertheless, in the context of its own times, the formulary was intended to do less than it has often been given credit for.[60] It represented not so much the creation of binding rules as the establishment of standards; its underlying principle, *dōri*, conveyed reasonable-

58 For example, a suit in 1244 involving a corner of Kyushu's Hizen Province led to the interrogation of at least twenty local persons; see *DKR*, doc. 144.

59 For example, the reference to seven summonses in a Bizen Province suit in 1255; see *KB*, doc. 50.

60 The existence of an early English translation of the formulary (1904) caused several generations of historians to rely unduly on this document. The potential influence of such translations is discussed by Jeffrey P. Mass, "Translation and Pre-1600 History," *Journal of Japanese Studies* 6 (Winter 1980): 61–88.

ness, not literalness. Thus, a judgment based on the particulars of a case was the closest approximation of *dōri;* Kamakura laws, as summation of current practice, were the next closest.

The *goseibai shikimoku,* then, was a sketch rather than a finished blueprint; its general concerns were more important than its specific content. Had the formulary, by contrast, sought to impose a uniform set of regulations, it would have conflicted with the limitless variety of estate-based customs. This would have rendered justice inoperable, as governance in the thirteenth century (Kamakura's or Kyoto's) could hardly have been reduced to formula. The *shikimoku*'s objectives were thus to define the parameters of the *gokenin's* world and to enunciate standards that would both exalt and restrain him. Because the society of the vassal was itself ever-changing, it was readily anticipated that the code, like a constitution, would be supplemented by legislation.

And so it was. Hardly was the ink dry on the 1232 document when new enactments began to pour from Kamakura's lawmakers. Some of these dealt with topics not covered in the *shikimoku,* but others were clearly corrective in nature. The latter condition was promoted by a development that Yasutoki had not foreseen. In its efforts to reconcile two competing social and political orders, Kamakura had forsworn interference in the affairs of *shōen* proprietors, specifically in *shōen* in which *jitō* did not hold land rights. This left non-*jitō gokenin,* who constituted the majority of the native western province vassals, legally unprotected, and estate owners were quick to take advantage of this situation.[61] Moreover, the *shikimoku,* though including *jitō* under its umbrella of protection, also restricted them in a number of explicit ways. Proprietors had merely to study the formulary and then bring suit against a *jitō* for alleged codal violations. Because the *shōen* proprietors themselves were immune from discipline by Kamakura, there was nothing, moreover, to prevent them from bringing trumped-up charges.[62] At any rate, the 1230s and 1240s witnessed a number of adjustments in the bakufu's laws as inequities in the original legislation were deemed needy of correction.

Notwithstanding such difficulties, the post-*shikimoku* era carried Kamakura justice to a new plateau of excellence. From about 1230 the Rokuhara deputyship in Kyoto became an adjunct to the system, fully empowered to judge suits independently of Kamakura. Although in practice Rokuhara functioned mostly as a lower court with appeal

61 *DKR*, pp. 108–12, docs. 76–77.
62 For example, a case in which a proprietor ignored an earlier judgment against itself and attempted to reopen the suit; see *DKR*, doc. 78.

eastward regularly used, the bakufu had diversified its judicial machinery and strengthened its reputation as Japan's most prestigious court. At the same time, Kamakura was also taking steps to improve its efficiency and overall performance. In 1249, it added another investigative office, the *hikitsuke-shū*, which gradually took its place as the principal organ of inquiry below the *hyōjōshū*.

As indicated earlier, dispute resolution was, from beginning to end, Kamakura's chief contribution to the age. More than policing, the collection of taxes, or any other of a myriad of responsibilities associated with governments, the settlement of land suits, broadly conceived, stood as the raison d'être for the bakufu's existence. On the other hand, this did not mean that Kamakura's authority was simply one-dimensional. It did exercise, for example, certain administrative responsibilities in its base area of the east. Yet this authority was far from fully articulated, and few data survive on Kamakura as a territorial power.

The explanation for this anomaly takes us back to the dual polity. During Kamakura times, the country was not divided into discrete territorial spheres. Authorities were overlapping within the context of the all-encompassing estate system. This meant that *shōen* holders and provincial proprietors maintained contacts with the east, whereas Kamakura, through its *shugo* and *jitō*, exercised influence in the west. Thus, the dual polity was a thoroughly integrated polity which, however, might be unequal. Although the bakufu had arguably the more important contribution to make, Kyoto, it seems clear, had the more varied. Preoccupied with its judicial burden, Kamakura eschewed many of the complementary duties of government, which remained the purview of traditional, court-centered authority.[63]

SHUGO AND *JITŌ*

The *shugo* and *jitō* were the period-defining figures of the Kamakura age, a condition that was recognized even at the time. The less significant of the two, the *shugo*, was created, as we have seen, as part of the bakufu's effort in the 1190s to inject coherence into its vassal network and to clarify the boundaries of the emerging dual polity. The plan was to assign a trusted easterner to each province of the country and to have this officer represent the bakufu as its ranking agent in that

63 These views are developed by Jeffrey P. Mass, "What Can We Not Know About the Kamakura Bakufu?" in Jeffrey P. Mass and William B. Hauser, eds., *The Bakufu in Japanese History* (Stanford, Calif.: Stanford University Press, 1985), pp. 24–30.

province. The *shugo*'s authority was to be threefold. He was to act as coordinator of his area's *gokenin*, in particular, commanding them in war and leading them in their peacetime guard duty in Kyoto. Second, he was to assume responsibility for controlling local rebellion and crimes of a capital nature, both duties hitherto discharged by the older civil governors. Finally, he was to serve as an adjunct to Kamakura's judicial system, performing in the joint roles of investigator, enforcer, and liaison.[64]

Only the first two duties breached the natural division between Kamakura's and Kyoto's authority, and as such they required official sanction from the court. We do not know the circumstances surrounding this arrangement or when it was secured, but by early in the thirteenth century *shugo* were active in these capacities. The Kyoto guard service, known as *ōbanyaku,* was a legacy from the Heian period that Kamakura inherited and made incumbent on its collective vassalage on a provincial basis. Service periods were normally three or six months, and the duty fell on individual provinces at irregular intervals, sometimes twenty years or more. The *ōbanyaku,* curious as it now seems, was the centerpiece of Kamakura's system of vassal services, which also included tribute obligations (labor, horses, etc.) but not regular taxes or rents. Part of the rationale for doing things in this way derived from the bakufu's ambivalent attitude toward noneastern vassals, relatively few of whom it honored. Although it wished to call these westerners to service from time to time, it did not desire their presence in Kamakura, which had its own *ōbanyaku* limited to easterners. At all events, *shugo* were placed in command of the imperial guard duty.

The *shugo*'s constabulary authority involved them (or their deputies) in fairly frequent conflict with estate owners, who sought immunity from *shugo* entrance. Historians have not been able to agree on the extent of the *shugo*'s jurisdiction here, that is, the stage in the criminal prosecution continuum to which his authority reached, or the precise social classes covered.[65] But it is noteworthy that Kamakura's ranking peace officers in the field, like policemen in other times and places, were the objects of censure rather than praise by the interests ostensibly being served. In this regard, *shugo* were no different from civil governors or their agents from whom estate holders also sought immunity. We may say, at any rate, that *shugo* were

64 The Kamakura *shugo* is treated in *WG*, chap. 8.

65 The debate has mostly been between Satō Shin'ichi and Ishii Ryōsuke; for a summary, see *WG*, pp. 213–20.

least successful in this aspect of their duties and were fairly frequently lawbreakers themselves.

These formal responsibilities of the *shugo* (the Kyoto *ōbanyaku,* rebellion, and murder) were incorporated into Kamakura law under the curious misnomer of *taibon sankajō,* the three regulations for great crimes. This was in 1231, long after the three duties, minus the name, had become an operational definition of the *shugo*'s authority. The notion of uniformity expressed by such a legalism goes to the very heart of the *shugo* conception. The holders of this title were viewed as public officers with responsibilities replicated in all provinces of the country. In that regard they were like their counterparts, the civil governors, and unlike the *jitō,* who, following *shōen* custom, all were perceived to be different. The *taibon sankajō,* with its slender authority, expressed the narrow limits of the *shugo*'s public presence.

As noted, there was a third aspect to the *shugo*'s authority, and this was centered on duties performed on behalf of the bakufu. In particular, the *shugo* assisted Kamakura in the latter's judicial endeavors. The range here was impressive – from interrogating local witnesses, summoning defendants, and subpoenaing relevant documents, to forwarding investigative reports, issuing enforcement orders, and announcing judgments. A question arises as to whether such activity (along with the *ōbanyaku*) allowed *shugo* to develop leverage over *gokenin* as a step toward fashioning private vassalages. On balance, this probably did not occur, as *shugo* were commonly obliged to take actions unfriendly to *jitō,* who were usually the defendants in legal actions, and as Kamakura was careful to hedge the autonomy of its provincial appointees. *Shugo,* for instance, held tenures that were revocable at will; they received assignments only in provinces of which they were not natives (save for the east); their posts were not normally identified with landholding; and they were restricted in the number and functioning of their deputies.[66] It is hardly surprising, given these conditions, that few *shugo* bothered to take up residence in their assigned provinces. With tenures that were considered nonheritable, most appointees remained in their eastern bases or else elected to live in Kamakura itself.

Although a handful of *shugo* did succeed in entrenching themselves in their provinces, this did not mean that their relations with Kamakura were in any way discordant. They continued to require the bakufu's active support and patronage, in return for which they pro-

66 Among these four, the only point that has been disputed is the landholding issue. Satō Shin'ichi argues in the negative, and Ishii Susumu takes the opposing view. I favor Satō here; see *WG*, pp. 225–7.

vided valuable and ongoing service. No *shugo* could survive, much less prosper, in isolation. In addition, as the years passed, the bakufu's leading house, the Hōjō, came to gather up an increasingly large portfolio of *shugo* titles, some thirty or more, almost half the national total, by the end of the period. We do not know enough about this development to judge whether it constituted a setback for the *shugo* system or rendered it more efficient. Certainly it limited the potential for the autonomy of other *shugo*, as "Hōjō neighbors" were now a reality for everyone. Our best guess is that the Hōjō aggrandizement of *shugo* posts did not appreciably distort the aims or operations of Kamakura's governance. Localism, society's larger trend, was not occurring at the level of the *shugo* or province anyway and was partly obstructed by them. Thus, far from hastening the decline of higher authority's sanction, the institution of *shugo* functioned as a major support for it. As we shall now see, the same can hardly be said for the Kamakura *jitō*.

If one has to search for multiformity among *shugo*, that condition was built in to the office of *jitō*. *Jitō* appointments could be made to land units of any size or description – or indeed not to land at all. Perquisites and authority were similarly diverse[67] and were expected to conform to the rights packages of the *jitō*'s predecessor, whether another *jitō* or a land manager bearing a different title, usually *gesu*. Once a *jitō* was appointed, he could look on his office as heritable property subject only to Kamakura's probate of his will. He could also expect immunity, as mentioned earlier, from the disciplinary authority of his absentee landlord. If the *jitō* committed any kind of offense against man or property, the estate owner had no recourse but to appeal to Kamakura for redress. This obliging of the *jitō* to manage lands on behalf of a proprietor exercising no direct control over him was what made the office revolutionary. It also ensured an unending need for a bakufu judicial authority.

In the hands of warriors, the post of *jitō* was trouble prone from the start. Kamakura made its appointments without knowledge of, and therefore without specifying, the limits of the managerial authority in question. It admonished its new *jitō* to obey local precedents – and left it to the *jitō* to discover what these were. Not surprisingly, *shōen* proprietors and *jitō* read these practices differently, which became the basis of litigation. Early on, Kamakura thus found itself making historical

67 For examples of the limitless variety in both physical shape and range of authority, see *WG*, pp. 171–2.

probes into the customs of remote areas. Where it erred was in not recording all its findings, not, that is, until Yasutoki's reforms. But even then, resourceful *jitō* were still free to choose new areas of activity to contest or to return to older subjects that retained ambiguities. The problem for the bakufu was that it could hardly afford to move too harshly against too many of its own men. Its judgments against *jitō* were never wavering, but most of its decisions were admonitory rather than overtly punitive. In Kamakura's view, dismissals were possible in extreme cases, but establishing the limits of a *jitō*'s authority would often be punishment enough. Henceforth, the *jitō* would be bound by a legal document that included the particulars of his earlier offenses.

What were some of the specific areas of dispute? *Jitō* received designated land units as compensation for their services. It was a common practice to claim adjacent units as falling within protected regions, to assert lower tax ratios or totals, and to invoke custom as the justification for imposing labor duties on cultivators. Points of quarrel in the sphere of *shōen* management centered on the extent of the *jitō*'s policing authority, the extent of his jurisdiction over local officials, the range of his competence to organize and oversee agriculture, and the nature of his involvement with the collection and delivery of *shōen* dues. Each of these topics was the source of endemic disagreement, as to control all of them was to dominate a *shōen*. Typically, however, the *jitō* enjoyed only a share of that authority, commonly expressed by some kind of formula. Thus, in the area of policing competence, a *jitō* might hold a one-third or one-half share,[68] which meant that confiscated property or fines in those amounts would redound to him. Or again, in regard to a *shōen*'s managerial corps, the *jitō* might control certain titled officials, which gave him the powers of appointment and dismissal over them.[69]

The normal antagonist of the *jitō* in all these areas was a special appointee of the proprietor who exercised the remaining jurisdiction. Thus, many *shōen* had dual tracks of authority, one under the *jitō* and immune from the proprietor, the other controlled by him through his agent. These agents were of two basic origins, either long-time residents of the area in question and possibly the original commenders of some or all of the land composing the *shōen*, or centrally dispatched professional managers. In any event, this bifurcation of authority and

68 See *KB*, docs. 90, 89, respectively. Or the share could be total; see *KB*, doc. 88.
69 See, for example, the several titles under a *jitō*'s authority in estates in Satsuma and Aki provinces; *KB*, doc. 78; *DKR*, doc. 41.

responsibility between *jitō* and custodians, as they were called,[70] provided the backdrop for some of the era's truly classic, long-running battles. We know a great deal about many of these from the bakufu's judicial edicts, which were the instruments of hoped-for settlement. In fact, we know a vast amount about the *jitō* in general, as they were the primary objects of complaint and control and thus the subjects of thousands of documents.

In their growing desperation, *shōen* proprietors evolved a series of direct approaches aimed at pacifying or constraining the *jitō*. The initiative here was taken by the *shōen* proprietors, who typically offered a compromise. Under the generic name *wayo*, compromises of two types predominated. The first, called *ukesho*, seems unusually remote from reality. Under it the *jitō* were given total administrative control of the *shōen*, even to the point of barring entrance by agents of the proprietor. In return, the *jitō* contracted to deliver a fixed annual tax, regardless of agricultural conditions. By agreeing to underwrite such arrangements, Kamakura was in effect promising that violations could and would be litigated. Yet because delivery of the tax was the *jitō*'s only obligation to the proprietor, amounts in arrears became the sole object of suits. The worst that might happen was that the *jitō*, deeply in debt but with his *ukesho* intact, would simply be ordered to pay, often on lenient terms.[71]

The second device aimed at mollifying the *jitō* was called *shitaji chūbun*, a physical splitting up of *shōen*. As with other divisions of authority, percentage arrangements were the norm here, and maps with red lines through them were drawn to demarcate shares.[72] The bakufu's formal approval, symbolic of its guarantorship, was standard here too.[73] It was long assumed that *shitaji chūbun* represented a more advanced form of settlement than did *ukesho* because ownership, rather than managerial authority, was involved. According to this view, the *jitō* now became Japan's first locally based holders of estate-sized properties, a revolutionary stage in the return of authority to the land. Although the general conclusion here seems accurate in hindsight, perceptions at the time were somewhat different. In particular,

70 The term here is *azukari-dokoro*. By mid-Kamakura times, a second term–*zasshō*–was coming into vogue. Sometimes they implied the same person and were used interchangeably (*DKR*, doc. 103), other times not (*DKR*, doc. 41).

71 The institutions of *wayo* and *ukesho* are treated by Jeffrey P. Mass, "Jitō Land Possession in the Thirteenth Century," in Hall and Mass, eds., *Medieval Japan*, chap. 7. For actual examples, see *KB*, docs. 117–25.

72 For an example, see the photograph on the jacket of Hall and Mass, eds., *Medieval Japan*.

73 For example, see *KB*, docs. 126–8.

shōen proprietors, not *jitō*, provided the main impetus toward *shitaji chūbun*. Their objective was to secure an unencumbered share of a property legally theirs but pressured incessantly by a *jitō*. As for the *jitō*, they too were thinking mostly in the present. Thus, they commonly resisted *shitaji chūbun* arrangements, as the loss of an authority embracing entire *shōen* would result. Or the case might be cited of a *jitō* seeking an *ukesho* over a whole *shōen* in place of the *shitaji chūbun* agreed to by his forebears.[74] History – in the concrete – did not always move forward.

Jitō titles, like other forms of property, were heritable within the holder's family. The bakufu permitted its *jitō* to bequeath their titles, in unitary or partible fashion, to legitimate relatives of their own choosing. They were not allowed to bequeath their offices to external parties. In the early part of this period, partible practices were the norm, with women included in the regular inheritance pool. Because distinguished families might hold multiple *jitō* offices, children sometimes received individual titles and established separate lines that gained recognition from Kamakura. Short of that, they received *jitō* portions entitling them to confirmation and protection by the bakufu as well as the right to bequeath shares to their own heirs. During Kamakura times, the tendency was strong to eschew lateral for vertical inheritance, which meant that clannishness in property matters remained relatively undeveloped. Even within the nuclear group there existed the potential for tension, because fathers (and mothers) could write and rewrite wills and progeny might be disinherited. Finally, it was left to the house head to select a principal heir, who might be a younger son. The possibilities were thus rife for family conflict and for recourse to bakufu courtrooms.[75]

Because new *jitō* posts could hardly be expected to keep pace with the number of junior generation candidates for them, practices developed that began to move warrior society toward a more unitary property system. In place of unencumbered, alienable rights to daughters, for example, life bequests and annuities were set up, with reversion to the principal heir or his heir as part of an emerging system of entail. Fathers, moreover, began enjoining inheriting sons to maintain the integrity of family holdings and to reduce or eliminate secondary recipients. Scholars, quite properly, have emphasized such develop-

74 The division had occurred in 1237; the attempt to replace it with an *ukesho* came sixty years later; see *KB*, doc. 129.

75 Jeffrey P. Mass, *Lordship and Inheritance in Early Medieval Japan: A Study of the Kamakura Sōryō System* (Stanford, Calif.: Stanford University Press, 1989).

ments. Yet at no time during the Kamakura age did these practices become universal; inheriting daughters and fragmented holdings can always be found.[76] Nor is it clear what Kamakura's attitude was toward the new tendencies. As Seno Seiichirō has shown, the chieftain's authority over his siblings remained undeveloped, and bakufu judgments did not tilt toward him and thus away from his brothers.[77] In any event, the competition for control of *jitō* posts and between these posts and proprietorships constituted the very lifeblood of Kamakura justice. The ambitions of *jitō* were the bane of most everyone, but the office itself marked the clear cutting edge of progress.

THE BAKUFU AT MID-CENTURY

Yasutoki died in 1242 at the age of fifty-nine. His death removed the greatest of the Hōjō from the helm at Kamakura and immediately plunged the bakufu into a period of uncertainty. His successor was his eighteen-year-old grandson Tsunetoki, who soon ran afoul of the shogun Yoritsune, now in his twenties and desirous of ruling in his own name. In 1244, Yoritsune was replaced by his own seven-year-old son, Yoritsugu, but the troubles did not end here. The ex-shogun was still present in Kamakura and began to line up support against the Hōjō. Two years later he was banished to Kyoto, though the faction that had formed around him remained active.

In the meantime, conditions in the capital were also in flux. During the same year that Yasutoki died the emperor also died, and the bakufu promoted a successor, Gosaga, who was not the preferred choice of Kyoto. Four years later Kamakura again forced an issue by elevating Gosaga to the ex-emperorship. In the same year (1246) Tsunetoki himself died and was followed as regent by his more vigorous younger brother, Tokiyori. Yet even with new leadership in the two capitals, harmony did not ensue. A rumor of rebellion by Nagoe Mitsutoki, a branch head of the Hōjō, reached Kamakura in the fifth month of 1246, which led to the dismissal of four anti-Tokiyori members of the *hyōjōshū*. Events came to a head in 1247 when the Adachi, a family allied with the main line of the Hōjō, maneuvered the distinguished house of Miura into challenging for control. The Miura were defeated, thus eliminating the bakufu's second most prestigious house after the Hōjō, and a further housecleaning of recalcitrants followed.

76 For example, an unencumbered bequest to a daughter in 1323; see Mass, *Lordship and Inheritance*, doc. 147.

77 Seno Seiichirō, *Chinzei gokenin no kenkyū* (Tokyo: Yoshikawa kōbunkan, 1975), pp. 375–88.

As a result of the Miura disturbance, the line of Tokiyori, hereafter known as *tokusō,* was more firmly entrenched than ever, though never wholly immune: The deaths of great leaders remained a problem in the absence of a fixed mechanism for succession. Nevertheless, the events of 1247 ushered in a generation of stability, which was not upset until the Mongol threat of the late 1260s.

It is noteworthy that even during the political infighting of the 1240s, Kamakura continued to discharge its judicial responsibilities. After 1247, certain reforms were introduced, whose culmination was the establishment of a new investigative organ, the *hikitsuke-shū,* in 1249. At the same time, with Gosaga as its accomplice, Kamakura encouraged the court to update its own machinery, now on the model of the bakufu. There can scarcely be a more revealing development than the formation in 1246 of a Kyoto *hyōjōshū,* designed as a clearing-house for disputes not affecting Kamakura's interests. In a sense, by this action, the era's dual polity was given its ultimate expression. The court now emulated the bakufu in a major structural advance, but the lines of jurisdiction separating them remained wholly intact. Cooperation between the country's two governments, Yoritomo's goal of an earlier day, had entered a new stage.

In 1252, Gosaga's son Munetaka was installed as Kamakura's first princely shogun. More than thirty years earlier, Hōjō Masako had sought a similar arrangement from a resistant Gotoba, but now at mid-century the Hōjō achieved this objective: The bakufu's leading house secured a puppet in each capital, who were conveniently father and son. Munetaka, indeed, is the final shogun whose name historians remember; his successors appear in lists of bakufu chieftains but are not considered players. The remainder of the era witnessed a number of important developments, among them the rise of lower-class social movements and the impoverishment or enrichment of different groups of warriors. The effects of the the Mongol invasions would be felt at many levels of society. But the bakufu by mid-century had reached its full maturity. Hereafter, the age belonged to the Hōjō, the future to the warrior class as a whole.

CHAPTER 2

THE DECLINE OF THE KAMAKURA BAKUFU

INTRODUCTION

The 1260s marked the beginning of a decisively new period for the Kamakura bakufu as it faced a set of increasingly complex problems caused by changing conditions both at home and abroad.[1] The political structure of the bakufu was about to undergo a major change after

1 I have used the following sources in writing this article: (1) the *Azuma kagami*, a history-chronicle in diary format written from the viewpoint of the bakufu and covering the years 1180 to 1266. Nothing replaces it after that date. (2) The "Kamakura nendai ki" and "Buke nendai ki" are helpful, albeit partial, substitutes. I also used other diaries such as (3) "Kenji sannen ki" and "Einin sannen ki." These and other diaries can be found in Takeuchi Rizō, comp., *Zoku shiryō taisei,* 22 vols. (Kyoto: Rinsen shoten, 1967). For political conditions within the bakufu, documents in (4) "Kanezawa bunko komonjo," which include letters exchanged among members of the Kanezawa (Hōjō) family, are important. The most inclusive document collection for the Kamakura period is (5) *Kamakura ibun, komonjo hen* (thirty-six volumes to date), compiled by Takeuchi Rizō. Other sources such as (6) *Kanagawa ken shi, shiryō hen,* vols. 1 and 2; and (7) Seno Seiichirō, comp., *Kamakura bakufu saikyojō shū, jō, and ge* (Tokyo: Yoshikawa kōbunkan, 1970) are useful. A comprehensive description and index to these and other published documentary sources can be found in (8) pt. 2 of Jeffrey P. Mass, *The Kamakura Bakufu: A Study in Documents* (Stanford, Calif.: Stanford University Press, 1976). There is no index of this magnitude anywhere else. For the Kyoto side of Kamakura history, diaries by nobles are important historical sources. The following are well known for this period: (9) "Kitsuzokki" by Yoshida Tsunenaga and "Kanchū ki" by Fujiwara Kanenaka – both in Sasagawa Taneo, ed., *Shiryō taisei* (Tokyo: Naigai shoten, 1937) – "Sanemikyō ki" by Sanjō Sanemi (unpublished); and "Hanazono Tennō shinki" by Emperor Hanazono, in Sasagawa, ed., *Shiryō taisei.* Historical chronicles such as the "Masukagami," "Godai teiō monogatari," and "Hōryakukan ki" are also helpful. Many of the documents mentioned here are included in the fifth edition of (10) the *Dai Nihon shiryō,* though the volumes covering the Kamakura era have reached only 1248. In the meantime, readers are referred to (11) Tōkyō daigaku shiryō hensanjō, ed., *Shiryō soran,* vol. 5 (Tokyo: Tōkyō daigaku shuppankai, 1965).

Although there are many secondary works, the following are especially noteworthy: Miura Hiroyuki, *Kamakura jidaishi,* vol. 5 of *Nihon jidashi* (Tokyo: Waseda daigaku shuppanbu, 1907, 1916), reprinted as *Nihonshi no kenkyū,* vol. 1 (Tokyo: Iwanami shoten, 1982) Ryō Susumu, *Kamakura jidai, jō, ge* (Tokyo: Shunshūsha, 1957); Satō Shin'ichi, "Bakufu ron," in *Shin Nihon shi kōza,* 7th series (Tokyo: Chūō kōronsha, 1949); Satō Shin'ichi, "Kamakura bakufu seiji no senseika ni tsuite," in Takeuchi Rizō, comp., *Nihon hōkensei seiritsu no kenkyū* (Tokyo: Yoshikawa kōbunkan, 1955), pp. 95–136; Kuroda Toshio, "Mōko shūrai," *Nihon no rekishi,* vol. 8 (Tokyo: Chūō kōronsha, 1965); Amino Yoshihiko, *Mōko shūrai,* vol. 10 of *Nihon no rekishi* (Tokyo: Shōgakkan, 1974); Amino Yoshihiko, "Kamakura makki no shomujun," in Rekishigaku kenkyūkai and Nihonshi kenkyūkai, comps., *Kōza Nihonshi,* vol. 3 (Tokyo: Tōkyō daigaku shuppankai, 1970), pp. 21–56; and Nitta Hideharu, "Kamakura kōki no seiji katei," in *Iwanami kōza Nihon rekishi,* vol. 6 (Tokyo: Iwanami shoten, 1975), pp. 1–40. Though dated, Miura Hiroyuki's *Kamakura jidaishi* has not lost its value. During the postwar period, Satō Shin'ichi's work led the field, and most recently, Amino Yoshihiko's "Mōko shūrai" merits special attention as an innovative history.

the death of Hōjō Tokiyori in 1263, which in effect ended the "Golden Period" characterized by the regency *(shikken)* system. At the same time, changes in the social, economic, and technological spheres were beginning to shake the *shōen* system, which had been flourishing since the eleventh century. As examples of these changes, improved agricultural technology increased arable acreage, and the technique of double cropping – planting wheat after harvesting the rice – also enhanced productivity. The greater surplus in turn led to the diversification of agriculture, and as witnessed by the opening of periodic markets, commerce and trade likewise became more important. Simultaneously, peasants with free time or surplus means produced various handicrafts to be sold at market. A cash economy made advances as a large quantity of coins was imported from China, giving rise to financial middlemen and the practice of paying *shōen* taxes in cash.

These changes could not have taken place without influencing the overall social fabric. In various regions, cultivators rose up against the local *jitō* or *shōen* proprietors. In the meantime, the *jitō* and proprietors themselves began to compete, the worst of such confrontations occurring in the home provinces and the west, often involving military forces. Various groups of marauders, called *akutō*, whether of peasant or warrior origins, upset the peace and undermined the bakufu's original stabilizing aim.[2]

These domestic troubles were compounded by the precarious political conditions prevailing in the neighboring countries of East Asia, which eventually led to an extensive takeover by the Mongols and then to a series of attempted invasions of Japan, the greatest external attack on Japan in premodern times. The bakufu responded to this threat by consolidating its own power, by extending its hitherto weak political influence in western Japan, and by tightening its hold on the affairs of the court in Kyoto. This expansion of power presented an ideal opportunity for factions within the bakufu to strengthen their influence. The Hōjō clan, especially its main *(tokusō)* line, confirmed its already dominant position, whereas the *miuchibito* (private vassals of the *tokusō)* also enhanced their power. The period of so-called autocratic rule by the *tokusō* began after the Shimotsuki incident of 1285, in which a group of powerful *gokenin* represented by Adachi Yasumori was eliminated.

At first, the rise of the *tokusō* and the *miuchibito* factions, accompany-

2 The most recent work on the topic of *akutō* is by Koizumi Yoshiaki, *Akutō* (Tokyo: Kyōikusha, 1981).

ing the strengthened national position of the bakufu seemed to mark the peak of Kamakura political power. However, this proved to be illusory, as the general trend was toward greater internal strife and dissatisfaction which soon mushroomed into a serious antibakufu movement. There were, in fact, many causes for the warriors' dissatisfaction, one being the lack of reward land in the aftermath of the Mongol invasions. Already by the time of the invasions many *gokenin* were impoverished, owing to the continued parcelization of landholding under the divided inheritance system, as well as to their involvement in the growing cash economy, which undermined their traditional economic base. Because the warriors were expected to bear the expenses of their military service, the invasions compounded their financial difficulties, and many ended up losing their lands, by either selling or pawning them. The presence of a large number of landless *gokenin* thus posed a major problem to the bakufu.

To rescue the small and medium-sized *gokenin* houses in the last stages of collapse, the bakufu used a radical measure, ordering the cancellation of the *gokenin*'s debts and the return of their pawned land at no cost. But this emergency relief measure saved the financially strained *gokenin* only temporarily, and many houses were subsumed by others – the *shugo, miuchibito,* or even *akuto* warriors who acquired wealth through commerce, trade, or financial activities.

Each warrior house was being reorganized as well, adding to the dissatisfaction of the displaced family members. This transformation was characterized by two concurrent patterns. First, the divided inheritance gradually gave way to unitary inheritance, which granted the entire family holding to the head, to whom his siblings were then required to subordinate themselves. Second, the link between the family's main line (*honke*) and its branch lines (*bunke*) gradually weakened, as the latter formed strong ties with other warrior houses in their geographical areas, becoming in the process more independent of their former blood relations.

Set against this turbulent background, the Hōjō's autocratic rule further intensified the warriors' dissatisfaction. But the greatest crisis for the bakufu occurred when a worsening intracourt rivalry propelled the emperor, Godaigo, to take the lead in an antibakufu movement. The imperial line had split into two branches which competed for both the imperial title and rights to *shōen*. Placed in the role of arbitrator, the bakufu resolved to have the two branches reign in alternate succession. The bakufu's involvement in these matters allowed it tighter control over the inner workings of the court but at the same time caused bakufu enmity and resentment from the losers in this competition. Emperor Godaigo, in particular, resented the bakufu's intervention in court affairs, which heightened his desire to return the country to a *tennō*-centered national governance. Godaigo thus took every opportunity to fan the anti-Hōjō and antibakufu sentiments manifested in the *gokenin*'s unrest and the *akuto*'s spreading activities. Godaigo's plan to topple the bakufu was not immediately successful, however, and its failure in 1331 led to his exile to Oki Island. But once this movement was under way, the rebellion spread quickly from the home provinces to the rest of the country. In 1333, the Kamakura bakufu was overthrown.

THE MONGOL INVASIONS AND THE KAMAKURA BAKUFU

The arrival of diplomatic messages from the Yüan

By the early 1260s, Kublai Khan, grandson of the great Genghis Khan, headed the Mongol tribes which had by then built an extensive empire encompassing a large portion of Eurasia.[3] To the Mongols, Japan was desirable owing to its proximity to Korea and its relations with the Southern Sung. In 1266, Kublai made his first overture to Japan by sending a letter through the king of Koryŏ, who was ordered to dispatch an intermediary to accompany the Yüan messenger. This first messenger, however, was prevented from crossing to Japan and

3 Much has been published on topics related to the Mongol invasions. A recent publication, *Mōko shūrai kenkyū shi ron*, by Kawazoe Shōji (Tokyo: Yūzankaku, 1977) contains a nearly complete bibliography that is concisely annotated. Here, I shall list only works of particular importance or those used in this essay. For nonspecialists, the following works are useful: Kawazoe Shōji, *Gen no shūrai* (Tokyo: Popurasha, 1975); Yamaguchi Osamu, *Mōko shūrai* (Tokyo: Jōsha, 1964, 1979); Hatada Takashi, *Genkō–Mōko teikoku no naibu jijō* (Tokyo: Chūō kōronsha, 1965); Abe Yukihiro, Mōko shūrai (Tokyo: Kyōikusha, 1980). The works of Yamaguchi and Hatada are important for their view from a wider East Asian perspective. Abe's work is the most recent, but because it is not entirely reliable, I would recommend Kawazoe's work more highly. As for document collections, Yamada An'ei's *Fukuteki hen*, 2 vols. (Tokyo: Yoshikawa kōbunkan, 1981) is still an extremely useful classic, unsurpassed by any later publications. The best compilation of materials related to the defense effort per se appears in Kawazoe Shōji, *Chūkai, Genkō bōrui hennen shiryō–Ikoku keigo banyaku shiryō no kenkyū* (Fukuoka: Fukuokashi kyōiku iinkai, 1971). This is an important work that includes many useful notes.

Several monographs should be mentioned. A treatment of the Mongols from an East Asian perspective was attempted by Ikeuchi Hiroshi in his *Genko no shin kenkyū*, 2 vols. (Tokyo: Tōyō bunko, 1931). A quarter of a century later Aida Nirō wrote *Mōko shūrai no kenkyū*, which analyzed the invasions from the angle of Japan's internal political conditions (Tokyo: Yoshikawa kōbunkan, 1971) This book had an immense impact on later research. In English, there is an article by Hori Kyotsu, "The Economic and Political Effects of the Mongol Wars," in John W. Hall and Jeffrey P. Mass, eds., *Medieval Japan: Essays in Institutional History* (New Haven, Conn., Yale University Press, 1974).

thus returned to China without accomplishing his diplomatic task. In the following year an angry Kublai issued a strict order to the king of Koryŏ to take responsibility for getting the Yüan letter to Japan. Given no choice, the Korean king attached a letter of explanation to the letter from the Yüan and provided, as before, a guide for the Yüan messenger. The group arrived in Dazaifu, Kyushu, in the first month of 1268.

The letter carried by the Yüan envoy contained roughly the following message:

> From time immemorial, rulers of small states have sought to maintain friendly relations with one another. We, the Great Mongolian Empire, have received the Mandate of Heaven and have become the master of the universe. Therefore, innumerable states in far-off lands have longed to form ties with us. As soon as I ascended the throne, I ceased fighting with Koryŏ and restored their land and people. In gratitude, both the ruler and the people of Koryŏ came to us to become our subjects; their joy resembles that of children with their father. Japan is located near Koryŏ and since its founding has on several occasions sent envoys to the Middle Kingdom. However, this has not happened since the beginning of my reign. This must be because you are not fully informed. Therefore, I hereby send you a special envoy to inform you of our desire. From now on, let us enter into friendly relations with each other. Nobody would wish to resort to arms.[4]

At this time, the man governing Dazaifu was Mutō (Shōni) Sukeyoshi, the *shugo* of three northern Kyushu provinces. Upon receiving this message, Sukeyoshi forwarded it to Kamakura.

Changes in the bakufu

The letter from Dazaifu reached Kamakura in 1268. But before examining the bakufu's response, I shall first discuss certain internal changes in Kamakura in the years following Hōjō Tokiyori's death in 1263. In the judicial sector, a new post, the *osso bugyō,* was created to examine judgments that might be appealed. The first appointees were Hōjō (Kanezawa) Sanetoki[5] and Adachi Yasumori, both former heads of courts in the bakufu's main investigatory agency, the *hikitsuke.*

4 Readers are referred to the writings left by the contemporary monk Soshō of Tōdaiji (called 'Mōko koku chō jō'), as well as the following published works: Yamada, An'ei, ed., *Fukuteki hen,* and Takeuchi Rizō, comp., *Kamakura ibun,* vol. 13 (Tokyo: Tōkyōdō, 1977) doc, 9564.

5 The son of Saneyasu, who was in turn the youngest son of Hōjō Yoshitoki. He was called Kanazawa because he had had a villa built in Kanezawa District (Musashi Province) just to the east of Kamakura. Sanetoki is particularly well known for the Kanezawa *bunko* (Kanazawa archive), a library housing a large number of Japanese and Chinese publications that he established at his villa.

Sanetoki was a brother of the new regent, Tokimune's mother, and he had been highly regarded by the late regent Tokiyori. Yasumori was the head of the Adachi family which for many generations had maintained close ties with the Hōjō. He was also the father of Tokisume's young wife. Thus the two men who represented the lines of Tokimune's mother and wife became leading figures in the reorganized bakufu. Inasmuch as they had played dominant roles in the bakufu under Tokiyori, their continuing positions of importance reflected the bakufu's desire to maintain Tokiyori's basic policies, which were strengthening the Hōjō grip over the bakufu's consultative structure and securing the *gokenin*'s trust by improving the operations of the judicial system. The appointments of Tokimune, Sanetoki, and Yasumori fulfilled the first goal, and the establishment of the *osso bugyō* sought to satisfy the *gokenin* who demanded fair judgments.

In general, these efforts were designed to counter certain internal conflicts that began to surface after Tokiyori's death. The Nagoe line of the Hōjō, descended from Yoshitoki's second son, was now in a position to challenge the main Hōjō line, the *tokusō*. The pattern of appointments to major bakufu positions illustrates this internal friction. For instance, in 1264, Tokiaki, the head of the Nagoe, secured the position of chief of the *hikitsuke,* the third most important job in the bakufu following those of regent and cosigner (*shikken* and *rensho*). Nevertheless, Tokiaki was not granted a post in the newly formed *osso bugyō*. Moreover, the *hikitsuke* itself was abolished suddenly in 1266/3, and its responsibilities were diverted to the regent and cosigner, assisted by the Board of Inquiry (*monchūjo*). This action effectively removed Nagoe Tokiaki from his primary base of power in the bakufu.

Several months later a private conference held at Tokimune's residence revealed the composition of a new power bloc. Itself an extension of the *yoriai,* a secret meeting initiated by Tokiyori years earlier to discuss critical matters, the conference was attended by Tokimune, Masamura, Sanetoki, and Yasumori. At the meeting the four men decided to replace the shogun, Prince Munetaka, with his three-year-old son Koreyasu. Although we do not know the motive behind this decision (an alleged affair between the shogun's wife and a certain monk was reported), the explanation given to Kyoto was simply a "rebellion by the shogun." More plausibly, the bakufu's leadership may have sensed a potentially threatening tie between the shogun and the opposition group and so took the offensive to foreclose any trouble.

It was just at the point when Kamakura was astir with rumors regarding the shogun's forced return to Kyoto that the messenger from Koryŏ arrived bearing the letter from the Mongols.

The bakufu's response to the Yüan letter

The Mongols' demand for a peaceful relationship with Japan posed a serious problem to the bakufu. The text of their letter did not seem threatening: It called for peace, not subjugation. In addition, the appended letter from the king of Koryŏ stressed that Kublai's goal was prestige for his dynasty rather than conquest. Yet at the same time, the wording of the Mongol letter could be interpreted more ominously, and thus the bakufu had to contemplate its response carefully.

Kamakura's first consideration may indeed have been Japan's ability to handle diplomatic negotiations. Even though Japan and the Southern Sung maintained commercial ties, formal diplomacy between the two countries had been in abeyance since the late ninth century, which meant that Japan lacked the necessary skill and confidence to assess international conditions. Second, it is likely that Japan's perception of the Mongols was extremely biased, inasmuch as the information it received about China came from either its Sung trading partners or from Buddhist monks, both of whom regarded the Mongols as unwelcome invaders. In particular, the Zen monks, many of whom were patronized by the Hōjō,[6] had come from Southern China and must have been vocal in their opposition to the Yüan request.

Moreover, the bakufu was not the ultimate diplomatic authority in Japan. The Yüan letter had been addressed to the "King of Japan," not to the bakufu, and thus in the second month of 1268 the letter was sent to Kyoto, where it was ignored. This decision, ostensibly made by the ex-emperor Gosaga, probably complied with the bakufu's own view of the matter.

In the meantime, the implementation of actual defense measures rested with Kamakura. Even before the court had reached its formal decision, the bakufu issued a directive to the *shugo* of Sanuki Province in Shikoku, stating: "Recently, we learned that the Mongols have become inclined toward evil and are now trying to subdue Japan.

6 Hōjō Tokiyori was a devout follower of Rankei Dōryū, a Chinese Zen monk who migrated to Japan in 1246 and built the Kenchōji in Kamakura. Tokiyori also patronized Gottan Funei, who arrived in Japan in 1260. In subsequent years, both Tokiyori and Tokimune invited Zen monks from the Southern Sung. Among the monks who came to Japan, Mugaku Sogen came to be highly respected among the Ji sect believers. Interestingly, he had been a victim of Yüan suppression in Sung China.

Quickly inform the *gokenin* in your province, and secure the nation's defense." Even though this is the only such directive that survives, we may assume that all *shugo* in the western region received a similar order.

The Mongols, of course, were active during this period. In the fifth month of 1268, Kublai ordered Koryŏ to construct one thousand battleships and to conscript ten thousand men, explaining that such preparations were necessary because of the possibility of rebellion by either the Southern Sung or Japan. Despite their public, diplomatic posture, the Mongols were in fact proceeding with their preparations for armed conflict. Nevertheless, Kublai continued to dispatch envoys and letters to Japan via Koryŏ. After the first envoy was forced to return to Koryŏ empty-handed, Kublai sent a second in the eleventh month of 1268. Together with a Korean guide, the Yüan envoy arrived in the second month of 1269 at the island of Tsushima. Instead of completing his mission, however, he had a confrontation with the local Japanese and so returned to Korea, taking with him two Japanese as captives.

The Japanese were taken to the Mongol capital to meet with the khan who stressed once again that his only desires were to have official representatives visit the Japanese court and to have his name remembered for generations thereafter. Kublai then ordered the return of the two Japanese, to be accompanied by another envoy carrying an imperial letter. Koryŏ was again made responsible for delivering the letter, and in the ninth month of 1269, this group arrived in Tsushima. The overture was no more successful than its predecessors – yet the Mongols persisted on the diplomatic front. For example, drafts of letters dated the first and second months of 1270 stated: "The use of military force without reason runs counter to Confucian and Buddhist teachings. Because Japan is a divine country [*shinkoku*], we do not intend to fight with force." Nonetheless, the bakufu advised the court not to respond, and as before, the envoy returned empty-handed.

The invasion's imminence

The timing and actual execution of a plan to invade Japan were closely tied to changing conditions in Koryŏ, which, from the sixth month of 1269, was in disorder, owing to the king's dethronement and reinstallment, and a civil war. By taking advantage of this situation, the Mongols were able to strengthen their hold on Koryŏ and thus facilitate their advance into Japan. In the twelfth month of 1270, Kublai appointed Chao Liang-pi as a special envoy to Japan and simultaneously stationed an army in Koryŏ. This led to Kublai's final campaign to induce a peaceful settlement. In the meantime, he launched a major offensive against rebel elements in Koryŏ itself, using a combined force of Mongols and Koreans. In the fifth month of 1271, these rebel elements were defeated, though some of them relocated to the south and continued their resistance.[7]

In 1271, Japan received a message from Koryŏ that warned of the Mongol advance and requested reinforcements of food and men. Recently discovered evidence suggests that the messenger carrying this letter to Japan was a member of the rebel force. It is evident that the rebels tried to retaliate against the Mongol expansion by warning Japan, even as their own country was serving as Kublai's agent. Although this overture did not yield concrete results, it does reveal the complex international relations of that time.

For their part, the Japanese were now induced to step up their defense by mobilizing even more warriors to protect Kyushu. Accordingly, the bakufu issued an order in the ninth month of 1271 that stated: "We have received news that an invasion is imminent. All *gokenin* who hold land in Kyushu must return to Kyushu immediately, in order to fortify the land and pacify local outlaws [*akutō*]."[8] Before this order was issued, only the *gokenin* living in Kyushu had been held responsible for preparing that island's defense.

Shortly thereafter, the Mongol envoy, Chao Liang-pi, arrived in Dazaifu with a letter. Although its message repeated much of what the previous letters had stated, Chao added the warning that unless Japan replied by the eleventh month, the Mongols were prepared to dispatch their battleships. The court's inclination was to issue an official response, but by the new year Chao was forced to return to Koryŏ without having obtained a reply. It seems that the bakufu had once again vetoed that court's decision to respond – even in the negative. After two more attempts to elicit a response (in 1272/5 and

7 Ishii Masatoshi, "Bun'ei hachinen rainichi no Kōraishi ni tsuite – Sanbetsushō no Nihon tsūkō shiryō no shōkai," *Tōkyō daigaku shiryō hensanjo hō* 12 (March 1978): 1–7.

8 It is important to note that the bakufu's order emphasized both the national defense and the suppression of *akutō*. Eastern warriors who were ordered to their holdings in Kyushu did not, however, leave immediately. For example, Shodai, a *gokenin* from Musashi Province, moved to his Higo Province holding only in the fifth month of 1275, and comparatively speaking, this was probably one of the earlier cases. At the end of 1286, the bakufu complained that there were still those who had not made the move. See Gomi Katsuo, "Nitta-gū shitsuin Michinori gushoan sonota," *Nihon rekishi*, no. 310 (March 1974): 13–26. Those warriors who held powerful positions within the bakufu were not obligated to move to Kyushu but were instead to send men of ability in their place.

1273/3), Chao finally notified Kublai of his failure. The Mongols subsequently gave Japan seven more opportunities to change its mind, but Japan's hard-line policy was already fixed. The Mongols eventually realized that force was the only means left for fulfilling their diplomatic goal.[9]

The Kamakura bakufu's response

As invasion seemed more and more inevitable the bakufu decided to consolidate its internal structure. First, it attempted to ease the split in the Hōjō family by reinstituting the *hikitsuke* system in the fourth month of 1269, three years after its abolition. The five units of the *hikitsuke* system now were made to include both main-line and anti-main-line Hōjō members: Nagoe Tokiaki (head of the first unit), Kanazawa Sanetoki (head of the second unit), Adachi Yasumori (head of the fifth unit), and two other Hōjō members. Each unit head represented a branch of the Hōjō, and together they formed a system similar to a coalition government. Nevertheless, the intrabakufu antagonisms intensified and exploded in 1272 in the form of the Nigatsu disturbance, in which many warriors and courtiers who opposed the *tokusō* were murdered. In Kamakura, the victims included Nagoe Tokiaki, his brother Noritoki, and a number of courtiers who had come from Kyoto to serve the shogun. In Kyoto itself, the most prominent person executed was Hōjō Tokisuke, who was the the Rokuhara *tandai* (a shogunal deputy stationed at Rokuhara in southeastern Kyoto to supervise the political, military, and judicial affairs of southwestern Japan) and an aggrieved elder brother of the regent Tokimune.

Soon after Tokiaki's death, the incident took on a new twist: Tokiaki was declared innocent, and instead, the five Hōjō *miuchibito* actually responsible for the murder were eliminated. The murderer of Noritoki received neither praise nor punishment, only ridicule. In sum, the incident was a concrete manisfestation of the serious instability within the bakufu. As far as we can determine, in the wake of the purge of the anti-main-line Hōjō by the *miuchibito*, the *miuchibito* themselves became the targets of condemnation and were accordingly eliminated. This bizarre episode was described as follows by an observer,

9 Some historians interpret the bakufu's rigid attitude toward this matter as a conscious policy to intensify the external crisis in order to deflect the impact of internal problems, such as the rise of *akutō*. This theory implies that the bakufu consciously invited the Mongols to attack Japan. For an example of this view, see Abe Yukihiro, *Mōko shūrai*. I would argue that this interpretation reflects too much the view of the world today.

Kanazawa Akitoki: "After 1269, life became disorderly for one reason or another. Mine or yours, one's life was never safe."

Once the Nigatsu disturbance had been settled, the bakufu issued an order to the provincial authorities to submit land surveys (*ōtabumi*) detailing the names of owners and the dimensions of local lands used as the basis for taxation and the conscription of *gokenin*. The timing of this order suggests that the bakufu was finally beginning to investigate the human and economic resources that could contribute to Japan's military potential. As early as 1267, the bakufu had issued an order prohibiting the sale, pawning, or transfer of *gokenin* land to nonrelatives and had authorized the return of holdings already sold or pawned in exchange for repayment of the original price. This order was rescinded in 1270, but a year after the submission of the *ōtabumi*, a new regulation was put into effect guaranteeing the return without cost of any pawned *gokenin* land. The bakufu further attempted to improve its vassals' situations by ordering the submission of lists containing the names of lands that had been lost as well as those of the new owners.

The invasion of 1274

In the second month of 1273, the Southern Sung defense line fell to the Mongols, and a collapse seemed close at hand. In the fourth month, the rebel elements of Koryŏ were finally put down. It had been two years since Kublai had changed the name of his dynasty to Ta Yüan in the Chinese style, and he was now ready to expand his empire even further. There remained no geographical obstacle to his moving forcefully against Japan.

Accordingly, the khan appointed joint commanders of an expeditionary force that was to sail in the seventh month of 1274. Koryŏ was likewise given an order to build and dispatch a fleet of nine hundred battleships and an army of five thousand men. Even though many of the ships of extremely poor quality – the product of hasty workmanship in response to the conqueror's order – the required number was prepared in time.

On the third day of the tenth month, three months later than the original plan, the expeditionary force consisting of 15,000 Yüan soldiers, 8,000 Koryŏ soldiers, and 67,000 ship workers sailed toward Japan. Departing from Koryŏ, they attacked Tsushima two days later and defeated Sō Munesuke, the deputy *shugo*, and about 80 other mounted soldiers. On the fourteenth day, they attacked Iki Island where the deputy *shugo*, Taira Kagetaka, fought valiantly with a force of 100 mounted soldiers but was eventually defeated. Two weeks later, the Yüan–Koryŏ allied force settled in Hakata Bay and began landing in the western area of the bay around Imazu, Sawaraura, and Momojibara. From these points, they planned to move east, eventually to attack Hakata.

On the Japanese side, two powerful *shugo*, Ōtomo Yoriyasu and Mutō (Shōni) Sukeyoshi, the bakufu's twin Kyushu deputies (Chinzei *bugyō*), commanded a *gokenin* defense force. The sources do not tell us the size of the Japanese army, but we can assume it was much smaller than the Yüan–Koryŏ expeditionary force. The figure of 100,000 that appears in a Chinese account is obviously exaggerated.[10]

Fatigue from the long voyage seems not to have reduced the skill of the Yüan–Koryŏ soldiers in the art of collective fighting. Moreover, they used poisoned arrows and exploding devices, which the Japanese had never seen before. The Japanese warriors' one-to-one fighting method had little effect here. Despite some minor successes, the defenders were therefore forced to retreat, although in the end they escaped defeat because of a great storm that struck the harbor and destroyed a large part of the Yüan–Koryŏ fleet.

A vivid depiction of this war comes from a picture scroll commissioned by a small-scale *gokenin*, Takezaki Suenaga of Higo Province, to illustrate his meritorious acts. The scroll, called *Mōko shūrai ekotoba*,[11] notes that on the twentieth day of the tenth month, Suenaga mobilized his followers to join the battle of Hakozaki Bay, but because he heard that Hakata was being attacked, he and his men quickly headed there. When they arrived at Okinohama in Hakata, they found that many other warriors were already there. At this point, the commander,

10 We know of roughly 120 warriors who received rewards in 1275. Large bands such as those of the Kikuchi and Shiraishi supplied over 100 soldiers and horses, but smaller-scale warriors (like Takezaki Suenaga) could contribute only a handful. If we take the number 50 as a hypothetical average of mounted fighting men per house, the total would have been something over 6,000 defenders. But if we take 30 as the average, then the total would be only 3,600.

11 This is the standard name for the scroll, though *Takezaki Suenaga ekotoba* would be more appropriate, as it reflects Suenaga's point of view exclusively. He commissioned the scroll quite late, around 1293. Over the centuries it has received some damage, and accordingly I have used only those sections whose interpretations are not open to dispute. Several reproductions of the scroll are available: *Gyobutsubon, Mōko shūrai ekotoba (fukusei)* (Fukuoka: Fukuokashi kyōiku iinkai, 1975), which is a reproduction at three-fourths the original size; *Mōko shūrai ekotoba*, in *Nihon emaki taisei*, vol. 14 (Tokyo: Chūō kōronsha, 1978); *Heiji monogatari emaki, Mōko shūrai ekotoba*, vol. 9 of *Nihon emaki zenshū* (Tokyo: Kadokawa shoten, 1964). The first two are in color, and the last two contain descriptions and research notes that are extremely useful. As for the pronunciation and interpretation of the main text of the *ekotoba*, see Ishii Susumu et al., eds., *Chūsei seiji shakai shisō, jō* vol. 21 of *Nihon shisō taikei* (Tokyo: Iwanami shoten, 1972), pp. 415–28.

Mutō Kagesuke (Sukeyoshi's second son), ordered a joint operation to push back the enemy force. Inasmuch as Suenaga had only five mounted soldiers under him, he determined that the situation at Okinohama provided little opportunity for glory, and thus he took his small force to another battle area called Akasaka. There the powerful warrior of Higo Province, Kikuchi Takefusa, was pushing the enemy into retreat, and Suenaga saw his chance. He joined the attack, but soon one of his men was shot, and Suenaga himself and the three others received heavy injuries and lost their horses. He was saved by Shiraishi Michiyasu of Hizen Province, who galloped in at this point at the head of a force of more than one hundred men.

Suenaga's performance exemplified the Japanese manner of fighting, which contrasted markedly with that of the enemy. The soldiers of Yüan–Koryŏ moved collectively in an orderly fashion with spears lined up, following the beat of drums and signals. But this is not to say that all Japanese fighting men were as eager as Suenaga to place personal distinction first. After the invasion, the bakufu complained that some warriors, though present, refused to fight or, in other cases, refused to change locations.

The war reached a climax at dusk on the twentieth day. The Japanese army abandoned the Hakata and Hakozaki areas and retreated to the remains of an ancient fortress at Mizuki in order to defend Dazaifu, located some sixteen kilometers from the shore. The Yüan–Koryŏ force, however, had also suffered losses. In particular, the deputy commander of the Yüan army, Liu Fu-heng, had been wounded by an arrow shot by Mutō Kagesuke. The Mongol leaders made a fateful decision to withdraw, because of manpower and supply problems. By the next morning a major portion of their fleet had simply vanished. It is not clear whether the storm struck while the ships were still in Hakata Bay or when they were passing the Islands of Iki and Tsushima on their way back to Koryŏ. In any case, the force's return trip took more than a month. On the twenty-seventh day of the eleventh month, after spending more than twice the time normally required to cross the channel, the fleet arrived back in Korea. A surviving record shows that more than 13,500 persons, roughly one-third of the entire expeditionary force, did not return. Contemporary Japanese sources called the great storm that saved Japan *kamikaze*, the "divine wind."[12]

12 The accepted theory of Japanese historians in the post-Meiji era is that the Yüan–Koryŏ fleet encountered the storm on the night of the twentieth day of the tenth month. But in 1958, a meteorologist, Arakawa Hidetoshi, published a controversial article entitled, "Bun'ei no eki

Japan after the Bun'ei invasion

The aftermath of any major premodern war in Japan was the occasion for granting rewards for meritorious service. Although this had been an external invasion that did not produce enemy lands to be distributed, the warriors who participated in the defense submitted their demands anyway. In 1275, the bakufu rewarded some 120 deserving warriors for their services in the recent fighting, though for many other there were disappointments. The case of Takezaki Suenaga is illustrative.

In the sixth month of 1275, Suenaga left his home in Higo Province for Kamakura. Despite his brave participation in the defense effort, his deeds had not even been reported to the bakufu. His trip was thus to make a direct appeal. It is interesting that his relatives opposed the plan and refused to give him the needed material support to make the trip. Because he had earlier lost land in litigation and had become otherwise impoverished, he had to sell his horses and saddles in order to earn sufficient traveling money.

In the middle of the eighth month, Suenaga finally reached Kamakura and immediately attempted to contact various officials of the bakufu. But perhaps because of his unimpressive attire he was not even granted an audience. Luck did turn his way, however. In the tenth month, Suenaga succeeded in making his appeal to Adachi Yasumori, chief of the bakufu's rewards office (*go'on bugyō*). Yasumori pressed hard with various questions to which Suenaga replied as follows: "I am not appealing merely because I want a reward. If my claim to having fought in the vanguard be proved false, please cut off my head immediately. I have only one wish: for my merit to be known to the shogun. That would serve as a great encouragement in the event of another war." In the face of such unwavering insistence, Yasumori acknowledged Suenaga to be a loyal servant of the bakufu and promised to inform the shogun and to assist in the matter of rewards.

Suenaga's scroll vividly portrays this meeting, noting that Yasumori apparently kept his word: Among the 120 warriors rewarded, Suenaga was the only one who received the personal investiture (*kudashibumi*)

no owari o tsugeta no wa taifū dewa nai" (It was not a typhoon that ended the Bun'ei war), *Nihon rekishi,* no. 120 (June 1958): 41–45. This article caused a reevaluation of the traditionally accepted theory, and as a result, many new views were introduced. For an introductory summary and critique of these views, see Tsukushi Yutaka, *Genkō kigen* (Fukuoka: Fukuoka kyōdo bunkakai, 1972); and Kawazoe, *Mōko shūrai kenkyū shiron.*

of the shogun. In addition, Yasumori presented Suenaga with a prize horse, an act of benevolence that the recipient did not forget. In the testament that Suenaga left to his heir, he admonished his descendants to continue to honor their noble benefactor.[13]

Anticipating a second invasion, the bakufu quickly moved to strengthen its defense program. In 1275, vassals of the Kyushu region were ordered to organize into combined units of two to three provinces, each of which would serve a defense tour of three months per year. This service, called *ikoku keigo banyaku,*[14] constituted a heavy burden for the warriors of Kyushu, even more so as they had to mobilize instantly – in the event of a crisis – during their off-duty periods.

Aside from the shoreline defense duties, the bakufu enforced a series of measures designed to fortify the nation. Many of these programs, however, were intended at the same time to boost the power of the bakufu vis-à-vis the court, as well as the power of the *tokusō* vis-à-vis other warrior families. An earlier illustration of this double program dates from 1274, just before the withdrawal of the Mongol fleet in the Bun'ei invasion. Taking advantage of the emergency situation, the bakufu ordered the *shugo* of the western provinces to mobilize both *gokenin* and non-*gokenin* alike. This represented a clear expansion of the limits of bakufu jurisdiction nationally and *shugo* jurisdiction locally. Thus, to cite one example, the *shugo* of Aki Province requisitioned more than one hundred ships and confiscated a shipment of rice that had been prepared as a tax (*nengu*) payment to a Kyoto *shōen* owner. Moreover, the bakufu ordered the eastern *gokenin* who held lands in the western part of the Sanyō and San'in areas to proceed to their holdings. This was a further attempt by Kamakura to concentrate more men in the strategic war zones. However, the Mongols retreated before any of these vassals might have been sent to the battle front.

After the Bun'ei invasion, politically influential warriors replaced the *shugo* of certain strategically located provinces. In eight of the eleven cases confirmed by historians, Hōjō family members were appointed as *shugo*. In the other three provinces, Adachi Yasumori and his allies were appointed as *shugo*. This allowed the Hōjō to increase the number of *shugo* posts under their control and meant that the nation's

13 The relevant section was appended to the *Mōko shūrai ekotoba* under the title "Yasumori no onkoto" (Honorable matters pertaining to Yasumori).

14 On this topic, see Kawazoe, *Chūkai, Genkō bōrui hennen shiryō*.

defense fell more and more under the direct supervision of the key figures occupying the center of the bakufu.[15]

Kamakura also made new arrangements for protecting the capital. It dispatched to Kyoto the elderly and respected Hōjō Tokimori and other warriors of renown. At the same time, all fighting men – *gokenin* and non-*gokenin* – of Yamashiro Province were made responsible for Kyoto guard duty (*ōbanyaku*), whereas warriors from Kyushu were now exempted. Moreover, so as not to burden the populace unnecessarily, the bakufu encouraged both warriors and courtiers to live frugally. Kamakura also ordered the country's *shugo* to urge provincial temples and shrines to dedicate special prayers for the defeat of the enemy and for protection of the divine land.

Finally, the plans for defense included a retaliatory strategy to attack Koryŏ, the Yüan base for invading Japan. Extant documents from Kyushu and Aki Province show that orders were issued from the last part of 1275 through the following spring to mobilize warriors and prepare battleships, as well as to recruit ships' crews for an expedition. Those recruited included not only *jitō* and *gokenin* but also warriors that were not vassals of the bakufu. From available sources we cannot determine the extent to which these plans were put into effect, although of course there was no actual attack on Koryŏ.

The monument that testifies to the bakufu's effort to secure the country is a series of stone walls along the coastline around Hakata Bay. Although only a portion of the original structure remains today, the walls stretched 20 kilometers east and west of Hakata and generally stood 50 meters inland from the shoreline and were approximately 1.5 to 2.8 meters high and 1.5 to 3.4 meters wide at the bottom. The official schedule for the wall's construction stipulated the third month of 1276 as the beginning date and the eighth month of the same year as the completion date. However, it seems that the construction did not proceed as quickly as planned. For instance, Satsuma Province did not complete its contribution to the project until early in 1277. The responsibility for constructing the wall fell not only on Kyushu *gokenin* but also on various *shōen* officials, the extent of the duty corresponding to the size of individual landhold-

15 See Satō Shin'ichi's classic study, "Kamakura bakufu seiji no senseika ni tsuite," in Takeuchi Rizō. ed., *Nihon hōkensei seiritsu no kenkyū* (Tokyo: Yoshikawa kōbunkan, 1955). Subsequently, it was Murai Shōsuke who confirmed that the transfer of these *shugo* occurred in the latter part of 1275. See Murai Shōsuke, "Mōko shūrai to Chinzei tandai no seiritsu," *Shigaku zasshi* 87 (April 1978): 1–43. I have followed Murai's theory.

ings. One document from Ōsumi Province records a ratio of one *shaku* of wall for each *chō* of land held.[16]

In this way, the national mobilization effort permitted the bakufu an unprecedented right of command over officials hitherto outside its jurisdiction. The following example shows Kamakura's changing position in the nation's power balance: In order to provide strong leadership for the Inland Sea defense zone, Hōjō Muneyori, the younger brother of the *tokusō,* was appointed *shugo* of Nagato Province. In 1276, he recruited for service all warriors in the Sanyō and Nankai circuits, irrespective of their vassal status.

At the center of the bakufu during this period were Hōjō Tokimune and Adachi Yasumori. Hōjō Masamura and Kanazawa Sanetoki, the two other prominent figures in the post-Tokiyori era, had already died. Yasumori was Tokimune's father-in-law and had a major impact on policymaking in Kamakura. Miyoshi Yasuari recorded in his diary, *Kenji sannen ki,*[17] that twice during 1277 (in the tenth and twelfth months), Tokimune held private conferences (*yoriai*) at his residence. Tokiyori had started the practice of *yoriai,* which continued during Tokimune's rule, replacing the *hyōjōshū* (deliberative council) as the key arena for decision making. According to the *Kenji sannen ki,* the most important political and personnel decisions were made at the *yoriai,* which were attended by the most influential men of the era. In the same year, the right to recommend *gokenin* for traditional court offices was withdrawn from the *hyōjōshū* and became instead the shogun's sole prerogative. Thus, Tokimune and Miyoshi Yasuari (head of the *monchūjo*) are listed in the *Kenji sannen ki* as having attended four times; Adachi Yasumori, twice; Taira Yoritsuna (who headed a group of *miuchibito*), three times; and two other powerful *gokenin,* twice. The strength of a certain group of *miuchibito* at this time can be attributed to the influence of Adachi Yasumori who, at the conclusion of the Nigatsu disturbance, succeeded in promoting the status of such men despite his initial opposition to them. However, this harmonious balance of interests did not last long, as antagonisms were already beginning to surface between Yasumori and Taira Yoritsuna.

16 Kawazoe Shōji summarizes concisely the present state of research on the wall construction; see his "Kaisetsu," in *Chūkai, Genkō bōrui hennen shiryō.*

17 The main text of "Kenji sannen ki" appears on *Gunsho ruijū, bukebu,* vol. 421, though with a few errata. A better text is Takeuchi Rizō, comp., *Zoku shiryō taisei,* vol. 10 (Kyoto: Rinsen shoten, 1967). Ryō Susumu gives a detailed analysis of this diary in "Kenji sannen ki kō," in *Kamakura jidai, jō,* pp. 217–31.

The second Mongol invasion, 1281

Overtures from the Yüan did not cease after the Bun'ei invasion. In the fourth month of 1275, an envoy arrived in Muronotsu in Nagato, instead of at Dazaifu. The bakufu's response to this mission was harsher than before. The bakufu summoned the entire Yüan entourage in the eighth month and in the following month summarily executed them in the suburbs of Kamakura. In the meantime, the Yüan destroyed the capital of the Southern Sung in 1276 and captured the reigning Chinese emperor. By early 1279, the Southern Sung empire was completely destroyed. At this time, the invasion of Japan was once again put at the top of the Yüan agenda. Destruction of the Sung provided the Yüan with a new approach route to Japan. Instead of going through Korea, the Mongols could use the surrendered Sung navy dispatched from China itself. Another favorable condition for the Yüan was that Koryŏ was growing more complacent as the Yüan expanded their borders ever closer to Korea itself. This new set of circumstances formed the background for the Yüan's plan to attack Japan a second time.

The old Sung territory provided many of the resources for the invasion. In 1279, Kublai ordered the people of the lower Yangtze area to construct six hundred warships and consulted a commander of the Sung army regarding specific plans of action. On the advice he received, the khan sent another envoy to Japan, carrying a message warning that if Japan failed to submit, it would suffer the same fate that had struck the Sung. This envoy arrived in Japan in the sixth month, but as before, the court and bakufu refused to receive him. All the members of his mission were executed in Hakata.

During this period, Koryŏ continued to bear the burden of preparing battleships and their crews. This time, Kublai ordered 900 ships. In China proper, Kublai reinforced his plan administratively by establishing a new governmental organ, the Ministry for Conquering Japan. The official order to attack came in the first month of 1281. The entire army was divided into two divisions – the Eastern Route Division dispatched from Koryŏ and the Chiang-nan Division dispatched from southeast China. The Eastern Route Division had a combined force of 10,000 Koryŏ soldiers and 30,000 Mongols. Some 900 battleships carried 17,000 crew members in addition to the soldiers. The Chiang-nan Division was composed of 100,000 previously defeated Sung soldiers sailing on as many as 3,500 battleships. The two divisions were to merge in Iki and then proceed together to attack Japan proper. Before their departure, Kublai, who was aware of the potential disunity of this invasion plan, strongly emphasized the necessity for cooperation.

Preparations were also under way in Japan. Evidence indicates that Japan knew of the impeding invasion. According to a letter the bakufu sent to the *shugo* Ōtomo Yoriyasu in Kyushu, Kamakura was anticipating the attack before the fourth month of the following year and warned the *shugo* to consolidate their defense strategies. In the same letter, the bakufu noted that there had been a recent tendency for *shugo* and *gokenin* not to cooperate effectively.

The pattern of mobilization in Japan was the same as for the Bun'ei invasion. Kyushu warriors assembled around Hakata Bay. Using the newly constructed stone walls as barriers, they were to fight under the command of the Ōtomo and Mutō. Although the exact size of the Japanese force is unknown, we can assume that this one was larger than the previous one.[18] Adachi Morimune (Yasumori's second son) and the Shimazu of Southern Kyushu also served as generals, and the powerful *miuchibito* Andō and Goda came down from Kamakura to serve as military officials. It is clear that the Hōjō main line was attempting, as before, to consolidate its control. Overall, we can surmise that the proportionate growth in size was much greater for the combined Yüan armies than for the Japanese force.

On the third day of the fifth month of 1281, the Eastern Route Division left Koryŏ and by the end of the month attacked Tsushima and Iki. The original plan had called for the Eastern Route Division to meet the Chiang-nan Division there on the fifteenth day of the sixth month. But in violation of this agreement, the Eastern Route Division moved on toward Hakata Bay early in the sixth month, though owing to the stone walls, it was unable to land and thus occupied Shiga Island instead.

The Japanese army did not hesitate to pursue this fleet that was stationed just off the coastline. By using small boats or running up the causeway connecting the island to the mainland, the Japanese mounted an offensive. Takezaki Suenaga was again present and fought at the forefront of the Higo Province army, and his meritori-

18 No extant record reveals the size of the Japanese army in 1281. However, we can identify the names of most warriors who received awards from some seven surviving award listings. During the third granting session alone, Kanazaki estate in Hizen was the site of awards to more than four hundred warriors, a figure that already exceeds by a factor of three the number of known rewards in the Bun'ei war.

ous deeds were recognized by his commander, Adachi Morimune. Before the middle of the sixth month, the Yüan force abandoned Shiga Island and retreated to Iki. The Japanese army chased them, and thus the fighting continued.

In the meantime, because of the death of the Chiang-nan Division's commanding general, it was not able to leave Ningpo until the middle of the sixth month. The plan to merge with the Eastern Route Division was redirected from Iki to Hirado. In the seventh month the two divisions met, and from Hirado they headed toward their original destination, Hakata Bay. By the end of the seventh month, they had arrived at Takashima Island near Hizen Province where they confronted the Japanese army.

But just before the Yüan–Koryŏ force was about to launch its final offensive, a devastating storm hit the bay on the night of the thirtieth day of the seventh month. The generals of the Yüan army commandeered the remaining ships in order to return to Koryŏ, leaving large numbers of stranded soldiers to the mercy of the Japanese. Takezaki Suenaga took part in this phase of the fighting, and the record he commissioned testifies to his gallantry.

In the second Yüan expedition against Japan, the Mongol army lost 69 to 90 percent of its men, a total of more than 100,000 dead. Japan's success was attributed once again to the intercession of the gods. During the crisis, the bakufu continued to strengthen its authority. It received permission from the court to collect a commissariat tax from the public and private estates of Kyushu and the San'in provinces of western Honshū. Moreover, on the ninth day of the intercalary seventh month, the bakufu requested imperial approval to the conscript warriors from nonbakufu lands. Because the news concerning the Mongol retreat reached Kyoto at precisely the same time, this latter request was not immediately granted. However, the bakufu continued to press the emperor on the point, and on the twentieth day, an imperial edict was issued granting the bakufu this new authority. Interestingly, however, the edict was dated the ninth day, instead of the twentieth day, in order to legitimize the bakufu's purported need to expand its control in the name of national security.

Immediately following the defeat of the Yüan–Koryŏ army, Kamakura revived its earlier plan to attack Koryŏ. The plan stipulated that either the Mutō or the Ōtomo would lead a fighting force of *gokenin* from three northern Kyushu provinces as well as *akutō* from the Yamato and Yamashiro provinces. Extant records do not disclose how far this interesting strategy was pursued, but there is no evidence of a counterinvasion. In fact, Japan itself remained under the threat of attack,[19] and as a result, additional Hōjō were dispatched as *shugo* to Kyushu and the Sanyō areas. The *gokenin* of Kyushu, however, were prohibited to travel to Kyoto and Kamakura without the bakufu's authorization. Moreover, the vassals of Kyushu were expected to continue to serve regular defense duty, which now included three to four months of guard service in Kyushu or Nagato, the construction and repair of stone walls, and the contribution of military supplies such as arrows, spears, and flags. These responsibilities now fell on all warriors from Kyushu and not merely the *gokenin*. Some *shōen* proprietors apparently resisted this change, for in 1286 the bakufu decreed that in the event of noncompliance, Kamakura would appoint a *jitō* to the offending estate.

JAPAN AFTER THE MONGOL WARS

The bakufu in the postcrisis period

The years immediately following the second Mongol attack were characterized by innovative regulations, judicial reform, and increasingly intense factional conflicts. In 1284, the regent Hōjō Tokimune died suddenly at age thirty-four and was succeeded by his fourteen-year-old heir, Hōjō Sakatoki. The new regent's advisers immediately enacted changes by issuing new codes and restructuring the judicial organ. In the fifth month of 1284, the bakufu issued a thirty-eight-article "new formulary" (*shin shikimoku*) and then followed this collection of behavioral standards with eighty specific regulations based on these codes.

The new legislation dealt with a wide range of concerns. For example, the shogun was to observe propriety and frugality in all aspects of his life and to devote himself to proper learning. The shogun's lands (the *kantō goryō*) were to be supervised more tightly, and the country's official provincial shrines and temples (*ichinomiya* and *kokubunji*) were to be protected, promoted, and repaired. In Kyushu, not only *ichinomiya* but all shrines received special attention; for instance, shrine land that has been pawned was to be returned to the shrine at no

19 In 1283, Kublai established the Office for Advancing East and, at the same time, sent another envoy to Japan who unfortunately encountered a storm and was forced to return to China. After suppressing a rebellion in the Chiang-nan area, Kublai dispatched another envoy in 1284 who got only as far as Tsushima before he was killed. Further plans for an advance against Japan were complicated as the Mongol Empire became increasingly embroiled in domestic rebellions. Kublai's death in 1294 ended further expeditionary attempts. Nevertheless, Japan did not abandon its defense measures until the end of the Kamakura era.

cost, as an expression of gratitude for the prayers that had been said at the time of the Mongol invasions.

Land rewards were to be granted to those Kyushu *shōen* officers and smaller holders (*myōshu*) who, despite their service during the wars, had not yet received compensation. The regulation further stipulated that land that had been sold or pawned be returned to them without penalty. To implement this provision, the bakufu dispatched a special envoy of three *hikitsuke* magistrates to Kyushu. These officials were called *tokusei no ontsukai* (agents of virtuous rule) and were viewed as the administrators of a rescue mission. There is evidence that around the same time, *gokenin* outside Kyushu were given similar protection.[20] These *tokusei* measures of 1284 were considerably more inclusive than the one issued in 1273, which guaranteed only pawned property.

With respect to the *akutō*, the bakufu dispatched special agents to suppress their activities in the Kinai and neighboring provinces. These agents were to cooperate with local *shugo* in maintaining peace and order in especially troubled areas.

Nevertheless, in 1284 the bakufu focused primarily on consolidating its rule in Kyushu. Until the 1260s, the powerful *shugo* families of Mutō and Ōtomo had jointly held the title of Chinzei *bugyō*. But under the changed circumstance of the invasion era, it was now deemed necessary to establish an autonomous judicial authority in Kyushu to prevent local *gokenin* from traveling to Kyoto or Kamakura to file lawsuits. Thus, the three *tokusei* agents, together with the Mutō and Ōtomo families and Adachi Morimune, came to form a three-unit judicial structure in which each unit was responsible for judging cases from three provinces each. This court was housed in a building in Hakata,[21] and this office served as the governmental organ responsible for enforcing *tokusei* measures as well as delivering judicial decisions.

The judicial system of Kamakura was also reformed in this year. In the eighth month, the bakufu issued an eleven-article code that enjoined the *hikitsu-keshū* and its magistrates to carry out their jobs faithfully and attempted to remove the influence of powerful persons in judicial decision making. Interestingly, much consideration was given to poor *gokenin* who needed to be rescued by the courts. There were some procedural changes as well. Previously, the *hikitsuke* official who

20 Kasamatsu Hiroshi, *Nihon chūsei-hō shiron* (Tokyo: Tōkyō daigaku shuppankai, 1979, p. 104.

21 Satō Shin'ichi, *Kamakura bakufu soshō seido no kenkyū* (Tokyo: Meguro shoten, 1946), pp. 287–91.

was assigned a suit drafted two or three alternative verdicts that were then presented to the *hyōjōshū* for the final decision. But under the new procedure, only a single verdict was forwarded to the *hyōjōshū*, and the authority of the *hikitsuke* was dramatically increased.[22]

Adachi Yasumori, the maternal grandfather of the young regent Sadatoki was influential in promoting these reforms. Since his initial appointment to the post of appeals magistrate (*osso bugyō*) after Tokiyori's death, he had consistently sought to maintain the support of the *gokenin* through efficient administration of the judicial system.[23] Moreover, although the Adachi family had built a strong power base by acting in concert with the Hōjō, they had always stressed as well their continuing close ties with the shogun.[24] In opposition to Yasumori and his followers was a group represented by Taira Yoritsuna, who was a partisan of both the *tokusō* and the *miuchibito*. Before his death, it had been the regent Tokimune who acted as the arbiter between these two contending groups, but after the accession of the youthful Sadatoki in 1284, conditions deteriorated rapidly.

The Shimotsuki incident: the fall of Adachi Yasumori

In the eleventh month of 1285, Taira Yoritsuna suddenly attacked Adachi Yasumori and his followers, claiming to have been ordered to do so by the regent. For half a day a fierce battle was fought in Kamakura, but Yasumori and his followers were surprised in the attack and were soon killed. Because this disturbance occurred in the month of the "frosty moon," a contemporary record referred to it as the "Shimotsuki" incident. The events leading up to the incident are not clear, but according to one theory, Adachi Munekage, Yasumori's heir, was accused of plotting to usurp the shogun's seat on the pretext that his ancestor Kagemori was actually a son of Yoritomo. In view of the traditionally close ties between the Adachi and the Minamoto families, Munekage's decision to change his surname to Minamoto cannot by itself be interpreted as masking some ulterior motive. It is

22 Satō Shin'ichi stresses this point in ibid., pp. 69–76.

23 Yasumori was not only the most remarkable political figure of his era; he was also a learned scholar of the Confucian classics and of Buddhism. For a biographical sketch, see Taga Munehaya, "Akita Jō-no-suke Adachi Yasomuri," in Taga Munehaya, *Kamakura jidai no shisō to bunka* (Tokyo: Meguro shoten, 1946), pp. 247–79.

24 The sister of Yasumori's grandfather Kagemori was the wife of Yoritomo's younger brother Noriyori. Kagemori took Buddhist vows after the death of Sanetomo, the third shogun, and Yasumori himself was highly regarded by Sanetomo's widow. On one occasion, Yasumori found a sword named Higekirimaru that had been left by Yoritomo in Kyoto, and he respectfully returned it to Kamakura.

safer to assume that the confrontation between Yasumori and Yoritsuna had simply attained a level at which an armed struggle could no longer be avoided.

The impact of this incident was deep and long lasting. According to extant documents, more than fifty men committed suicide after the incident. Among these were various members of the Adachi family and a branch line, the Ōsone, as well as warriors from other influential houses.[25] The sources also tell of many *gokenin* from the Musashi and Kōzuke provinces committing suicide and one entry in the record mentions as many as five hundred victims. But the latter were probably attacked on suspicion of partisanship with Yasumori.

It is understandable that many Kōzuke *gokenin* should have died along with Yasumori, who held the fourth generation *shugo* post there. However, the large number of deaths in Musashi, with which the Adachi had no prior association, deserves special attention. Musashi Province had long contained several small-scale warrior bands, which leads us to conclude that Yasumori enjoyed a strong following among houses of this size. Moreover, Yasumori's ties with those close to the shogun can be surmised from the suicide of Fujiwara Sukenori, a courtier in service to the shogun. Thus, by identifying the dead we can help clarify the overall network of support. Yasumori's partisans consisted mostly of small-scale *gokenin* and those close to the shogun.

Some men who had been on Yasumori's side escaped death but lost political power. A well-known example here is Yasumori's daughter's husband, Kanazawa Akitoki, a member of a branch of the Hōjō. He had been serving as head of the fourth *hikitsuke* unit and held the third-ranking position in the *hyōjōshū*. Accused of complicity, Akitoki was removed from his positions and exiled to Shimōsa. The day before his exile, he sent a letter to a monk of the Shōmyōji, a temple that might be called the Kanazawa clan temple. He stated, "For the last decade or so, since 1269, I have lived as though stepping on thin ice."[26] This statement vividly conveys the degree of insecurity at the center of the bakufu's political structure. Others who fell from power included Utsunomiya Kagetsuna and Ōe Tokihide, both members of the *hyōjōshū* and the husbands of Yasumori sisters. Indeed, we can

25 *Kanagawa ken shi, shiryō hen* vol. 2, nos. 1016–20. For example, the Ogasawara, the maternal line of Yasumori, lost its chieftain (*sōryō*) and several others. Other suicides and persons disgraced included the powerful Sagami family of Miura; the Itō of Izu; the Kira, a branch family of the Ashikaga; Nikaidō Yukikage, a *hikitsuke* member and the hereditary holder of the *mandokoro shitsuji* post; Mutō Kageyasu, another *hikitsuke;* the Hatta, *shugo* of Hitachi; and the Ōe, Kobayakawa, Amano, Iga and others. Many of these were famous *gokenin*.

26 *Kanagawa ken shi, shiryō hen* vol. 2, no. 1023.

gauge the extent of Yasumori's influence by noting that five out of sixteen *hyōjōshū* members and seven out of thirteen *hikitsuke* elected to join with the Adachi.[27]

The repercussions from this incident were felt throughout Japan. In Hakata, the second son of Yasumori, Adachi Morimune, who had replaced his father as the deputy *shugo* of Higo, was murdered. Also, in the scattered provinces of Hitachi, Tōtomi, Shinano, and Harima, Yasumori's sympathizers were killed. Not long after, Mutō Kagesuke, the commander who had led Takezaki Suenaga, rebelled at Iwato Castle in Chikunzen, which had been built as a fortress against the Mongols. The Mutō, along with many warriors from northern Kyushu, were defeated in the battle of Iwato.[28]

Autocratic rule by Taira Yoritsuna, a miuchibito *representative*

The immediate outcome of the Shimotsuki incident was the concentration of political power in the hands of Taira Yoritsuna, the leader of the *miuchibito*. A courtier's diary described the situation: "Yoritsuna alone holds power and all live in fear."[29] Yoritsuna himself was said to be a great-grandson of Taira Morikuni who had served Kiyomori during the latter's period of ascendancy. At the time of the Taira defeat, Morikuni was taken to Kamakura as a hostage and placed in the custody of the Miura. Subsequently, Yoritsuna's father, Moritsuna, served Hōjō Yasutoki and wielded significant power as manager of the Hōjō household. Yoritsuna rose by serving Hōjō Tokimune, and his wife was the wet nurse to Tokimune's son Sadatoki. Yoritsuna thus held all the requisite qualifications to be the head *miuchibito*.

Who were these *miuchibito*?[30] From the time of Hōjō Yasutoki, the notable *miuchibito* houses were the Bitō, Andō, Suwa, Nanjō, and Seki. Their residences were located inside Yasutoki's mansion. The families themselves came mostly from outside the east and were originally incorporated into the Hōjō household during the early thirteenth

27 Taga Munehaya was the first to focus on the Shimotsuki incident and analyze it in detail. See "Hōjō shikken seiji no igi," in his *Kamakura jidai no shisō to bunka*, pp. 288–320. Satō Shin'ichi clarified the incident's historical significance in his *Kamakura bakufu soshō seido no kenkyū*, pp. 76–78, 96–97. Also see Ishii Susumu, "Shimotsuki sōdō oboegaki," in *Kanagawa ken shi dayori, shiryō hen* vol. 2 (Yokohama: Kanagawa ken, 1973), pp, 1–4.

28 For a detailed study of this battle, see Kawazoe Shōji, "Iwato gassen saihen – Chinzei ni okeru tokusō shihai no kyōka to Mutō shi," in Mori Katsumi hakase koki kinen kai, ed., *Taigai kankei to seiji bunka*, vol. 2 of *Shigaku rōnshū* (Tokyo: Yoshikawa kōbunkan, 1974), pp. 217–49. 29 "Sanemi kyōki," 1293/4/26.

30 The classic study of *miuchibito* appears in Satō, *Kamakura bakufu soshō seido no kenkyū*, pp. 104–21.

century.[31] Later, a new group of eastern *miuchibito* appeared with base lands in areas once held by shogunal *gokenin.*

This new group of eastern *miuchibito* included the Kudō, Onozawa, Soga, Shibuya, Uji, Shiaku, Aihara, and Homma, among others. The function of these private vassals centered on the management of lands held by the *tokusō* or lands controlled by other Hōjō who were *shugo.* In addition, the *miuchibito* exercised certain administrative duties in Kamakura, for instance, overseeing the paperwork for the Hōjō's growing portfolio of holdings.

As a category, *miuchibito* differed from *gokenin* in several significant ways, as the case of Andō Renshō shows.[32] Renshō was born at the end of Yasutoki's tenure as regent, and he died in 1329, shortly before the fall of the bakufu. He was a near contemporary of Taira Yoritsuna. One of Renshō's special achievements was his patronage of the Kumedadera, a temple in Izumi Province, where his portrait still hangs. Renshō is credited with reviving the temple in 1277, by commending to it three plots of land in Izumi and another in Tajima. With other temples, however, Renshō's activities led to trouble. His inability to collect a loan he had made to a priest of the Ninnaji caused him to seek the assistance of a usurer-monk of the Enryakuji, who in turn attempted to seize certain rents in default of the loan. The affected chapel in Ninnaji brought a suit against Renshō with the bakufu.

In his service to the Hōjō, Renshō held administrative posts in the Tada-in estate of Settsu Province and in three other *shōen,* all belonging to the *tokusō.* He also held the deputy *shugo* post for Settsu. As it happened, two of the three *shōen* under his administrative control bordered Osaka Bay and probably functioned as ports. The port of Fukudomari in Harima Province was constructed in large part by expenditures borne by Renshō alone. The project required more than fifteen years of labor and cash running into the several hundreds of *kan.* Ultimately, Fukudomari developed into a port that was as significant as the older harbor town of Hyōgo in Settsu was. For his part, Renshō collected high rents and dallied in commerce.

Andō Renshō, therefore, was not simply a man of arms but was also a crafty entrepreneur deeply involved in transportation and usury.

31 Like Taira Moritsuna, the Seki were descended from Taira Morikuni. The Bitō came from a family that had lost its holdings at the time of the Gempei War and sought refuge with Yoritomo in Kamakura. The Suwa were Shinto priests from a shrine of the same name in Shinano Province. The only prominent *miuchibito* house originally from the east appears to have been the Nanjō.

32 A number of articles describe Andō Renshō and his activities. For a concise description, see Amino, *Mōko shūrai,* pp. 115–16, 296–300.

Other members of the Andō clan managed additional *tokusō* holdings along the Inland Sea, in Kyushu, and in northern Tōhoku (the Tsugaru peninsula). Members of the Andō family in Tsugaru served as deputies for Ezo (Ezo *daikan*) from the time of Hōjō Yoshitoki and also controlled the premier northern seaport, Tosa, in the same area. Other port towns from Tosa south through Wakasa to Kyoto were likewise controlled by the Hōjō.[33]

The leader of the *miuchibito*, Taira Yoritsuna, occupied the dominant position in the bakufu in the post-Shimotsuki era. He encountered many problems, however, the greatest of which was winning the trust and support of the disaffected *gokenin* class. Instrumental to this effort was the distribution of the post-Mongol reward lands. The reward program began in 1286 when some twenty-five Kyushu warriors (including *shugo* and members of the Hōjō house) were chosen as the first recipients, with the shogun personally administering the operation. Lists of names and rewards were sent down to the Ōtomo and Mutō, but processing them proved complicated, and there was a delay of two years. The rewards themselves were of three sizes – paddy grants of ten, five, and three *chō*, along with proportional awards of residence areas and dry fields.

To solve the problem of land shortages, the bakufu adopted several measures: It utilized a share of the shogun's personal holdings (called *kantō goryō*); it confiscated the landed interests of some *shōen* proprietors; and it exchanged lands outside Kyushu for those located within. Another source of rewards was land confiscated from warriors implicated in the Shimotsuki incident. Because it was the bakufu's policy to confine the grant program to Kyushu, a major shift resulted in the pattern of landholding there. Unfortunately, small-scale warriors were helped little. The greatest tracts of land went either to the Hōjō or to warriors who supported them. It is even possible that for most reward lands, the Hōjō came to hold a superior authority for holdings distributed at a lower level to *gokenin*.

Under Yoritsuna, offices in the bakufu tended to go to persons friendly to the Hōjō, and policymaking was similarly compromised. Thus the *tokusei* measures of 1284, which were aimed at rescuing shrines, *shōen* officials, and *myōshu* (*shōen* cultivators) in Kyushu, were, in effect, nullified when another order was issued to return

33 A flag with the Hōjō family emblem that survives from 1272 authorized free passage for ships passing through Tagarasu Bay in Wakasa. Another record from 1306 shows that twenty large ships from the Tsugaru area carried the bakufu's authorization to enter the port of Mikuni in Echizen Province, loaded with salmon and kimono.

conditions to their pre-1284 status. The bakufu also replaced the system of justice by the three *tokusei* agents in Hakata with a new office, the Chinzei *dangijo,* in 1285. This office, staffed by the Mutō and Ōtomo families, Utsunomiya Songaku, and Shibuya Shigesato, was to function as the new central judicial and administrative organ for the entire Kyushu region. Even though the latter two were *gokenin,* their interests were evidently closely tied with those of the *tokusō.*[34] At any rate, the Chinzei *dangijo* was established as a judicial center in Hakata that could handle land-related disputes and criminal cases.

These structural reforms were accompanied by the appointment of *miuchibito* to an ever-increasing number of key positions within the bakufu. For instance, in 1291, two *miuchibito* received supervisory posts in the Chinzei *dangijo;* whereas several other *miuchibito,* from the *hikitsuke,* were given responsibility for justice pertaining to temples, shrines, and courtier landowners. Five powerful Hōjō vassals, including two of Yoritsuna's own sons, came to function in the *hikitsuke.*

Tokusō *autocracy*

Yoritsuna's leadership, however, proved in the end to be ephemeral. In the fourth month of 1293, less than ten years after his rise, he was accused of attempting to advance his son Sukemune to the position of shogun, and so he was killed along with more than ninety of his sympathizers by forces of the regent Sadatoki. This incident, called the Heizen-Gate disturbance after the gate at which the armed conflict took place, ended Yoritsuna's era and ushered in a period of *tokusō* rule by the then-twenty-four-year-old Sadatoki.

Within a month's time, Sadatoki had collected oaths from the membership of the *hyōjōshū, hikitsukeshū,* and *bugyōnin* corps. In particular, the last were required to swear that they would not take bribes. Overall, Sadatoki's aim was to assist struggling *gokenin* and to extend favor to honest persons. He thus reconfirmed as vassals those warriors whose great-grandfathers had been recognized as such, irrespective of the present condition of their holdings. In other words, *gokenin* were theoretically secured in that status even if they had pawned or sold lands granted to them by the bakufu.

Contemporary records also called these new measures *tokusei* measures, suggesting an awareness of their similarities to the 1284 policy

34 Utsunomiya Songaku came to serve as the deputy *shugo* of Higo Province under a *tokusō*-held *shugo* post. Also, various members of the Shibuya came to be recognized as *miuchibito.*

changes of Adachi Yasumori. There was even a restoration to favor of some of Yasumori's sympathizers. For example, the previously disgraced Nagai Munehide was appointed as an appeals magistrate (*osso bugyō*) along with Hōjō Munenobu. Moreover, in the tenth month, Sadatoki abolished the *hikitsuke* organ and created a system of six "reporters" (*shissō*) in its place, assigning three Hōjō who were previously *hikitsuke* unit leaders, Utsunomiya Kagetsuna, Kanazawa Akitoki, and Hōjō Munenobu, who doubled as *osso bugyō*.[35] In addition Settsu Chikamune, who had been head (*shitsuji*) of the *monchūjo* since the end of 1285, was replaced by Miyoshi Tokitsura, another of Yasumori's sympathizers. Finally, the *mandokoro* leadership was shifted from Nikaidō Yukisada to Nikaidō Yukifuji, who had similarly been close to Yasumori.[36]

This revival of Yasumori's sympathizers, however, proved to be superficial. The new post of *shissō*, for example, was wholly subservient to Sadatoki, with responsibilities limited to the submission of details or reference materials with bearing on cases being litigated. By contrast, the former *hikitsuke* unit heads had had much greater freedom of action under Yasumori's reform measures.

In 1294, Sadatoki decreed that no further awards or punishments would be imposed for participation in the Shimotsuki incident. To Sadatoki, then, the prior affiliation of warriors was less important than their current absolute submission to him. In this year also, he extended the face-to-face confrontation procedure to cover a larger number of suits. Moreover, in the tenth month of 1294 he revived the *hikitsuke* but retained the power to issue independent judgments.[37] He did make one important concession, however, by recognizing second hearings for cases that he himself had judged, a reversal of his prior position on the subject.

Despite Sadatoki's efforts to eliminate factional strife within the bakufu, pressures continued to mount from the *miuchibito* collectively and from the more disadvantaged members of the *gokenin* class. A diary written by Miyoshi Tokitsura in 1295, the *Einin sannen ki*,[38]

35 Both Kagetsuna and Akitoki were at one time supporters of Yasumori.

36 For further details, see Ishii Susumu, "Takezaki Suenaga ekotoba no seiritsu," *Nihon rekishi*, no. 273 (1971): 12–32. The year 1293 was also when Takezaki Suenaga, another supporter of Yasumori, began to promote his plan of producing a scroll that depicted his own military valor. The timing of this effort following the Heisen-gate disturbance could hardly have been mere coincidence.

37 The *Kamakura nendai ki* dates the revival of the *hikitsuke* as 1295, and many historians have adopted this. However, the correct date is 1294/10, as first pointed out by Satō Shin'ichi, in "Kamakura bakufu seiji no senseika ni tsuite," pp. 121–22.

38 As noted, Miyoshi Tokitsura was *monchūjo shitsuji*. The text was published and introduced for the first time in 1953 by Kawazoe Hiroshi, "Einin san'nen ki kōshō," *Shichō* 50 (January 1953): 33–51. It also appears in Takeuchi, ed., *Zoku shiryō taisei*, vol. 10.

describes this strife through the following incident: a report by a *miuchibito* of blunders committed by the *hyōjōshū* led to Sadatoki's punishment of his own vassals rather than the perpetrators of the error. Although it can be argued that the *tokusō*'s ultimate aim was to alleviate the suffering of the *gokenin* class, his policies also characteristically promoted his own autocratic rule. This ambiguity is best illustrated by the famous *tokusei* edict of 1297, which stipulated (1) abolition of the appeal suit system (*osso*), (2) prohibition of further pawning or sale of *gokenin* property and a guaranteed return of previously sold property to the original owner at no cost,[39] and (3) refusal by the bakufu to accept any litigation involving the collection of loans, in order to curtail excessive usury practices.

The second and third items represented a bold remedial measure for financial depressed *gokenin*, going one step beyond Yasumori's *tokusei* edict. Responding to these regulations, *gokenin* from many regions demanded the reform of their surrendered lands, and the bakufu regularly supported their claims.[40] The first item, however, was more clearly a device to enhance Sadatoki's rule, for it overturned his authorization of three years earlier confirming the right to appeal. The 1297 *tokusei* edict, at any rate, is symbolic of the ambiguity that characterized this period.[41]

These policies, in fact, remained highly fluid. In the following year, the system of appeal was once again revived, and litigation bearing on the collection of loans was recognized as a legitimate cause for complaint. Only the measure guaranteeing the return of previously pawned or sold *gokenin* land was maintained.

The appeal system underwent further changes. In 1300, two years after its revival, the appeal magistrate's office (*osso bugyō*) was abolished, and instead five *miuchibito* took over that responsibility. Here was an attempt to maintain the appeal system itself while concentrating authority in the hands of the *tokusō*.[42] One year later, however, the *osso bugyō* was reinstituted, a testimony to the difficulties that Sadatoki encountered in seeking to consolidate his rule.

However imperfect this "autocracy," the bakufu under Sadatoki

39 Except for land already possessed for twenty years or more.

40 For a more detailed study of this *tokusei* edict, see Miura Hiroyuki, "Tokusei no kenkyū," in Miura Hiroyuki, *Hōseishi no kenkyū* (Tokyo: Iwanami shoten, 1919), pp. 767–835.

41 See Kasamatsu Hiroshi, "Einin tokusei to osso," in Kasamatsu, *Nihon chūsei-hō shiron*, pp. 103–21.

42 According to Kasamatsu, the *miuchibito* decided whether a case warranted reexamination, but the actual review was carried out by the *hikitsuke*. In other words, the *miuchibito* did not handle the entire *osso* process themselves.

was experiencing its most complete domination to date. In 1285, immediately after the Shimotsuki incident, Hōjō house members controlled twenty-nine of the country's sixty-eight *shugo* posts, whereas other families held twenty-two. Five provinces had no *shugo*, and the identity of *shugo* in the twelve remaining provinces is unknown. At any rate, more than half of the known *shugo* posts were held by the Hōjō. By 1333, that family held thirty-six *shugo* titles; other families held twenty-one; five provinces had no *shugo;* and the figures for six provinces are unknown.[43] The provinces in which the Hōjō held their titles were widely distributed.

Not all the *jitō* posts held by the Hōjō have been identified by historians,[44] but most seem to have been concentrated in the Tōhoku region, the eastern part of the Tōkaido (especially Izu and Suruga), and Kyushu. In Kyushu at least sixty *jitō* posts constituting 22,000 *chō* of paddy land, or about 20 percent of the entire paddy total for Kyushu, were under Hōjō control.[45] The overall strength of the Hōjō house derived largely from this ever-expanding portfolio of land.

The akutō

One of the serious problems confronting the bakufu in the late thirteenth century was the rise of the *akutō. Shōen* were increasingly requesting Kamakura to suppress this banditry, and in 1296, proprietors, the bakufu ordered the *shugo* to construct policing stations on all major roads and to employ *gokenin* in the growing suppression effort. In 1300, the bakufu dispatched a powerful warrior to each of the provinces of Kyushu, to help the *shugo* maintain the peace. In 1301, to control the pirates, all ships in Kyushu were required to display the name of the shipowner and the port of registry. In 1303, night attacks and piracy, which had previously been punishable by exile, were redefined as crimes punishable by death. Thieves, gamblers, and arsonists were also to receive stricter punishments.

The bakufu's *akutō* control measures did not yield quick results. In 1308, for example, Kōno Michiari, a magnate from Iyo Province posted

43 These statistics are based largely on Satō Shin'ichi, *Zōho Kamakura bakufu shugo seido no kenkyū* (Tokyo: Tōkyō daigaku shuppankai, 1971). I have made some minor adjustments.

44 There is currently much local study being done on the landholding patterns of the Hōjō. The most comprehensive study is by Okutomi Takayuki, *Kamakura Hōjōshi no kisoteki kenkyū* (Tokyo: Yoshikawa kōbunkan, 1980), especially the section entitled "Hōjōshi shoryō gairyaku ichiran," pp. 258–78.

45 These figures represent an update of my "Kyūshū shokoku ni okeru Hōjōshi shoryō no kenkyū," in Takeuchi Rizō hakase kanreki kinenkai, ed., *Shōensei to buke shakai* (Tokyo: Yoshikawa kōbunkan, 1969), pp. 331–93.

to Kyushu, was ordered home to assist in the effort to control pirates in the bays of western Japan and especially in Kumano. A year later, warriors from as many as fifteen provinces were mobilized to fight against these same Kumano pirates.[46] On another occasion, in 1301, five *akutō* from Yamato Province refused to submit to the bakufu's conscription order, thereby forcing the bakufu to call out *gokenin* from Kyoto and seven other provinces to attack their fortifications.[47]

Kamakura's increasing reliance on the use of military force came to be reflected in its criminal codes. For example, in 1310, *karita rōzeki* (the pilfering of harvests from property in dispute at court), which had frequently been treated as a land-related issue, was placed under the jurisdiction of the criminal courts. Similarly, in 1315, *roji rōzeki* (the theft of movables as payment for uncollected debts) was also placed under criminal jurisdiction, also a departure from past practice.

Sadatoki continued to attend *hyōjōshū* meetings and maintained his role as the central figure of the bakufu, even after taking Buddhist vows in 1301. His tenure as *tokusō*, however, was beset with internal rivalries. For example, Hōjō Munekata, a member of the *tokusō* line and a cousin of Sadatoki, placed himself in the same functional category as the *miuchibito*, in disregard of his family background, and attempted to steal political power by assuming the position of *uchi kanrei*, an officer of the *samurai-dokoro*. In 1305, Munekata murdered his rival, Hōjō Tokimura, who was cosigner (*rensho*) at the time. Soon thereafter, Munekata himself was killed by a conspirator. This "Fifth-Month disturbance," named after the month of Munekata's death, reveals that even Sadatoki was not able to eliminate the factional disputes among members of the Hōjō. When Sadatoki died, at the age of forty-one in 1311, a contemporary remembered him in his later years as a tired politician but also as a man who had decreed innumerable death sentences.

During Sadatoki's leadership, the bakufu continued to prepare for a Mongol invasion by consolidating its Kyushu region's administrative and judicial organs. In 1292, at the end of the Taira Yoritsuna period, two sets of communications arrived from China: a document from a Yüan official entrusted to a Japanese merchant ship and a messenger from Koryŏ carrying an order from Kublai Khan. Interpreting these messages as premonitory signs of another invasion, the bakufu urgently dispatched Hōjō Kanetoki, a cousin of Sadatoki and a

46 Amino Yoshihiko, "Kamakura bakufu no kaizoku kin'atsu ni tsuite – Kamakura makki no kaijō keigo o chūshin ni," *Nihon rekishi*, no. 299 (April 1973): 1–20.

47 "Kōfukuji ryaku nendaiki," in *Zoku gunsho ruijū*, no. 29, *ge*, p. 172.

Rokuhara *tandai*, and Nagoe Tokiie, another Hōjō member, to Hakata. These two men were granted the authority to judge court cases as well as to command military forces. To facilitate the exercise of their authority, the bakufu established the Chinzei *sōbugyō sho* in 1293. Scholars differ as to whether this agency should be regarded as the de facto beginnings of the Kyushu deputyship (Chinzei *tandai*).[48]

Kanetoki and Tokiie returned to Kamakura in 1294. Then Kanazawa Sanemasa, who had been *shugo* of both Nagato and Suō provinces, was delegated to Hakata to judge *gokenin* suits in Kyushu. This transition marked the final step toward full establishment of the Chinzei *tandai*, a powerful political organ in Hakata that administered defense measures against external attack and executed judicial decisions for the entire Kyushu region. Although the scale of the office was smaller than those of the main headquarters in Kamakura or of the Rokuhara *tandai*, the judicial structure of the Chinzei *tandai* came to be equipped with the same lower-level accoutrements, such as a *hyōjōshū*, *hikitsukeshū*, and *bugyōnin*.

Parallel to this development was the strengthening of *shugo* authority in Suō and Nagato provinces on the western extremity of Honshū. The *shugo* in those provinces, who were Hōjō, were granted more extensive authority than that enjoyed by other *shugo* and were sometimes referred to as the Nagato and Suō *tandai*.

The Chinzei *tandai* administered the defense service rotation (*ikoku keigo banyaku*). From 1304, the provinces of Kyushu were divided into a total of five units, with service for each based on one-year tours. This change from the previous mode of duty was implemented in hopes of lightening the service burden, and this system continued until the end of the Kamakura period.

THE FALL OF THE KAMAKURA BAKUFU

Conflicts in the court

Although Tokusō Sadatoki's high-handedness contributed to the general malaise of the late Kamakura era, the more immediate cause for

48 Two contrasting theories regarding the establishment of the Chinzei *tandai* are represented by Seno Seiichirō in *Chinzei gokenin no kenkyū* (Tokyo: Yoshikawa kōbunkan, 1975), pp. 391–2; and Satō, *Kamakura bakufu soshō seido no kenkyū*, pp. 304–11. Seno argues that because the power of Kanetoki and Tokiie did not include a definitive authority to issue decisions, the Chinzei *tandai* as such did not yet exist. Satō, on the other hand, advances the notion that even without this definitive authority, the possession of adjudicative powers themselves was tantamount to the beginnings of the Chinzei *tandai*.

the bakufu's demise was the instability at court.[49] In the second month of 1272, immediately after the elimination of the anti-*tokusō* elements in Kamakura, the retired emperor Gosaga died. He (r. 1242–6) had been enthroned at the pleasure of the bakufu and, after a brief reign, had ruled as ex-sovereign for almost thirty years. During this period, the bakufu was dominated by the regents Tokiyori and Tokimune, and court–bakufu relations remained relatively peaceful. The appointment of Gosaga's own son, Prince Munetaka, as shogun in 1252 reflected this absence of tension.

In policymaking as well, there was substantial cooperation between the two capitals. As early as 1246, Gosaga had complied with the bakufu's demand for a general administrative restructuring that included the expulsion of the influential Kujō Michiie. The reforms adopted followed the Kamakura model. Thus, five nobles came to staff a *hyōjōshū*, which served as the highest-ranking organ at court. Two nobles of ability were appointed as "liaison officials" (*densō*), each of whom attended to court business on alternative days. They had the power to decide on daily political matters but were to defer important decisions to the discretion of the Kyoto *hyōjōshū*. Matters concerning court–bakufu relations fell under the authority of the *kantō mōshitsugi*, to which Saionji Saneuji was appointed, replacing the discredited Kujō Michiie. From this time on, the office became a hereditary position within the Saionji family. Reforms initiated by Gosaga set a standard for future retired emperors, and his tenure was known later as the "revered period of Gosaga-in."[50] His death thus caused considerable consternation in both Kyoto and Kamakura.

The first of many problems to develop was the matter of the imperial succession. In many ways this dispute was of Gosaga's own making. Before his death he had shown great affection for his second son, the future emperor Kameyama (r. 1259–74), and had arranged for him to succeed his eldest son, the emperor Gofukakusa (r. 1246–59). Gosaga, moreover, indicated his desire to perpetuate the line of

49 Some of the more prominent works describing conditions at court are the following: Miura Hiroyuki, "Kamakura jikai no chōbaku kankei," in *Nihonshi no kenkyū*, vol. 1 (Tokyo: Iwanami shoten, 1906, 1981), pp. 14–115; Miura Hiroyuki, "Ryōtō mondai no ichi haran," in *Nihonshi no kenkyū*, vol. 2 (Tokyo: Iwanami Shoten, 1930, 1981), pp. 17–36; Yashiro Kuniharu, "Chōkōdō-ryō no kenkyū," in Yashiro Kuniharu, ed., *Kokushi sōsetsu* (Tokyo: Yoshikawa kōbunkan, 1925), pp. 1–115; Nakamura Naokatsu, *Nihon shin bunka shi, Yoshino jidai* (Tokyo: Nihon dentsū shuppanbu, 1942), pp. 41–144; and Ryō Susumu, *Kamakura jidai, ge: Kyoto – kizoku seiji no dōkō to kōbu no kōshō* (Tokyo: Shunshūsha, 1957).

50 For this description of Gosaga's government, I have relied greatly on Hashimoto Yoshihiko, "In no hyōjōsei ni tsuite," in Hashimoto Yoshihiko, *Heian kizoku shakai no kenkyū* (Tokyo: Yoshikawa kōbunkan, 1976), pp. 59–84.

Kameyama by naming the latter's son crown prince (the later emperor Gouda.) Gosaga, however, had failed to designate which of his two sons (Gofukakusa or Kameyama) should control the succession and instead deferred this decision to the bakufu. Inasmuch as Gosaga owed his own enthronement to Kamakura's recommendation, he may have believed that the bakufu should once again intervene.[51] Instead, however, Kamakura asked Gosaga's empress about her late husband's true wish, and in the end Kameyama was chosen. Throughout, the bakufu had attempted to act prudently rather than to risk conflict by making an independent selection.

In this way, the young twenty-four-year-old emperor became the "senior figure" in Kyoto. Although the political center at court was transferred from a retired emperor to a reigning emperor, the administrative structure remained virtually unchanged. The *hyōjōshū*, under Gosaga was renamed the *gijōshū*, but its function remained the same. Likewise, both the *kantō moshitsugi* and the *densō* continued to operate as before. At the apex of this system stood the *chiten no kimi* (supreme ruler), who could now be either a reigning or a retired emperor. Thus for the first time since the eleventh century, a sitting emperor (Kameyama) came to be recognized as dominant over a retired sovereign (Gofukakusa),[52] marking the first in a series of adjustments that eventually led to Godaigo's Kemmu restoration.

In 1274, the year of the first Mongol attack, Kameyama yielded his emperorship to his son Gouda.[53] Gofukakusa registered clear dissatisfaction with this and in 1275 announced his intention to take Buddhist vows. At this point the bakufu suddenly abandoned its earlier indifference and proposed that Kameyama adopt Gofukakusa's son and name him as crown prince. We do not know the exact motive behind this proposition; perhaps Kamakura intended to perpetuate the friction between the two brothers and thereby attenuate the court's potential power. Or perhaps it was the doing of Saionji Sanekane (the *kantō mōshitsugi*) who had close ties with the bakufu. He may have wished to exploit this friction in order to undermine the Tōin, a branch of the Saionji recently set up by Sanekane's uncle Saneo, who was wielding much influence through his ties to Kameyama. But the most plausible

51 This sentiment is recorded in "Godai teiō monogatari," a historical writing of Emperor Fushimi. See Yashiro, "Chōkōdō ryō no kenkyū," pp. 50–52.

52 In 1273, Kameyama issued a twenty-five article edict (the "Shinsei" edict) pronouncing this change. See Miura Hiroyuki, "Shinsei no kenkyū," *Nihonshi no kenyū*, vol. 1, pp. 614–18.; and Mitobe Masao, *Kuge shinsei no kenkyū* (Tokyo: Sōbunsha, 1961), pp. 232–41.

53 At this point, the new *gijōshū* organ reverted to a *hyōjōshū*, marking the shift back to a retired emperor.

reason for this sudden intervention was the increasing need of the bakufu, confronted by the Mongol threat, to bring Japan as much as possible under its control. Juggling the imperial succession was just another weapon aimed at national control.[54]

Kameyama complied, but in so doing, he was in fact sowing the seeds of even greater problems. After securing the position of the prince, the supporters of Gofukakusa then demanded that Kamakura enthrone this prince as emperor after Gouda's retirement. In the meantime, perhaps knowing that his own line would not always occupy the imperial seat, the retired emperor Kameyama energetically implemented new policies. In the eleventh month of 1285, Kameyama issued a twenty-article regulation that, for example, prohibited the transfer of temple and shrine land to other temples and shrines or to lay people.[55] This and other articles marked an important advance in the development of legal procedures bearing on land transfers and also marked a radical progress in the formulation of courtier law (*kuge hō*).

In the following month, the *hyōjōshū* of the retired emperor made public a code of behavior prescribing the proper etiquette for inside and outside the palace. It was called the *kōan reisetsu* and included the appropriate format for writing documents. The purpose of these various regulations seems to have been to freeze the hierarchical status system of the day by legalizing the decorum required of each social and official level.[56]

A further reform of Kameyama was to bring courtier justice even more in line with the Kamakura system.[57] Thus in 1286, the *hyōjōshū* classified its responsibilities as follows: (1) *tokusei sata,* for which it met three times a month, to deal with problems relating to religious matters and official appointments, and (2) *zasso sata,* for which it met six times a month, to investigate litigation. Regarding the latter, the *hyōjōshū* set up a system of face-to-face meetings between litigants in an office called *fudono,* at which a judgment might be issued immedi-

54 Murai, "Mōko shūrai to Chinzei tandai no seiritsu," p. 11.

55 This edict appears in printed form in *Iwashimizu monjo,* no. 1, doc. 319. Recently it was included in Kasamatsu Hiroshi, Satō Shin'ichi, and Momose Kesao, eds., *Chūsei seiji shakai shisō, ge* vol. 22 of *Nihon shisō taikei* (Tokyo: Iwanami shoten, 1981), along with notes and its Japanese reading, see pp. 57–62. As for analysis of the content of this edict, see Kasamatsu Hiroshi, "Chūsei no seiji shakai shisō," in Kasamatsu Hiroshi, *Nihon chūsei-hō shiron* (Tokyo: Tōkyō daigaku shuppankai, 1977), pp. 178–9.

56 The Kōan *reisetsu* appears in *Gunsho ruijū, zatsu bu,* no. 27. For its historical significance, see Kasamatsu, *Nihon chūsei-hō shiron,* pp. 191–2.

57 See Kasamatsu, *Nihon chūsei-hō shiron,* pp. 157–202; also Kasamatsu Hiroshi, "Kamakura kōki no kuge hō ni tsuite," in Kasamatsu et al., eds., *Chūsei seiji shakai shisō, ge,* pp. 401–16.

ately. Before this, the *fudono* had served as a management bureau for retired emperors' documents, though now it was transformed into a full-scale judicial organ.[58]

The Daikakuji and Jimyō-in lines: a split in the court

Just as the retired emperor Kameyama was reorganizing his government, a rumor spread that he was plotting against the bakufu. The rumor may have originated with the supporters of Gofukakusa at court or with the bakufu itself which may have feared the ex-emperor's potential power. At this time, the bakufu was in the hands of the *miuchibito* under Taira Yoritsuna. At any rate, in 1287 Kamakura demanded the enthronement of Gofukakusa's son as the emperor Fushimi. Although Kameyama pleaded against this, Emperor Gouda was forced to resign and was replaced by Fushimi (r. 1288–98). Gofukakusa then took the position of "supreme ruler" in place of Kameyama. Two years later, at the bakufu's insistence, the son of Fushimi was named crown prince. It was in the same year, 1289, that the shogun, Prince Koreyasu (the son of the former shogun Munetaka, himself the son of Gosaga), was accused of plotting against the bakufu and was sent back to Kyoto. "The prince was exiled to Kyoto," people in Kamakura gossiped. At this point, the thirteen-year-old son of Gofukakusa, Prince Hisaakira, was made the new shogun.

In both Kyoto and Kamakura, then, the Taira Yoritsuna clique succeeded in filling the top hierarchy with members of Gofukakusa's line. The Yoritsuna–Gofukakusa connection was underscored by Yoritsuna's dispatching of his second son, Iinuma Sukemune, to Kyoto to receive the new shogun.

Resentment was felt in many corners. Having been stripped of any real power, Kameyama took Buddhist vows in 1289. For a different reason, Gofukakusa also took Buddhist vows in the following year and yielded his political power to emperor Fushimi. At around this time, a member of a warrior house purged in the Shimotsuki incident attacked the imperial residence and attempted to murder the emperor. Kameyama ultimately was blamed for this intrigue, and he was very nearly confined at Rokuhara, following the example of the Jōkyū disturbance. Only a special plea allowed him to escape this fate.

Unlike his father Gofukakusa, who was a compromiser and follower of precedents, Fushimi, the new supreme ruler, proved to be an ener-

58 Hashimoto, *Heian kizoku shakai no kenkyū*, p. 77.

getic reformer.[59] In 1292 he issued a thirteen-article code regulating judicial procedures.[60] In 1293 a new appeal system called *teichū* was adopted by one of the court's traditional tribunals, the *kirokujo*. *Teichū* proceedings were heard by six courtier judges (*shōkei*), six legal experts (*ben*), and sixteen assistants (*yoriudo*). *Shōkei* and *ben* were each organized into six rotating units, and *yoriudo* into eight rotating units. Each of these units heard appeal cases in rotation for twenty-eight days each month.

At the same time, regularized court sessions were held six times a month to hear new cases. These were attended by three rotating units of the *gijōshū* and three other rotating units of *ben* and *yoriudo* who belonged to the *kirokujo*.[61] Fushimi's reforms reflected once again Kamakura's own judicial system and marked a significant advance in court judicial practices.

Fushimi's personal position at court did not remain secure, however, mainly because of a split among those close to him. One of the courtiers closest to Fushimi was Kyōgoku Tamekane. Grandson of the famous poet Fujiwara Teika, Tamekane was a gifted and innovative *waka* poet himself. But this poet had another side. He was notorious as a narrow-minded, unscrupulous politician with extraordinarily high self-esteem.[62] He was resented for having managed to become the husband of the wet nurse to the emperors Fushimi and Hanazono, a position of great influence at court. Among Tamekane's enemies, the most significant was Saionji Sanekane, the *kantō mōshitsugi*. To undermine Tamekane, Sanekane withdrew from Emperor Fushimi and joined Kameyama's supporters. This change in Fushimi's support network in turn endangered his position. Soon enough, Fushimi, too, became the object of the same kind of rumor that caused Kameyama's fall. To counter his precarious position, Fushimi wrote a religious supplication that read, "There are a few who are spreading an unfounded rumor in order to usurp the imperial seat."[63]

By this time, the composition of the bakufu had changed; Taira

59 At this time, the emperor's court set up a *gijōshū*, following the precedent of Emperor's Kameyama in the years 1272–4. A *gijōshū* was equivalent to a retired emperor's *hyōjōshū*. Subsequent governments under incumbent emperors followed this basic pattern.

60 Miura Hiroyuki discusses this edict in "Shinsei no kenkyū," pp. 619–22; also see Mitobe, *Kuge shinsei no kenkyū*, pp. 241–4. Gotō Norihiko gives a full translation in "Tanaka bon Seifu – bunrui o kokoromita kuge shinsei no koshahon," *Nempō, chūseishi kenkyū*, no. 5 (May 1980): 73–86.

61 Hashimoto, *Heian kizoku shakai no kenkyū*, p. 78.

62 Kyōgoku Tamekane has tended to receive fuller treatment as a poet than as a politician. A representative work is by Toki Zenmaro, *Shinshū Kyōgoku Tamekane* (Tokyo: Kadokawa shoten, 1968), which contains a bibliography of related works on Tamekane.

63 Quoted in Miura, *Kamakura jidaishi*, p. 567.

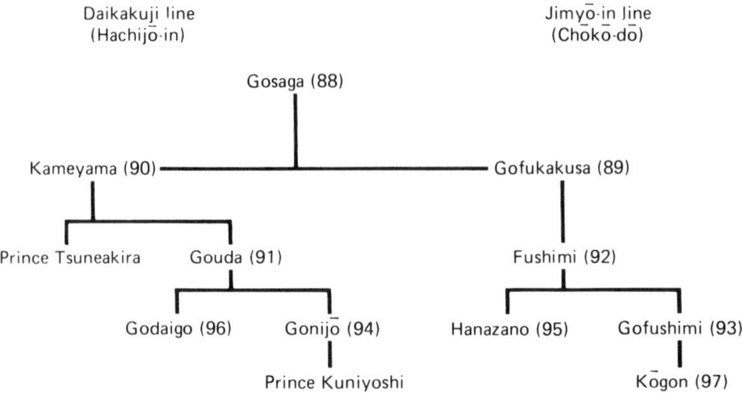

Figure 2.1 System of alternate succession between Gofukakusa and Kameyama lines. (Order of succession is given in parentheses.)

Yoritsuna had fallen, and the autocratic rule of Hōjō Sadatoki was well under way. In 1297, the bakufu arrested Tamekane and exiled him to Sado. Having eliminated this troublemaker, the bakufu then arranged for the resignation of Fushimi and the enthronement of Fushimi's son Gofushimi (r. 1298–1301). The grandson of Kameyama and son of Gouda (the future emperor Gonijō) was designated as the new crown prince. Subsequently, the bakufu began to consider seriously a system of alternate succession between the lines of Gofukakusa and Kameyama.[64] Figure 2.1 shows their lineage and order of succession.

In order to implement the practice of alternate succession, the bakufu demanded Gofushimi's resignation in 1301, only four years after his enthronement. Gonijō, the grandson of Kameyama, then succeeded him. The selection of the crown prince became a major issue, but the bakufu adhered to the practice of alternate succession by designating the younger brother of Gofushimi (later Emperor Hanazono) as the heir apparent.

By this time, the antagonism between the Kameyama and Gofukakusa lines had lasted for thirty years, and it had become a significant part of the imperial institutional tradition. Not only immediate family members but also nobles at court became embroiled in this conflict. The antagonism, moreover, applied to more than just the question of imperial succession. The economic interests of each line, which affected holders of land rights at all levels of the *shōen* hierarchy, deepened the rapidly growing tension at court.

64 Miura, *Nihonshi no kenkyū*, pp. 98–100.

The two lines were identified by the location of their private residences. The line of Kameyama was called the Daikakuji line, taking the name of Gouda's residence, whereas Gofukakusa's line was known by the residence of Fushimi, the Jimyō-in. As many as one hundred to two hundred *shōen* supported each line. *Shōen* units held by each line were collectively named the Hachijō-in-ryō for the Daikakuji line and the Chōkōdō-ryō for the Jimyō-in line.[65]

If the two lines were to share the imperial seat alternately, their economic resources would need to be balanced as well. But sometimes the death of a large property holder could easily upset the balance. In 1300, for example, the ownership of nearly one hundred *shōen* became subject to dispute after Muromachi-in, the previous holder of these lands, died. Muromachi-in's mother had been a member of the Jimyō-in, and after her son's death, her daughter inherited the whole share. But the land slipped out of the Jimyō-in line's possession when this daughter became a wife of Gouda, a member of the Daikakuji line. Fearing further problems of this kind, the bakufu arranged to have the entire portfolio divided in half and assigned to each line.[66]

The deepening hostility between the two lines, which had first begun as a succession dispute, now affected the entire court structure. Even in the cultural and religious spheres, the split was apparent. Whereas the Daikakuji line patronized the new Chinese culture–Sung-style Confucianism, Zen Buddhism, and the Chinese style of calligraphy – the Jimyō-in line preferred the traditional Japanese (Heian) culture in literature, calligraphy, and Buddhism.[67]

The situation at court worsened as the waves of antagonism among courtiers went beyond the original gulf that separated the two camps and caused further splits in each line. In the Jimyō-in line, the retired emperor Gofushimi and his younger brother (the future emperor Hanazono) were showing signs of hostility. The situation was far more grave for the Daikakuji line, however. Initially, the retired emperor Kameyama favored Emperor Gonijō's younger brother, Prince Takaharu (the future emperor Godaigo), as the next emperor. But in 1303, when the daughter of Saionji Sanekane bore Kameyama a son

65 The patterns of transfer and division of imperial family holdings, such as the Chōkōdō-ryō and the Hachijō-in-ryō, have been much studied. Among the more important works are the following: Yashiro, "Chōkōdō-ryō no kenkyū"; Nakamura, *Nihon shin bunka shi, Yoshino jidai;* Ashida Koreto, *Goryōchi-shikō* (Tokyo: Teishitsu Rinya kyoku, 1937); Nakamura Naokatsu, *Shōen no kenkyū* (Kyoto: Hoshino shoten, 1931, 1978); and Okuno Takahiro, *Kōshitsu gokeizai shi no kenkyū* (Tokyo: Unebi shobo, 1942).

66 Nakamura, *Shōen no kenkyū,* pp. 382–85.

67 A detailed discussion of this point appears in Miura, *Nihonshi no kenkyū,* pp. 106–7.

(Prince Tsuneakira), Kameyama changed his mind and began to promote this young son for the throne. This change of heart caused those affiliated with the Daikakuji line to split into three smaller factions, supporting Gonijō, Prince Takaharu, and Prince Tsuneakira.

The internal strife at court worsened after the successive deaths of Gofukakusa and Kameyama in 1304 and 1305, followed by the death of Gonijō in 1308. Before these three died, the Saionji family had hoped to enthrone Prince Tsuneakira by forcing Gonijō's abdication. But this proved unnecessary; with Gonijō dead, the principle of alternate succession allowed Emperor Hanazono of the Jimyō-in line to occupy the throne. In the meantime, the retired emperor Fushimi, also of the Jimyō-in line, actually dominated the court and ruled from the office of *in*. The Daikakuji line retained the position of crown prince. With the understanding that the imperial rank and lands would be transferred to the son of Gonijō, Gouda designated Prince Takaharu (Gonijō's brother and the future emperor Godaigo) as the heir apparent.

Godaigo's reign

Fushimi's rule an ex-sovereign was just as energetic as that as emperor. He delegated much responsibility to Kyōgoku Tamekane, who by this time had returned to Kyoto from exile. The organs of justice were further reorganized, and an appeals court (*teichū*) was incorporated into the *fudono*.[68] However, the earlier friction between Tamekane and Saionji Sanekane resurfaced and reduced the effectiveness of Fushimi's rule. Once again, in 1315, Tamekane was accused of plotting against the bakufu and was arrested by the Rokuhara *tandai*. As before, he was exiled to Tosa.

The fall of Tamekane naturally affected the well-being of Fushimi. A rumor spread that Fushimi, too, was involved in an antibakufu plot, and the ex-emperor was forced to prove his innocence by writing a letter of denial in his own hand. It seemed that both the bakufu and Saionji Sanekane were giving greater support to the Daikakuji line than to Fushimi's Jimyō-in line.

In 1317, the bakufu sent a message to the court that recommended Hanazono's resignation and the selection of a new crown prince by way of agreement between the two lines. But the rival lines could not so easily reach an accord. Before a decision could be made on the new crown prince, the retired emperor Fushimi died, leaving the Jimyō-in

68 Hashimoto, *Heian kizoku shakai no kenkyū*, pp. 82–83.

line powerless without a central figure. In the following year, 1318, the bakufu proposed to designate the son of Gonijō as the heir apparent and to place Godaigo on the throne. Gouda, the father of Godaigo and Gonijō, thus began his rule as retired emperor. The Daikakuji line thus came to dominate the highest levels of the imperial hierarchy.

But it was not the bakufu's intention to tip the balance permanently. At the same time as the Daikakuji surge, Kamakura set down specific conditions for that line to follow. Later documents reveal the terms of this "*bumpō* mediation": (1)The next succession was to be secured for the Jimyō-in line by designating the son of Gofushimi, Prince Kazuhito (later Emperor Kōgon), as crown prince as soon as the incumbent Prince Kuniyoshi became emperor; (2) the reign of each emperor was not to exceed ten years; and (3) the offspring of Godaigo were not to seek the throne.[69] At his enthronement, therefore, Godaigo faced several limitations. It was particularly unsatisfactory that Godaigo, then in his prime at age thirty-one, should have to surrender all hope of having an imperial heir. And he feared that without an heir, his grandiose plans for reviving "the golden age" of Daigo, an early Heian emperor, would not bear fruit. His strong personality only reinforced the dissatisfaction caused by the circumstances surrounding him. As a first step out of this quandary he sought to become the supreme ruler himself. The resignation of Gouda-in from active politics in 1321 gave Godaigo the opportunity to both reign and rule.

Godaigo began his rule by staffing his court with men of ability. His interest in Sung Confucianism led him to select such famed scholar-politicians as Yoshida Sadafusa and Kitabatake Chikafusa, both of the Daikakuji line, and Hino Suketomo and Hino Toshimoto, men of less prestigious family backgrounds but of equal ability. Moreover, reflecting the changed conditions after Gouda's withdrawal from public life, Godaigo shifted the *teichū* appeals court from the *fudono* of the retired emperor's government back to the *kirokujo* of his own imperial government. Here, Godaigo himself sometimes participated in judging cases.[70]

A noteworthy aspect of the Godaigo's rule was his attempt to consoli-

69 For an extensive description of the "Bumpo no wadan," see Yashiro, "Chōkōdō-ryō no kenkyū," pp. 72–81.

70 A number of works treat topics such as these as the essential historical ingredients presaging the Kemmu restoration. See, for example, Miura, *Kamakura jidaishi;* Tanaka Yoshinari, *Nambokuchō jidaishi* (Tokyo: Meiji shoin, 1922), pp. 23–82; Hiraizumi Kiyoshi, "Nihon chūkō," in Kemmu chūkō roppyakunen kinenkai, comp., *Kemmu chūkō* (Tokyo: Kemmu chūkō roppayakunen kinenkai, 1934), pp. 1–177; and Nakamura Naokatsu, "Godaigo tennō no shinsei," in *Nakamura Naokatsu chosaku shū,* vol. 3: *Nanchō no kenkyū* (Kyoto: Tankōsha, 1978), pp. 55–67.

date imperial power by tapping the growing commercial sector as a source of revenue. In 1322, for example, he ordered imperial officials to collect taxes from saké brewers in Kyoto on a regular basis, the first time that this was ever attempted.[71] The emperor's court, moreover, demonstrated concern over fluctuating prices. During a famine in 1330, he accordingly issued an edict stabilizing prices and also decreed that merchants who were hoarding rice would be required to sell it at a special market. All tariffs were suspended for three months.[72]

Approaching crisis in the bakufu

Meanwhile, Sadatoki's autocratic rule in Kamakura was giving way to renewed *miuchibito* dominance. In 1311, Sadatoki died, and his nine-year-old son Takatoki became *tokusō*. The young *tokusō* had two advisers: Nagasaki Enki (the son of Taira Yoritsuna's brother), who had long been serving as *uchi kanrei*, and Adachi Tokiaki (the grandson of Adachi Yasumori's brother and Takatoki's father-in-law). In 1316, when he was fourteen, Takatoki assumed the post of regent (*shikken*), but he proved to be an effete politician. A contemporary chronicle, the "Hōryaku kanki," noted that Takatoki was "weak-minded and unenergetic . . . it was difficult to call him *shikken*."[73] As a result, the real political power fell to the new *uchi kanrei*, Nagasaki Takasuke, Enki's son. In alliance with other *miuchibito*, Takasuke began to dominate the bakufu.

Takatoki's resignation from the post of regent in 1326 encouraged internal disunity. Nagasaki Takasuke immediately forced Kanazawa Sadaaki (Akitoki's son), who had been serving as cosigner (*rensho*), to become the next *shikken*. This greatly angered Hōjō Sadatoki's widow, who had planned to elevate Yasuie, the younger brother of Takatoki, to the regency. After only a month of service as *shikken*, Sadaaki was forced to resign his post when Sadatoki's widow attempted to have him murdered. In the meantime, Takatoki preoccupied himself with cultural pursuits and completely ignored politics. However, in 1330 Takatoki ordered Nagasaki Takayori and another *miuchibito* to murder Nagasaki Takasuke. Perhaps Takatoki was angered by Takasuke's domination of the bakufu. The plot, nonetheless, was discovered, and Takatoki was forced to pretend complete innocence.

71 Amino Yoshihiko provides a detailed treatment of this subject in "Zōshushi kōjiyaku no seiritsu ni tsuite – Muromachi bakufu sakayayaku no zentei," in Takeuchi Rizō hakase koki kinenkai, comp., *Zoku shōensei to buke shakai* (Tokyo: Yoshikawa kōbunkan, 1978), pp. 359–97.

72 Hiraizumi, "Nihon chūkō," pp. 93–100; and Nakamura, "Godaigo tennō no ichi rinji," pp. 76–79.

73 The "Hōryaku kan ki" appears in *Gunsho ruijū, zatsu bu*.

At the same time that conspiracies were rife in the bakufu's capital, the most conspicuous problem in the provinces continued to be the *akutō*. According to records from Harima Province and to the chronicle "Mineaiki," the *akutō* at the turn of the century – whether pirates, mountain bandits, or robbers – were spreading rapidly. They wore outrageous clothing and were equipped with pitiful-looking swords or long bamboo poles, and they also congregated into small groups, gambled regularly, and were talented petty thieves.[74]

The bakufu officially set out in 1318 to bring these people under control in twelve provinces of western Japan (the Sanyō and Nankai regions). Three *miuchibito* of renown were dispatched to each province where they demanded oaths from the *shugo*, deputy *shugo*, and *jitō-gokenin* to destroy existing *akutō* bases. According to the "Mineaiki," in Harima alone, over twenty stone forts were destroyed, and a number of *akutō* members killed. In addition, although arrest warrants for fifty-one famous outlaws were issued, the "Mineaiki" tells us that none was actually captured. At the same time, the bakufu mobilized those warriors holding land along the Inland Sea coastline to defend against pirates and to protect important ports.[75] These efforts produced some positive, but not lasting, results. In Harima, for instance, the *akutō* activities diminished for two or three years but then started up again with even greater vigor.

The style and behavior of the Harima *akutō* changed over the years. In the latter part of the 1330s, previously small and unimpressive *akutō* elements began to appear in large groups of fifty to one hundred, magnificently outfitted men all riding splendid horses. Many of these men came from neighboring provinces to form a band (*tō*) through mutual pledges of loyalty. They were highly imaginative in the violent methods they employed to effect their ends, and most *shōen* in Harima fell prey to their depredations. The "Mineaiki" reports, indeed, that more than half of all warriors in that province sympathized with the *akutō*.

It is now apparent that many of these *akutō* were none other than the local warriors themselves, not "bandits" in the original sense of the word. It is thus understandable that the bakufu's effort to control them by issuing pacification orders would have had little effect. For example, the bakufu's threat in 1324 that it would confiscate *shōen* that failed to hand over captured *akutō* to the *shugo* failed to have much impact.

74 The "Mineaiki" appears in *Zoku Gunsho ruijū, Shakuka bu.*
75 Amino, "Kamakura bakufu no kaizoku kin'atsu ni tsuite."

In the northeast the problem was not one of *akutō* but of antibakufu rebellions in a region of the country largely dominated by the Hōjō. In Ezo, for instance, a rebellion that started in 1318 became aggravated two years later when the hereditary officials of the area, the Andō, suffered a severe internal split. Although Kamakura attempted to quell the disturbance by dispatching a large army, the fighting continued unabated.[76]

The demise of the Kamakura bakufu

Because the bakufu was faced with a variety of problems, Emperor Godaigo began to contemplate bringing it down by force. His initial task was thus to tap various sources for potential allies. The monks of the large temples in the Kyoto region were the first to be approached. In particular, Godaigo recognized the potential military power of the Enryakuji monks and accordingly placed his sons, the Princes Morinaga and Munenaga, at the top of the clerical hierarchy, as Tendai *zasu*. Outside the religious orders, Godaigo's close collaborators Hino Suketomo and Toshimoto made contacts with dissatisfied warriors and with *akutō* in the Kinai and neighboring provinces. Gradually, an antibakufu movement began to develop. Sympathizers often assembled in the most casual attire without regard to rank or status and held banquets to discuss strategy and logistics. These meetings were called *bureikō,* that is, discussions without propriety.

There were setbacks at times. In the ninth month of 1324, for example, a plan to mobilize Kyoto warriors under the leadership of the Toki and Tajimi warrior houses of Mino Province was exposed, and a bakufu army dispatched by the Rokuhara *tandai* captured the ringleaders. Significantly, Hino Suketomo and Toshimoto were also implicated and arrested in what became known as the Shōchū disturbance. Godaigo himself fell under suspicion and had to defend his innocence in the matter. The bakufu, at any rate, failed to heed the warning signals in this incident and satisfied itself with blaming Hino Suketomo for the trouble and exiling him to Sado.

Meanwhile at court, a further development in the ongoing imperial succession dispute provided Godaigo with another reason to challenge the bakufu. Crown Prince Kuniyoshi died suddenly in 1326, and there were disagreements as to who should succeed him. There were three

76 Kobayashi Seiji and Ōishi Naomasa, comps., *Chūsei ōu no sekai* (Tokyo: Tōkyō daigaku shuppankai, 1978), pp. 80–82.

candidates: the son of Kuniyoshi, the son of Godaigo, and Prince Kazuhito of the Jimyō-in line. Much to the frustration of the emperor, the bakufu chose Kazuhito, who later became Emperor Kōgon.

In the fourth month of 1331, a second antibakufu conspiracy was exposed, and this time Hino Toshimoto and his followers were arrested. Having lost his commanders, the emperor himself now took the lead in the antibakufu movement, and at the end of the eighth month, he left Kyoto for Nara, where he fortified himself on Mount Kasagi. Godaigo's personal involvement sparked additional support, such as that of Kusunoki Masahige from neighboring Kawachi Province and that of other warriors from the more distant Bingo Province.

Responding to this emergency, Kamakura took the offensive and by the end of the ninth month had captured the emperor. This Genkō incident, as it was called, seemed to mark the end of Godaigo's hopes to destroy the bakufu. In the meantime, Prince Kazuhito had already been enthroned as the new emperor Kōgon, and the retired emperor Gofushimi now became active, restoring power to the Jimyō-in line. Because Godaigo was no longer emperor or an active retired emperor, the bakufu exiled him to Oki, the same punishment meted out to Gotoba for his antibakufu Jōkyū disturbance in 1221. Also following the precedent set by the Jōkyū disturbance, the bakufu punished many of Godaigo's followers with death or banishment. Yet unlike that earlier episode, such forcefulness by Kamakura did not succeed in eradicating all of the antibakufu elements. In the absence of his father, Prince Morinaga, the former Tendai *zasu*, now assumed leadership of the movement.

For some time actually, Morinaga had been secretly encouraging *akutō* in the southern sector of the home provinces. But beginning in 1332, his activities suddenly became overt, and by the eleventh month, he was openly mobilizing warriors in the Yoshino area of Yamato Province. Hearing this news, Kusunoki Masashige came out of hiding and reorganized his army in Kawachi. At the same time, the *akutō* followers of Prince Morinaga became active in the vicinity of Kyoto. By the first month of 1333, Kusunoki advanced from Kawachi into Settsu and there, around Shitennōji, defeated an army of the bakufu's Rokuhara *tandai*.

The bakufu had hardly been routed as yet, and in the second month it took a strategically located castle (Akasaka in Kawachi), seized earlier by Masashige, and then moved its army into Yoshino. In the meantime, Morinaga eluded capture and continued to organize antibakufu forces on his way to Kōyasan in Kii, whereas Masashige fortified his troops at Chihaya Castle on Mount Kongō and – using techniques typical of the *akutō* – fired rocks and branches from the mountaintop on the bakufu army below.

The forces of rebellion now snowballed everywhere. For example, a wealthy local warrior of Harima, Akamatsu Norimura, took up arms late in the first month, whereas the Doi and Kutsuna of Iyo Province rebelled in the second month. The Sanyōdō and Inland Sea areas thus became major battlefields. Continuing their offensive, the Akamatsu moved in the direction of Kyoto and soon pushed into Settsu.

Having been informed of the improving situation, Godaigo escaped from Oki in the second month, arriving on the shores of Hōki Province where he was welcomed by the influential warrior Nawa Nagatoshi. By the third month, the Akamatsu, leading the warriors and *akutō* from Harima and other home provinces, entered Kyoto but were unable to occupy it. A month later reinforcements were provided by Chigusa Sadaaki, a close collaborator of Godaigo, but even then the bakufu succeeded in preventing the imperial loyalists from taking the capital.

At this time the leadership in Kamakura dispatched a new army to Kyoto, led by Ashikaga Takauji. Chief of a distinguished eastern warrior house, Takauji had long held an antipathy toward the Hōjō *tokusō* and his *miuchibito,* and even before entering Kyoto, he was in touch with Godaigo. At first he attacked Kamakura's enemies but soon switched sides, returning to Kyoto to attack the Rokuhara deputyship, which fell early in the fifth month. In disarray, the warriors of Rokuhara fled to Kamakura, carrying Emperor Kōgon with them, but they ran into blockades set up by various *akutō*. On the ninth day of the fifth month, the imperial entourage was captured by these *akutō*, and numerous bakufu fighting men committed suicide.

Exactly one day before this incident, Nitta Yoshisada of Kōzuke Province mounted a challenge against the bakufu in the east, and by the twenty-first day of that month the city of Kamakura fell. There were numerous suicides by the Hōjō and their *miuchibito,* and for all practical purposes the Kamakura bakufu had been destroyed. Four days later the Mutō and Ōtomo families in Kyushu led a successful campaign against the Chinzei *tandai*, and on the same day, Godaigo, who was now heading toward Kyoto, issued an order rejecting Kōgon as emperor. Atop the debris of Japan's first shogunate, the restoration was about to begin.

CHAPTER 3

THE MUROMACHI BAKUFU

INTRODUCTION

The Muromachi bakufu, the second of the three military governments that held power in Japan from 1185 to 1867, was founded between 1336 and 1338 by Ashikaga Takauji (1305–58). The name Muromachi was taken from the district in Kyoto where the Ashikaga residence and administrative headquarters were located after 1378. The end of the regime is dated either 1573, when the last Ashikaga shogun was ousted from Kyoto, or 1597, when the ex-shogun died in exile.

The period in Japanese history defined by the existence of the Muromachi bakufu has been judged in two quite contradictory ways. Measured on the basis of effective centralized rule, it has been seen as a time of political weakness and social unrest. Yet in cultural terms it has been recognized as one of Japan's most creative periods of artistic achievement. There is, of course, no necessary contradiction between political instability and cultural brilliance. And modern historians have tended to play down the apparent paradox. They stress instead the significant social and institutional changes of the time: when military government (the bakufu system) came into its own, when the military aristocracy (the *buke* or samurai estate) became the real rulers of the country, and when profound changes were wrought in the distribution of rights over land and in the organization of the cultivating class. Recent assessments have suggested that even with respect to government effectiveness, the Ashikaga should not be dismissed too lightly. After all, the Muromachi bakufu lasted for more than two hundred years. At the height of its power, under the third and sixth shoguns, a military government for the first time gained possession of all aspects of secular authority. It was only in the exercise of that authority that the Ashikaga shoguns had difficulty.[1]

1 Beginning in the late 1940s, Japanese scholars literally transformed the field of Muromachi studies, along four main lines. (1) Studies by Matsumoto Shimpachiro, Satō Shin'ichi, Ishimoda Shō, Nagahara Keiji, and Kuroda Toshio explored the political institutions of the period to comprehend the balance of power between civil and military, central and local

In extending its influence beyond its Kamakura headquarters, the first shogunate had relied on a network of military land stewards (*jitō*) and provincial constables (*shugo*), whose reliability was presumably guaranteed by their enlistment, when possible, into the shogun's band of vassals. The Kamakura bakufu's authority, though limited to certain aspects of military recruitment, judicial and police action, and the expediting of estate payments, was exercised effectively within what remained of the legal institutions of imperial provincial administration. The Ashikaga shoguns, however, had less support from this inheritance and were required to depend more upon institutions of their own making; hence their reliance on the provincial constables to whom they delegated much local authority. Under the Muromachi bakufu, the *shugo* acquired political influence by combining the authority the post had commanded under the Kamakura bakufu with that customarily available to the civil provincial governors under the imperial system. The chain of command among shogun, *shugo*, and provincial retainers now carried almost the entire burden of government, both nationally and locally.

But the Ashikaga contribution to the evolution of Japanese government has not been easy to define. Although the Muromachi bakufu handled a greater volume of administrative, judicial, and military transactions than the Kamakura system had done, neither shogun nor *shugo* acquired the capacity for enforcement needed to fully exercise their legal authority. The command imperative and the balance of power on which the Ashikaga house rested its rule was weakened by the fact that the Ashikaga shoguns were not able to perfect either a fully bureaucratic administrative or a fully "patrimonial" delegation of lord to vassal. As chiefs of the military estate, the Ashikaga shoguns did maintain a private bureaucracy and a guard force drawn from their extensive but individually weak *jitō*-grade vassals. But these direct retainers were limited in number, and in regard to serious military action, or to the staffing of important bakufu offices, the Ashikaga were heavily dependent on the *shugo* support. And because the ability

interests; (2) studies such as those by Satō Shin'ichi who, in yet another dimension of his work, began analyzing the inner workings of the Muromachi bakufu as a central government – a lead that has been followed most notably by Kuwayama Kōnen; (3) studies by Nagahara Keiji and Sugiyama Hiroshi began the serious exploration of *shugo* local administration and its articulation with bakufu interests above and with lesser military houses at the provincial level below; and (4) those studies, beginning with Sugiyama Hiroshi's pioneer analysis of the Muromachi bakufu's economic structure, and more recently those by Kuwayama Kōnen, give a more accurate picture of the fiscal practices and policies of the Muromachi regime. Close on the heels of such Japanese historians have come a number of Western specialists in Muromachi history. References to their writings will appear in the later pages of this chapter.

TABLE 3.1
Ashikaga shoguns

	Name	Reign as shogun
1.	Takauji (1305–58)	1338–58
2.	Yoshiakira (1330–67)	1359–67
3.	Yoshimitsu (1358–1408)	1368–94
4.	Yoshimochi (1386–1428)	1394–1423, 1425–8
5.	Yoshikazu (1407–25)	1423–5
6.	Yoshinori (1394–1441)	1429–41
7.	Yoshikatsu (1434–43)	1441–3
8.	Yoshimasa (1436–90)	1443–73
9.	Yoshihisa (1465–89)	1473–89
10.	Yoshitane (1466–1523)	1490–3, 1508–21
11.	Yoshizumi (1480–1511)	1493–1508
12.	Yoshiharu (1511–50)	1521–46
13.	Yoshiteru (1536–65)	1546–65
14.	Yoshihide (1540–68)	1568
15.	Yoshiaki (1537–97)	1568–73 (abdicated 1588)

to hold the loyalty of such support shifted over time and circumstance and from shogun to shogun, it is necessary to start any inquiry into the Muromachi bakufu by first looking at the Ashikaga house, its rise as a prominent *shugo* family under the Kamakura bakufu and its role in destroying the Hōjō and in establishing a new bakufu.

THE RISE OF THE ASHIKAGA HOUSE

The Ashikaga house, as seen in Figure 3.1 and Table 3.1, was descended from the same Seiwa branch of the Minamoto lineage as was Yoritomo (1147–99), the founder of the Kamakura shogunate.[2] The name Ashikaga was derived from the family's original landholding, Ashikaga-no-shō in Shimotsuke Province. The Minamoto house began its association with estates, or *shōen*, in Shimotsuke under Yoshiie (1039–1106). His grandson Yoshiyasu (?–1157), after receiving the estate manager's rights *(gesu shiki)* of Ashikaga-no-shō, took the estate's name to identify his newly established branch line. Proprietary rights to the estate were held by the retired emperor Toba (1103–56). Throughout the Kamakura period Ashikaga-no-shō remained an important holding of the estates controlled by the "junior," or Daikakuji,

2 The following description of the Ashikaga house and its early rise relies on Toyoda Takeshi, "Genko tōbatsu no shoseiryoku ni tsuite," in Ogawa Makoto, ed, *Muromachi seiken*, vol. 5 of *Ronshū Nihon rekishi* (Tokyo: Yūshōdō, 1975).

I. The early years

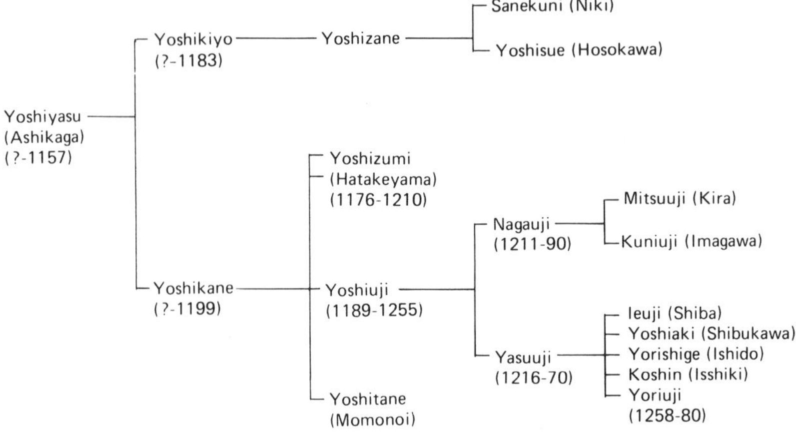

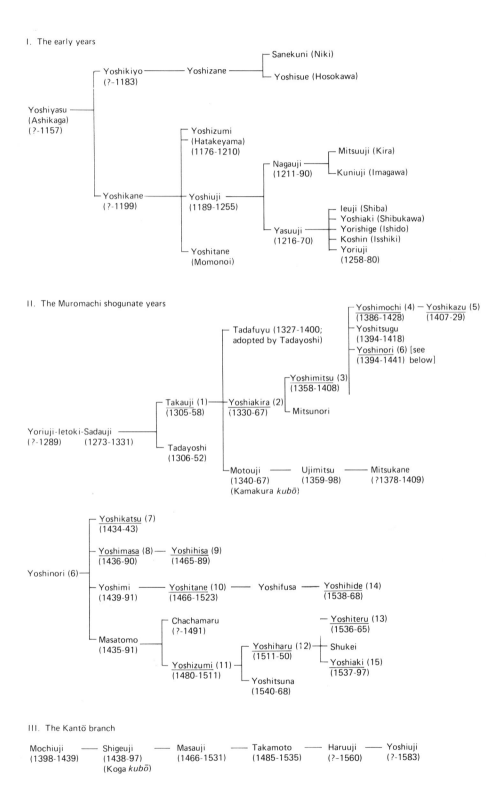

II. The Muromachi shogunate years

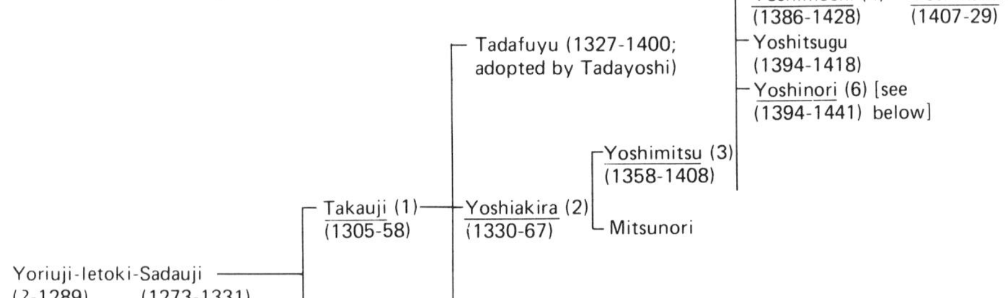

Motouji (1340-67) (Kamakura *kubō*) — Ujimitsu (1359-98) — Mitsukane (?1378-1409)

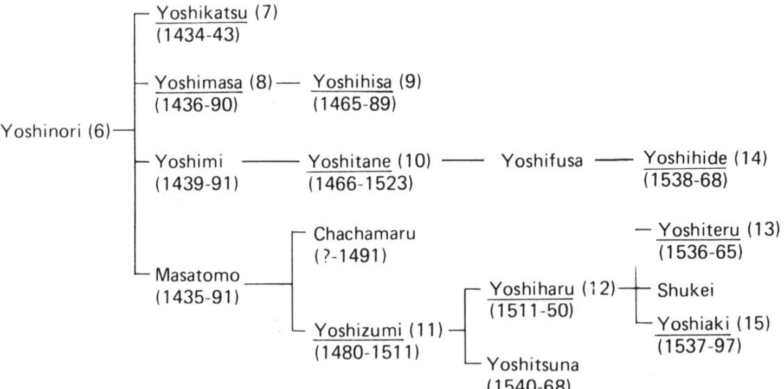

III. The Kantō branch

Mochiuji (1398-1439) — Shigeuji (1438-97) (Koga *kubō*) — Masauji (1466-1531) — Takamoto (1485-1535) — Haruuji (?-1560) — Yoshiuji (?-1583)

branch of the imperial house. As a consequence, the Ashikaga family observed two loyalties: one to the shogun and the Hōjō regency and the other to the imperial house. Ashikaga Takauji, whose defection led to the demise of the Kamakura shogunate, made his move in part in the name of Godaigo (1288–1339), head of the Daikakuji line.

It was Yoshiyasu's son, Yoshikane (?–1199), who joined Minamoto Yoritomo's cause in 1180 and thereby brought the Ashikaga family into the service of the Kamakura military government. Before 1180, Yoshikane had married one of Hōjō Tokimasa's daughters. Another daughter, Masako (1157–1225), had married Minamoto Yoritomo. Thus Yoshikane found himself married to the sister of the wife of Yoritomo, the first shogun. The Hōjō connection was actively maintained thereafter, so that during the Kamakura period, of seven generations of Ashikaga chiefs, five took Hōjō wives. Takauji, at the time of his defection, was married to the sister of the last regent. It is significant, however, that Takauji did not have a Hōjō mother; his father had married into the Uesugi, an important military house based in Tamba Province, west of the capital.

In the third generation after Yoshiyasu, the Ashikaga lineage began to segment and spread out beyond the home province. Two of Yoshikane's sons were the first to move out of Shimotsuke. One went to Kōzuke and took the name Momonoi and the other went to Musashi and took the name Hatakeyama. Three members of the next generation moved into Mikawa Province, where they took the place names Niki, Hosokawa, and Togasaki as their own. Then, other members of the lineage established three more branch families, the Kira, Imagawa, and Isshiki in Mikawa. This concentration of holdings in Mikawa probably explains why the head of the house was appointed *shugo* of Mikawa in 1238. The Ashikaga were awarded Kazusa as well, in 1259, but Shimotsuke, the locus of their ancestral holding, remained in the hands of the long-entrenched Koyama family.

Although there is some information about the number of branch families and the location of their holdings, there are almost no data on the size and value of these possessions. Collateral families constituted a first line of support for the chief of the Ashikaga line. By Takauji's generation, these included the Momonoi, Hatakeyama, Niki, Hosokawa, Kira, Imagawa, Isshiki, Ishido, Shibukawa, and Shiba

Figure 3.1 Ashikaga lineage genealogy. (Shoguns are underlined and numbered; names in parentheses are branch family names adopted from location of primary landholding.)

families. Another family that played an important role in the Ashikaga fortunes was the Uesugi, the only family other than the Hōjō that had provided wives for the Ashikaga chiefs. The collaterals provided much of the manpower of the Ashikaga armies. The area of their greatest concentration, Mikawa and adjoining provinces, was clearly a pivotal base, close, but not too close, to Kyoto. Added to this was the fortuitious circumstance that the Uesugi's ancestral holding was in Tamba, just to the west of the capital. It is no accident that Takauji should have started his attack on the Hōjō from Tamba.

Another group that contributed importantly to the Ashikaga power base was the household retainers. Referred to generically as *hikan*, they occupied subordinate positions on the Ashikaga lineage chief's landholdings, serving as estate managers and providing military service. There is little information about this group of families, but a significant piece of documentation in the Kuramochi archives lists what is believed to be the landholdings (*goryō*) of the main Ashikaga house and the stewards serving on them.[3] The document is undated, but internal evidence shows it was drafted between 1293 and 1301.

The Kuramochi document lists thirty-five landholdings located in ten provinces. There is no indication of the size of any of these properties or the income they produced. The locations of those that can be identified are indicated on Map 3.1.[4]

As the map shows, the holdings of the Ashikaga main line were more widely scattered than were the base holdings of its collateral branch families. A correlation between these two sets of holdings makes it clear that the lineage chief could not have depended on his collateral branches to oversee his lands but, rather, had to have them managed by intendants drawn from his own hereditary retainers. The Kuramochi document lists twenty-one such intendants, bearing nineteen surnames.

In 1333, Ashikaga Takauji was called to arms against the threat posed by Emperor Godaigo's machinations. Takauji had already contemplated Godaigo's defection, but Takauji's motives were mixed. First, being of the Minamoto lineage, he felt abused by the Taira Hōjō, who relied on his military support but nonetheless treated him as a vassal, ordering him to commit his troops in defense of Kama-

3 The initial analysis of these documents, now held by Tohoku University, is by Kuwayama Kōnen, "Muromachi bakufu no sōsōki ni okeru shoryō ni tsuite," *Chūsei no mado* 12 (April 1963): 4–27.

4 Of the thirty-five pieces referred to in the documents, only some twenty-five can be identified by location.

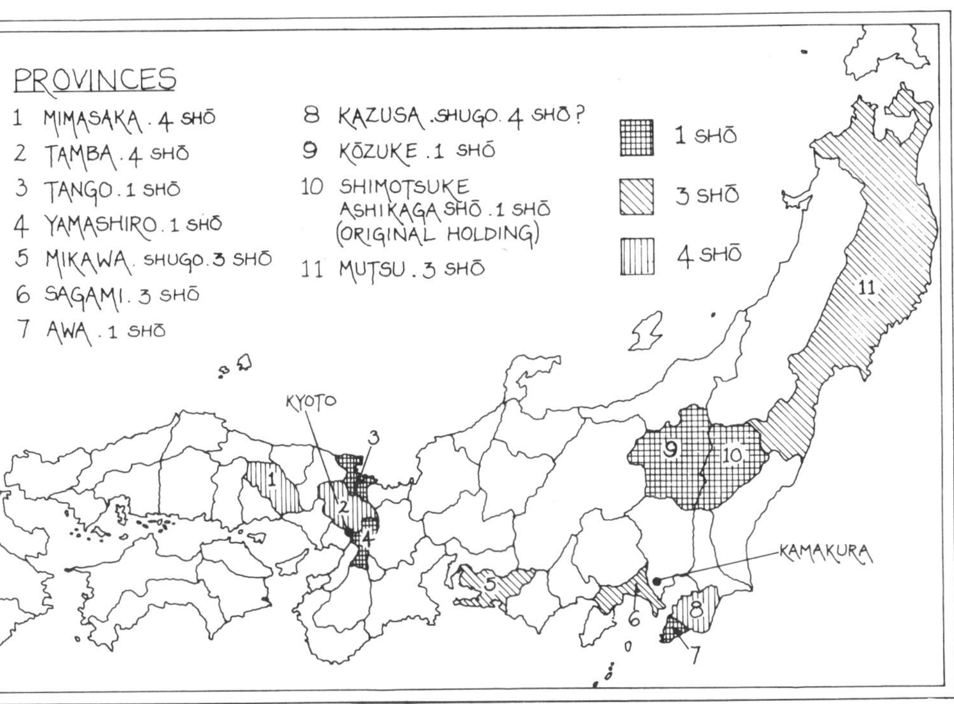

Map 3.1 The Ashikaga house, ca. 1330

kura and requiring him to take a special oath of loyalty. Takauji's complaint against Hōjō Takatoki, as reported in the *Taiheiki*, was at first personal:[5]

Takatoki is but a descendant of Hōjō Tokimasa, whose clan long ago came down among the commoners, while I am of the generation of the house of Genji, which left the imperial family not long since. Surely it is meant that Takatoki should be my vassal instead of contemptously handing down orders such as these![6]

Once Takauji made public his resolve to defect, however, more justification was needed. He, of course, had every right to consider Godaigo's call a superior one, particularly as the emperor still held the proprietary rights to Ashikaga-no-shō. But Takauji could claim a still

5 The *Taiheiki*, written presumably by a priest attached to Godaigo's exiled court in 1345 and added to as late as 1370, covers events from about 1318 to 1368. Its historical reliability is moot, but its content is not by any means fictional. Passages quoted in translation are taken from Helen C. McCullough, trans., *The Taiheiki: A Chronicle of Medieval Japan* (New York: Columbia University Press, 1959). Hereafter cited as *Taiheiki*.

6 *Taiheiki*, pp. 237–38.

higher cause which was publicized in his prayer to Hachiman, the patron diety of the Minamoto lineage. Passing through the village of Shinomura in Tamba on his way to attack the Hōjō at Rokuhara in 1333, Takauji stopped at a shrine to Hachiman and stated his case. His purpose, he protested, was to destroy the "Eastern descendants of the house of Taira . . . [who] wickedly for nine generations have walked in the ways of violence."[7] But such propagandistic expressions were merely rationalizations. Japan in the 1330s was disturbed by more than private or family rivalries.

Toyoda Takeshi, in his treatment of the forces that undid the Hōjō regency, began with the so-called *akutō* (evil band) phenomenon.[8] The term *evil band* was applied to various types of illegal activities, but the most significant, from the point of view of this analysis, was the work of purposefully organized groups of local warriors who resorted to violence in disputes, usually over land rights. A classic example of such a dispute is that over the Tōdaiji estate of Kuroda in Iga Province. The trouble on this estate was caused by the temple's estate manager (*gesu*). During the 1260s the *gesu* joined with the *jitō* that the bakufu assigned to Kuroda in opposing the temple, withholding dues payments, and the like. The temple appealed for redress to Rokuhara, the bakufu headquarters in Kyoto. To settle the case, Rokuhara called on the deputy *shugo* of adjoining Omi Province and a Kamakura *gokenin* in Iga. But the order had no effect, and Rokuhara was eventually obliged to mobilize a punitive force on its own. Kuroda-no-shō continued to experience trouble periodically until the end of the Hōjō regency.

In the Kuroda case, there is a pattern of growing conflict between central authority and local autonomy. The fact that Rokuhara was unable to suppress the Kuroda *akutō* by calling on the bakufu's regional agents bespoke a growing antagonism between the *jitō*-type of vassals of Kamakura and the Hōjō family that monopolized more and more of these high appointments. In central Japan in particular, local *bushi* houses like these found connections in the imperial court to be a useful device for legitimizing their defection from the Hōjō. Thus, when Godaigo began the plot to rescue the imperial government from domination by the Kamakura bakufu, he received strong support from dissident military houses in all quarters of the country.

Akutō behavior was symptomatic of the two great themes of disaffec-

7 Ibid., p. 250.

8 Toyoda, "Genkō," pp. 1–5. For a recent study in English, see Lorraine Harrington, "Social Control and the Significance of Akutō," in Jeffrey P. Mass, ed., *Court and Bakufu in Japan: Essays in Kamakura History* (New Haven, Conn.: Yale University Press, 1982).

tion that led to nearly eighty years of civil war, beginning with the destruction of the Hōjō-dominated Kamakura bakufu in 1333. On the one hand, Godaigo awakened among the court nobility and the major religious establishments the hope that the mounting encroachment of military houses on local administration and land-derived wealth could be stemmed. On the other hand, in the provinces the pressure was toward the reverse – the continuing effort by local houses as estate managers to avoid having to serve the Kyoto nobility and to be able to retain the estates' income for themselves. These two movements were not compatible, and in the final analysis, the second was destined to win out as the powers of lordship passed into the hands of those who could defend them at the village level. During the first half of the Muromachi era, however, the Ashikaga shoguns, by occupying the middle ground between these two positions, managed to stave off the demise of the *shoen*-based nobility for yet another two centuries.

THE FOUNDING OF THE MUROMACHI BAKUFU

Emperor Godaigo, who began his reign in 1318, gave early evidence of his determination to recapture the powers lost by the throne to both the high court nobility *(kugyō)* and the Kamakura bakufu. In 1321, Godaigo discontinued the system of government in which political control was exercised by the retired emperor *(insei)* and by the Fujiwara regency *(sekkan)*. Instead, he proposed to engage directly in the affairs of state. As a first step in this direction, he revived the office of land records *(kirokusho),* first established in 1069 to oversee the documentation of *shōen* and to regulate the illegal acquisition of land by noble houses and religious institutions in an effort to prevent the flight of taxable land from the purview of court-designated local officials. Godaigo's plots against the Hōjō came to the attention of the bakufu, and in 1331, he was exiled to the remote island of Oki. But Godaigo had set in motion more than a privately motivated attack on the Hōjō-dominated bakufu. When in 1333 he managed to escape from Oki, he found himself at the center of a broadly based movement of resistance against the Hōjō. Among the many provincial military leaders who came to his support were Ashikaga Takauji and Nitta Yoshisada.

In the winter of 1333, upon word of Godaigo's return to the mainland, Ashikaga Takauji was dispatched from Kamakura in command of a large army to safeguard the Hōjō headquarters at Rokuhara in Kyoto. Already he intended to change his allegiance if the opportunity presented itself. Upon reaching Ōmi Province, he received a written commission from Godaigo that legitimized his defection. Bypassing Kyoto, Takauji marched directly to Tamba, the home province of the Uesugi house. There, in the fourth month of 1333, Takauji raised the banner of Minamoto resistance to the Hōjō and called for supporters. He was joined immediately by warrior bands from all parts of the country. As the *Taiheiki* narrates, a force of twenty thousand in Tamba had swelled to fifty thousand by the time that Takauji was at the gates of Kyoto.[9] To take a local example, in Harima the head of a leading local warrior house, the Akamatsu, destined to be named *shugo* of Harima, was one of the first to join Takauji. Along with him came a band of local samurai families from the neighboring Bizen and Bitchū provinces, among them the Matsuda, who later became *shugo* of western Bizen. Sporadic but fierce fighting ensued, but Takauji had little difficulty in destroying the Hōjō establishment in Kyoto and in capturing the city for Godaigo. At nearly the same time, Nitta Yoshisada led his forces to the destruction of the Hōjō in Kamakura. Thus, the two men were destined to become rival leaders in Godaigo's service.

Godaigo returned to the capital intent on setting himself up as a true monarch. To that purpose he activated the records office and established an awards commission (*onshō-gata*). Through these and other organs of government, he began to make appointments to central and provincial posts and to distribute titles to landholdings. Almost immediately there was a falling out with Takauji. Although they had fought to destroy the Hōjō and to return Emperor Godaigo to the throne, neither Takauji nor his followers were prepared to go along with the emperor's plan to create a government centered on the throne in which military leaders would be of equal or lower rank than the court nobles, men without experience in warfare or statecraft. Takauji personally was well treated by Godaigo. Designated "first to be rewarded," he received the fourth court rank junior grade, the privilege of using one of the characters from the emperor's private name, the governorships of two provinces and the position of *shugo* of another, and numerous landholdings. Takauji, however, had already petitioned for the posts of *seii tai shōgun* (literally, "barbarian-subduing generalissimo)" and *sō-tsuibushi* (constable general), the positions that would give him the authority to establish a new bakufu. Although Godaigo did name Takauji *chinjufu shōgun* (general of the northern pacification command) and, later, *sei-tō shōgun* (general of the eastern pacification command), he refused during his lifetime to grant Takauji's request. In-

9 *Taiheiki,* p. 151. All such figures are, of course, conjectural.

stead, he successively named his sons, the princes Morinaga and Norinaga, to the post, thus giving form to a polity in which civil authority would outrank or displace the military.

Godaigo's conception was bold, but the execution of his plan was inept and highly prejudiced. As the *Taiheiki* records, although men like Takauji and Yoshisada received special attention, "the offices of *shugo* and governor in more than fifty provinces were received by nobles and court officials; likewise confiscated estates and great estates were given them until they became . . . rich and powerful. . . . "[10] Following the destruction of the Hōjō, a considerable amount of vacated land and a large number of provincial posts were available for award to those who had assisted in Godaigo's return to the throne. But by including court nobles among the recipients, the emperor ran out of resources with which to reward his military supporters. Among those poorly treated were local leaders such as Akamatsu Norimura, who, once having been appointed *shugo* of Harima, later had the appointment withdrawn. Such arbitrary action led to a general disillusionment among military leaders in the provinces. Takauji, aspiring chief of the military estate and potential shogun, became the most prominent alternative to Godaigo. But he was not alone, as his rivalry with Nitta Yoshisada was to prove.

In 1333, after crushing the Hōjō in Kyoto, Takauji set up a secretariat (*bugyō-sho*) to administer the city in the manner of the recently destroyed Rokuhara headquarters. As the winning general, Takauji assumed the right to reward his followers with grants of confiscated landholdings and to make appointments to the posts of *shugo* and *jitō*. Obviously there was a conflict of authority and jurisdiction here that could not long remain unresolved. During most of 1334 Takauji and Godaigo managed a precarious coexistence in Kyoto. The emperor publicly announced his plan, called the Kemmu restoration, and established various organs of central government. Takauji did not take office in any of these, nor did he disband his own secretariat. When Godaigo dispatched his young son Prince Norinaga to Kamakura in an effort to assert the imperial presence in the Kantō, Takauji had his brother Tadayoshi appointed military guardian to the prince. When Takauji complained to Godaigo that the newly appointed shogun, Prince Morinaga, was plotting his death, the emperor had Morinaga sent to Kamakura to be placed in Ashikaga Tadayoshi's custody.

10 *Taiheiki*, p. 365. In this case, there is good evidence that the *Taiheiki* gives an accurate report.

In 1335, Hōjō remnants recaptured Kamakura and drove out Tadayoshi and Prince Morinaga. In the confusion, Tadayoshi had Prince Morinaga killed. Takauji now led his own army, without imperial orders, to the Kantō and quickly retook Kamakura. This time Takauji remained in Kamakura for a year and began to put on the mantle of shogun, giving out land patents and confirmations. When it was clear that Nitta Yoshisada was siding with Godaigo, Takauji declared Nitta's lands confiscated and began to distribute them to his followers. Godaigo retaliated by declaring Takauji an "enemy of the throne" (*chōteki*) and stripping him of his titles and honors. He commissioned generals loyal to his cause, among them Nitta Yoshisada and Kitabatake Akiie, to recapture the Kantō.

Takauji was now in full rebellion against Godaigo, and his break with rival military leaders like Yoshisada was complete. Taking to the field again, he fought his way back to Kyoto in the second month of 1336, against heavy opposition from forces supporting Godaigo's cause. Takauji managed to hold the city for only four days before being driven out toward the western provinces. His retreat was not complete until he had reached the island of Kyushu.

Although Kyushu and the western Honshū provinces were not areas in which the Ashikaga had many direct military connections, Takauji used to his advantage a commission of chastisement against Nitta Yoshisada that he obtained from the retired emperor Kōgon-in, head of the senior branch of the imperial house. Also, by representing the Minamoto cause and professing to champion basic warrior interests in the event of his becoming shogun, Takauji was able to build up a considerable following along the path of his retreat. When possible, he found opportunities along the way to place his collateral followers in favorable positions, promising the most powerful local families and the heads of Ashikaga collateral branches who supported him the military governorships of various provinces and districts, depending on the success of his cause. To the Hosokawa he promised the entire island of Shikoku; to the Imagawa, Bitchū; to the Akamatsu, Harima; and to the Niki, Tamba. By the time he arrived in Kyushu, Takauji had already won over most of the local military lords, such as the Shimazu, and only a brief military campaign was needed to gain the support of the remainder.

By the fifth month of 1336, with some of his house retainers and collateral commanders and contingents led by his newly won allies from western Japan, Takauji began the countermarch toward Kyoto. His forces moved by both land and water. At the critical battle of

Minatogawa in Settsu, the Ashikaga won a decisive victory, forcing Nitta back to Kyoto and Emperor Godaigo to take refuge with the monks of Hieizan. Takauji entered Kyoto in the company of Prince Yutahito, the brother of Kōgon-in who had previously given Takauji his imperial mandate. Takauji generously endowed the Kōgon-in faction with lands and guarantees of protected income. Somehow the imperial regalia was obtained from Godaigo. These emblems, which were given to Prince Yutahito, became the basis for his installation as Emperor Kōmyō. Takauji began the construction of a new imperial palace, the first permanent one in many years, which was completed the following year. Takauji had now played the supreme role of having installed an emperor with his military power. He further legitimized himself by taking high court rank and adopting the role of chief of the warrior estate. The secretariat he had established three years before had remained in operation and was now turned into a bakufu in all but name. Takauji's public posture was further enhanced when he promulgated the Kemmu *shikimoku* (the Kemmu injunctions), making public the policy he proposed to follow when named shogun.[11] But the appointment did not come until 1338.

There was work yet to be done. Kyoto was still not safely in Ashikaga hands, nor would the enemies of the new bakufu leave the field. Godaigo, claiming that he had given up only replicas and that he still possessed the authentic regalia, kept his cause alive from the mountainous region of Yoshino. There he set up a court in exile, which, because it was located south of Kyoto, was called the Southern Court. The court that remained in Kyoto, which served to legitimate the Ashikaga shogun, was, by the same token, called the Northern Court. Fighting in the name of these two courts continued until 1392, when a settlement was arranged. The existence of two imperial courts, each claiming legitimacy, each calling on the warrior houses throughout Japan to fight for its cause, justified the resort to arms, often for purely private objectives. The basic motivations were not always apparent, but in the years to follow intense rivalries for power among the most powerful military houses in the provinces were fought out.

Takauji's two primary military rivals from the beginning were Nitta Yoshisada and Kitabatake Akiie, both of whom had their largest bases

11 For a translation of this document and the 452 supplementary laws (*tsuikahō*) that succeeded it, see Kenneth A. Grossberg, ed., and Kenneth A. Grossberg and Nobuhisa Kanamoto, trans., *The Laws of the Muromachi Bakufu: Kemmu Shikimoku (1336) and the Muromachi Tsuikahō* (Tokyo: *Monumenta Nipponica* and Sophia University, 1981). Herewith cited as *Kemmu Shikimoku and Tsuikahō*.

of support east and north of the capital. Although both men were killed in battle in the summer of 1338, and despite Godaigo's death in the summer of 1339, the fighting did not end. Godaigo's son Prince Norinaga succeeded to the "junior" line under the name Gomurakami. In the central provinces, Kusunoki Masatsura, *shugo* of Kawachi, kept the Ashikaga forces on the defensive. In Kyushu, Godaigo's other son, Prince Kanenaga, succeeded in establishing himself at Dazaifu as the chief agent of the capital. The divided polity and the civil war it engendered continued. But the main issue regarding the establishment of a bakufu in Kyoto had been settled.

For a few years the capital area remained sufficiently quiet, so that the work of organizing the new bakufu could move ahead. The Kemmu *shikimoku* was followed by supplementary orders (*tsuikahō*) that sought to resolve the many problems that had been left unsettled during the years of heavy fighting.[12] But in 1350, events took another sudden turn, this time brought on by conflicts within the Ashikaga leadership. For several years, a rift over basic policy had been growing between Takauji and his brother Tadayoshi. This was the consequence of the division of responsibilities that had been worked out between the two men. The division was a natural one to make: Takauji was responsible for military strategy and personnel, and Tadayoshi concerned himself with the bakufu's administrative and judicial organs. But policy differences soon developed between the brothers. Takauji, more sensitive to the interest of the local military houses on whose support he depended, tended to be soft regarding the military encroachment on civil estates. Tadayoshi was more inclined to permit the bakufu courts, staffed to considerable extent by hereditary legal experts, to support the proprietary interests of the capital elite.[13] Eventually factions among the Ashikaga collaterals formed behind the brothers.

In 1349, Takauji, having been persuaded of Tadayoshi's disloyalty, dismissed his brother from his bakufu assignments, withdrawing the expectation that he would be next to inherit the title of shogun. The next year Takauji was forced to take to the field against Tadafuyu, his own troublemaking natural son who had been adopted by Tadayoshi.

12 *Kemmu Shikimoku and Tsuikahō*, pp. 25–41. Fourteen *tsuikahō* were issued between 1336 and 1345. But in the year 1346 alone, forty such orders were issued.

13 This analysis was first made by Satō Shin'ichi, "Muromachi bakufu kaisōki no kansei taikei," in Ishimoda Shō and Satō Shin'ichi, eds., *Chūsei no hō to kokka* (Tokyo: Tōkyō daigaku shuppankai, 1960). For a statement in English, see Shin'ichi Sato, with John Whitney Hall, "The Ashikaga Shogun and the Muromachi Bakufu Administration," in John Whitney Hall and Takeshi, Toyoda, eds., *Japan in the Muromachi Age* (Berkeley and Los Angeles: University of California Press, 1977), pp. 45–52.

In the winter of 1351–2, Tadayoshi was captured and killed, presumably by poisoning on Takauji's orders. But Tadayoshi's death only increased the anti-Takauji sentiment in the Kantō. It was not until the spring of 1355 that Takauji, after perhaps the most destructive battle of the civil war, in which several sections of the city were destroyed, retook Kyoto conclusively.

Takauji died in 1358 and was succeeded as head of the Ashikaga house and shogun by Yoshiakira, then in his twenty-eighth year. As might be expected, the second shogun at first had trouble keeping the Ashikaga forces in line, but the intensity of the civil war had subsided. The most powerful *shugo* houses capable of opposing the Ashikaga – the Shiba, Uesugi, Ōuchi, and Yamana – had settled their differences and had joined forces with the bakufu. Yoshiakira died in 1368, to be succeeded by his ten-year-old son Yoshimitsu, who lived to preside over the most flourishing era of the Muromachi bakufu.

THE PATH TO ASHIKAGA LEGITIMACY

One of the major accomplishments of the Ashikaga house was its success in legitimizing the post of shogun within a polity still legally under the sovereign authority of the emperor. We have already noted that Minamoto Yoritomo, the first shogun, did not depend solely on the title of shogun to establish his legitimacy.[14] Rather, it was the Hōjō regents who built up the importance of the title as a device through which to exercise leadership over the *bushi* class. After Yoritomo's death, the office of shogun became identified with the powers that Yoritomo had acquired both as the foremost military leader and by virtue of the high ranks and titles bestowed on him by the court. Although the office of shogun never received written definition or legal formulation, under the Ashikaga the title was recognized as giving to its recipient and holder the status of chief of the military estate (*buke no tōryō*), the keeper of the warriors' customary law, and the ultimate guarantor of the land rights of the *bushi* class.

The concept of *buke* rule, in the context of the imperial tradition of civil government, was the subject of considerable discussion in fourteenth-century Japan. Political philosophers in both Kyoto and Kamakura were fully aware of the issues raised by the emergence of military rule. Godaigo's Kemmu restoration, and the long drawn-out

14 Jeffrey P. Mass, *Warrior Government in Early Medieval Japan: A Study of the Kamakura Bakufu, Shugo, and Jitō* (New Haven, Conn.: Yale University Press, 1974). Also see his chapter in this volume.

civil war that followed, naturally stimulated attempts at special pleading on both sides. One of the foremost efforts to address the issue of imperial rule was the *Jinnō shōtōki,* written between 1339 and 1343 by Kitabatake Chikafusa, a supporter of Godaigo in exile.

Chikafusa began with the premise that the *tennō* line, by means of correct succession from the Sun Goddess, was "a transcendent source of virtue in government, which was above criticism."[15] On the other hand, individual emperors were accountable for their private acts and could be criticized if their intrusion into political and military affairs should have unfortunate results. According to Chikafusa, not even Godaigo was above criticism. Having failed to recognize the changed nature of the time, his appointments to office and his rewards to courtiers and military leaders had been capricious, and the results proved harmful to the state.

Statements justifying military rule, written from the point of view of the *buke* class, were even more direct. The court aristocracy, they claimed, had had their day and had failed. It was the destiny of the samurai estate, through its ability (*kiryō*), to bring the state back to a peaceful and well-administered condition. This essentially was what Ashikaga Takauji asserted when he prayed publicly before the Shinomura Hachiman Shrine of Tamba. The same premise underlines the preamble to the Kemmu *shikimoku* of 1336.[16] Neither statement was critical of the emperor or his court but, rather, of the maladministration of the Hōjō regents. As to what constituted good government, the obvious answer was the maintenance of peace, law, and order, a condition in which all the people could prosper. The basic intent of the Kemmu *shikimoku* was to offer guidelines on how to achieve good government.[17]

Even more philosophically explicit on what constitutes good government is a document known as *Tōji-in goisho* (Takauji's testament) and written in 1357, though most likely not by Takauji.[18] This document sets forth in a Confucian manner the proposition that the state (*tenka*) is not the possession of any person, neither emperor nor shogun, but of itself and that rulers must conform to the "essence of the polity" (*tenka no kokoro*). Within the *tenka,* the task of the shogun and his followers is to ensure peace.

15 H. Paul Varley, *Imperial Restoration in Medieval Japan* (New York: Columbia University Press, 1971). 16 *Shigaku kenkyū* 110 (April 1971): 72–97.

17 Henrik Carl Trolle Steenstrup, "Hōjō Shigetoki (1198–1261) and His Role in the History of Political and Ethical Ideas in Japan" (Ph.D. diss., Harvard University, 1977), p. 236.

18 Ibid., p. 234.

One is struck by the pragmatic spirit of these general statements on government and statecraft. They clearly stand on a middle ground in placing military rule into the context of a polity that included both an emperor and a large court (*kuge*) community. No model excluded the emperor. Nor was there any thought to bring *kuge* and *buke* together into a single ruling class. *Buke* remained a separate branch of the aristocracy. The shogun, though recognized as chief of the warrior estate, was never conceived of as a self-proclaimed or self-appointed official. The office of shogun was an imperial appointment. Even though the emperor personally might be a creature of the military hegemon, having been assisted to the throne by a victorious military leader, investiture as shogun was an act that only the emperor and his courtiers could perform.

Political ideas of this sort were reflected in the real world. The struggle that preceded the final Ashikaga military victory shaped the complex interdependence between *buke* and *kuge* interests. Takauji had depended on the imperial patent to legitimate his chastisement of Nitta Yoshisada, his own brother, and his natural son Tadafuyu. He had installed Emperor Kōmyō, who in turn had named him *seii tai shōgun*. In the years that followed, the court community became almost totally reliant on military government to preserve its livelihood; yet military leaders avidly competed for apparently hollow court ranks and functionally meaningless court titles. No matter how powerful a military hegemon, if he aspired to recognition as ruler of the entire country, he needed more than a conquering army. He needed also a sufficiently high court status to demonstrate publicly his right to rule.

Having settled in Kyoto, the Ashikaga house was quickly assimilated into the high aristocracy, that is, into the select group of families of third court rank and above who were known as *kugyō*. The third shogun, Yoshimitsu, best illustrates the capacity of the Ashikaga leaders to penetrate court society. Having attained the first court rank in 1380 at age twenty-two, he received successively higher appointments until attaining in 1394 the highest court title available, that of prime minister (*daijō daijin*). Yoshimitsu's successive steps up the ladder of court rank were accompanied by his adoption of a commensurate life-style.

In 1378, the Ashikaga house had built a residential palace in the grand manner at Muromachi, soon referred to as the Palace of Flowers (Hana no gosho). This complex of buildings occupied twice the space of the imperial palace that had been built for the emperor by Takauji as a grand gesture of patronage. When in 1381 Yoshimitsu managed to entertain Emperor Goenyū in his own residence, the occasion confirmed his status as *kugyō*. That Yoshimitsu fully understood this is revealed in his conscious adoption of two separate ciphers, one for use as a member of the military aristocracy and the other as a courtier. Increasingly from this time on, he used the latter almost exclusively.

After his successful reconciliation of the rival branches of the imperial house in 1392, Yoshimitsu was in the most exalted position in both the *kuge* and the *buke* worlds. A supreme patron of the arts, he is best remembered for his Kitayama villa and its centerpiece, the Golden Pavilion, built between 1397 and 1407. In 1408 he made known his hopes of having his son Yoshitsugu receive a ceremonial standing comparable to that of an imperial prince, thus setting in motion the rumor that he intended to gain for the Ashikaga house access to the imperial throne itself. But Yoshimitsu died shortly thereafter.

Historians continue to debate whether Yoshimitsu did in fact intend to usurp the throne and whether he could have succeeded. There is not enough documentation to settle the issue on the basis of written evidence. The fact that he did not do so and that his son and successor Yoshimochi dissuaded the court from bestowing on his father the posthumous title of *daijō-hōō* (priestly retired monarch) indicates that an overt act of usurpation would have been difficult, if not impossible, to carry out.

But whether or not Yoshimitsu intended to displace the emperor, he and his successors as shogun did preside over the demise of the tradition of imperial rule as it had been up to that point. As Nagahara Keiji pointed out so clearly, by this time, the warrior aristocracy had absorbed the functions of the imperial government over which the *tennō* and the *kuge* had presided. Yoshimitsu possessed all the formal rights of rulership: to grant or withdraw holdings in land, to staff posts in central and provincial administrations, to establish central and provincial courts, and to maintain the flow of taxes. Yoshimitsu as chief of the *buke* had achieved a general takeover of the functional organs of government.[19]

Can it then be said that Yoshimitsu had attained the status of monarch? As shogun, and hence chief of the *buke* estate, and as prime minister, and thus the highest-ranking official of the noble estate, he held the credentials of ultimate authority in both. Under the Ashikaga,

19 Nagahara Keiji, "Zen-kindai no tennō," in *Rekishigaku kenkyū* 467 (April 1979): 37–45. In English, see Peter Arnesen, "The Provincial Vassals of the Muromachi Bakufu,"in Jeffrey P. Mass and William B. Hauser, eds., *The Bakufu in Japanese History* (Stanford, Calif.: Stanford University Press, 1985), pp. 125–6.

the shogun had become more powerful than any previous secular official. But he was not sovereign, nor were his peers likely to have permitted him to become such.

The monarchical issue is raised in yet another context. Yoshimitsu's acceptance in 1402 of a mission from China that brought to the shogun documents investing him as "King of Japan" and calling on him to adopt the Ming imperial calendar. How did Yoshimitsu justify his break with the Japanese tradition of refusing to acknowledge the sovereignty of a foreign country? Certainly trade was a major consideration. But a final assessment of the encounter may not rest in the field of trade. Tanaka Takeo, for instance, suggests that involvement in trade with the continent was a conscious effort by Yoshimitsu to project Japan into the mainstream of East Asian affairs, an effort to gain recognition as a member of the wider East Asian community. Within Japan, the shogun's successful negotiations with China became a means to confirm the principle that as chief of the military estate, he had full control of Japan's foreign affairs. Yoshimitsu had in fact shielded the emperor from facing the actuality of a letter of investiture from the Ming emperor. But he also made clear that the emperor need not be troubled by diplomatic affairs in the future.[20]

SHOGUN, *SHUGO*, AND PROVINCIAL ADMINISTRATION

It is sometimes claimed that Takauji, in his effort to attract and hold *shugo*-grade warriors in his command, gave away resources vital to the sustenance of his own position as shogun. But the reverse is more likely true. By adding to the stature of *shugo* as provincial administrators, he added equally to the reach of the bakufu's authority. And as long as they worked together in a context that admitted the shogun's primacy, the growth of *shugo* power in the provinces was to the advantage of the bakufu's rule.

At the outset of his attack on the Hōjō, Takauji depended primarily on members of the Ashikaga house, cadet branches, and direct retainers for support in the field. His first appointments to *shugo* were picked from among house retainers like the Kō brothers and were placed over provinces in the Kantō where the Ashikaga already had some reliable bases. As the war spread and Takauji was widely opposed by rival military houses, he was obliged to name trustworthy

20 Takeo Tanaka, with Robert Sakai, "Japan's Relations with Overseas Countries," in Hall and Toyoda, eds., *Japan in The Muromachi Age*, p. 178.

TABLE 3.2

Control of provinces by Ashikaga collaterals and other families, ca. 1400

Province	Family	Province	Family
Yamashiro	Bakufu	Tango	Isshiki
Yamato	Kōfukuji	Tajima	Yamana
Kawachi	Hatakeyama	Inaba	Yamana
Izumi	Niki	Hōki	Yamana
Settsu	Hosokawa	Izumo	Kyōgoku
Iga	Yamana	Iwami	Yamana
Ise	Toki	Iki	Kyōgoku
Shima	Toki	Harima	Akamatsu
Owari	Shiba	Mimasaka	Akamatsu
Mikawa	Isshiki	Bizen	Akamatsu
Totomi	Imagawa	Bitchū	Hosokawa
Suruga	Imagawa	Bingo	Hosokawa
Ōmi	Kyōgoku	Aki	Shibukawa
Mino	Toki	Suo	Ōuchi
Hida	Kyōgoku	Nagato	Ōuchi
Shinano	Shiba	Kii	Hatakeyama
Wakasa	Isshiki	Awaji	Hosokawa
Echizen	Shiba	Awa	Hosokawa
Kaga	Togashi	Sanuki	Hosokawa
Noto	Hatakeyama	Iyo	Kawano
Etchū	Hatakeyama	Tosa	Hosokawa
Echigo	Uesugi		
Tamba	Hosokawa		

collaterals and friendly allies to all the provinces.[21] Between 1336 and 1368 the composition of the Ashikaga house band changed dramatically as a number of the cadet houses who joined the Tadayoshi faction were destroyed and as new allies were put in places of trust. Naturally Takauji sought to bring as many provinces as possible under *shugo* appointed from among Ashikaga kinsmen. By the end of the fourteenth century, of the provinces of central Japan, twenty-three were held by Ashikaga collaterals, twenty by noncollaterals, and two by institutions, as can be seen from Table 3.2[22] (see also Maps 3.2 and 3.3).

It is natural to assume that the collateral houses were the most important in the eyes of the shogun. But as events proved, the

21 Imatani Akira, "Kōki Muromachi bakufu no kenryoku kōzō – tokuni sono senseika ni tsuite," in Nihonshi kenkyūkai shiryō kenkyū bukai ed., *Chūsei Nihon no rekishizō* (Osaka: Sōgensha, 1978), pp. 154–183 reveals how in certain strategic but precariously held provinces in central Japan, like Settsu, Yamato, and Izumi, *shugo* were appointed by *kōri* (districts) for strategic reasons.

22 These figures were developed from the listings of *shugo* appointments by Sugiyama Hiroshi in *Dokushi sōran* (Tokyo: Jimbutsu ōraisha, 1966), pp. 115–18.

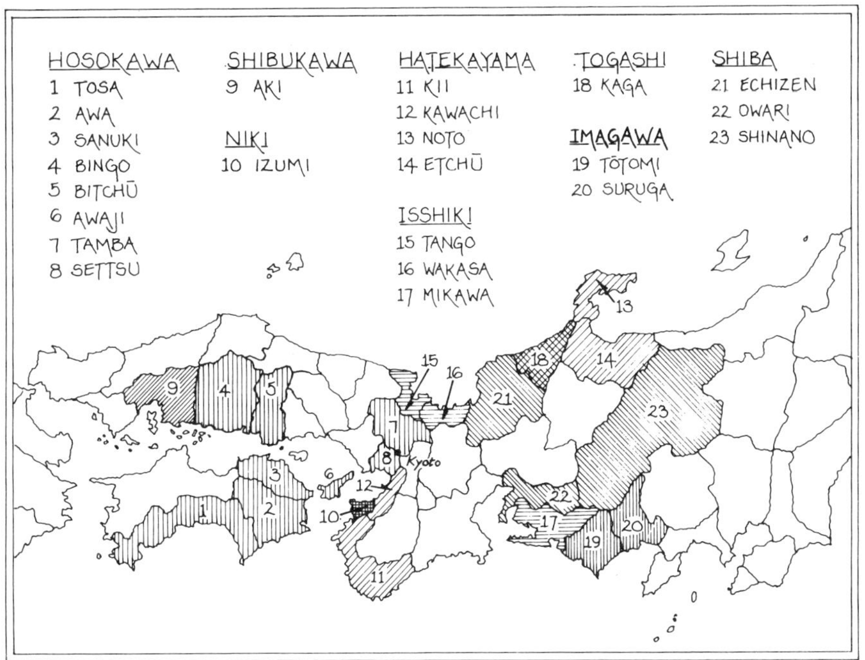

Map 3.2 Provinces in central bloc held by Ashikaga collateral *shugo*, ca. 1400.

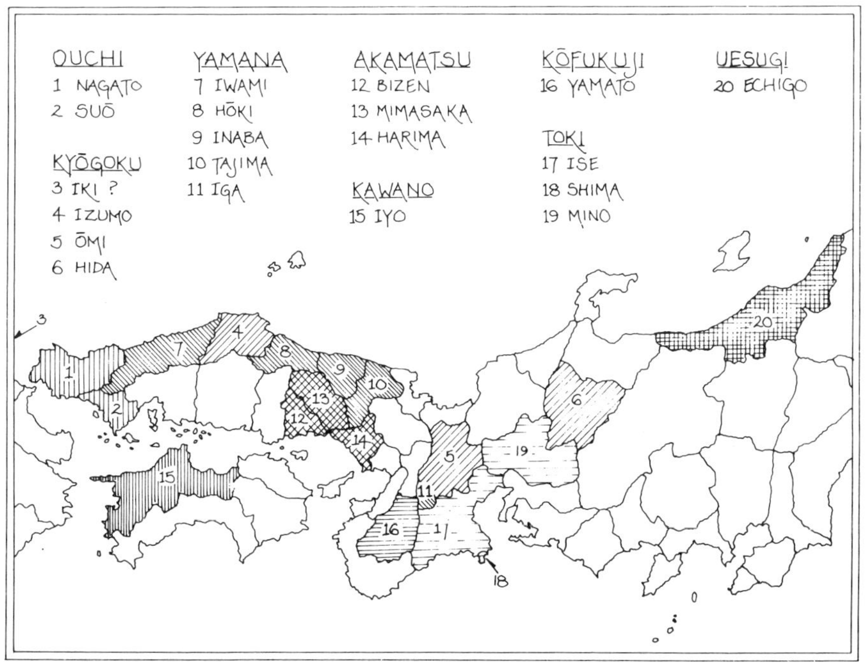

Map 3.3 Provinces in the central area held by noncollateral *shugo* houses, ca. 1400.

noncollateral *shugo*, all being to some extent "creations" of the Ashikaga and having been confirmed or put in place by Takauji or one of his successors, often were even more reliable. The Ashikaga naturally had greater difficulty with entrenched military houses from the Kamakura period that could not be dislodged from their provinces.

Among the noncollateral creations, the Akamatsu house of Harima is typical of the first type.[23] The Akamatsu had served as Kamakura-appointed stewards of the Sayo estate in Harima Province. In 1333, Akamatsu Norimura joined Godaigo and assisted in his escape from exile. In reward Akamatsu was named *shugo* of Harima, but at a later date the reward was withdrawn. Norimura subsequently changed his loyalty to Ashikaga Takauji, and his support in the battles that led to the recapture of the capital placed him high on Takauji's reward list. In 1336 he was appointed *shugo* of Harima, and shortly thereafter his sons were appointed to Settsu and Mimasaka. As the bakufu organization was formalized in the years of the third shogun, Yoshimitsu, the Akamatsu house held the posts of *shugo* in Harima, Bizen, and Mimasaka and was recognized as one of the four families from which the heads of the bakufu's Board of Retainers (*samurai-dokoro*) were chosen.

The Ōuchi of Suō are a good example of the second type of *shugo* house.[24] As the *shugo* of Suō under the Kamakura regime, Ouchi Nagahiro joined the Ashikaga cause in 1336 and assisted in the recapture of Kyoto that year. As reward, Takauji confirmed his possession of Suō. Thereafter the Ouchi were to serve the Ashikaga house, and at the time of its greatest expansion it held six *shugo* posts.

The post of *shugo* had not been fully developed under the Kamakura bakufu. In the provinces the civil governor's office (*kokuga*) and the attached resident officials still provided the machinery of administration and judicial process, and except for the Kantō, these facilities remained accountable to civil officials based in Kyoto. As the power of these civil authorities declined, the need for a greater bakufu presence in the provinces became apparent. The agency through which this was accomplished was the office of *shugo*. When in the later years of their regency, the Hōjō openly attempted to monopolize the *shugo* appointments (they succeeded in filling twenty-eight of the fifty-seven appoint-

23 See John Whitney Hall, *Government and Local Power in Japan, 500–1700: A Study Based on Bizen Province* (Princeton, N.J.: Princeton University Press, 1966), pp. 137–206 for a description of the Akamatsu as *shugo* of Bizen. Kishida Hiroshi offers a detailed study of the Akamatsu rule in Harima. See his "Shugo Akamatsushi no Harima no kuni shihai no hatten to kokuga," in Ogawa, ed., *Muromachi seiken*, pp. 139–76.

24 See Peter Arnesen, *The Medieval Japanese Daimyo: The Ōuchi Family's Rule in Suō and Nagato* (New Haven, Conn.: Yale University Press, 1979), pp. 139–76.

ments), it was clear that the importance of the post was being recognized. In the Kantō, where the bakufu possessed broad powers of appointment, the practice of awarding remaining provincial "public lands" to incumbent *shugo* was gaining currency, and Godaigo continued the practice. From the beginning, the Ashikaga shoguns conceived of the provinces as administrative units to be governed by *shugo* who were freely appointed by the shogun.[25]

Article 7 of the Kemmu code of 1336 equated the office of *shugo* with that of provincial governor in the imperial bureaucracy.[26] To that end the Muromachi bakufu sought to make the provincial headquarters and their attached lands (*kokugaryō*) available to the *shugo*. The size of these lands varied widely, but whether or not they were of significant economic value, authority over the seat of provincial government had important political implications. For example, the Akamatsu, as newly appointed *shugo* in Harima, worked steadily to obtain control over the provincial headquarters, by reducing local resident officials to vassalage. By the 1360s they were being referred to as *kunikata*, a recognition that as *shugo* they were the "ruling authority of the province."[27] Contemporary documents record that the Akamatsu chiefs granted land to their subordinates. For a house like the Ōuchi, with a long history of serving as resident officials, the advent of the new bakufu did not demand a radical departure from customary practice.[28]

Most of the newly posted *shugo* in central and western Japan appointed by the first two Ashikaga shoguns were brought in from outside the provinces to which they were assigned. These early appointees did not have ready-made and secure positions in which to settle. The Muromachi bakufu soon realized that it had to give its *shugo* greater administrative, judicial, and fiscal authority. Between 1333 and 1346, important changes were made in the legal nature of the office of *shugo*. Godaigo's policy of naming courtiers as *shugo* or of appointing the same individual (most often a military leader) to both the office of *shugo* and provincial governor had the effect of fusing the two offices into one.

Under the Kamakura bakufu, *shugo* had been given three specific functions: (1) enrolling bakufu retainers for guard duty at Kyoto and Kamakura, (2) suppressing major crimes like murder and piracy, and

25 Kurokawa Naonori, "Shugo ryōgokusei to shōen taisei," in Ogawa, ed., *Muromachi seiken*, pp. 107–22. 26 *Kemmu Shikimoku and Tsuikahō*, pp. 18–19.
27 Kishida, "Shugo Akamatsu," p. 165.
28 Arnesen, *Ōuchi Family's Rule*, pp. 99–115.

(3) punishing treason. In 1346, the Muromachi bakufu added two more important powers. The first conferred the right to deal with the unlawful cutting of crops – a favorite act of *akutō* bands. The second, in practical terms, meant the right to carry out the bakufu's orders to confiscate or redistribute land rights. Together, these legal provisions gave the *shugo* the authority to exercise major judicial and fiscal powers that heretofore had been exercised by organs of the central government.[29] But a number of specific military privileges were still to be defined.

Considering the amount of warfare that accompanied the establishment of the Muromachi bakufu, it is not surprising that the acquisition of supply and support resources would be a primary concern. Those military leaders who, like Takauji or Yoshisada, commanded large house bands, were under constant pressure to underwrite the military expenditures of their followers. Takauji's practice was either to dip into his own family holdings or to promise grants from future acquisitions by conquest. Neither of these sources was fully reliable, nor were land grants in themselves easily or quickly converted into economic products-in-hand. A more immediate source of support thus was needed. The answer was to invoke the precedent of the wartime commissariat surtax.

It had been customary for some time for warriors in the field, or after an extended engagement, to receive from the central authority the right to collect commissariat rice (*hyōrō-mai*) from designated areas. For example, after his victory over the Taira in 1185, Minamoto Yoritomo was empowered to use the newly created military land stewards to collect a nationwide tax of three *shō* per *tan* of cultivated land – about a 3 percent charge on the annual harvest – for commissariat support. When Takauji recaptured Kyoto in 1336, he issued permits to some of his followers to collect extraordinary imposts on certain types of land in areas in which warfare had actually taken place. These permits were issued specifying the lands to which the tax right pertained as military provisions (*hyōrō-ryōsho*). The permits were to be temporary. But privileges of this sort were more easily granted than withdrawn. Before long, the taking of the "military's share" of the country's annual product was institutionalized through the practice of the *shugo*-levied half-tax (*hanzei*).

The adoption of half-tax procedures illustrates the conflicting demands placed on early Muromachi bakufu policy. The first supplemen-

29 Kurokawa, "Shugo ryōgokusei,", pp. 117–19.

tary law, issued in 1337, shows that the bakufu's principal concern was to recall the previously awarded "temporary" tax powers to protect the interests of the most highly placed noble and priestly proprietors. It demanded that lands held by *shugo* and other military officers for commissariat support "be immediately returned to the estate agents of the civil proprietors."[30] A directive issued in 1338 accused the *shugo* of abusing this privilege, by taking permanent possession of lands occupied for military support and even distributing them among their own retainers. The bakufu was clearly in a bind. Its primary interest in the provinces was to build up the strength of its *shugo;* yet it could not deny entirely the interests of the capital nobility and priesthood.

In 1352, in Supplementary Article 56, the bakufu began to protect certain limited and specified proprietary interests.[31] The bakufu order of 1368 singled out for protection "properties of the emperors and empresses, of fully protected shrines and temples, and the hereditary properties of the Fujiwara regents." Moreover, those parts of the estates to which *jitō* rights *(shiki)* had been awarded to the civil proprietor by the bakufu were to remain protected.[32] This policy thus protected the estate incomes of the most prestigious of the court nobility and religious institutions, whose preservation was of vital concern to the Ashikaga. Furthermore, because such a policy of selective application of the half-tax at the provincial level could be carried out only by the *shugo,* the court nobility accordingly became dependent on the shogun as the only authority capable of dealing with the *shugo.*

Already the *shugo* had become involved in another fiscal practice that increased the court's dependence. This was the practice of tax contracting *(shugo-uke).* Under this system, Kyoto-based absentee proprietors entrusted the *shugo* with collecting and delivering the taxes due from their provincial holdings. The amount was generally agreed upon in the abstract as a set figure or quota. Once a proprietor entered into such a relationship, he relinquished all direct contact between him and the estate.

Another fiscal device that derived from the practice of the civil governors was the right to collect provincewide extraordinary taxes *(ikkoku heikin no yaku).* The most common of these, known as *tansen,* were imposts levied to pay for certain special events such as imperial

30 *Kemmu Shikimoku and Tsuikahō,* pp. 25–26; Prescott B. Wintersteen, "The Muromachi Shugo and Hanzei," in John Whitney Hall and Jeffrey P. Mass, eds., *Medieval Japan: Essays in Institutional History* (New Haven, Conn.: Yale University Press, 1974), p. 212; Shimada Jirō, "Hanzei seido no seiritsu," in Ogawa, ed., *Muromachi seiken,* pp. 61–65.

31 *Kemmu Shikimoku and Tsuikahō,* p. 48.

32 *Kemmu Shikomoku and Tsuikahō,* pp. 64–65.

enthronements and abdication ceremonies or for the rebuilding of palaces or important temples. Under the Muromachi bakufu, the *shugo* first served simply as executors of the bakufu's orders to collect such taxes.[33] But gradually the practice was extended so that *shugo* could authorize *tansen* on their own initiative and even convert the tax from an occasional impost to a regular one. The importance of this development cannot be overemphasized. The collection of *tansen* had become a private right. Beyond that it became possible for a *shugo* to grant the use of this right to a subordinate as a "fief," instead of land, to cement a lord–vassal relationship.[34]

The expanded authorities acquired by the *shugo* under the Muromachi bakufu provided them not so much with power in hand as with the tools with which to accumulate such power. A *shugo* could be appointed to a whole province whether or not he possessed a power base in that province. Even if a *shugo* did have such a power base, as in the case of the Ōuchi, many of the proprietary rights in his province of assignment would still be held by court nobles, religious organizations, other *shugo* houses, and other lesser military houses.

The most prevalent practice by which *shugo* sought to gain control of their provinces was not the acquisition of private landholdings but, rather, the enlistment of local warrior families as vassals.[35] In order to accomplish this the *shugo* had to be accepted as the primary lawgivers of the provinces and have the capacity to make, or pass on, grants of office or land to the local warrior families. It is for this reason that the added authority to carry out judicial actions involving land transfers and the awards of *hanzei* or *tansen* privileges were so important to the *shugo*. The ultimate objective of *shugo* policy was to reduce, when possible, all lesser warrior families in the province to a subordinate status.[36] The trend toward the privatization of superior–inferior relations at the provincial level eventually resulted in the appearance of what Japanese of the time called *daimyo* and what modern historians call *shugo* daimyo, a condition in which *shugo* authority had been translated into a considerable amount of actual regional power.

Up to a point, the increase in local influence that the *shugo* acquired was beneficial to the bakufu. But there were limits to the amount of independence that the bakufu could, or should, tolerate from its

33 During 1346, a large number of *tsuikahō* dealt with the problems of the violent seizure of crops and property in the provinces. See *Kemmu Shikimoku and Tsuikahō*, pp. 33–47.

34 Arnesen, *Ōuchi Family's Rule*, pp. 165–9.

35 Ibid., p. 23.

36 Sugiyama Hiroshi, "Muromachi bakufu," in *Nihon rekishi kōza*, vol. 3 (1957): 51; Arnesen, *Ōuchi Family's Rule*, pp. 182–4.

shugo. In many instances, the interests of shogun and *shugo* were at odds with each other, and the bakufu would have to assert its primacy. Of course, in principle the shogun himself, or the collective will of his main *shugo* supporters, had the authority to exercise discipline. The Ashikaga shoguns had a number of means for directly intervening into provincial affairs. Unfortunately, we do not yet have sufficient information concerning the shogun's own vassals' serving as *jitō-gokenin* in the provinces, but it does appear that the shogun could go over the heads of his *shugo* by relying on less powerful but more directly controlled provincial houses.[37]

THE MUROMACHI DISTRIBUTION OF POWER

Once the battles of consolidation were over, the major *shugo* houses were put in place, and the division between the Northern and Southern Courts was brought to an end; that is, in the years immediately after 1392 when Shogun Yoshimitsu was in full command of the bakufu, a reasonably stable balance of interests appears to have been achieved among shogun, court, and *shugo*. This condition held for roughly three-quarters of a century. The balance had both territorial and political dimensions.

The usual impression is that the Muromachi bakufu, being located in Kyoto, maintained a more or less uniform hold over the entire country. In actuality, however, the bakufu had to accept a considerable amount of regional variation in its political reach. The debate within the Ashikaga leadership over whether to establish the bakufu in Kyoto or Kamakura had been an issue of real consequence. It was recognized that the Kantō, with its history of separatism from Kyoto and its reputation as the place of origin of the *buke* estate, would be hard to govern from Kyoto. And so it turned out to be. Takauji tried to set up a branch bakufu for the Kantō area at Kamakura but never really succeeded. The bakufu, however, had even greater problems in two other areas: the Ōu district in the far north and Kyushu in the southwest. The separatist tendencies of these regions were not caused only by their distance from the capital alone but by political and economic factors as well. The dominant military houses in these regions, left to their own devices, tended to form their own local coalitions through which they tried to ward off outside interference. The difficulty that

37 Arnesen, "Provincial Vassals," in Mass and Hauser, eds., *Bakufu in Japanese History*, pp. 99–115.

the Ashikaga shoguns had in maintaining control over the more distant regions of the country was a consequence of their failure both to develop the necessary machinery of government and to acquire the power to impose a full military hegemony. Each area had its special problems.

The Kantō area

It was clearly the intent of the early Ashikaga shoguns to retain direct control of the Kantō provinces from Kyoto.[38] But this was easier wished than done. The destruction of the Hōjō regime had been achieved by men like Takauji, heads of provincial warrior families, who were seeking to extend their landholdings and their regional influence. Those who survived the lengthy civil war had gained both land and a sense of local independence. The central authorities were no longer able to control the provinces by directive or by posting a deputy there.

As the system of provincial administration by bureaucratic extension from a central authority failed, other forms of command had to be found. Godaigo had tried to extend his political reach by capitalizing on the imperial house's charisma. Fortunately for him, eight of his sons survived into adulthood. In 1334 he sent his son Norinaga to Kamakura as governor of Kozuke Province. In this instance, Takauji insisted on supporting with military authority the prestige adhering to the imperial person, by dispatching his brother Tadayoshi with the prince to serve as guardian. This practice of combining the prestige of royalty or of nobility with the enforcement capacity of a powerful military family was a favorite device. But Tadayoshi lost Kamakura, making it necessary for Takauji to lead his own forces into the Kantō to restore the primacy of the Ashikaga house.

When Takauji returned to Kyoto, he left behind his young son, Yoshiakira, then four years old, as his own representative in the Kantō. As guardians he appointed three kinsmen related by blood or marriage: Hosokawa Kiyouji, Uesugi Noriaki, and Shiba Ienaga. It was expected that this combination of a main-line member of the Ashikaga house backed by powerful military kinsmen could control the Kantō. In 1349 Takauji sent his second son, Motouji, to Kama-

38 The main source for this section is Itō Kiyoshi, "Muromachi ki no kokka to Tōgoku," *Rekishigaku kenkyū* (October 1979): 63–72. More recent is Lorraine F. Harrington's study, "Regional Outposts of Muromachi Bakufu Rule: The Kantō and Kyūshū," in Mass and Hauser, eds., *Bakufu in Japanese History*, pp. 66–88.

kura with the title of Kantō *kanrei* and under the guardianship of Uesugi Noriaki. The jurisdiction of the branch shogunate, now called Kamakura-fu, included the "eight Kantō provinces" plus Izu and Kai. Within these provinces the Kantō *kanrei* was given broad administrative and judicial powers. These included the authority to raise military forces, to make or withdraw grants of land, to make appointments to local offices (including the naming of *shugo*), and to superintend the affairs of temples and shrines. The Muromachi bakufu apparently reserved for itself only the authority to approve succession in the Uesugi house. To carry out its functions, Kamakura-fu created a full assemblage of administrative offices based on the model of the Muromachi headquarters.

Despite these efforts to keep the Kantō subservient to Kyoto, the arrangement never worked well and ultimately failed. The sense of separation remained strong in Kamakura, and this was kept alive by the fact that among the leading Ashikaga collaterals on whom the bakufu had to rely, many had been supporters of Tadayoshi and remained resentful of the manner in which Takauji had brought about his death. Furthermore, after Motouji's death in 1367, members of the Kamakura branch of the Ashikaga house proved ill inclined to take directives from Kyoto. Before long, the head of the Kantō Ashikaga house had adopted the style of *kubō* (an honorific title reserved for the shogun) and had passed the office of *kanrei* to the head of the Uesugi house who had served up to that point only as guardian and chief officer. The Kamakura *kubō* Ujimitsu and his successors, far from keeping the Kantō tranquil, aggressively tried to expand their influence, thereby provoking a series of disturbances. The wide gap between the two branches of the Ashikaga house is symbolized by the Kantō *kubō*'s eventual confiscation of Ashikaga-no-shō. Differences between Muromachi and Kamakura came to a head between the sixth shogun, Yoshinori, and the fourth Kamakura *kubō*, Mochiuji (1398–1439). Mochiuji, who spent much of his time in Kyoto, had hopes of being named shogun himself, to succeed Yoshimochi. He resented the selection of Yoshinori and created trouble by refusing to use the era name (*gengo*) that was identified with Yoshinori's shogunate. Finally, in 1432 Yoshinori felt obliged to send a punitive force into the Kantō to punish Mochiuji for insubordination. Mochiuji was killed and Kamakura-fu destroyed.

The Muromachi bakufu, however, was not prepared to lose the Kantō. In 1449 and again in 1457, members of the Ashikaga shogunal line were sent to the Kantō to reestablish a branch shogunate. But

Kamakura-fu could not be revived. The Uesugi house, having taken the title of Kantō *kanrei,* exerted as much of a centralizing force as was possible under the circumstances. But this was exerted less and less on behalf of Kyoto.

Ironically, despite the Kantō origin of the Ashikaga house, once Takauji had pulled out of the area, he left behind remarkably few supporters. Around 1400, *shugo* appointments in the Kantō provinces were held by eight houses, not one of which was a cadet branch. Clearly, the Kantō was too distant a region to be controlled by proxy from Kyoto, given the means of communication and the military technology of the day. Failure to control the Kantō, however, did not greatly affect the staying power of the Kyoto-based Muromachi bakufu.

The Ōu area

The two large undeveloped provinces of Mutsu and Dewa, known together as the Ōu region, north of the Kantō, suffered even more from its remoteness from Japan's political center.[39] Under the Muromachi bakufu, neither province was brought under the *shugo* system. Yet because the region lay "behind" the Kantō, no government based at Kamakura could ignore its existence and its potential as a place of military buildup or of refuge for enemies of Kamakura. Minamoto Yoritomo had struggled with this problem in the aftermath of the Gempei War and had posted agents there to keep the peace. The provinces played a considerable role in the military action of the Kemmu era, which began when Godaigo sent Kitabatake Chikafusa, one of his important courtier generals, to the region as governor of Mutsu. Takauji countered by naming Shiba Ienaga as the supreme commander of Ōu (Ōu *sotaisho.)* In 1335 Takauji dispatched another of his collateral generals, Ishidō Yoshifusa, to the Mutsu provincial office as protector (Mutsu *chinjō).* In the next few years, Yoshifusa distinguished himself in battles with Southern Court adherents of the region. In 1345, Takauji established the office of governor general for the two provinces, to which he named two house generals, Hatakeyama Kunikiyo and Kira Sadaie. But the two generals proved to have irreconcilable differences, having been on opposite sides of the Tadayoshi quarrel. Muromachi next sent Shiba Iekane and Uesugi

39 Endo Iwao, "Nambokuchō nairan no naka de," in Kobayashi Seiji and Ōishi Naomasa, eds., *Chūsei Ōu no sekai* (Tokyo: Tōkyō daigaku shuppankai, 1978), pp. 84–124.

Noriharu to serve jointly as *kanrei*. At one time there were four *tandai* designates in Mutsu contesting for the office. In 1392, the Kantō *kubō*, Ashikaga Ujimitsu, brought Mutsu and Dewa into the jurisdiction of Kamakura-fu and named his son as *kanrei*. But with the end of Kamakura-fu, the office of *kanrei* lost its political meaning and its strategic importance to the Muromachi bakufu.

The Kyushu area

Kyushu presented the Ashikaga with quite different problems of control.[40] Western Japan as a whole had never been securely dominated by military regimes based in central or eastern Japan. Historically, the provinces of Kyushu and of the western end of Honshū had been the domains of strongly entrenched military houses like the Shimazu of Satsuma and Ōsumi; the Shōni of Higo, Buzen, and Chikuzen; the Ōtomo of Bungo; and the Ōuchi of Suō. Takauji and his successors had little choice but to leave these powerful houses in place as *shugo*.

Yet even though the western provinces had their own history of independence from control from either Kyoto or Kamakura, it had been customary to place a representative of the central government in northern Kyushu as an outpost for the conduct of foreign affairs. Since Nara times the Hakata region had been the location of Dazaifu, an office of the central government with authority over foreign relations and trade. The Kamakura bakufu established the post of Kyushu commissioner (Chinzei *bugyō*) to deal with local affairs and to keep peace among the Minamoto vassals. In 1293, in the wake of the Mongol invasions, the office of military governor of Kyushu (Chinzei *tandai*) was created and given powers similar to those of the Rokuhara *tandai*. The office was abolished at the end of Hōjō rule. But during the period of rivalry between the North and South Courts, both sides used these Kyushu regional offices to establish their presence in the western provinces.

As a result of Takauji's retreat to Kyushu in 1336, we find him establishing a regional office, the Kyushu intendant (Kyūshū *tandai*).[41] To this office he appointed a succession of collateral family heads, starting with Isshiki Noriuji. But there was strong support for the Southern Court cause in Kyushu, and this was not easily overcome. Emperor Godaigo had managed to send one of his many sons,

40 See Kawazoe Shōji, "Chinzei kanrei kō," in Ogawa, ed., *Muromachi seiken*, pp. 77–106.

41 This office was given a number of names such as Chinzei *kanrei*, Chinzei *tandai*, and Chinzei *taishōgun*. See ibid., pp. 78–79.

Prince Kanenaga, to Kyushu with the title of general of the western pacification command (*sei-sei shogun*). During the next thirty years the Northern Court faction was kept on the defensive against forces mobilized by Prince Kanenaga from local *shugo* families like the Kikuchi and Aso. When envoys sent from China by the Ming emperor reached northern Kyushu in 1369, it was with this office that they negotiated. In 1371 the Muromachi, recognizing its weakness in the west, sent one of its ablest generals, Imagawa Ryōshun, to Kyushu as intendant. After strenuous fighting, in 1381 the Imagawa chief finally managed to defeat the local partisans of the Southern Court. In 1395 he was replaced by Shibukawa Mitsuyori who had less success in maintaining military command. But the office itself remained in the hands of this family for the rest of the Muromachi period. Kyoto was never fully able to rule the western end of the Inland Sea, so critical to the foreign trade that flourished from the fourteenth century on. On the other hand, the *shugo* of Kyushu were more apt voluntarily to support the shogun, taking up residence in Kyoto in order to take part in the cultural life of the capital.

The central provinces

Between the Kantō and northern Kyushu lay the forty-four provinces of central Japan over which the Muromachi bakufu exerted its most direct and effective control. When historians write about the "Muromachi state" or the "Muromachi government" they are usually referring to this more limited portion of the country. *Shugo* appointments to these provinces were drawn from some twenty-two houses. Of these, the majority were collateral branches of the Ashikaga house; the rest were allies by marriage or pledge of loyalty, and as such were considered "outside lords" (*tozama*).[42]

A stable balance among *shugo* appointments was not easily achieved. The war between the Northern and Southern Court factions, which continued for more than fifty years after the founding of the Muromachi bakufu, encouraged flux. The *shugo* were intensely competitive and frequently switched allegiances to pursue their private interests.[43] Even Yoshimitsu was forced to put down rebellions of trusted *shugo,* among them the Akamatsu in 1383, the Yamana in 1394, and the Ōuchi in 1399. Yoshimitsu's successful termination of

42 Sugiyama, "Muromachi bakufu," pp. 58–59.

43 Ogawa Makoto, *Ashikaga ichimon shugo hatten shi no kenkyū* (Tokyo: Yoshikawa kōbunkan, 1980), presents the most insightful account of the early competition among the *shugo*.

the rift between the court factions in 1392 removed a major obstacle to the achievement of a general cooperation between the shogunate and the *shugo* of central Japan. The bakufu by that time was functioning effectively as a central government, and the *shugo* found it to be in their best interests to join with, rather than compete against, the bakufu.

Besides the shogun's capacity as chief of the warrior estate to generate superior military force, two administrative practices proved crucial to maintaining this climate of cooperation: One was the requirement that the *shugo* of the central provinces take up residence in Kyoto, and the other was the *kanrei* system of decision making. Given the difficulty of communication in fourteenth-century Japan and the lack of enforcement power in what remained of the court-based institutions of provincial administration, any would-be hegemon was dependent on direct, ideally face-to-face, contact with his subordinates to ensure that his commands were carried out.

Yoshimitsu used various combinations of military force, political manipulation, and intimidation in his efforts to keep the *shugo* in line. His military actions against the Akamatsu, Yamana, and Ōuchi have been noted. His less militant displays of power took the form of grand provincial progresses in the guise of religious pilgrimages, such as his journey in 1389 into the western provinces to visit the Itsukushima Shrine in Aki and, incidentally, to put pressure on the Ōuchi house. The private forces readily available to the shogun, though insufficient to defend unassisted against a determined attack by a major *shugo*, were large enough to turn the balance in the capital area and to impress local military houses. Of course, in the case of punishing a recalcitrant *shugo* or quelling provincial unrest, the shogun had to call on contingents from his *shugo*. The ability of a shogun to assemble mixed armies of this sort depended on his continued success in motivating a sufficient number of *shugo* to obey his commands. And to this end the *kanrei* system proved to be of great value.[44]

During the first few years of the Muromachi bakufu, Takauji and Tadayoshi had used the post of general manager (*shitsuji*) as chief administrative officer, to which a succession of hereditary retainers like Kō Moronao were assigned. In 1362 this office was upgraded and renamed *kanrei* (deputy shogun). The new post was assigned to the heads of some of the most powerful of the shogun's cadet houses in

44 Sato, with Hall, "The Ashikaga Shogun," in Hall and Toyoda, eds., *Japan in the Muromachi Age*, pp. 48–49.

hopes of pulling the *shugo* of the central bloc more closely together behind the shogun. In 1367 Hosokawa Yoriyuki was named deputy just as Yoshimitsu became shogun. Because Yoshimitsu was only thirteen years old, Yoriyuki's first years as *kanrei* resembled a regency. But unlike what happened in Kamakura after Minamoto Yoritomo's line ran out, the *kanrei* was not permitted to dominate the Ashikaga shoguns. Nor was the post of *kanrei* allowed to become monopolized by a single family until the end of the fifteenth century. Rather, it became the practice to pass the appointment among the three foremost *shugo* houses of Shiba, Hosokawa, and Hatakeyama. These houses, known as the Sankan (the three *kanrei*), among them held seventeen provinces in Yoshimitsu's day. Together they formed an inner bloc of *shugo* committed to support the Ashikaga house. The *kanrei* functioned in two directions. As head of the assembly of senior *shugo (yoriai)*, he gave to the *shugo* a sense of involvement in bakufu affairs. To the shogun, the *kanrei* was able to present the *shugo*'s points of view and advise against extreme action that they would resent.

In the early years the *shugo* were naturally preoccupied with establishing their presence in the provinces to which they had been assigned. But by the start of Yoshimitsu's rule, most of the *shugo* of the central bloc had taken up more-or-less permanent residence in Kyoto.[45] Although unlike the *sankin-kotai* requirement of the Tokugawa shogunate, *shugo* residence in Kyoto was not mandated by written precept, by the end of Yoshimitsu's rule such residence had become compulsory in practice. If a *shugo* left his Kyoto residence for his home province without the shogun's permission, it was considered tantamount to an act of rebellion. This obligation of residence in Kyoto appears to have fallen only on the *shugo* of the central provinces; the *shugo* of the Kantō bloc were expected to live in Kamakura. In western Japan, the Kyushu *tandai*, being simply another form of *shugo*, made no residence demands on the other *shugo*. But although not compelled to do so, most of the *shugo* of the Kyushu provinces built residences in Kyoto, both to keep in touch with affairs at the center and to participate in the cultural life of the capital.

Enforced residence away from their assigned provinces meant that the *shugo* themselves had to administer their provinces indirectly through subordinates. The most common practice was to establish one or more deputy *shugo (shugo-dai)* from among the *shugo*'s closest retain-

45 Masaharu Kawai, with Kenneth A. Grossberg, "Shogun and Shugo: The Provincial Aspects of Muromachi Politics," in Hall and Toyoda, eds., *Japan in the Muromachi Age*, pp. 68–69.

ers to manage local affairs in his absence. Frequently, even the deputy *shugo* was called to Kyoto, thus necessitating the appointment of a subdeputy *(shugo-matadai)*. As can be imagined, *shugo* residing in Kyoto found it difficulty to develop a reliable chain of command between capital and province. Vassal *shugo-dai* could play a critical role in either expanding and safeguarding the *shugo*'s local authority or undermining it. The problem was especially acute in situations in which the *shugo* were exercising jurisdiction over an unfamiliar province. In such cases, the *shugo* were often forced to depend on the head of a prominent local family, a *kokujin,* to serve as deputy. In many cases, these families eventually turned against their Kyoto-based superiors so as to grasp local military hegemony.[46]

Contact between *shugo* and shogun was at first personal and direct. But with the adoption of the *kanrei* system, the shogun's relations with the *shugo* were mediated through the *kanrei,* and certain decisions were made subject to the assembly of senior *shugo*. There was, of course, an inherent contradiction in a procedure that put the deputy and the assembly between the shogun and his vassal *shugo*. A strong-minded shogun, like the mature Yoshimitsu or Yoshinori, resented the restrictions this imposed on his freedom of command. The *kanrei–yoriai* system as a check on shogunal absolutism worked well up through the time of Yoshikazu, the fifth shogun. And even the sixth shogun, the strong-willed Yoshinori, was forced to accept from time to time the collective will of the *kanrei* and *yoriai*.

The third shogun, Yoshimitsu, had brought the status and power of the office to its highest level. Yet his grandiose behavior and autocratic rule were tolerated, even admired, by the *shugo,* who were themselves caught up in the heady experiences of aristocratic life in Kyoto. Yoshimitsu's two successors retreated from this autocratic posture and acknowledged a greater acceptance of the *kanrei–yoriai* system. Yoshikazu, living with the knowledge that his father, Yoshimitsu, had intended to pass over him as his heir, was not inclined to offer personal leadership to the bakufu, and so died without naming his own successor. As a result, his successor was determined by lot by the Ashikaga family council, and Yoshinori, Yoshimitsu's sixth son, was chosen. Yoshinori was at the time a mature man of thirty-four. Early in his life, with no apparent hope of becoming shogun, he had entered the priesthood, and at the time he was named shogun he was serving as chief abbot *(zasu)* of the Enryakuji and head of the Tendai sect on Mount

46 Hall, *Government and Local Power,* pp. 227–33.

Hiei. He immediately showed himself to be a leader who intended to become personally involved in bakufu affairs. He was a good politician and was determined to increase the power of the Ashikaga house.

Yoshinori's first move was to change bakufu administrative procedures by reorganizing the Corps of Administrators (*bugyōnin-shū*) and instituting what was called the shogunal hearing (*gozen-sata*).[47] Under this procedure, briefs on policy matters were prepared by the administrators and brought directly to the shogun for decision. This meant that in most instances the *kanrei* was not consulted, as evidenced by the appearance of *bugyōnin* directives that expressed the shogun's will without the customary countersignature of the *kanrei*. This change was correctly perceived as a move toward greater shogunal personal rule.[48]

Another line of action that Yoshinori pursued proved even more disquieting, for it involved the shogun's effort at directly interfering in *shugo* domestic affairs. Using his authority to approve *shugo* appointments and inheritances, Yoshinori began to manipulate the lines of succession among *shugo* houses so as to bring to Kyoto *shugo* more amenable to his direction.[49] One device in particular available to Yoshinori was his authority to enlist the lesser members of *shugo* houses into his private military force as guardsmen. Such appointments were usually of second or third sons in *shugo* families, men not normally in line for the family headship. But as a result of the personal relationship between shogun and guardsmen, the shogun was able to intervene on behalf of those he favored to ensure their succession.

This was the motivation for a series of seemingly arbitrary actions taken by Yoshinori that came to a head in 1441. In that year, the shogun appeared to be taking steps to block the appointment of Akamatsu Mitsusuke's chosen heir to the post of *shugo* in Harima and Bizen. It was to forestall this move that Mitsusuke killed Yoshinori while the shogun was being entertained in the Akamatsu residence in Kyoto. This incident, known as the Kakitsu affair, marks a turning point in Muromachi bakufu history. That a prominent *shugo* could murder the shogun who was a guest in his own house was disquieting enough but that the murderer could survive the incident and return to his provincial base without suffering an immediate punitive attack

47 Kuwayama, with Hall, "Bugyōnin," in Hall and Toyoda, eds., *Japan in the Muromachi Age*, pp. 58–61. *Tsuikahō* numbered 183, 184, 189, and 190 to 197 issued in 1428 dealt with this issue.

48 Imatani Akira, *Sengokuki no Muromachi bakufu no seikaku*, vol. 12 (Tokyo: Kadokawa shoten, 1975), pp. 154–6. 49 Arnesen, *Ouchi Family's Rule*, p. 187.

implies that there were strong feelings of sympathy for the Akamatsu leader's actions.[50] Mitsusuke, however, was finally chastized. Having fortified himself in his provincial headquarters, he fought to the finish against a shogunal army led by the Yamana, the *shugo* of several nearby provinces. The Yamana invasion was not in reluctant compliance with bakufu orders, for the Yamana had long coveted the Akamatsu provinces of Mimasaka, Bizen, and Harima. As expected, the Yamana received these provinces as a reward for Mitsusuke's destruction.

The Kakitsu incident brought an end to a brief period of what some have called "shogunal despotism." But the weakening of shogunal power did not lead to a return to *kanrei–shugo* council ascendancy either. As a result of Yoshinori's meddling, one of the three *kanrei* houses, the Shiba, was greatly weakened, and the house served as *kanrei* only once in the ensuing years. In the aftermath of the Kakitsu incident, competition over the post of *kanrei* was largely confined to the Hosokawa and Hatakeyama houses. Moreover, the nature of the post itself changed. After 1441, the post of *kanrei* carried little of its former responsibility of supporting the shogun and mediating with the *shugo*. Rather, the post was regarded as a means to exercise private influence over the bakufu. Because such influence could result in tangible benefits to both the *kanrei* and his favored *shugo*, there was a tendency for the *shugo* houses to divide into factions behind the two remaining *kanrei* houses. How this situation led to the weakening of the bakufu power base became clear during the time of Yoshimasa, the eighth shogun. But before I turn to the events of this period, I shall discuss in more detail the bakufu rule.

THE MUROMACHI BAKUFU: INSTRUMENTS OF ADMINISTRATION AND ENFORCEMENT

The Kemmu *shikimoku*, by announcing the Ashikaga's intent to follow in the footsteps of the previous regime, implicitly laid claim to whatever powers that had accrued to the post of shogun under the Hōjō regents. By 1350, the Ashikaga government had assumed a reasonably stable form in which many of the organs of administration bore the same names as used by the Kamakura shogunate. But identity in name did not necessarily mean identity in function. The Ashikaga leaders approached quite pragmatically the task of building a bakufu.

50 Sugiyama Hiroshi, "Shugo ryōgokusei no tenkai," in *Iwanami koza Nihon rekishi (chūsei 3)* (Tokyo: Iwanami shoten, 1963), pp. 109–69.

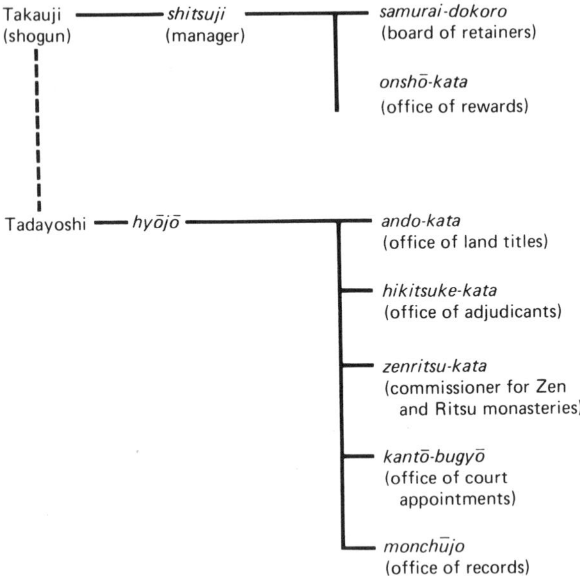

Figure 3.2 Organization of the bakufu, 1350. (Solid horizontal line indicates formal authority relationship; solid vertical line, a more or less equal formal status; and dashed line, an informal equality or division of authority.)

As of 1350, when Tadayoshi was still working closely with his brother, the organization of the bakufu followed the form outlined in Figure 3.2.[51] Satō Shin'ichi has emphasized the importance of the division of responsibility that had been worked out by the Ashikaga brothers.[52] Takauji, the elder brother, as shogun and head of the *buke* estate, assumed the direction of the bakufu organs dealing with such functions as the appointments to military posts, the distribution of rewards for military service, the enlistment of vassal followers, and the management of Ashikaga lands. Satō described these powers as basically feudal. By contrast, Tadayoshi was in charge of what Satō called the more "bureaucratic," or administrative and judicial, functions of government. Under Tadayoshi was organized the deliberative council, consisting of selected professional bureaucrats, and a number of offices that kept land records, adjudicated lawsuits, and handled relations between the bakufu and the imperial court and the religious orders.

51 Imatani, *Sengokuki*, pp. 151–81. 52 Satō, "Kaisoki," pp. 472–86.

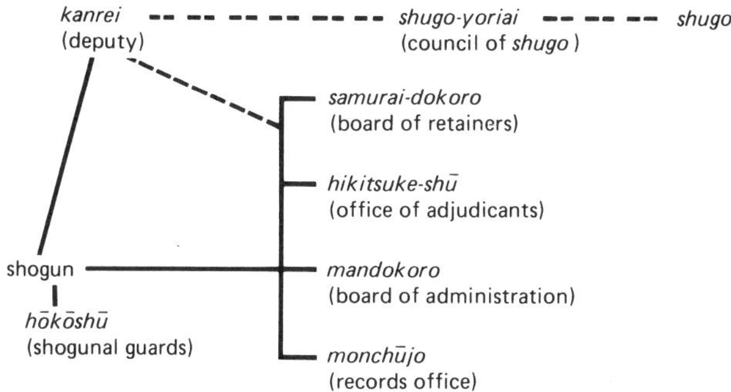

Figure 3.3 Changes in bakufu structure after Tadayoshi's expulsion, 1352. (Lines same as in Figure 3.2; double dashed line indicates an informal authority relationship.)

With Tadayoshi's expulsion from Kyoto in 1352, the bakufu structure underwent a significant change, and many of the offices inherited from Kamakura were either abolished or drastically modified in function. The most important such change, as seen in Figure 3.3, was the conversion of the office of *shitsuji* (the bakufu's chief of operations) into that of *kanrei* (deputy shogun) and the creation of the *shugo* council (*shugo yoriai*).[53]

The top of the Muromachi shogunal government was characterized by both a greater direct involvement in the affairs of state by the shogun and a more influential participation by the *shugo* houses in the decision-making process and in the bakufu administration.

The main bakufu offices with specialized functions were the Board of Retainers (*samurai-dokoro*), the Office of Adjudicants (*hikitsuke-shu*), the Board of Administration (*mandokoro*), and the Office of Records (*monchūjo*). Of these, at the outset the Board of Retainers was the most important. It alone was headed by a major *shugo* house. Charged with controlling the shogun's direct retainers, the Board of Retainers was made responsible for securing the capital area from lawlessness and administering the home province of Yamashiro. With the establishment of the office of *kanrei*, the *samurai-dokoro* lost much of its powers of control over the shogun's household retainers and over the *shugo* houses. But its administrative and judicial functions in the capital area continued to expand. The board, for instance, took over the powers of the Imperial Capital Police (*kebiishi*) and became the main police and

53 Satō, with Hall, "Muromachi Bakufu Administration," in Hall and Toyoda, eds., *Japan in the Muromachi Age*, pp. 47–49.

judicial authority in Kyoto.[54] In 1385, moreover, the chief (*shoshi*) of the Board of Retainers was given the added duty of serving as *shugo* of Yamashiro Province. It became customary to rotate this assignment among four major *shugo* houses: the Yamana, Isshiki, Akamatsu, and Kyōgoku.

The actual day-to-day running of the Board of Retainers was delegated to a deputy chief (*shoshidai*), appointed by the chief from among his own private retainers. Hence the identity of the deputy changed according to who served as chief. As a bureaucratic entity, the board was given a certain stability and continuity of operation by its permanent administrative staff, a group of individuals composed independently of the chief and his deputy, drawn from a class of hereditary administrators or professional bureaucrats, which will be described later.

Despite the many important functions of the Board of Retainers, after the Ōnin War (1467–77), it lost its central importance to the Administrative Council.[55] At first the council was almost exclusively concerned with the shogun's household and its fiscal management.[56] Its first chief officer was a hereditary administrator carried over from the Kamakura bakufu, a member of the Nikaidō house. In 1379, the Nikaidō were replaced by the Ise family, a line of hereditary retainers who, among other duties, had traditionally served as guardians of the Ashikaga shogun's heirs. The council came into its own as the bakufu's main administrative office when the shogun Yoshinori began to use it as the organ through which to bypass the *kanrei*. As the sphere of shogunal government narrowed, however, this single agency was able to handle nearly all of the shogunate's administrative functions. Moreover, as the shogun found fewer and fewer opportunities to assert political initiative, procedures in the bakufu became increasingly routinized under what Kuwayama Kōnen has called the "*bugyōnin* system."[57]

Throughout the Muromachi period there were more than fifty families of professional administrators available for service, many of whom had served the imperial court and the Kamakura bakufu. Such families were now brought into Ashikaga service because of their special

54 Haga Norihiko, "Muromachi bakufu samurai dokoro kō," in Ogawa, ed., *Muromachi seiken*, pp. 25–55.

55 Imatani, *Sengokuki*, p. 165. 56 Haga, "Samurai dokoro," p. 50.

57 Kuwayama, with Hall, "Bugyōnin," in Hall and Toyoda, eds., *Japan in the Muromachi Age*, pp. 53–54.

administrative skills. In time they formed the Corps of Administrators, the *bugyōnin-shu*. At any one time, between fifteen and sixty members might be assigned to the finance, justice, and administrative organs of the bakufu.[58] A study of the fluctuating numbers of administrators retained by the Muromachi bakufu shows that in the period before the Ōnin War, the numbers reflected the shifting balance of power between the *kanrei–yoriai* system and the shoguns' effort to exert their own influence on the bakufu. Thus the fewest numbers were in evidence under Yoshimitsu, Yoshikatsu, and Yoshimochi, all of whom followed the *kanrei* principle.[59] Yoshinori's efforts to exert his direct shogunal prerogative was reflected by an immediate increase in the size of the corps. This upward trend continued until Yoshimasa's death. Thereafter, the number of members declined, to remain at around fifteen until the end of the Muromachi bakufu. Members of the corps were drawn from the following eleven families: Iio, Suga, Saitō, Jibu, Eno, Sei, Nakazawa, Fuse, Matsuda, Yano, and Ida.

The drop in staff numbers reflected, first of all, a loss of power by the Ashikaga house and also a change in function. Perhaps because of the shogun's weakening power, the administrators increasingly became an entrenched and self-perpetuating group of families that, more than any other single factor, accounted for the continued existence of the bakufu during its last hundred years. These families became the agents through which members of the capital elite establishment dealt with one another. For instance, administrators serving as members of the Office of Adjudicants were assigned specifically to handle the affairs of important shrines like the Iwashimizu Hachiman Gū or Tsurugaoka Hachiman Gū, and great temples like the Enryakuji, Tōdaiji, Kōfukuji, Tōji, and Tenryuji. In other words, these hereditary administrators had begun to serve as agents of these institutions in case of litigation before the council, receiving retainer fees for serving as their spokesmen.[60] This was obviously a profitable arrangement. To keep it alive, it was to the advantage of all concerned to maintain the prestige of the shogun and the efficacy of the bakufu's remaining organs of adjudication. That this happened is revealed by the fact that the Ashikaga's supplementary laws continued to be issued into the

58 Haga, "Samurai dokoro," p. 27; Kuwayama, with Hall, "Bugyōnin," in Hall and Toyoda, eds., *Japan in the Muromachi Age*, pp. 56–60.

59 Kenneth A. Grossberg, "Bakufu and Bugyonin: The Size of the House Bureaucracy in Muromachi Japan," *Journal of Asian Studies* 35 (August 1976): 651–4.

60 Kuwayama, with Hall, "Bugyōnin," in Hall and Toyoda, ėds., *Japan in the Muronmachi Age*, p. 62.

1570s and that there are many records of action taken by the Office of Adjudicants in the last decades of the Ashikaga regime.[61]

But to say that the Muromachi bakufu continued to function until the mid-sixteenth century is also to say that the scope of its competence narrowed. By the time of the last shogun, the scope of the bakufu's control had been reduced almost solely to the city of Kyoto and its close environs. Control of Kyoto, in and of itself, was an important achievement, and the fact that Kyoto became subject to bakufu administration was of major significance for the Ashikaga house's staying ability.

At the time the Ashikaga established their bakufu in Kyoto, the city was still under the control of the civil and religious nobility. Takauji's claim of chieftainship of the military estate gave him the authority to exercise military, judicial, fiscal, and appointment powers over *bushi* but not over the civil elite. The organs of imperial administration that had been revived by Godaigo were soon in disarray. Yet the establishment of the Muromachi bakufu did not automatically rectify the situation.

In Kyoto the imperial house, the high court nobility, and the great religious institutions remained free to govern, through their own house staffs, their estates and other dependent groups like the merchant and craft guilds. In fact, these groups and organizations can be conceived of as a distinct power structure with remarkable staying power, to which modern historians have applied the term *kenmon seika*.[62] Essential to this condition was the maintenance of a secure capital area, a functioning judicial process, and a reasonably effective machinery for the delivery of tax payments. The chief instruments available for this were the Imperial Capital Police (*kebiishi*) and the various management systems maintained by the Kyoto-based headquarters (*honjō*) of the major civil and religious proprietary interests. In its early policy, the bakufu sought only to assist in maintaining law and order in the capital, in order to protect the provincial interests of the most important civil and religious proprietors. Kyoto was administered under what was essentially a dual polity.[63]

61 Kuwayama Kōnen, *Muromachi bakufu hikitsuke shiryō shūsei*, vol. 1 (Tokyo: Kondo shuppansha, 1980).

62 This concept, most closely associated with Kuroda Toshio, is best described in English by Suzanne Gay in "Muromachi Bakufu Rule in Kyoto: Administration and Judicial Aspects" in Mass and Hauser, eds., *Bakufu in Japanese History*, pp. 60–65.

63 Prescott B. Wintersteen, "The Early Muromachi Bakufu in Kyoto," in Hall and Mass, eds., *Medieval Japan*, p. 202.

Tension between the bakufu's Board of Retainers and the capital police was quick to develop, especially in matters of conflicting jurisdiction. The failure of the court-maintained police to carry out their duties effectively induced the bakufu to claim the need to increase its police role in the capital. And the court was inclined to agree. A court decree of 1370, noting the capital police's ineffectiveness in curbing violence against the nobility by religious bill collectors, invited the bakufu to provide assistance. Once the bakufu began enforcing the court decrees, it began also to move into the court's economic affairs. By decree in 1393 the bakufu took over the collection of dues from brewers and moneylenders.

The bakufu relied on several types of personnel to enforce its will. One already noted was the body of professional bureaucrats who served as administrators. The shogun also had at his disposal armed forces with which to ensure compliance with his decisions. Both the *kanrei* and the chief of the Board of Retainers relied on their own armed retainers to provide a military presence in the capital. Resident *shugo* also kept on hand contingents of a few hundred mounted men. In addition, the shogun and the bakufu offices not headed by *shugo* military houses could call on the services of a category of personal retainers of the shogun known as *hōkōnin* (see Maps 3.4 and 3.5).[64]

Those men for whom we might use the term *guardsmen* were direct Ashikaga retainers settled on shogunal lands (*goryōsho*) and accountable to the shogun alone. Their use was political and economic as well as military. The largest number were from lesser branches of Ashikaga cadet and nonkin *shugo* houses. Such were the Hosokawa, Hatakeyama, Isshiki, or Shiba among the cadet houses, and the Sasaki, Toki, Ogasawara, Ōuchi, and Kyōgoku, but not the Akamatsu, among the nonkin *shugo* houses. From these houses the shogun selected individuals who may have borne the same surname as the main house but who were not in line to succeed to the family headship. Another group was recruited from houses that had long served the Ashikaga as hereditary retainers. An outstanding family of this type was the Ise. Finally, some members of provincial houses rose to local prominence, the kind of military proprietor referred to as *kokujin*. The best known of such appointments was the Kobayakawa of Aki Province.[65]

64 Fukuda Toyohiko, "Muromachi bakufu no hōkōshū," *Nihon rekishi* 274 (March 1971). 46–65.

65 See the analysis of the Kobayakawa by Arnesen, "Provincial Vassals," in Mass and Hauser, eds., *Bakufu in Japanese History*, pp. 106–112.

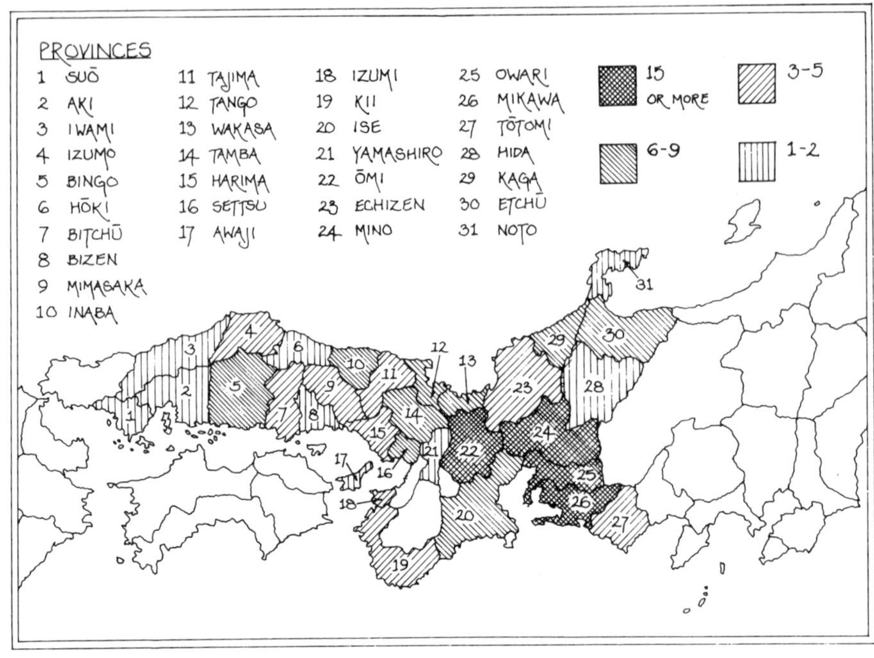

Map 3.4 Location of *hōkōnin*, 1444–9. (Shaded areas indicate number of families per province.)

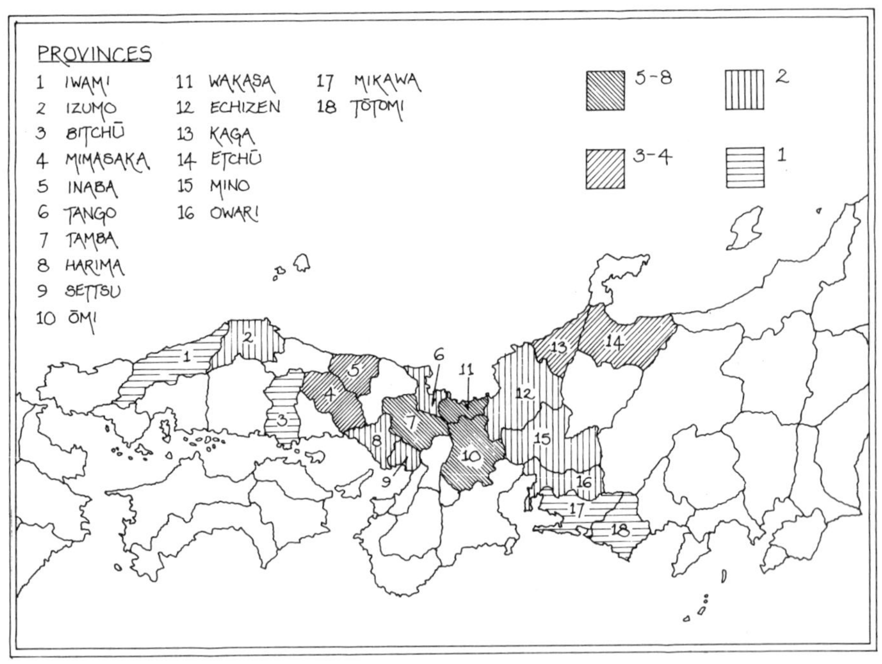

Map 3.5 Location of *hōkōnin*, 1565. (Shaded areas indicate number of families per province.)

Once they reached the capital the guardsmen were mustered into five groups (*ban*) headed by officers drawn from the Hosokawa, Hatakeyama, Momonoi, and Ōdate houses. In the 1450s, guardsmen administered holdings located in thirty-two of the forty-four provinces of central Japan. These were concentrated in the central region, stretching from Mikawa westward to Tango.[66] Interestingly, there were virtually no placements in the closest of the home provinces, such as Yamashiro, Iga, Yamato, very few in Harima, Settsu, Izumi, Kawachi, or Kii, and none at all in Shikoku. The numbers of guardsmen varied over time and circumstances. Takauji is said to have employed 30; Yoshimitsu, 290; and Yoshinori, 180. Satō Shin'ichi estimated that these numbers enabled the shogun to muster at a given time between 2,000 and 3,000 mounted fighters.[67]

All guardsmen were totally dependent on the shogun's favor for the status they held in his service. Thus the guardsmen, like the administrators, comprised an element in the bakufu that was identified with the well-being and continued existence of the Ashikaga house. Although the guardsmen did not constitute a force capable of imposing the shogun's will on even a single hostile *shugo*, in situations in which there was a balance of power, they could swing that balance in the shogun's favor or, as in the years of the Ōnin War, help maintain the shogun's neutrality.

BAKUFU FISCAL AND MANPOWER SUPPORTS

Historians have sought to explain the economic foundations of the Muromachi bakufu in terms of land and landed income. It is troublesome, therefore, not to be able to draw a clear picture of the bakufu's landholdings that might account for the shogunate's fiscal operation. It is on the basis of only a single document in the Kuramochi archives that it is known that as of around 1300 the Ashikaga possessed some thirty holdings (*goryōsho*) located in twelve widely scattered provinces. Beyond this, there is almost no information on what happened to this portfolio in subsequent years. No effort to document a continuous analysis of Ashikaga landholdings has yet succeeded. This failure is partially a result of insufficient diligence on the part of historians and not on the absolute lack of documentation. In the last few years, for

66 Fukuda Toyohiko, "Muromachi bakufu hōkōshū no kenkyū: sono jin'in to chiikiteki bumpu," in Ogawa, ed., *Muromachi seiken*, p. 231.

67 Satō Shin'ichi, "Muromachi bakufu ron," in *Iwanami kōza Nihon rekishi* (*chūsei* 2) (Tokyo: Iwanami shoten, 1963), p. 22.

instance, the number of identifiable Ashikaga holdings at the end of the fourteenth century has risen from sixty to some two hundred, as reported by Kuwayama Kōnen.[68] And the count is still rising. But how these items came into existence, how they related to earlier holdings, and what their fiscal value was is not at all clear. All the evidence so far has had to be extrapolated from documents that were not drafted to answer such questions directly.

First, as a result of its defeat of the Hōjō, the Ashikaga house's estates were presumably augmented by a package of forty-five pieces in twenty provinces given to Takauji and Tadayoshi by Godaigo. Recent studies have confirmed the retention of a number of these holdings into the 1390s, but not much beyond.[69] A list of sixty holdings dating from shortly before the end of the fifteenth century does not coincide with earlier lists. Clearly, there was a great deal of movement in the bakufu's land base.

The latest scholarship suggests that the search for a "land base" to explain the finances of the Ashikaga house has put its emphasis in the wrong place.[70] The Ashikaga did not create, as did the Tokugawa house, a large bloc of centrally administered lands from which revenues were collected to benefit central bakufu storehouses. Rather, it was the practice to assign landholdings to others to be administered on behalf of the bakufu and also as a means of private support. By far the greatest portion of the *goryōsho* appears to have been allotted in this way to members of the guards. Such grants tended to become hereditary possessions. But up to the end of the regime, the close relationship between the shogun and his provincial housemen guaranteed at least some return to the shogun from this practice.

Fortunately, there are three sets of documents covering the activities of the shogunal guards for the years 1444 to 1449, 1450 to 1455, and 1487 to 1489. Fukuda Toyohiko, in his careful study of these documents, concludes with the following table (Table 3.3), in which he lists the number of guardsmen holdings, by province.[71] In this table he offers two sets of figures based on the three sets of documents, Column I being a more conservative count than Column II. Column III is based on a roster of guards under Shogun Yoshiteru before his death in 1565 (see Maps 3.4 and 3.5).

The lists of guardsmen's holdings demonstrate graphically the shift-

68 Kuwayama Kōnen, "Muromachi bakufu keizai no kōzō," in *Nihon keizaishi taikei (chūsei 2)* (Tokyo: Tōkyō daigaku shuppankai, 1965), pp. 193–9. 69 Kuwayama, "Sōsōki," p. 18.
70 Imatani, "Sengokuki," pp. 18–22; Kuwayama, "Keizai no kōzō," pp. 219–20.
71 Fukuda, "Hōkōshū," p. 231.

TABLE 3.3
Guardsmen holdings by province

Province	I	II	III
Ōmi	21	25	8
Mikawa	17	44	1
Owari	16	19	2
Mino	15	30	2
Tango	9	18	2
Etchū	9	10	3
Kaga	9	10	4
Wakasa	8	9	7
Tamba	7	11	5
Ise	7	9	–
Inaba	7	9	3
Bingo	7	7	–
Settsu	6	7	2
Mimasaka	5	9	3
Harima	5	6	2
Izumo	5	5	2
Echizen	5	5	2
Tōtōmi	4	6	1
Bitchū	3	4	1
Tajima	3	3	–
Izumi	3	3	–
Kii	3	3	–
Aki	2	4	–
Noto	2	3	–
Yamashiro	2	2	–
Iwami	1	2	–
Suō	1	2	–
Hida	1	1	–
Awaji	1	1	–
Hōki	1	1	–
Bizen	1	1	–
Kawachi	–	1	–
	186	270	50

ing distribution of the bakufu's provincial connections. It is surprising to find such a large number of holdings up to and after the Ōnin War and even more surprising to note how many remained as late as 1565. Of course, distribution alone tells us little about the nature and size of revenues that the bakufu derived from these lands. A number of scattered case studies, however, indicate the pattern of estate management of the *goryōsho* by the guardsmen.

The guards normally resided in Kyoto, and so like the *shugo*, they were obliged to entrust local administration to deputies (*daikan*). A document of about 1450, referring to a *shōen* in Etchū Province, is typical.[72] Out of a total annual tax assessment of 780 *kan*, 340 *kan* were lost through poor harvest and the illegal encroachment of neighbors, leaving 430 *kan* as the reduced tax base. Of this, one-fifth (86 *kan*) was absorbed for managerial services by the guard and his agents, and another one-fifth was spent in transportation fees, leaving three-fifths (250 *kan*) for delivery to the bakufu. No claim can be made that a hard-and-fast rule of one-fifth for the guardsmen and three-fifths for the shogun was enforced. But clearly, besides guard duty the guards were expected to facilitate the delivery of a tangible amount of income to the bakufu. Because these holdings, as seen in Column III, tended increasingly to cluster near the capital, the capacity of the Kyoto-based guards to hold on to them and to derive income from them for their own support and for that of the shogun was relatively high.

Yet another category of land that could benefit the shogun were those that had been donated to patronized temples, like the Gozan. Many properties that the shogun gave to temples as pious gestures were in later years called on to help support the bakufu. In certain locations it appears that members of the Zen monasteries' fiscal administrations, the *tōhanshū*, served as managers of lands that were held in a manner not unlike the regular *goryōsho*.[73]

The fiscal base of the Muromachi bakufu was not limited to income from the *goryōsho*. A growing portion was derived as a consequence of the shogun's authority to levy taxes on special groups and activities in the city of Kyoto and the commercial community at large.

One feature of the Muromachi bakufu's fiscal structure was that several bakufu agencies were supported by direct endowments in land or in rights to income for specific services rendered. For example, as the Administrative Council took over more of the burden of administration in Kyoto, sources of support were sought within the city. In turning to this "inner" source of income, the bakufu took advantage of the urban commercial tax base that had been the historical preserve of the civil and religious aristocracy. One of the main sources of such income came from the categories of merchants known as *sakaya* (saké brewers) and *dosō* (storehouse keepers). The right of the capital police to tax these organizations had been recognized for years on the basis that those responsible for maintaining law and order in the city should be supported by the recipients of this protection. The practice began with the collection of special contributions for special events, such as

72 Morisue Yumiko, "Muromachi bakufu goryōsho ni kansuru ichi kōsatsu," in Ogawa, ed., *Muromachi seiken*, pp. 254–5. 73 Imatani, *Sengokuki*, pp. 11–60.

imperial enthronement ceremonies or the rebuilding of temples and palaces. A levy in 1371, to cover the enthronement expenses of Emperor Goenyu, imposed a payment of thirty *kan* per warehouse and two hundred *mon* in cash per vat on the breweries. In 1393, having taken over control of the city's administration, the bakufu made imposts of this kind a regular practice. The 1393 order issued from the council refers to a figure of six thousand *kan* as the amount customarily paid to the monks of the Enryakuji and states that this now should come to the bakufu.[74]

Kuwayama suggests an even closer relationship between the *mandokoro* and the *dosō*. The latter were at first not so much moneylenders as storehouse keepers, whose fireproof storage houses were used for safekeeping by the aristocracy. Later, as an extension of such a service, *dosō* began to serve as fiscal managers, extending credit on the basis of stored goods. *Dosō* also appear to have been appointed as officials of the shogun's treasury (*kubō mikura*). Hence they became both the objects of taxation and the means of tax collection.[75] The bakufu in time developed a number of other commercial and transport taxes derived from the patronage of merchant guilds, the establishment of toll barriers on highways, and the sponsorship of foreign trade. The importance of trade with Ming China to the political, cultural, and economic life of Muromachi Japan has been dealt with extensively elsewhere. It has been suggested that in addition to the "enormous profits" derived from it, the trade gave to the bakufu monopoly control over the Chinese coins imported into Japan and thereby a status equivalent to that of a central mint.[76] But the various benefits that accrued to the bakufu from this trade are still not wholly understood.

Another complex area of bakufu and shogunal house income pertains to revenues derived from the shogun's aristocratic and military status. For instance, the shogun could count on the support of his *shugo* vassals for both military and nonmilitary assistance. For a given military action, it was generally the responsibility of one or more *shugo* to mobilize private forces on the shogun's behalf. Of course, this meant the prospect of tangible reward if the action proved successful. The 1441 Yamana attack on the Akamatsu referred to earlier is a case

74 Prescott B. Wintersteen, "The Early Muromachi Bakufu in Kyoto," in Hall and Mass, eds., *Medieval Japan*, pp. 208–9.

75 Kuwayama Kōnen, "Muromachi bakufu keizai kikō no ichi kōsatsu, nōsen-kata kubō okura no kinō to seiritsu," *Shigaku zasshi* 73 (September 1964). 9–17.

76 Takeo Tanaka, with Robert Sakai, "Japan's Relations with Overseas Countries," in Hall and Toyoda, eds., *Japan in the Muromachi Age*, p. 170.

in point. As a result of the successful campaign, Yamana was made *shugo* of two provinces vacated by the Akamatsu.

In the area of nonmilitary expeditions, the shogun had the right to requisition from his *shugo* contributions for public works, such as the building of shogunal residences. The 1437 requisition of ten thousand *kan* for the shogun's residence was imposed differentially on *shugo* according to the number and size of the provinces that each held. The impost was distributed among twenty-two *shugo* on the basis of two hundred *kan* for those who held only one province and one thousand *kan* for houses holding three or more. Other forms of contribution from *shugo* were the standard practice that *shugo* build their residences in Kyoto, that they maintain their own armed forces of from three hundred to five hundred horsemen, and that when appointed to a bakufu office, such as the Board of Retainers, they staff their offices with their own men. One notable example is the case of Ashikaga Yoshimasa's project to build the Higashiyama villa, the central structure of which was the Silver Pavilion (Ginkaku). The actual fund raising began in 1481, only four years after the termination of the Ōnin War. Yet *shugo* were dunned for contributions as part of their duty toward the shogun. Despite the war-torn condition of the country, the money was collected. As Kawai Masaharu writes, the shogun himself was a person of charismatic prestige who could still expect support of this kind even in the aftermath of a ten-year war that he himself had brought on. It remained a matter of political value for an aspiring provincial daimyo to contribute toward, or build himself, palaces for the *tennō* or shogun in the capital.[77]

Another source of income for the shogun resulted from his powers of appointment. Among aristocratic circles it was standard practice for those appointed to a high court or temple rank by the shogun to pay him a gratuity. Imatani Akira estimates that the flow of treasure into the bakufu coffers from this practice was a major source of support for the bakufu, especially in its declining years. The income from appointments alone has been estimated at 3,600 *kanmon* annually.[78] Of course, this flow of wealth within elite circles was not all in one direction. The shogun himself was obligated to give gifts and to contribute funds for the building of palaces and temples and for the performance of various rituals such as imperial enthronements and funerals. In such situations the shogun was more apt to use his powers to require national compli-

77 Kawai Masaharu, *Ashikaga Yoshimasa* (Tokyo: Shimizu shoin, 1972), pp. 147–50.
78 Martin Collcutt, *Five Mountains: The Rinzai Zen Monastic Institution in Medieval Japan* (Cambridge, Mass.: Harvard University Press, 1981), pp. 235.

ance with bakufu requisitions rather than to draw funds himself from the bakufu's stores.[79] Such requisitions generally took the form of a provincewide *tansen* tax.

For much of the Muromachi period, *tansen* represented a major source of income for the bakufu, to the point that the Administrative Council (*mandokoro*) maintained an officer in charge of *tansen* revenues. The *hōkōshū* were used as collecting agents in the provinces. The picture that emerges, therefore, is one in which land, by being dispersed as private enfeoffments, served mainly to support the many families and institutions that constituted the "governing establishment." The resources that powered the actual functions of government appear to have come from general taxes, like *tansen*, whose collection depended on the continuing prestige of the Ashikaga house as a charismatic entity within what essentially was a structure inherited from the imperial bureaucracy.

THE LAST HUNDRED YEARS

The final century of Muromachi bakufu rule has given historians a number of difficult interpretive problems. During these years the bakufu was obviously in decline, and the shogun was increasingly inconsequential as a political force. In fact, Japanese historians commonly divide the time from the outbreak of the Ōnin War in 1467 until Oda Nobunaga's entrance into Kyoto in 1568, as the Sengoku period, the era of warring provinces, thus shifting the main focus of their attention from the capital and the shogun to the provinces where the daimyo successors to the *shugo* fought among themselves for territorial hegemony. But it is increasingly apparent that the ground swell of change in Japanese government and society that took place in the years following the Ōnin War should not be described simply in terms of denouement or breakdown. The bakufu, as separate from the shogun as person, did retain a function throughout the last hundred years. And although these were times of instability, they gave rise to the structures and institutions that were to support a new, and in many ways revolutionary, centralized order.[80]

Although the political and social order of the mid-Muromachi period may have appeared to differ fundamentally from what it had been

79 Nagahara, "Zen-kindai," pp. 39–40.

80 Mitsuru Miyagawa, with Cornelius J. Kiley, "From Shōen to Chigyō: Proprietory Lordship and the Structure of Local Power," in Hall and Toyoda, eds., *Japan in the Muromachi Age*, pp. 89–105.

at the end of the Kamakura era, the main premises on which Japanese government rested remained basically unchanged. Despite the "encroachment of military government" on civil authority, the polity at large, the *tenka,* was still conceived as before. The same touchstones of legitimation were recognized, and authority was still regarded as a legal right granted or justified from above.

But by the end of the fifteenth century, this order was being challenged by the appearance of groups or communities that sought, from the higher central authority, autonomy in their local affairs. At the upper level, this took the form of "*kokujin* lordships" (*zaichi ryōshu)* whereby local *buke* families became the sole proprietors of their own lands, managing to protect themselves from higher authority by their own strength of arms or by the formation of leagues or compacts (*ikki*) with neighboring *kokujin.* At first, these compacts were small in scale, but as in the case of Aki Province, some were able to counter the interference of both the bakufu and neighboring *shugo.* The revolutionary aspect of such compacts was that they were organized on the basis of territory and were held together by mutual agreement for the purpose of self-defense. By the end of the fifteenth century, local military lords emerged out of the ranks of *kokujin,* many of them heads of *ikki* leagues, whose territory was made large enough to give them the status of daimyo. This, as Kawai has shown, was a major impetus for the formation of the so-called *sengoku* daimyo.[81]

Unlike the *shugo* daimyo whose legitimacy was derived from the bakufu, the *sengoku* daimyo drew their primary authority from their ability to exercise power and to maintain local control over the other *kokujin* and peasant communities within their sphere of command. They might on occasion, however, declare themselves successors to *shugo* or other provincial officials. But their main reliance, besides their own military strength, was on their capacity to secure the loyalty of their military followers and to convince the other inhabitants of their territories of their ability, or at least intent, to work for the good of the territorial community. This situation was reflected in the large body of legal codes issued by *sengoku* daimyo, in which the daimyo territory was conceived of as an organic entity, a *kokka,* over which the daimyo exercised public authority (*kōgi*).[82]

81 Kawai, with Grossberg, "Shogun and Shugo," pp. 80–83.
82 Shizuo Katsumata, with Martin Collcutt, "The Development of Sengoku Law," in John Whitney Hall, Keiji Nagahara, and Kozo Yamamura, eds., *Japan Before Tokugawa: Political Consolidation and Economic Growth, 1500–1650* (Princeton, N.J.: Princeton University Press, 1981), pp. 114–17.

The trend toward local autonomy was evident at the lower levels of Japanese society as well, as the cultivator class underwent a major transformation during the late Muromachi period.[83] One aspect of this was the increased freedom won by agricultural villages to organize their lives according to the community's desire. This was reflected in the appearance of village assemblies *(yoriai)* and village-established codes for internal regulation. It was reflected further in the success of some communities in winning from higher authority the rights to water use, autonomy of internal administration, and adjudication of disputes. Some even earned the right of immunity from entrance by officials of higher authority, as long as an agreed-upon annual tax was delivered. Many of these concessions were won by the use of the only weapons the villages possessed: the organization of village compacts and mass demonstrations, both called *ikki*. It was in this context of local unrest that the incipient daimyo of the Sengoku age recognized the need to accommodate the demands of the peasantry and thus declared themselves the protectors of all classes within their realms (*kokka*). By professing their regard for the common good, they claimed the right to govern their territory on the strength of the support they received from those they governed. Thus they invoked a new legitimacy, not derived from *tennō* or shogun, but established by the implied consent of the public will. This was the making of a new rationale for government, a radically new *tenka*.[84]

Although these changes were taking place in the provinces, their full impact did not reach the capital region until after the mid-sixteenth century. The capital and the surrounding agricultural lands in the provinces of Yamashiro, Ōmi, Kawachi, Settsu, and Yamato and a few other locations made up a central region that retained its own configuration throughout the last century of Ashikaga rule. And in this region in which the economy and society were still dominated by the interests of the court nobility and the central religious orders, the bakufu still had a role to play. During the last century, though the bakufu may have lost its ability to affect national affairs, it still was an important mechanism through which the noble houses, the great temples, and the wealthy merchant houses integrated their interests. Thus the bakufu continued to adjudicate disputes and to issue decrees until 1579.[85]

83 Keiji Nagahara, with Kozo Yamamura, "Village Communities and Daimyo Power," in Hall and Toyoda, eds., *Japan in the Muromachi Age*, pp. 107–23.

84 Ibid., pp. 121–3.

85 Ashikaga legislation, as revealed in the supplementary orders (*tsuikahō*), increasingly narrowed its scope to the capital city and its environs. See items 400–530 (1520–1570) in *Kemmu Shikimoku and Tsuikahō*, pp. 145–64.

The event that so dramatically started the downward slide of the Muromachi bakufu was the "War of Ōnin and Bummei," (1467–77), usually referred to simply as "Ōnin." A war that involved nearly all of the *shugo* houses of central Japan, it was doubly destructive because it was fought out in the streets of Kyoto. The issue that brought on the war was a conflict between the Hosokawa and Yamana families over the choice of heir to the shogun Yoshimasa. In the fighting, much of central Kyoto and the northern fringe of the city was destroyed, and many courtiers and priests fled the capital for the provinces. The shogun Yoshimasa remained aloof, maintaining his usual standard of aristocratic life.

If Yoshimitsu emerges in Muromachi history as the heroic model of the noble military ruler, Yoshimasa is generally pictured as the tragic ruler whose effete behavior brought on the declining fortunes of the ruling house.[86] Yoshimasa, the second son of the murdered Yoshinori, was named shogun in 1443 at the age of eight. Being a minor at the time, he was placed under the guardianship of the *kanrei,* Hosokawa Katsumoto. He was declared of age in 1449 and served as shogun until 1473, when he retired in favor of his son Yoshihisa. He lived on until 1489. In Yoshimasa's early years the bakufu had still not recovered from the shock inflicted by the murder of the shogun in 1441. At the same time, the country as a whole was suffering from acute economic problems. Rural mobs frequently broke into the capital, demanding relief from debts and taxation and forcing the bakufu to issue debt cancellation edicts (*tokusei-rei*). Widespread famine conditions during the 1450s led to death by famine in parts of Japan. Yet Yoshimasa and his *kuge* and *buke* colleagues engaged in politics as usual, building costly residences and bickering over court preferment and family inheritance. In 1458, Yoshimasa rebuilt the shogunal palace at great expense.

Meanwhile, political tension among the *shugo* was building up to the point of general warfare.[87] Yet during the fighting that started in 1467, Yoshimasa built a special residential palace for his mother. He had started in 1465 a retirement residence in the eastern foothills but had dropped the project when war broke out in Kyoto. In 1482, however, he began in earnest to build the Higashiyama villa that was to contain his monument, the Silver Pavilion (Ginkaku). In 1483, Yoshimasa moved to Higashiyama where he lived out his life as a patron of the arts, setting a style that was to leave an enduring mark on Japanese cultural history.

86 Kawai, *Ashikaga Yoshimasa,* offers the most complete modern biography.
87 Iikura Kiyotake, "Ōnin no ran ikō ni okeru Muromachi bakufu no seisaku," *Nihonshi kenkyū* (1974). 139–51.

By the end of the Ōnin War, most *shugo* had abandoned Kyoto and returned to their provinces to consolidate their forces. Kyoto itself was no longer a source of power for them. That was to be found in the provinces. As the *shugo* belatedly returned their attention to their provincial bases, most found that the times had already passed them by. Their vassals, being close to the real sources of military support and having for many years served as deputies for their Kyoto-based and increasingly remote *shugo* overlords, were showing signs of insubordination. Under these conditions, only the provincial daimyo domainal lord could survive. *Shugo* houses either were forced to adapt to these conditions or were quickly displaced by stronger provincial leaders. From this point on, affairs in the capital were conditioned on the struggle for power in the provinces.

But the capital and its government, the bakufu, retained some of its importance.[88] Although the last four or five shoguns had no personal power, the Hosokawa family that monopolized the office of *kanrei* managed to give a certain stability to the capital area, at least until the 1530s. During the Ōnin War, the *bugyōnin* had sided with the Hosokawa cause, and after the end of the fighting they remained cooperative with the Hosokawa. The pattern displayed in these years, in which a figurehead aristocratic house was kept alive by provincial military leaders as a means of acquiring national influence, was not new to Japanese history. The story of the last shogun, Yoshiaki, the emperor Ōgimachi, and the rising military hegemon, Oda Nobunaga, reveals how a "puppet shogun" could prove useful and yet cause trouble for his puppeteer.[89]

By the 1560s, the aristocratic houses of Kyoto were faced with more than the usual crises. The last *kanrei*, Hosokawa Ujitsuna, had been ousted by former vassals, the Miyoshi and the Matsunaga. In 1565, this group had assassinated the shogun, Ashikaga Yoshiteru, and had substituted Ashikaga Yoshihide as their puppet shogun. Another potential heir to the Ashikaga shogunate, Yoshiaki, at the time abbot of a subtemple of the Kōfukuji, escaped to the east to find support for his own cause. Oda Nobunaga seemed a likely candidate on whom to rely. Although still unproven as a national leader, he had had a string of notable military successes, especially the defeat in 1560 of a great army led by Imagawa Yoshimoto of Suruga. By 1565, Nobunaga was being

88 Ibid., pp. 142–3.
89 The remainder of what follows relies on Hisashi Fujiki, with George Elison, "The Political Posture of Oda Nobunaga," in Hall, Nagahara, and Yamamura, eds., *Japan Before Tokugawa*, pp. 49–93.

courted by both *tennō* and shogunal claimants to offer his military support on their behalf. Nobunaga responded to these offers in 1568, entering the capital in force "in the interest of" the emperor and "as champion for" Ashikaga Yoshiaki.

Once Nobunaga was in control of the city, the emperor, Ōgimachi, named Yoshiaki as the shogun and gave orders that both Yoshiaki and Nobunaga aid in the restoration of the estates lost by the imperial family. Nobunaga's status was left uncertain, but it appears that Yoshiaki wished to name him as *kanrei*. Had Nobunaga accepted this appointment, he would have become a party to a return to the triangular balance of power that had existed among *tennō*, shogun, and *kanrei* a century or so earlier. But Nobunaga refused to subordinate himself to the shogun. He rejected the offer and instead attempted to dominate the shogun through sheer force. From what transpired during the next few years, it is clear that the shogun was not powerless in such a situation. He could still count on the services of the Ashikaga house retainers, the civil administrators, and the guardsmen. The bakufu continued functioning as a legal office, affirming land grants and inheritances. Moreover, through his staff, the shogun still exercised considerable behind-the-scenes influence by playing factional politics among the provincial daimyo.

In early 1573, Yoshiaki sent out letters to nearby daimyo and religious institutions hostile to Nobunaga, calling for military action against him. He took refuge in a fortification south of Kyoto and waited for developments. Nobunaga made short work of the shogun's move. Yoshiaki was defeated, but not killed, and was allowed to live out his life in exile. But for all intents and purposes, the Ashikaga shogun and the Muromachi bakufu had ceased to exist.

Within a week after disposing of Yoshiaki, Nobunaga managed to have the emperor change the era name to Tensho as a sign of legitimation for a new political order. Nobunaga's *tenka* differed fundamentally from that of the Ashikaga shoguns. Yoshimitsu's or Yoshimasa's *tenka* had envisioned a fusion of *kuge* and *buke* rule conducted through the provincial administration of the shogun's *shugo* vassals. But by the time of Yoshiaki, the Ashikaga mandate to rule had been reduced to the narrowest of private interests, the shogun's simple desire to stay alive. Against this, Nobunaga was able to pose a broader conception of *tenka,* one that included a place for not only the *kuge* and *buke* but also the common people. It was this larger *tenka* that Yoshiaki proved unfit to govern.

CHAPTER 4

THE *BAKUHAN* SYSTEM

The political structure established by the Tokugawa house in the early years of the seventeenth century is now commonly referred to as the *bakuhan* system (*bakuhan taisei*). This term, coined by modern Japanese historians, recognizes the fact that under the Edo bakufu, or shogunate, government organization was the result of the final maturation of the institutions of shogunal rule at the national level and of daimyo rule at the local level.[1] Although Tokugawa Ieyasu became shogun in 1603, it was not until the years of the dynasty's third shogun, Iemitsu, that the Edo bakufu reached its stable form, that is, not until the 1630 and 1640s. And it took another several decades before the *han*, or daimyo domains, completed their evolution as units of local governance.[2] Scholars now agree, however, that most of the institutional components of the *bakuhan* system had made their initial appearance under the first two of the "three great unifiers," Oda Nobunaga and Toyotomi Hideyoshi.

This chapter will trace the formation and the evolution of the *bakuhan* structure of government from the middle of the sixteenth century to the end of the eighteenth century. Because the following chapters will treat separately the daimyo domains as units of local administration, the primary emphasis of this chapter will be the Edo shogunate and the nationwide aspects of the *bakuhan* system. As noted in the introduction to this volume, historians increasingly identify the broader dimensions of shogunal rule by using the concept of *kokka* (nation or state) to replace *taisei* (system), thus coining the expression

1 The use of the term *bakuhan* is essentially a post–World War II phenomenon, although the pioneers in this field had begun to conceive of Edo government as a dyarchy by the late 1930s. See Itō Tasaburō, "Bakuhan taisei ron," in *Shin Nihonshi kōza* (Tokyo: Chūō kōronsha, 1947); and Nakamura Kichiji, *Nihon hōkensei saihenseishi* (Tokyo: Mikasa shobō, 1940).

2 The new interest in the daimyo domain was also led by the two scholars cited in footnote 1. After the war the field was introduced by Fujino Tamotsu, in his *Bakuhan taiseishi no kenkyū* (Tokyo: Yoshikawa kōbunkan, 1961); and by Kanai Madoka, *Hansei* (Tokyo: Shinbundō, 1962). Harold Bolitho describes in greater detail the emergence of the *han* studies field in Chapter 5 in this volume.

bakuhansei-kokka (the *bakuhan* state).[3] Though not explicitly adopting this usage, this chapter will treat the Edo shogunate as a total national polity, not simply as a narrowly defined political system.

The political and social institutions that underlay the *bakuhan* polity had their origins in the "unification movement" of the last half of the sixteenth century, especially in the great feats of military consolidation and social engineering achieved by Toyotomi Hideyoshi during the last two decades of the century.[4] Although neither Nobunaga nor Hideyoshi became shogun, they succeeded in advancing to absolute proportions the capacity to rule over the daimyo and other political bodies that comprised the Japanese nation. In the parlance of the day they succeeded in winning the *tenka* (the realm) and serving as its *kōgi* (its ruling authority).[5] At the same time however, the daimyo enhanced their own powers of private control over their local domains (their *kokka* in a limited local sense), borrowing support from the very central authority that sought to constrain them. The most significant feature of the resulting national polity was that unification was carried only so far. The daimyo domains, though giving up a portion of their hard-won autonomy, managed to survive as part of the system.[6]

Tokugawa Ieyasu and his immediate successors brought to its fullest development the bakufu system of rule under a military hegemon. But despite the preponderance of military power that the Tokugawa shoguns held, their legal status was not qualitatively different from that of the fifteenth-century Muromachi shoguns. On the other hand, the powers exercised by the daimyo within their domains had expanded tremendously since the time of the Muromachi military governors, the *shugo* daimyo. In fact it was probably in the *han* that the machinery of centralized bureaucratic administration proceeded the farthest. In many instances the Edo shogunate based its governing practices on

3 See the treatment of this approach to Japanese political history by Sasaki Junnosuke in "Bakuhansei kokka ron," in Araki Moriaki et al., comps., *Taikei Nihon kokka shi* (*kinsei* 3) (Tokyo: Tōkyō daigaku shuppankai, 1975).

4 For a recent overview in English of Hideyoshi's social policies, see Bernard Susser, "The Toyotomi Regime and the Daimyo," in Jeffrey P. Mass and William B. Hauser, eds., *The Bakufu in Japanese History* (Stanford, Calif.: Stanford University Press, 1985), pp. 128–52. For greater detail, see Mary Elizabeth Berry, *Hideyoshi* (Cambridge, Mass.: Harvard University Press, 1982).

5 A penetrating treatment of these terms appears in Chapter 2 in this volume. For the early use of these terms by the large regional daimyo of the sixteenth century, see Shizuo Katsumata, with Martin Collcutt, "The Development of Sengoku Law," in John Whitney Hall, Keiji Nagahara and Kozo Yamamura, eds., *Japan Before Tokugawa: Political Consolidation and Economic Growth, 1500–1650* (Princeton, N.J.: Princeton University Press, 1981), pp. 119–24.

6 The previously cited symposium by Mass and Hauser on bakufu rule is a pioneer effort to analyze the evolution of military government in historical–structural terms.

techniques adopted from times when the head of the Tokugawa line was simply one of many daimyo competing for local supremacy in central Japan. In analyzing the creation of the Edo bakufu, then, we must deal with two separate but interrelated strands of institutional development. And it is this that is suggested by the term *bakuhan*.

THE TOKUGAWA HOUSE AND ITS RISE TO POWER

The story of the rise of the Tokugawa family to become the foremost military house of Japan follows a pattern common among a whole class of active regional military families who competed for local dominion during the fifteenth and sixteenth centuries.[7] The stages of growth, from local estate manager (*jitō*) to small independent military lord (*kunishū*), to minor regional overlord (daimyo), and then to the status of major regional hegemon were typical of the day. As of the 1550s, there were daimyo leaders in almost every region of Japan poised to contest the national *tenka*. Why Ieyasu rather than another of his peers managed to gain the prize, rested, no doubt, on his native ability and on such unpredictable factors as the length of his life (he lived to be seventy-three), his ability to father capable sons (he had eleven), and the location of his original power base. The Mikawa–Owari region was clearly one of the more favorable locations from which to take and hold the imperial capital. It was the starting point for all three of the unifiers.

The Tokugawa house genealogy as officially adopted by Ieyasu in 1600 claimed descent from the most prestigious of military lineages, the Seiwa Genji, through the branch line begun by Nitta Yoshishige (1135–1202). The originator of the Nitta line took his name from the locality in the province of Kōzuke to which he was first assigned as estate manager. In the generations that followed, the Nitta line branched, giving rise to numerous sublines, each of which followed the custom of adopting the name of its residential base as its identifying surname. One such branch took the name Tokugawa from the village of that name in the Nitta district of Kōzuke. Eight generations later the head of this Tokugawa family is presumed to have left Kōzuke and established himself as the adoptive head of the Matsu-

7 Among the large number of narrative histories on the rise of the Tokugawa house, I have relied on Tsuji Tatsuya's *Edo kaifu,* vol. 4 of *Nihon no rekishi* (Tokyo: Chūō kōronsha, 1966); and Kitajima Masamoto, *Edo bakufu,* vol. 16 of *Nihon no rekishi* (Tokyo: Shōgakkan, 1975). An outstanding scholarly analysis of the establishment of the Tokugawa hegemony can be found in the work of Kitajima Masamoto, notably his *Edo bakufu no kenryoku kōzō* (Tokyo: Iwanami shoten, 1964).

daira family, chiefs of a village bearing the same name in neighboring Mikawa Province. According to the official genealogy, Ieyasu was the ninth head of this Matsudaira line, and it was he who in 1566 petitioned the Kyoto court to recognize a change of surname to Tokugawa. See Figure 4.1.

There are numerous questions about the authenticity of the official Tokugawa family descent chart, particularly in the Kōzuke years. In premodern society, pedigree played an essential role in the establishment of a family's political status. Descent from noble lineage, whether or not supported by authentic documentation, was commonly claimed by local members of the provincial warrior aristocracy. When such families reached national importance, the need to prove genealogical correctness became critical. In Ieyasu's own case, not only did he change his surname, he also for a time kept two descent charts, thus keeping open a choice of two pedigrees, one tied to the Fujiwara (the foremost court family) and the other to the Minamoto (one of the primary military lineages). His decision to settle for the Minamoto was taken in the wake of his victory at Sekigahara in 1600, when the possibility of becoming shogun seemed within his grasp.

Whether the Kōzuke years recorded in the official genealogy are to be taken seriously is not of great consequence. In fact, most recent studies of the Tokugawa house begin with the Mikawa years, starting roughly from the middle of the fifteenth century. Only then do the sources permit a reasonably reliable account. We begin, then, at a time in Japanese history when the old order that had been maintained by the Muromachi shoguns and their provincial agents, the *shugo* daimyo, was being challenged. A new generation of provincial military lords was on the rise. These Sengoku daimyo, as they have been called, built up tightly knit housebands of increasing size and military effectiveness. The strength of these organizations lay in the closeness of the lord–vassal relationships that held the housebands together. Other than the steady increase in the size of these organizations, the most visible index of the growth of these new organizations could be seen in the nature of their military establishments.

Village samurai were distinguished from common cultivators by their possession of proprietary lordships and residences protected by rudimentary moats and earthen embankments. As fighting became more technologically advanced, these local warrior families took to building small fortifications, usually on the ridges of nearby hills, in which the local chief and his band of followers could take shelter and hold off predators. During the sixteenth century these little "hill cas-

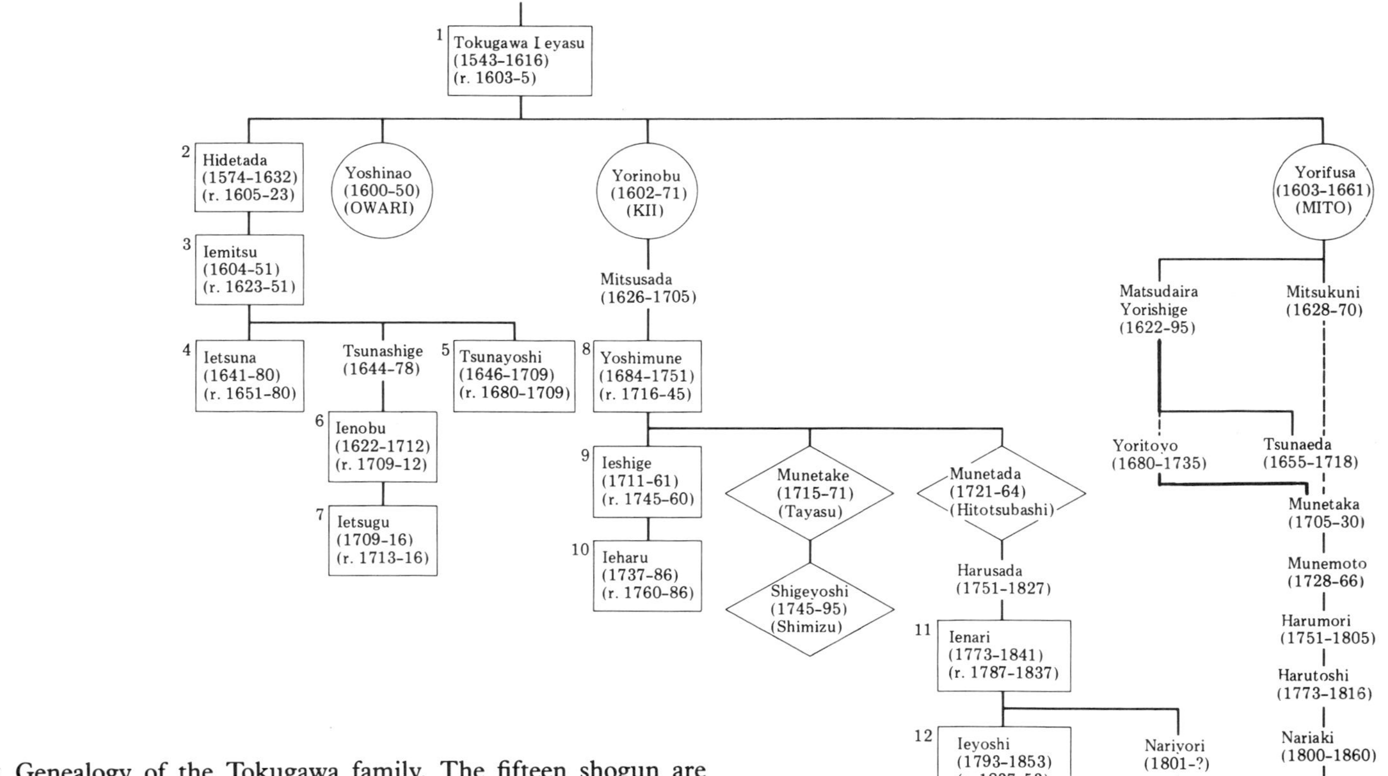

Figure 4.1 Genealogy of the Tokugawa family. The fifteen shogun are enclosed in rectangles; heads of the three successor houses (*gosanke*), in circles; heads of the three lords lines (*gosankyō*), in diamonds. Fathers are connected to actual sons by solid lines, to adopted sons by dashed lines. (Based on *Tokushi sōran*, *Nihonshi sōran*, and *Encyclopedia of Japan*.)

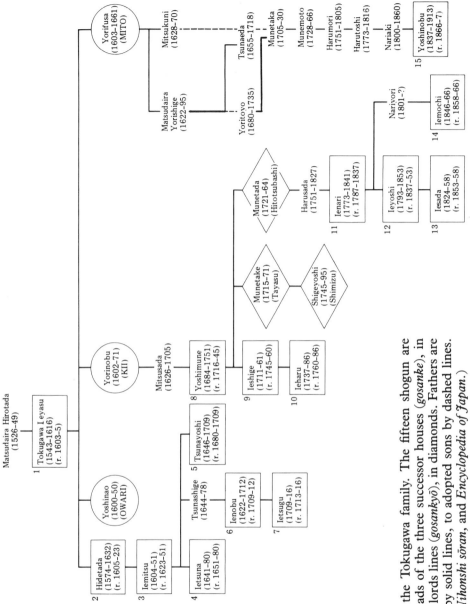

tles" proliferated throughout the country. In Mikawa we can trace the establishment of the Matsudaira branch families by noting the appearance of numerous hilltop forts above the valleys of the Yahagi River and its upper tributaries. The village of Matsudaira was itself on the Asuke River some distance above its confluence with the Yahagi. The first two Matsudaira generations were confined to this mountainous environment, but the third chief, Nobumitsu (?–1488) greatly expanded the family's reach, pushing into the middle plain of Mikawa and occupying the castle of Anjo in 1471.

For roughly fifty years the Matsudaira based themselves at Anjo. But its location to the west and south of Matsudaira village made it hard to hold, particularly in the face of the growing power of the Oda establishment to the west in Owari Province. In 1524 the family chief Kiyoyasu (1511–35) consolidated his position by pulling back to the east of the Yahagi river, adopting the castle of Okazaki as his headquarters. This castle was to serve the Matsudaira on and off until Ieyasu's time. Okazaki was well placed for purposes of military defense and economic growth, and by the 1550s the family had asserted itself over several districts covering roughly the interior one-third of Mikawa Province.[8]

The Matsudaira were not yet in a position to stand on their own. Historically they existed, as did others in this area, within a regional power structure built around the Imagawa house, whose heads were military governors (*shugo*) of Suruga, and at times of Mikawa and Tōtōmi as well. As a vassal of the Imagawa, the Matsudaira aspired to the vice-governorship of Mikawa. But they were hard pressed by the head of the Oda house who, as vice-governor of Owari, was actively pushing beyond its provincial borders. During the 1550s the Matsudaira household split over whether to realign themselves toward the Oda. The move to Okazaki Castle was an implicit decision to continue to look toward the east and the Imagawa. But Kiyoyasu was killed in 1535 by one of his own men over this issue, and when his successor Hirotada (1526–49) (Ieyasu's father) acknowledged the Imagawa overlordship, a faction of the Matsudaira leadership broke off and joined the Oda. As a child Ieyasu was a victim of these unsettled circumstances. From age six to fourteen he was kept as a hostage first by the Oda and then by the Imagawa. Technically he had inherited the family headship following Hirotada's death in 1549. But Okazaki was occu-

8 The Okazaki years are thoroughly covered in the documentary history published by Okazaki City: Shibata Akimasa, ed., *Tokugawa Ieyasu to sono shui*, 3 vols. (Okazaki shi: Okazaki shiyakusho, 1926).

pied by Imagawa officers. It was only in 1556 that Ieyasu was able to return to Okazaki as head of the Matsudaira main line.

Ieyasu found the Matsudaira houseband in disarray. On top of this, between 1556 and 1559 he was constantly in the field fighting at the behest of his overlord, Imagawa Yoshimoto (1519–60). Nevertheless, he did what he could to repair the damage done to the houseband during the years of internal dissension, thereby strengthening the bonds between himself and the numerous cadet houses and several classes of house vassals.

The Tōkai years

By the middle of the sixteenth century, the temptation to contest for national overlordship was becoming increasingly seductive to some of the more powerful daimyo. Imagawa Yoshimoto was one of the first to make the attempt. But when in 1560 he led an army of some 25,000 men across Mikawa on his way to the capital to gain legitimacy from the emperor, his army was decisively defeated, and he himself was killed by a greatly inferior force under the command of Oda Nobunaga. Yoshimoto's death released Ieyasu from his bond to the Imagawa house. As a sign, he adopted the given name Ieyasu at this time. (It had been Motoyasu, the "Moto," of couse, having come from Imagawa Yoshimoto.) Nobunaga was now clearly the coming power in the area, and Ieyasu lost little time in entering into a formal alliance with him.

Thus began a new chapter in the evolution of the Matsudaira house.[9] Using Okazaki as his central castle and protected on his western flank by Nobunaga, Ieyasu began to press eastward at the expense of the now-weakened Imagawa of Tōtōmi and the still-powerful Takeda in Suruga. By 1565 he had succeeded in placing his men in the key castles of Mikawa. In other words, Mikawa was safely his. Symbolic of his new sense of confidence, in 1566 he petitioned the court to have his surname changed to Tokugawa, leaving the name Matsudaira attached to the principal cadet families and also available for use as an honorary "gift name" with which Ieyasu could reward daimyo who became his allies. Along with official recognition of his change of surname, Ieyasu received appointment to the now largely honorary title of governor of Mikawa and to the fourth court rank junior grade.

9 The map of the Matsudaira house's castle holdings in Mikawa Province printed in Kitajima, *Kenryoku kōzō*, p. 7, reveals the close relationship of the Matsudaira house to the province's physical configuration – hills and rivers.

By such means Ieyasu began to acquire recognition as a member of the military aristocracy.

During the next few years Ieyasu beat into shape the kind of houseband and enfeoffment pattern required of a successful daimyo. Whereas the Matsudaira chieftains up to this point had relied heavily on kinsmen as their main supports in battle and administration, Ieyasu adopted the practice of converting even heads of collateral houses into dependent hereditary vassals (*fudai*), thus gaining a firmer grip over his senior military commanders. At the same time he enlarged his vassal band, particularly at the lower levels, by incorporating into his fighting forces large numbers of rural samurai. These he assigned to the command of his enfeoffed vassals to form new and expanded military units. At yet another level he worked to stabilize the relationship between his samurai retainers and the land-cultivating peasantry. As other daimyo were doing at this time, Ieyasu began a systematic survey of the land of his domain. He also confronted the troublesome issue posed in Mikawa by the militant and politically independent Ikkō religious communities, eventually bringing them around to his support.

Nobunaga and Ieyasu worked closely together during the next few years. Ieyasu's hold on Mikawa protected Nobunaga's advance on Kyoto in 1568, whereas the Oda presence in Owari gave Ieyasu the freedom to concentrate on his eastern front. By 1570 the Tokugawa chief had taken all of Tōtōmi from the Imagawa and had moved his castle headquarters to Hamamatsu, a port town in Tōtōmi. Ieyasu now began with Nobunaga's help an all-out effort to destroy the Takeda of Suruga and Kai. It turned out to be a lengthy operation. Not until 1582 were the Takeda finally defeated and Ieyasu could receive investiture of Suruga from Nobunaga.

By this time Ieyasu had acquired control over all or parts of the five provinces of Mikawa, Suruga, Tōtōmi, Kai, and Shinano. These all being in the Tōkaidō circuit, Ieyasu was commonly referred to as "lord of five Tōkai provinces." He stood among the dozen or so largest daimyo of the land, and he was already gaining a reputation for having one of the most effective administrative and military organizations in the country.

Nobunaga's assassination in 1582 by Akechi Mitsuhide threw the existing power structure into momentary confusion. Ieyasu himself, a likely figure to come to the defense of the Nobunaga legacy, was caught without his following in the port city of Sakai. He thus was forced to make his way to Okazaki in secret. Before he could gain full command of his forces for a possible military move, Hideyoshi had already killed Akechi and was in the process of winning over the Oda coalition. Ieyasu had been outmaneuvered, and he realized it. But he also knew that it was not politically wise to give in too precipitously to Hideyoshi's takeover.

Over the next several years Ieyasu worked off the formal obligations of his oath of allegiance to Nobunaga by taking up the cause of Nobunaga's second son Nobukatsu (1558–1630) against Hideyoshi. This involved him in some actual tests of strength with Hideyoshi. In 1589, Ieyasu invaded Toyotomi territory in Owari, winning a limited engagement at Nagakute. But his forces fought to a stalemate at Komaki. Although these at the time seemed to be minor engagements, in retrospect it is clear that they constituted something of a turning point. Militarily they instilled in each man a respect for the other. Modern historians have suggested that this was Ieyasu's first "political war," one that he shrewdly ended by agreeing, for political effect, to a formal compact of submission with Hideyoshi. Obviously Hideyoshi also found it expedient not to push to the limit. The agreement was consummated in 1586 by Ieyasu's formal visit of submission to Hideyoshi at Osaka Castle.[10] Ieyasu's second son was given to Hideyoshi for adoption; one of Hideyoshi's sisters was given in marriage to Ieyasu; and for a period Hideyoshi's mother was kept as a hostage in Ieyasu's household. At the time these exchanges were being negotiated, Ieyasu moved his castle headquarters farther to the east at Sumpu.

From 1586 to Hideyoshi's death in 1598, Ieyasu served as a willing ally. Having stood his own in battle against Hideyoshi, he was treated with respect and caution by the latter. As a consequence he was able to avoid depleting his own military resources by fighting Hideyoshi's battles. While Hideyoshi was sending gigantic armies into Shikoku and Kyushu to carry his conquest into western and southern Japan, Ieyasu managed to stay in the east expanding his holdings, improving his military capacity, and perfecting his administrative machinery. He also greatly enlarged his castle at Sumpu, to which he gathered large bodies of retainers and merchant and service personnel. It was during these same years that he carried forward the systematic survey of cultivated land, now definitely adopting the method preferred by Hideyoshi that stressed payment of the annual land tax in rice. The survey became the base on which an effective system of material extraction was built and the recruitment of military manpower from both samurai and peasants was standardized.

10 Tsuji, *Edo kaifu*, pp. 43–50.

By 1589, after the subjugation of Kyushu, the only major daimyo holdouts requiring Hideyoshi's attention were the Hōjō of the Kantō and the Date, Gamō, Tsugaru, and others in the far north. Hideyoshi attempted to win over the Hōjō by using Ieyasu as a go-between. Ieyasu had previously given his daughter in marriage to Hōjō Ujinao (1562–92). But unlike the daimyo of Shikoku and Kyushu, Ujinao refused to capitulate. Hideyoshi prepared for battle. This time Ieyasu was obliged to assist Hideyoshi in the attack on Odawara Castle, the headquarters of the great Hōjō domain that included the six Kantō provinces of Izu, Sagami, Musashi, Shimōsa, Kazusa, and Awa. In the investment, Ieyasu took the initiative, leading an army of some thirty thousand men in six divisions. The Hōjō held out for some three months, but the end was inevitable. Odawara Castle surrendered in the summer of 1590. Before this the Date and other daimyo to the north sought out Hideyoshi's camp and quickly pledged their allegiance. Hideyoshi had pacified the realm. All daimyo were now his vassals, and he could claim to be the chief of the military estate (*buke no tōryō*).

The early Kantō years

Following the Hōjō surrender, Hideyoshi ordered Ieyasu to move out of his home Tōkai provinces and to occupy the domain vacated by the Hōjō.[11] The assignment was on the surface an advancement. Possession of six of eight Kantō provinces made Ieyasu's holdings the largest in the land, larger in fact than Hideyoshi's. But the transfer moved Ieyasu farther from the center of political affairs, and it uprooted him and his followers from the areas where their historic roots were deepest and most secure. The move thus came as a shock to Ieyasu's senior vassals, who saw it as tantamount to exile.

The rapidity with which Ieyasu accomplished the Kantō transfer is amazing. Literally thousands of families had to pick up their entire households and equipment and find new houses in unfamiliar territory. And this had to be done with great expedition. Ieyasu received Hideyoshi's formal command on the thirteenth day of the seventh month. He had had some prior warning dating back to the fourth month and hence had been able to make some advance plans.[12] He entered the small castle of Edo, his new headquarters, by the first of

11 Kitajima, *Kenryoku kōzō*, pp. 189ff.
12 Kitajima, *Kenryoku kōzō*, p. 190; and Kitajima, *Edo bakufu*, pp. 132ff.

the eighth month. This was the official completion of his move, although it took nearly a year longer to settle in. Just as rapidly, Hideyoshi filled the castles given up by Ieyasu in the Tōkai provinces with his own trusted vassals.

The transfer into the Kantō was a major turning point in the Tokugawa fortunes, with results that were in many ways unanticipated, at least by Hideyoshi. The move out of the ancestral Mikawa homeland was bound to break the long-established ties of command among Ieyasu's vassal band, the lower village samurai, and the peasantry, thereby forcing Ieyasu to establish a network of command over an unfamiliar base.

There is some evidence that Hideyoshi expected the village samurai of the Kantō to give Ieyasu a difficult time. But Ieyasu's earlier experience in handling territories obtained by conquest – Kai Province won from Takeda was a good example – proved critical in the Kantō. Rather than displace the rural samurai and even some enfeoffed vassals left behind by the Hōjō, Ieyasu used them as best he could, recognizing the status they had held under the Hōjō and using them as rural intendants or recruiting them into his and his retainers' vassal bonds.

For all the difficulties that attended the transfer, possession of the Kantō – the historic homeland of the bushi class – provided Ieyasu with what was to prove the ideal base from which to win the national hegemony. Moreover, from the point of view of institutional development, the major difference between the domain structure of the daimyo of the Sengoku era and those of the Edo era was visible in the greater degree to which the latter had reduced the independence of their vassals. During the Sengoku era most bushi remained in the countryside living off their hereditary landholdings. This was true even for the high-ranking military officers with personal fiefs and even castles. Although independent enfeoffment meant that the daimyo overlord was less burdened by the need to provide shelter and maintenance for these members of his vassal band, he was at a disadvantage when it came to asserting his authority over them. The so-called Sengoku daimyo was lord of a decentralized domain made up of a patchwork of daimyo demesne and vassal fiefs. The daimyo of the seventeenth century had drawn their housemen, down to a fairly low level, away from their fiefs, thereby making them dependent on stipends paid out of the daimyo's granaries.[13] This condition is seen by

13 This practice distinguishes the possession of a land fief (*chigyō-chi*) from the rice stipend (*hōroku*). See Kanai, *Hansei*, pp. 38–43.

some scholars as indicative of the degree to which daimyo achieved the ultimate Edo period norm in sociopolitical evolution. Moreover it is apparent that in those parts of Japan where either the daimyo or the rural samurai, or both, had remained in place for several generations, daimyo authority over houseband vassals was harder to achieve. "Daimyo absolutism," as the capacity to exact domainwide compliance with directives from the castle headquarters has been called, flourished best where the private tie between the daimyo's houseband and the peasantry – in other words, the *jizamurai* system – had been completely destroyed.[14] The resulting structure was one in which the samurai had been drawn into the daimyo's castle headquarters and the peasantry had been placed under an impersonal field administration controlled from the central castle. There was thus a hidden advantage for Ieyasu in the forced transfer to the Kantō, for it obliged him to reorganize from scratch the relationship of his vassal band to the peasantry. The domain transfer was an experience that nearly all the daimyo who made the transition into the Edo period were to encounter at least once. One could say that it was almost a precondition for a successful transition into the *bakuhan* era.

Possession of the Kantō made Ieyasu lord of the largest domain in the country, well over twice the size of his Tōkai holdings. There is no accurate record of the total productive base of Ieyasu's Tōkai domain, but it is possible to get a general idea by extrapolation from the holdings of the daimyo who were placed in the territory vacated by Ieyasu in 1590. These add up to just over 1 million *koku*.[15] The extent of the Kantō domain taken over from the Hōjō is also not precisely known because of the complexity of the transfer and the fact that different methods of calculation were used at the time. In gross terms, however, the total was in the neighborhood of 2.5 million to 3.0 million *koku*. The task of administering and defending this greatly expanded territory meant that Ieyasu had either to delegate more authority to officers of his field administration or to expand his military and administrative personnel. He chose the latter method, relying on the services of both old and newly enrolled vassals. He, of course, took with him as many as possible of his own housemen. But he was still shorthanded and had to adopt into his service numerous samurai who had been left behind

14 For an analysis of the evolution of the "mature" *han* in terms of the progressive withdrawal of the samurai from their land fiefs, see Junnosuke Sasaki, with Ronald P. Toby, "The Changing Rationale of Daimyo Control in the Emergence of the Bakuhan State," in Hall, Nagahara, and Yamamura, eds., *Japan Before Tokugawa*, pp. 271–94.

15 Nakamura Kichiji, *Tokugawa*, p. 111.

by the Hōjō or who had been cast adrift in other provinces by the fortunes of war.[16]

As a master plan for his new domain, Ieyasu adopted Edo as his capital and distributed his retainers around Edo according to certain guidelines. Lands directly held by the head of the Tokugawa house as granary lands (*kurairi-chi* or *goryō,* later *tenryō*) were located close to Edo; small fief holders were placed not more than a single night's stopover away from Edo; and holders of large domains were placed at a greater distance from the center. These last were, for the most part, set out as castle holders and were situated with an eye to strategic location.

Ieyasu put the actual task of fief assignment into the hands of a team of officers with experience in land-tax administration. The team was under the supervision of Sakakibara Yasumasa (1548–1606), the first among his daimyo-class retainers and shortly to occupy the castle of Tatebayashi. The transition team worked quickly and effectively. It set aside lands with a total assessed value of roughly one million *koku* (the new standard unit of land assessment based on assessed rice production) for Ieyasu's private granary land. This, being about 39 percent of the total, was considerably more than the Hōjō chief had held. Granary land was placed under the administration of Ina Tadatsugu (1550–1610) and a group of subordinate land stewards. The latter were drawn in large part from personnel who remained in their ancestral villages and who had previously served the Takeda, Imagawa, or Hōjō. They were selected for their familiarity with the area.

The remaining territory was divided among Ieyasu's enfeoffed vassals. Of these, thirty-eight were assigned holdings of from 10,000 to 120,000 *koku.* This meant that they were of daimyo size and function, but they were not considered daimyo because they were rear vassals in the eyes of the national overlord. All together, this group held about 1 million *koku.* Thirty-two retainers holding from 2,000 to 5,000 *koku* accounted for another 142,000 *koku,* and several hundred lesser housemen each enfeoffed at less than 2,000 *koku* took up the remaining 426,000 *koku.* The initial fief distribution was carried out on the basis of the cadastral records obtained from the Hōjō. Because the Hōjō had retained the old monetary payment system of calculation (*kandaka*), the Tokugawa soon initiated a round of new surveys using

16 For a more limited example of vassal band organization by accretion, see my "The Ikeda House and Its Retainers in Bizen," in John W. Hall and Marius B. Jansen, eds., *Studies in the Institutional History of Early Modern Japan* (Princeton, N.J.: Princeton University Press, 1968) pp. 79–88. Also see Tsuji, *Edo kaifu,* pp. 54–6.

the rice-tax system.[17] It would take the next several decades for the Tokugawa to convert their Kantō holdings to the specifications of Hideyoshi's survey system (Taikō *kenchi*). Aside from the assignment of his military followers, Ieyasu was occupied with a mass of logistical problems. He faced the construction of a suitable castle, the draining of swampy land for urban construction, the drawing of fresh water into the city, and the improvement of port facilities.

Hideyoshi's last years

In the eight years from the fall of Odawara to the time of his death in 1598, Hideyoshi worked energetically, though rather erratically, to institutionalize his military power into a national government. Despite his domestic military successes, Hideyoshi still felt the need to demonstrate his powers of command over his vassal daimyo, even by compelling them to engage in foreign invasions. This would appear to be his main reason for the conquest of China that he attempted in 1590.[18] When the invasion ended in failure, many of the participating daimyo had been measurably weakened. And because the invasion was still in progress when Hideyoshi died, the fact that several important daimyo were out of the country at the time contributed to the political confusion that followed the hegemon's death.

Meanwhile Ieyasu, and a number of daimyo whose domains were located at great distances from the takeoff point for the invasion of Korea, had been spared a debilitating involvement in the venture. Ieyasu sent only a token backup force to northern Kyushu in 1592, and this did not see action. Ieyasu cleverly took the opportunity to expand and strengthen his Edo Castle and carry out military and civil administrative programs. Thus at the time of Hideyoshi's death in 1598, Ieyasu enjoyed a much more secure and powerful position than he had when he first acquired the Kantō provinces.

Although remarkably successful as a military leader, Hideyoshi proved less capable as a political organizer. Having beaten the daimyo into submission, he had difficulty in devising a governmental framework that would institutionalize his charismatic overlordship. What he eventually did was to graft his military power onto the social pres-

17 The earlier *kandaka* system of tax management, calculated in terms of monetary currency, is explained in Keiji Nagahara, with Kozo Yamamura, "The Sengoku Daimyo and the Kandaka System," in Hall, Nagahara, and Yamamura, eds., *Japan Before Tokugawa*, pp. 27–63.

18 The thesis that Hideyoshi used the invasion of Korea to safeguard his legitimacy is developed in Chapter 2 in this volume.

tige of the high nobility, legitimizing himself through the title of *kampaku* and by his close proximity to the throne.[19]

It was not until Hideyoshi realized that he was near the end of his life and that he was putting the fate of his succession on Hideyori (1593–1615), a child of five, that he tried to devise a formal system for delegating political authority. The task of safeguarding Toyotomi rule, he placed in the hands of a board of five regents (*go-tairō*). They were selected from among the most powerful of Hideyoshi's allies: namely, Tokugawa Ieyasu, who was to remain in Fushimi Castle as chief policymaker and head of the board; Maeda Toshiie (1538–99), who was assigned to Osaka Castle as guardian to Hideyori; Mōri Terumoto (1553–1625); Kobayakawa Takakage (1533–97) (later succeeded by Uesegi Kagekatsu); and Ukita Hideie (1573–1655). The more administrative aspects of government became the responsibility of a board of five commissioners (*go-bugyō*): Asano Nagamasa (1544–1611), Maeda Gen'i (1539–1602), Ishida Mitsunari (1560–1600), Mashita Nagamori (1545–1615), and Natsuka Masaie (?–1600). All five had served for many years as members of Hideyoshi's house administration.

This arrangement did create a central authority of sorts, able to make and carry out national policy in the immediate aftermath of Hideyoshi's death, as it did in calling off the Korean campaign. But the structure was inherently unstable, and once Hideyoshi passed from the scene it began to fall apart. The members of the two boards were too involved in their own domestic problems, so that one by one they abandoned the capital area on grounds of urgent business. The death of Maeda Toshiie in 1599 made Ieyasu by far the most experienced and powerful among the regents, and when on his own initiative he moved into the position in Osaka Castle vacated by Maeda Toshiie, he was recognized as the obvious *tenka-dono* (lord of the realm).

Winning the tenka

Ieyasu's path from here to the acquisition of recognized national leadership was not easily traversed. There were a number of powerful daimyo heads of large daimyo leagues, located mainly in western Japan, who were not ready to accept a takeover by Ieyasu without a struggle. There were also a number of lesser daimyo whose entire careers had been spent in the service of Hideyoshi and whose fortunes were thereby tied to a continuation of the Toyotomi polity.

19 See footnote 4.

This group consisted of house daimyo, like the five magistrates, and Hideyoshi's close field generals like Katō Kiyōmasa, Kuroda Nagamasa, and Fukushima Masanori. Their center of activity was Osaka Castle. But their cause lacked a single charismatic leader who could keep them united, and it soon became apparent that major differences of opinion divided the so-called administrative (*bugyō*) group from the generals.

Ieyasu did not openly declare his ambition to succeed Hideyoshi to national hegemony, but increasingly he began to act the part. For instance, he entered into marriage alliances with other daimyo on his own authority. In early 1600, after Maeda Toshiie's death, he moved from Fushimi into the western enclosure of Osaka Castle. The numerous letters he directed to his fellow daimyo at this time were couched in statesmanlike terms of concern for the maintenance of peace.[20] When Uesugi Kagekatsu (1555–1623), who had joined the ranks of the regents after Maeda Toshiie's death, was reported to be mobilizing troops in his domain centered on Aizu, a location that threatened the Tokugawa rear, Ieyasu expressed alarm and called for a countermobilization, ordering nearby daimyo to prepare a move again Aizu.

By now Ieyasu was issuing orders as though he had full national authority, and he was being courted by daimyo members of the Toyotomi coalition who began to offer him pledges of support, even sending hostages as a safeguard for the future. Among these were members of the Toyotomi "generals" group and others like the Ikeda (of Bizen) and the Yamanouchi (of Tōtōmi). By the summer of 1600, the country divided increasingly between those who saw an advantage to supporting the Osaka group based on Hideyori's potential as a symbol of national unity and those who saw Ieyasu as the inevitable hegemon of the future. The Osaka faction had among its most powerful supporters the Ukita, Chōsokabe, Mōri, Konishi, Nabeshima, and Shimazu, daimyo whose lands were mainly in provinces west of Osaka and out of Ieyasu's immediate reach. The supporters who clustered around Ieyasu were mainly based in the east.

Ishida Mitsunari, the prime mover of the western faction, denounced Ieyasu's move against Aizu as a usurpation of national authority and called for punitive action. He assembled a large military force and began to march toward the Kantō. Ieyasu, having anticipated this move, left the Aizu operation to others, notably Date Masamune and

20 Ieyasu's correspondence is conveniently arranged by Kuwata Tadachika in *Tokugawa Ieyasu, sono tegami to ningen* (Tokyo: Shin jimbutsu ōraisha, 1971).

Yūki Hideyasu, and quickly prepared to meet the threat from Osaka. As he led his army out of the Kantō, all the daimyo along the way opened their castles to him, detaching forces to join the mobilization. On the fifteenth day of the ninth month (October 21, 1600), the combined armies of the two factions met in battle at Sekigahara. It is estimated that the eastern league committed some seventy thousand men to the engagement. The western league fielded some eighty thousand men, but they were poorly positioned and of uncertain reliability. Only about half of them went into action. The battle was in doubt throughout the morning, but the defection of Kobayakawa turned the tide. Victory went to the eastern coalition.

Ieyasu used the victory at Sekigahara to assert his national authority over the military estate and to make drastic changes in the composition and placement of the daimyo and their holdings throughout Japan.[21] In the immediate aftermath of the battle, eighty-seven daimyo who had opposed Ieyasu were defeated and their lands confiscated. The lands of three others were drastically reduced in size. All together, a total of 6,221,690 *koku* were taken from Ieyasu's daimyo opponents. Another 1.35 million *koku* were taken from the Toyotomi house and made available for reallocation to other daimyo or for inclusion in Ieyasu's personal holdings. Even greater changes were brought about by the transfer of forty-three daimyo from one location to another and the creation of new daimyo. The authority to invest new daimyo rested on Ieyasu's claim to hegemony over the warrior estate. Prior to the battle Ieyasu counted among his cadet branch heads and hereditary housemen forty whose holdings were of 10,000 *koku* or more. He was now able to set these men out as full-fledged daimyo under his own patent. All were given domain increases. Another twenty members of his houseband who, as of 1600, held fiefs of less than 10,000 *koku* were raised to daimyo status. Finally, he granted daimyo status to eight rear vassals who had distinguished themselves in Ieyasu's eyes.

All these confiscations, reassignments, and new creations added up to the greatest transfer of landholding in Japanese history. As a result, the balance of power was heavily tilted in Ieyasu's favor. But it was not by any means secure or properly legitimized. In the immediate aftermath of Sekigahara, as the troops of the eastern coalition poured into Osaka, Ieyasu undoubtedly had the military capacity to take over Osaka Castle, at the time defended by Mōri Terumoto on behalf of

21 The most recent and detailed treatment of the Sekigahara settlement is found in the work of Fujino Tamotsu, especially *Bakuhan taisei shi no kenkyū*, p. 150.

Toyotomi Hideyori and his mother Lady Yodo. But Ieyasu was a sworn trustee of the Toyotomi polity, and many of his most powerful supporters in the recent confrontation still had strong emotional ties to Hideyoshi. Ieyasu was also sobered by the fact that he had few trustworthy allies in the western provinces. Hideyori, though suffering a loss of nearly two-thirds of the domain left by his father, was therefore allowed to retain Osaka Castle and a 650,000-*koku* domain in the surrounding provinces of Settsu, Kawachi, and Izumi. Although reduced to the status of daimyo in the world of the military hegemon, in the eyes of the court, Hideyori merited high rank as heir to Hideyoshi, who had retired with the high rank of Taikō. It was clear to all that the Tokugawa reality and the Toyotomi memory could not coexist for long, but Ieyasu, hoping to avoid a war that would reopen the question of the ultimate loyalty of the military houses, felt constrained to put off the final confrontation until 1614–15.

FORMATION OF THE EDO BAKUFU

In 1602, the Shimazu house of southern Kyushu acknowledged Ieyasu's overlordship, thus completing the Sekigahara settlement. A year later Ieyasu was installed as *sei-i tai-shōgun* by Emperor Goyōzei. In anticipation of this appointment that would legitimize him as chief of the warrior estate (*buke no tōryō*), Ieyasu had put together a genealogy that showed his descent from the Minamoto line. Concurrently with his new appointment he received the traditional designations *Genji no chōja* (chief of the Minamoto lineage), *Junna, Shōgaku ryōin bettō* (rector of the Junna and Shōgaku colleges), second court rank, and *udaijin* (minister of the right). These grandiloquent titles did not in themselves add new political or military weight to Ieyasu, but as tokens of legitimacy, they all were important. And their importance was underlined by the fact that Hideyori, although only ten years of age, received the title of inner minister (*naidaijin*) at the same time. Osaka Castle, because of Hideyori's high court rank, held certain powers of appointment and recommendation to the court that paralleled those of Ieyasu. Obviously Hideyori was the darling of the court and was being used as a means of court involvement in warrior political affairs. The closer the center of warrior officers came to Kyoto, the deeper this involvement became.

In 1605, Ieyasu turned over the office of shogun to his son Hidetada. Adopting the style of *ōgosho* (retired shogun), he established himself in the subsidiary castle of Sumpu where he surrounded himself with advisers of his own selection.[22] Hidetada was inducted as shogun at the Tokugawa residence in Kyoto. Entering Kyoto at the head of more than 100,000 men he used the occasion to impress on the country the power of his house. The great bulk of these troops were provided by the daimyo of eastern Japan who thereby reiterated their loyalty to the shogun.

Ieyasu's move was no retirement, no effort to ease the pressures of official life. Rather, it was a way of making the Tokugawa succession more secure, both by setting a precedent of direct succession and by making sure that the next shogun was safely in place before Ieyasu's death, thus frustrating any effort to promote Hideyori as an alternative head of state. Most important to the future of the bakufu, it gave Ieyasu a free hand to develop basic strategy and policy. At Sumpu, Ieyasu assembled what has been called a private "brain trust" to assist him in devising policy. Among these were the Tendai priest Tenkai (1536–1643), who served as Ieyasu's spiritual adviser and was instrumental in having the first shogun's grave established at Nikkō; Hayashi Razan, the Confucian scholar who assisted Ieyasu in drafting the legal codes; Ina Tadatsugu, a specialist on local administration; Gotō Mitsutsugu, founder of the Silver Mint (Ginza) and adviser on currency policy; and even the English navigator, William Adams.

There was much to be done. The administrative organs of shogunal government were yet to be adequately designed. The organization and assignment of the bakufu officials were not complete. The relocation of daimyo for political and strategic purposes would require many more years and many more moves and confiscations before the Tokugawa house could feel secure. There were numerous problems of overall political control of such groups as the emperor and his court, the temples and shrines, the peasants and merchants, and the foreign intruders from Europe and China.

But what most pressed on Ieyasu's mind was the threat of Toyotomi Hideyori and Osaka Castle. The problem became more acute each year as Hideyori came ever closer to maturity. There was already talk in the court circles of his being ready for appointment as *kampaku*.[23] And there were those in Kyoto who saw no harm in creating a dual head of state, one military and the other civil. In 1611 Ieyasu's greatest fears were confirmed when he arranged to meet Hideyori at Nijō

22 Naohiro Asao, with Marius B. Jansen, "Shogun and Tenno," in Hall, Nagahara, and Yamamura, eds., *Japan Before Tokugawa*, pp. 259–60.

23 The Hideyori threat to Ieyasu is analyzed in Harold Bolitho, *Treasures Among Men: The Fudai Daimyo in Tokugawa Japan* (New Haven, Conn.: Yale University Press, 1974), pp. 3–6.

Castle in Kyoto. Ieyasu's nervousness was reflected in his demand shortly thereafter, on the occasion of celebrations in honor of Emperor Gomizunoo's accession, that all daimyo swear a special oath of allegiance to him as the head of the military estate.

But Ieyasu knew full well that such an oath was not a solution. And so he resorted to a number of strategems to weaken the Osaka faction. One was to encourage them to exhaust the huge bullion supply stored in Osaka Castle to build temple monuments in Hideyoshi's memory. But in the end it took military action. Over a contrived issue in the winter of 1614, Ieyasu launched an attack on Osaka Castle. Although Hideyori failed to recruit a single active daimyo to his cause, Osaka Castle filled with ex-daimyo defeated at Sekigahara and masterless warriors set adrift by the destruction of so many daimyo housebands. An estimated ninety thousand defenders, many of them Christian, managed to hold off a force estimated at twice that number under Tokugawa command. Despite the use of newly acquired firearms by the attacking force, Osaka Castle proved impregnable. The first siege failed at a heavy cost in lives, and Ieyasu realized that a continuation of the assault using the same strategy could lead to humiliating defeat. Clearly, he had come to the most critical juncture of his career: An obvious victory by the Osaka faction would likely turn against him a large number of daimyo who had once been pledged to Hideyoshi but who joined the Tokugawa between 1598 and 1600. In this extremity Ieyasu called for a political compromise and a military truce, one provision of which called for the elimination of parts of the moats and defenses surrounding the castle. Hideyori, or rather his mother Lady Yodo, agreed to the truce only to realize too late that the Tokugawa work gangs brought in to fill in moats had gone too far. Once the castle's defenses had been seriously weakened, Ieyasu renewed his attack in May of 1615. In this so-called summer campaign, he was successful. Osaka Castle was entered and burned. Hideyori and his mother committed suicide. At long last the Toyotomi memory had been destroyed.

Hidetada and Iemitsu

Barely a year after the destruction of the Osaka faction, Ieyasu died. But he left for his successors a firm foundation on which to base an enduring political order. He had achieved what neither Nobunaga nor Hideyoshi had been able to do, the creation of a structure of political allegiances that could transcend the person of the hegemon, making the office of shogun the permanent object of national loyalty and obedience. This obviously was Ieyasu's main intent when he resigned the office of shogun. During the "Ōgosho era" he was able to take a number of important steps toward the institutionalization of the post of shogun. Toward the Kyoto court he exploited every occasion to impose his authority. A particularly sensitive issue was control over the award of court titles to members of the bushi class. In 1613, on the occasion of a court intrigue involving Hideyori, Ieyasu had promulgated a code of regulations, the Kuge shohatto, directed toward the nobility and restricting their involvement in political affairs. Documents of this sort were reworked and resubmitted after the victory at Osaka. The result was the Kinchū narabini kuge shohatto, a set of regulations that applied to the emperor and the Kyoto nobles, restricting them to the traditional arts and ceremonials and limiting their appointment authority. It effectively screened the civil nobility from the military aristocracy and their government.

Toward the daimyo Ieyasu had directed numerous regulations and demands for pledges of loyalty. The first such command following the victory at Osaka was the order limiting each daimyo to a single castle (*ikkoku ichijō rei*), an action that signaled the start of a new order of peace in which warfare among the daimyo was not to be countenanced. A few months later, the Buke shohatto (Laws for military households) was issued in a new and extended form.

Despite all that Ieyasu had achieved, the two shoguns who followed him did not have an easy time, for it was they who were given the task of consolidating the relations among shogun, emperor, and daimyo. As Asao Naohiro has pointed out, neither Hidetada nor Iemitsu received automatic recognition as national hegemon.[24] Whereas Ieyasu was accepted as chief of the military estate on the basis of his military successes, his successors did not have the opportunities to enhance their charisma through military exploits. Hidetada did see action in the Osaka investments, but under his father's command. Following Ieyasu's death he thus felt the need to pursue several lines to back up his claim to leadership of the bushi class. First, he made conspicuous display of the shogun's authority to act in matters of high national policy. His strict enforcement of prohibitions against Christianity and his early steps toward the regulation of foreign trade were calculated to gain general recognition for the shogun as the political head of state. In

24 The problem of legitimation faced by Ieyasu's successors as shogun is discussed by Asao, "Shogun and Tenno," pp. 265–90.

both instances Hidetada could claim to be the "protector" of the Japanese homeland against foreign enemies.

Second, the Tokugawa shoguns, as had Nobunaga and Hideyoshi, used the emperor for political effect. On the one hand, posing as patrons of the emperor, the shogun expended or requisitioned conspicuous financial resources to build palaces and residences for members of the court. On the other hand, he did everything to make the emperor the shogun's private legitimizer. This was accomplished in part by the enforcement of regulations limiting the court's contact with members of the warrior elite and by deepening relations between the Tokugawa house and the court, ultimately through intermarriage. In 1620 Hidetada's daughter was married to Emperor Gomizunoo. A daughter of this union born in 1623 took the throne as Meishō in 1629. This was the first time since the eighth century that a woman had been named empress, a clear demonstration that the Tokugawa house had succeeded in acquiring supreme status in both the military and noble hierarchies.

We are reminded of the close relationship that existed between the shogun and the imperial institution under the Ashikaga house. But the location of the Edo bakufu in the Kantō, some three hundred miles to the east, meant that the Tokugawa relationship was more institutional than personal. Much greater emphasis was placed on control. The Edo bakufu's presence in Kyoto was exhibited in the massive Nijō Castle, home of the shogun's deputy, the Kyoto *shoshidai*. Furthermore, the provisions that squeezed the more than three hundred aristocratic families into the palace enclosure (*gyoen*) in Kyoto exemplified the restraints that the shogun was capable of imposing.[25]

The crowning touch to the effort to legitimize the Tokugawa house was the successful deification of Ieyasu as Tōshō daigongen (Great shining deity of the east). Under the third shogun, Iemitsu, a shrine to Ieyasu was established at Nikkō. In time, daimyo, presumably on their own initiative, set up in their home territories scaled-down versions of the Nikkō shrine where they could hold services in memory of Ieyasu. The Nikkō Tōshōgu received from the emperor the same rank as the imperial shrine at Ise. The periodic grand progresses to Nikkō called by later shoguns served to direct national attention to Ieyasu's special place in history.[26]

25 For a map of the *kuge* quarters in Kyoto, see my "Kyoto As Historical Background," in John W. Hall and Jeffrey P. Mass, eds., *Medieval Japan, Essays in Institutional History* (New Haven, Conn.: Yale University Press, 1974), pp. 33–8.

26 Willem Jan Boot, "The Deification of Tokugawa Ieyasu," a research report in *Japan Foundation Newsletter* 14, no. 5 (1987): 10–13.

THE *BAKUHAN* POWER STRUCTURE

In the final analysis it was the shogunate's capacity to govern the daimyo that gave stability to the *bakuhan* state. In turn, this capacity rested on the maintenance of a favorable balance of power. The concept of balance implies differences in degree of attachment or of reliability under shogunal command among several categories of daimyo, particularly between the "house" daimyo (*fudai*) and the "outside" daimyo (*tozama*). At the time of Ieyasu's death, the balance could not yet be considered secure from the Tokugawa point of view, and the process of rearrangement continued for the rest of the seventeenth century. (See Map 4.1.) Whereas changes in the composition and location of daimyo were a natural outcome of victory or defeat in battle, in times of peace other justifications had to be given for making such changes. By keeping the relationship between daimyo and shogun a precarious one and by making the daimyo accountable to bakufu regulations and codes of conduct, the shogun was given numerous opportunities to transfer, reduce in size, or disinherit any daimyo. Transfers, of course, were not necessarily ordered for punitive reasons; they most often were ordered as a sign of favor from the shogun, usually involving assignment to a larger domain in a strategically more important location. Reductions and seizures were the result of disciplinary action by the shogun. Using the provisions of the Buke shohatto, the shogun could penalize a daimyo for failing to produce a natural heir, for making repairs on his castle without obtaining permission, for making unauthorized marriage alliances, and many other seemingly minor acts that violated the code.

Fujino Tamotsu calculated the total figures for confiscations of daimyo holdings for each shogun of the Edo regime.[27] The figures for the first five shoguns are shown in Table 4.1. Not counting the Sekigahara settlement, a total of some 13.2 million *koku* (equivalent to one-half of the country's total taxable land base) changed hands under the first five Tokugawa shoguns. These lands were reassigned to other daimyo or added to the shogun's demesne. In the process, a large number of outside daimyo were eliminated, among them such notable participants in the Tokugawa rise to power as Katō Kiyomasa (1562–1611) and Fukushima Masanori (1561–1624), while the number of house daimyo increased in numbers. All told, under these shoguns some 200 daimyo had been destroyed; 172 had been newly created; 200 had received increases in holdings; and 280 had their domains

27 Fujino Tamotsu, "On'ei roku – haizetsu roku," in his *Bakusei to hansei* (Tokyo: Yoshikawa kōbunkan, 79), pp. 42–3.

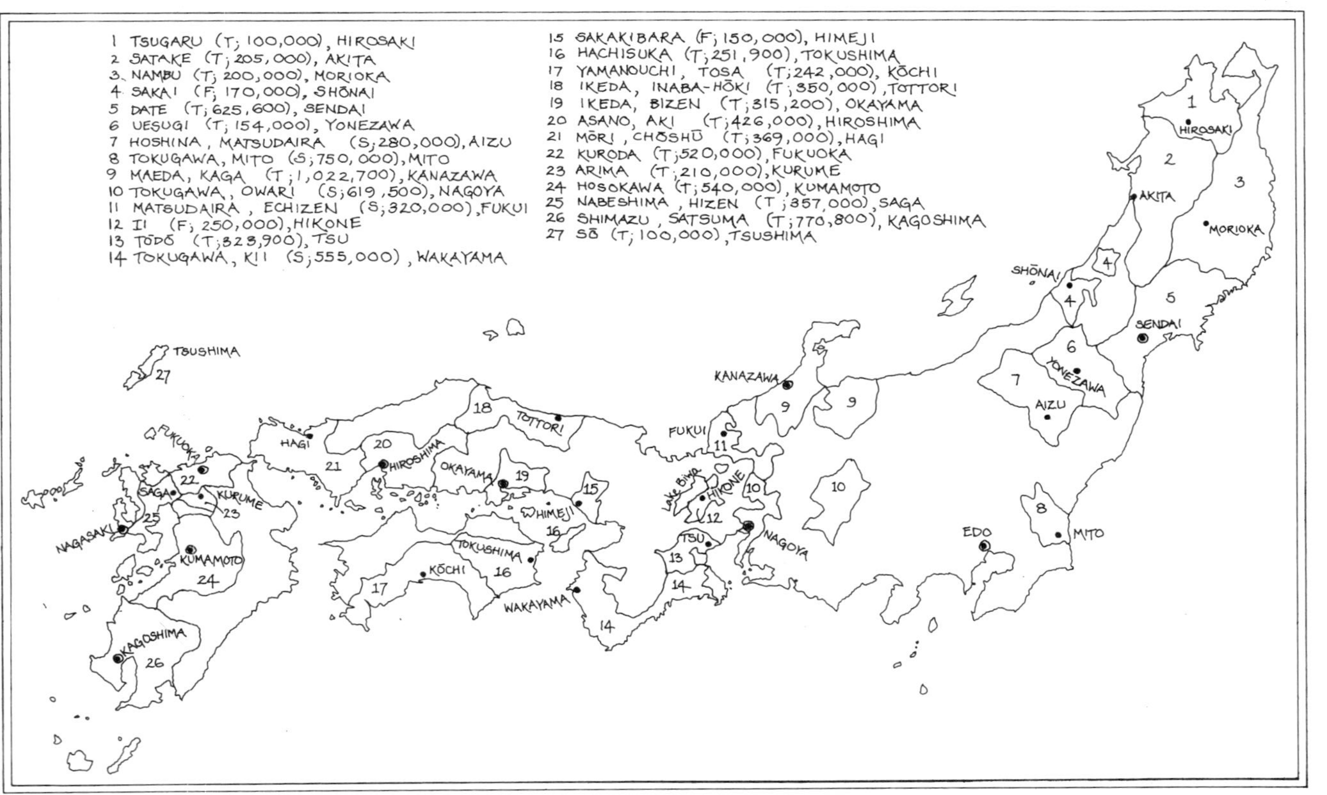

Map 4.1 Major daimyo domains and capital cities, mid-seventeenth century. The information on daimyo domains is listed in the following order: daimyo house name, province, status (T *tozama*, F *fudai*, S *shimpan*), domain size in *koku*, and capital city.

TABLE 4.1
Confiscations of daimyo holdings, 1601–1705

Shogun	Daimyo (No.)	(*tozama*/*fudai*)	Amounts confiscated (*koku*)
Ieyasu (1601–16)	41	(28/13)	3,594,640
Hidetaka (1616–31)	38	(23/15)	3,605,420
Iemitsu (1632–50)	46	(28/18)	3,580,100
Ietsuna (1651–79)	28	(16/12)	728,000
Tsunayoshi (1680–1705)	45	(17/28)	1,702,982
Total	198	(112/86)	(13,211,142)

transferred. By the time of Tsunayoshi's death in 1709 the purposeful reassignment of daimyo had been carried out in sufficient favor of the shogunate that the rate of attainder fell off dramatically.

The structure of power over which the Tokugawa shogun ultimately presided was conceived as a balance among several classes of daimyo and the interests of the shogun. The elements of this balance need further clarification. To begin, at the top of the hierarchy were the collateral houses, the so-called *shimpan* (or *ichimon* or *kamon*). These eventually numbered 23. The house or hereditary daimyo, or *fudai*, by the end of the eighteenth century numbered 145. The remnants of the daimyo who had been brought into being by either Nobunaga or Hideyoshi, the so-called outside lords (*tozama*), numbered 98. The Tokugawa house itself constituted the single largest power bloc. In 1722 the shogun's enfeoffed bannermen (*hatamoto*) numbered as many as 5,200 individuals, while his stipended housemen (*gokenin*) numbered an estimated 17,399. The latter were sustained on stipends derived from the shogun's granary lands. In addition there were nonofficer-grade foot soldiers (*ashigaru*) and clerks (*dōshin*) in the uncounted thousands. At the end of the first century after the founding of the Edo shogunate, the division of taxable landholdings among these several groups was calculated as follows:[28]

Imperial house land	141,151 *koku*
Shogun's granary land (*tenryō*)	4,213,171 *koku*
Shogun's bannermen (*hatamoto*)	2,606,545 *koku*
Shogun's house daimyo (*fudai*) and collateral daimyo (*shimpan*)	9,325,300 *koku*
Outside lords (*tozama*)	9,834,700 *koku*

28 A convenient listing of the 243 daimyo existing in 1698 is reproduced in Kanai, *Hansei*, pp. 60–73. In English, see a similar list in Conrad Totman, *Politics in the Tokugawa Bakufu 1600–1843* (Cambridge, Mass.: Harvard University Press, 1967), pp. 264–8.

Domainal productive capacity, as expressed in *koku,* was the first and most easily demonstrated measure of the relative strength of the several classes of daimyo.[29] Other factors such as geographical distribution and control of strategic and economically valuable locations were taken into account as well. The shogun's granary lands were located in forty-seven of the sixty-eight provinces, accounting for roughly a sixth of the country's productive base. If we add to this the bannermen's holdings, the percentage rises to close to a quarter. These holdings were heavily concentrated in the Kantō and the Tōkai provinces, but they also extended into central and western Japan. The actual distribution of *tenryō* by region shows 1.026 million *koku* in the Kantō, 687,000 in the capital area, 688,000 in the Tōkai provinces, 1.353 million in the region north of the Kantō, 412,000 in western Honshu and Shikoku, and 176,000 in Kyushu.[30] As European visitors to Japan in the seventeenth century commented, it was possible to travel from Osaka to Edo without having to leave bakufu territory. Not only was the *tenryō* well located to serve the tax need of the bakufu, it also contained most of the important urban centers, such as Edo, Osaka, Sakai, Kyoto, Fushimi, Nara, and Nagasaki. The shogun had also gained possession of the country's active silver and copper mines. The bakufu, through its authority over the *tenryō* and the fief lands of the bannermen, was directly in control of a commanding section of the country, whether measured in terms of land, manpower, commercial capacity, or institutional importance. But however large the shogun's direct holdings, government under the Tokugawa house remained a coalition between shogun and daimyo, as the term *bakuhan* reminds us.

To understand the several types of daimyo, their relationship to the shogun, and the significance of their geographic distribution, we need first to look back to origins.[31] There were, first, the self-made daimyo, those who had come into existence before the appearance of Oda Nobunaga. Among these were the Shimazu of southern Kyushu and the Nabeshima of northern Kyushu, the Mōri of western Honshu, and the Satake, Date, Nambu, Mogami, and Uesegi in the provinces north of Edo. These long-established houses had managed to survive the wars of consolidation, in many cases holding on to their original do-

29 Harold Bolitho has cautioned that *kokudaka* figures were not a sure sign of daimyo power, nor should one expect that these figures would hold constant throughout the era. See Chapter 5 in this volume.

30 Kitajima, *Kenryoku kōzō,* p. 332.

31 The difficulty that scholars have in classifying daimyo types is well explained in Chapter 5 in this volume.

mains and gaining acceptance as *tozama* from each of the unifiers, including the Tokugawa shogun. For the most part, their domains were of considerable size but were located on the fringes of the Japanese islands. Next were the daimyo who owed their existence to Oda Nobunaga. Only a few of these survived, among them the Maeda of Kaga, the Ikeda of Bizen, the Yamanouchi of Tosa, and the Kuroda of Buzen. Next came the daimyo created by Hideyoshi. Again, precious few of these survived Sekigahara. Among them were some of the "generals" groups such as Kato Kiyōmasa of Higo, who had managed to cast his lot with Ieyasu before Sekigahara.

In the middle of the seventeenth century, the vast majority of daimyo lines had been created by the heads of the Tokugawa house. The Tokugawa daimyo, as noted earlier, were divided first into the collaterals (*ichimon*) and the house or hereditary daimyo (*fudai*). Ieyasu, in contrast with Nobunaga and Hideyoshi, fathered a large number of capable offspring; moreover, he lived long enough to see to the survival of more than enough cadet branches to safeguard the Tokugawa line. The collaterals were used in two particular ways: first, to protect the Tokugawa family from failure to provide an heir and, second, to hold strategically important locations. Among the collaterals, three lines established by direct descent from Ieyasu were given the privilege of bearing the Tokugawa surname. Ieyasu's ninth son was assigned the Owari domain (619,500 *koku*) centering on Nagoya. His tenth son was given the Kii domain (555,000 *koku*) in Wakayama, and his eleventh son was placed in the province of Hitachi (250,000 *koku*). These three Tokugawa branches, collectively known as the three houses (*sanke*), were available for shogunal succession should the main line started by Hidetada fail to produce an heir. In fact, this did happen following the death of Ietsugu, the seventh shogun, and Yoshimune was brought in from the Kii branch of the house to serve as the eighth shogun.

Strictly for the purpose of safeguarding the succession, three additional collateral lines were established in the mid-eighteenth century, two by Yoshimune and one by his son Ieshige. These were the Hitotsubashi, Tayasu, and Shimizu families, collectively called the three lords (*san kyō*). Not strictly daimyo, they had no domains but were assigned residential quarters in Edo Castle and received stipends of 100,000 *koku* each from the shogun's treasury. These three houses in time played important roles in shogunal politics, as is shown by the fact that both the eleventh and fifteenth shoguns came from the Hitotsubashi line.

There were other collaterals and simulated cadet houses. Under the first three shoguns, various favored sons were given the Matsudaira surname and provided with suitable domains. Such were the Matsudaira houses of Aizu and Echizen. All in all, the Tokugawa house was remarkably successful in safeguarding its succession, thereby avoiding debilitating succession quarrels or the possibility of takeover by a subordinate house exercising power through a puppet shogun.

Fudai daimyo held status within the shogun's houseband in early protocol according to the time and place of the first enrollment in the houseband. The oldest of these lines can be traced back to the Okazaki Castle or the Sumpu Castle years, although the majority were products of later stages in the rise of the Tokugawa house. From the standpoint of power politics, of course, size and location were more significant. At the end of the Edo era, of the 145 house daimyo, 14 held domains of 100,000 *koku* or more; 36 had domains assessed between 50,000 and 99,000 *koku;* 64 between 11,000 and 49,000 *koku;* and 31 held the minimum of 10,000 *koku.*

The majority of the *fudai* were placed in the Kantō close to Edo. This was true particularly for those at the lower levels of the *koku* scale. The larger among the *fudai*, however, were placed at strategically important spots across the country. The Okudaira of Utsunomiya (77,000 *koku*) for instance, were located to provide additional protection to Edo from one of the city's northern approaches. The Ii were given the critically important domain of Hikone (350,000 *koku*) that stood guard at the approach to Kyoto from the east. On the other side of the capital, the domain of Himeji (150,000 *koku*) was considered guardian of the western approach. First held by the Ikeda house (*tozama*), it was eventually placed in the hands of the Sakai house (*fudai*).

Farther to the west, house daimyo were placed at Matsue, Tsuyama, and Fukuyama. On Shikoku, daimyo bearing the Matsudaira surname held Takamatsu and Matsuyama on the island's two northern corners. On Kyushu, however, the Tokugawa were not well represented. The Ogasawara at Kokura (150,000 *koku*) and the Ōkubo of Karatsu (60,000 *koku*) were the prime daimyo representatives of the shogun, and the port of Nagasaki, held in rotation by bakufu-appointed governors, served as the shogunate's main bureaucratic center for the control of foreign trade.

Why, given the number of daimyo destroyed by the shogun in the years after Sekigahara, did not Ieyasu and his successors simply preempt domains at will and assign their own men to them at their own discretion? To some extent, this is what was done on a small scale by the expansion of the shogun's granary lands. But the scale was modest. The fact is that the Tokugawa shoguns, from the first to the last, considered the daimyo a necessary element of national administration. That is, the daimyo were not thought of as enemies of effective government but, rather, as necessities. Throughout the formative period of the Edo shogunate, the effort was to find capable and reliable daimyo, not to destroy them. Clearly, daimyo could not be artificially fabricated. Experience in the handling of men and lands at one level was a prerequisite for advancement to a higher level. For example, a small fief holder, say a bannerman of 1,000 *koku,* could not be raised to daimyo status in a single move. Among the house daimyo, those who after the move into the Kantō had received domains of 100,000 *koku* were later advanced into the 150,000-*koku* range but no higher, and those in the 30,000 range were held below the 100,000 range. A sense of proportion was clearly involved.

THE EDO SHOGUNATE: THE AUTHORITY STRUCTURE

By taking the office of shogun as his prime means of legitimation Tokugawa Ieyasu followed the precedent established by the two previous shogunates. As shogun, he claimed recognition as chief of the bushi estate and, as the emperor's delegate, the rights and responsibilities of national governance. In describing the Edo regime in its early phases, historians until recently have dwelt on the factor of rights and perquisites, almost to the exclusion of responsibilities. But the existence of an implicit compact on the part of the shogun to serve as guardian of the state (the *tenka*) and protector of its people was acknowledged by the shoguns themselves, particularly with regard to matters involving foreign relations, as in the cases of the spread of Christianity in the mid-seventeenth century and of foreign intrusion in the mid-nineteenth century. It was this publicly acknowledged responsibility, and right, to conduct foreign relations that most clearly distinguished the Edo bakufu's status in the hierarchy of national affairs.

In domestic affairs the most important of the shogun's rights and responsibilities derived from his position as the ultimate proprietor of the country's taxable land. This right was comprehensive and applied to all proprietary holding of land, whether by members of the court nobility or of the religious orders. The corresponding responsibility was the shogun's duty to provide good government, a task that he shared with the daimyo. Under the Edo polity, the proprietary possession of land was legally possible only when certified by the shogun's seal. This was particularly significant in the case of the daimyo, all of whom were the shogun's sworn vassals who held their domains as personal grants from him.

As supreme proprietary overlord, the shogun assumed the right to regulate all lesser proprietors, be they courtier, priest, or warrior aristocrat. This regulatory authority was spelled out in a series of codes (*hatto*) directed toward each of these groups. Note has already been taken of the orders covering the court and the daimyo; a closer look needs to be taken of the latter.[32] Ieyasu had anticipated this document in the three-clause oath of allegiance he had demanded of all daimyo in 1611 and 1612. Its provisions called for obedience to bakufu laws and agreement not to harbor disloyal or criminal samurai. The Buke shohatto in its first extended form of thirteen clauses was issued in 1615 following the Tokugawa victory at Osaka. It began with what was to become a trademark of the Edo shogunate's political philosophy for a military government functioning in an era of peace: "The study of letters and the practice of military arts, including archery and horsemanship, must be cultivated diligently." There followed admonitions against unruly conduct, luxurious living, and failure to abide by dress regulations. But the heart of the code was concerned with matters of control. Daimyo must not harbor antibakufu criminals in their domains. They must not repair or enlarge their castles without permission from the bakufu. They must gain shogunal approval before contracting a marriage. And they must report suspicious activities in neighboring domains.

From the time of Ieyasu the Buke shohatto was read before the assembled daimyo at the inauguration of each new shogun. Iemitsu, the third shogun, made the most changes in its content, increasing the provisions to twenty-one with the addition of prohibitions against private trade barriers, against ships of more than a five hundred-*koku* burden, and against the propagation of Christianity. This version clarified as well the provisions of alternate attendance (*sankin-kōtai*) and reiterated the decree that all laws emanating from Edo be obeyed as the law of the land.[33]

Unquestionably the most effective mechanism developed by the

32 Translation of this and other Tokugawa bakufu laws can be found in Ryusaku Tsunoda, William Theodore de Bary, and Donald Keene, eds., *Sources of Japanese Tradition* (New York: Columbia University Press, 1958).

33 Toshio G. Tsukahira, *Feudal Control in Tokugawa Japan: The Sankin Kotai System* (Cambridge, Mass.: Harvard East Asia Research Center, 1966).

Tokugawa shoguns was the alternative attendance requirement. At first applied selectively to *tozama* daimyo, it was made mandatory for all daimyo, including *fudai*, by Iemitsu in 1642. This extension of the common practice among the bushi commanders of taking hostages to ensure the loyalty of vassals and military allies obliged all daimyo to establish residences in the environs of Edo Castle so as to be available to pay regular attendance on the shogun. In their Edo residences, daimyo were required to domicile their wives, children, and a certain number of chief retainers, together with the necessary staff to maintain the official residences. Daimyo were permitted to return to their home domains in alternate years (in some instances, in alternate half-years) but were required to leave their wives and children and ranking retainers in Edo as hostages.

As a method of assisting shogunal authority, this practice continually affirmed Edo's political centrality. By means of alternate attendance, the shogun was able continuously to assemble the daimyo in Edo Castle for rituals and other gatherings. Communication between the bakufu and the daimyo was thereby made immediate and personal. Aside from these considerable advantages to the bakufu, there were other, perhaps unintended, side effects of alternate attendance. The maintenance of dual residences, at home and in Edo, and the expenses of frequent travel between them imposed a massive drain on the daimyo's treasury, especially for the lords in western Japan. By the end of the eighteenth century for many daimyo, alternate attendance was costing a third or more of their annual income, and as a result many were in serious debt to merchant financiers.

It should be recognized that the provisions of the Buke shohatto and other similar codes were couched in generalities so that enforcement could be at the whim of the enforcer. The first three shoguns, as we have seen, frequently used presumed violations of the code to justify their numerous attainders. In the early years, the bakufu kept the daimyo under constant scrutiny through such agents as the itinerant inspectors (*junkenshi*), created in 1633 to conduct periodic inquiries into daimyo domains. Their eyes were focused particularly on political conditions, the enforcement of anti-Christian edicts, and the state of daimyo military forces. Another type of bakufu official, the provincial inspectors (*kuni metsuke*) were used to watch over critical periods in a domain's existence, such as when succession passed into the hands of a minor. The bakufu also required the daimyo to submit a great variety of reports. Maps of the domain (*kuni ezu*) gave visual evidence of the location and *kokudaka* figures of the taxpaying villages. Population registers compiled as a by-product of the annual religious inquiry (*shūmon aratame*) were made available to the bakufu's inspector general (*ōmetsuke*). And periodic reports on judicial actions taken by daimyo had to be submitted to bakufu scrutiny.[34]

Although the daimyo gave up critical portions of their political autonomy to the bakufu, in actual practice they were left with considerable freedom in the administration of their domains. The bakufu did not tax them directly, on the principle that the daimyo's responsibilities to maintain order in their domains and to share in the regime's military defense constituted a sufficient contribution to the common good. The maintenance of a domain military force was, for a daimyo, both a right and a responsibility. The rules governing the performance of military service (*gun'yaku*) had both positive and negative implications.[35] The bakufu found itself caught between the desire to reduce daimyo military capacity so as to lessen the likelihood of rebellion, and the necessity, for purposes of defense and the maintenance of domestic peace, to keep a certain level of military force in readiness. The 1615 order restricting "one castle to a province" denied the daimyo the maintenance of more than one military establishment. The 1649 regulation on military service (Gun'yaku ninzuwari) set standard figures on the size of armed forces permitted to, or required of, daimyo according to their domain size. A 100,000-*koku* domain, for instance, was made accountable for 2,155 men, of which 170 were mounted, 350 carried firearms, 30 carried bows, 150 were spearmen, and 20 were trained in signal flags. A samurai with an enfeoffment of 200 *koku* was accountable for 5 men: himself with a horse, a horse leader, a spear bearer, an armor bearer, and a porter.

Although the bakufu tended to discourage the expansion of daimyo military establishments, daimyo were obliged to contribute heavily to the bakufu program of castle building. On the theory that construction for the bakufu was a public service, daimyo were obliged to contribute manpower, material, and funds for the construction and rebuilding of a series of shogunal castle and residences, palaces for the court nobility, and various public works projects. Daimyo were required to build or expand castles at Edo, Nijō (Kyoto), Hikone, Sumpu, Nagoya, and Osaka. Work on Edo Castle continued into the

34 The annual religious investigation registers required of all Japanese beginning in the 1630s, as a means of stamping out Christianity, have been used by modern demographers to reconstruct Edo population history. See Susan B. Hanley and Kozo Yamamura, *Economic and Demographic Change in Japan 1600–1868* (Princeton, N.J.: Princeton University Press, 1977).

35 The 1649 regulations for military service are published in Shihōsho, *Tokugawa kinrei kō*, 6 vols. (Tokyo: Yoshikawa kōbunkan, 1931–2), vol. 1, p. 129.

1630s and required the efforts of daimyo from all parts of the country, as far distant as the Mōri of Choshu and the Date of Sendai.[36]

Like every centralizing government, the Edo shogunate pursued the objective of standardizing weights and measurements and unifying the currency. The latter goal was facilitated by the shogun's acquisition of the country's major gold, silver, and copper mines. As one after another major city fell within its area of authority, the bakufu was able to exercise a powerful influence on the country's commercial life. The bakufu also succeeded in regulating foreign trade by channeling it through chosen instruments at Nagasaki, Tsushima, and Kagoshima. Thus step by step in the course of its efforts to govern the cities and villages under its direct administration, the bakufu established policies that set the national norm. The so-called Regulations of Keian (Keian ofuregaki) issued to the agricultural population of the shogunal demesne in 1646 and the 1655 Regulations for Edo (Edo machijū sadame) took their place among the principal legal documents of the age.

The dominance of military authority over the great monastic orders had been largely achieved by Oda Nobunaga and Toyotomi Hideyoshi. Until that time, monasteries held independent proprietary rights to extensive territories, and religious communities had built castles and recruited large bodies of armed men for their defense. Under the Edo bakufu, the religious bodies were further reduced in their landholdings, and the priesthood was regulated under the provisions of the 1655 Shoshū jiin hatto. The popular Honganji sect was divided into two branches, east and west, to reduce the sect's influence. But although the Buddhist orders were denied political influence and were greatly reduced in income, they were given a new and secure place in the Tokugawa order as the agents of anti-Christian policy. Under the *tera-uke*, or temple register, system, all Japanese were obliged to adopt a family temple of registry (*dannadera*). These temples in turn were given the task of making annual inquiries into the religious belief of their parishioners. The practice of religious inspection (*shūmon aratame*) was then institutionalized by the creation in 1640 of a bakufu office for that purpose.[37]

Finally, the shogun as national overlord exercised the right and responsibility to settle disputes and hear cases involving daimyo and other elements of the Tokugawa order. Whereas previously such dis-

36 See the example of Osaka Castle in William B. Hauser, "Osaka Castle and Tokugawa Authority in Western Japan," in Mass and Hauser, eds., *The Bakufu*, pp. 153–88.

37 George Elison, *Deus Destroyed: The Image of Christianity in Early Modern Japan* (Cambridge, Mass.: Harvard University Press, 1973), p. 195.

putes had been settled by direct military action, under the Edo bakufu, as spelled out in the Buke shohatto, the bakufu was to provide the mechanisms for settlement. A supreme court (*hyōjōsho*) staffed by daimyo and bannermen members of the shogun's upper administration was established in Edo Castle in 1722.

The commonly given description of the power structure that supported the Edo bakufu inevitably leaves the impression that the Tokugawa shogunate was all-powerful. If this indeed had been true, it would raise the question of how such a structure could have collapsed so suddenly after 1853. The truth is that many of the elements of power in the seventeenth century failed to retain their meaning in the nineteenth. Why did the Tokugawa house not follow the pattern, for instance, of the nearly contemporaneous Tudor monarchy in England and work toward a greater centralization of power?[38] There were, of course, some uncontrollable factors of decline. Mines of precious metals were unexpectedly exhausted. Epidemics, droughts, and famines debilitated whole regions and required the bakufu's material assistance. Economic conditions worsened for the entire samurai class.

Unlike the European monarchs, however, the shogunate, once a stable power structure had been achieved, did little to extend the powers of the central government and instead allowed many of these powers to decay. Not only was there no effort made to do away with the daimyo, but the many restrictions that proved so essential in the early years were softened or even abandoned. The 1651 decision to allow "deathbed adoptions" eliminated one of the most effective weapons the shogun had in finding reasons to dispossess daimyo.

By virtue of its dependence on a balance of power between shogun and daimyo, the *bakuhan* system was particularly vulnerable to the effect of time once the central authority abandoned its aggressive effort to build up its strength at the expense of the daimyo. When control regulations became routine, when the surveillance of the daimyo by bakufu inspectors was carried out halfheartedly, as economic problems affected the samurai class, and as the bakufu's finances deteriorated, the central authority was weakened disproportionately.

BAKUFU ORGANIZATION

The organs of shogunal administration evolved from the Tokugawa house organization as the Tokugawa family worked its way from the

38 Bolitho, *Treasures*, p. 18.

status of village samurai to head of a major regional daimyo coalition and finally to national hegemon. Early patterns of military and civil organization were carried over into the institutions of national governance, expanded, refined, or modified to handle changing requirements. Military and administrative service remained the expected "return" for the "favor" granted by the shogun as overlord. The consequences of this evolutionary process are most clearly seen in the manner in which the shogun staffed his military forces and administrative offices. For although Tokugawa authority extended over the entire country, the bakufu itself was manned only by the houseband, that is, the house daimyo, the bannermen, and the direct retainers or housemen. This was the inner group of dependent personnel under the shogun's direct command. The outside lords and even the cadet and collateral daimyo were treated as allies existing outside this circle.

An early view of the Matsudaira (Tokugawa) house organization comes into focus during the latter years of its Okazaki phase. By this time, the Matsudaira chief had pulled together a houseband consisting of related families (most of them bearing the Matsudaira surname), local gentry (*kunishū*) who had been reduced to vassalage, and stipended housemen (*kenin*). Already the practice was developing whereby the chief, as daimyo, was relying increasingly on direct military subordinates, *fudai* and *kenin*, rather than members of his kinship group, to carry the burden of enforcement and defense. Whereas many daimyo continued to rely heavily on senior collaterals and hereditary vassals with a long history of association with the daimyo's house, the Matsudaira policy, at least under Ieyasu, was more flexible and responsive to the needs of the chief. As head of the Matsudaira (Tokugawa) main line, Ieyasu had persistently kept his options open and relied when possible on nonkin vassals and on direct retainers of the *hatamoto* and *gokenin* variety, on the assumption that they would be more responsive to his command. The problem with kinsmen was that because they were eligible for family succession, they were potential rivals to the existing family head. Thus, when possible, kin branch heads were reduced to military vassalage. This practice was facilitated by the constant move and expansion of the locus of the Tokugawa domain. For example, the Tokugawa houseband that started with a preponderance of members from Mikawa Province was enlarged by recruits from Suruga, Tōtōmi, Kai, and Shinano, as Ieyasu added these provinces to his control.

A document of 1567 is useful for its insight into the military and civil organization of the Tokugawa domain.[39] For command purposes the Tokugawa houseband was organized on two separate levels: at the top between the daimyo and his direct vassal commanders, and below that between the commanders and their own military bands or units (*kumi*). For military purposes the majority of the daimyo's vassals were assigned to two divisions under separate leaders. In one, Sakai Tadatsugu was placed over eighteen vassal commanders (seven bearing the Matsudaira surname). In the other Ishikawa Kazumasa took the lead of thirteen vassal commanders (three of them Matsudaira). In addition there were five commanders of bannermen companies and two commanders of rearguard companies. Units under ten vassal commanders were designated keepers of the castle (*gorusui shū*), and fifteen headed units of foot soldiers (*ashigaru*). Other officers were placed in charge of flags and communications, ships, packhorses, and supplies. The civil affairs of the domain were assigned to the so-called three magistrates (san bugyō), to which Ieyasu appointed his trusted retainers, Ōsuga Yasutaka, Uemura Masakatsu, and Kōriki Kiyoyasa. Under them were three chief intendants (*daikan gashira*) charged with collecting land taxes, and a variety of officers responsible for currencies, weights and measures, the kitchen, the secretariat, documents, and the like. Among special service personnel there were attendant priests and physicians. The establishment of a bureaucracy with numerous functionally specific offices had already begun to take shape. And supporting this were personnel organized into three categories of *karō* (elders), *bugyō* (functional unit heads), and *daikan* (intendants).

As this houseband organization expanded into the Kantō in 1590 and then across the entire nation after 1600, the basic composition of the inner command structure did not change. The Tokugawa bakufu remained essentially an expanded houseband in which the chieftain (now the shogun) governed through his hereditary vassals and other types of direct retainers. But in addition there were now two new groups of daimyo located outside the houseband that had to be accommodated. These were the cadet or collateral houses and the *tozama* allies. Neither of these groups of daimyo routinely held office in the bakufu.

The central bureaucracy

The massive bureaucracy that eventually took shape under the Tokugawa shoguns was not yet fully organized at the time Ieyasu became

39 Fujino, *Bakuhan taisei*, p. 29.

shogun.[40] Many offices and administrative procedures we think of as having been part of the bakufu practice from the start actually were not adopted until well into the second half of the century. At the time of Ieyasu's death, a number of basic problems in the transition of governance from charismatic leadership to bureaucratic routine had yet to be solved. Most critical was the continuing disagreement over the locus of policymaking authority, whether it should reside with the shogun alone or in council with the chief advisory positions in the bakufu.[41]

Tokugawa Ieyasu had been fairly successful in defending himself and his immediate successors against interference from the collaterals. As it turned out, it was the leading members of the house daimyo who gave the shoguns the most trouble. The neat table of organization charts of the Edo bakufu, which list upwards of four hundred posts in chain-of-command order, mask the problems of competition for control of policy and enforcement authority that plagued Edo bakufu politics. While Ieyasu was still alive, it would have been hard to imagine that differences of policy would develop between the shogun and the house daimyo, whose interests as a whole were represented by the *rōjū* (senior councilors). Historically, shogun and *fudai* had worked together to win the *tenka,* with the bakufu being simply the mechanism through which the shogun activated the daimyo and governed the country. But as time passed, the *fudai* found their private interests as daimyo diverging from those of the Tokugawa house. As a result, control over bakufu policy became a prize sought by a number of special interests, including the shogun, the collateral daimyo, and the house daimyo.

The first three shoguns managed to assert their political leadership by controlling a circle of personal favorites whom they placed in high advisory posts such as the Senior Council. Ieyasu's use of his own "brain trust" is well documented. Hidetada's reliance on Doi Toshikatsu (1573–1644), his youthful companion, and Iemitsu's reliance on Hotta Masamori (1608–51) exemplify the ability of strong shoguns to govern through chosen instruments. But later shoguns found it increasingly difficult to have their own way in making appointments to high office. Each shogun thereafter was obliged to fight for his own identity, in a number of different ways with varying degrees of success.

40 There are numerous versions of the Edo bakufu's table of organization. A complete and informative one is "Edo bakufu," in Kokushi daijiten henshū iinkai, comp., *Kokushi daijiten* (Tokyo: Yoshikawa kōbunkan, 1980), vol. 2, pp. 331–6.

41 Harold Bolitho has clarified the nature of the tensions between the wishes of the *fudai* daimyo and the interests of the shogun. See his chapter "Fudai Daimyo and Bakufu Policy: 1600–1857," in his *Treasures*, pp. 154ff.

Iemitsu's successor as shogun, Ietsuna, being but ten years old and physically weak, was quickly captured by the senior *fudai* houses. Later shoguns found it expedient to rely on more easily controlled "inner officers" such as the chamberlains. Tsunayoshi, the fifth shogun, who came to the office as a mature man, began his tenure by dismissing the distinguished Tairō Sakai Tadakiyo. It was rumored that Sakai had plotted to install a courtier as a figurehead shogun, in order to gain control of bakufu policy. Tsunayoshi was thus the first to use successfully the inner office route to bypass the senior *fudai*.

The shogun in theory was a despot, accountable to none but the emperor. (See Figure 4.2.) The emperor in turn represented the "will of Heaven" that placed on the shogun the responsibility to ensure the well-being of the people. A child or an incapacitated shogun could be guided by a regent, and on occasion collateral members of the Tokugawa house could intervene in situations affecting the well-being of the extended Tokugawa lineage. A case in point would be the choice of an heir to the shogun. Informal or irregular involvement by members of the three houses and other Tokugawa collaterals was made possible by the fact that the daimyo of this category sat together in the shogun's palace on ceremonial occasions. But in legal terms there was no higher authority between the shogun and "shogunal policy."

In making policy, the head of the Tokugawa house followed the common daimyo practice of recognizing certain senior vassals as "elders." Ieyasu and Hidetada used such terms as *toshiyori* and *shukurō* to designate members of a senior advisory council. Under Iemitsu the term *kahan no retsu* (seal bearer) was applied to senior daimyo with powers to represent the shogun's authority. This practice was eventually formalized by the creation of two advisory boards of retainers. A group of four to six senior councilors (*rōjū*) constituting a high administrative council was brought into place in stages beginning in 1623. Staffed by high-level *fudai* daimyo, the Senior Council was given authority over matters of national scope, including supervision of the Kyoto court, the daimyo of all classes, religious bodies, foreign affairs, defense, taxation, currency, and other matters of major importance. A second board or council of three to five junior councilors (*wakadoshiyori*) was formalized in 1633 to handle the more domestic aspects of shogunal rule. Composed of *fudai* daimyo of lesser rank, it had jurisdiction over the bannermen and housemen, their assignment to office and promotion in rank. The Junior Council also was charged with the peacetime training and assignment of guard units, the procurement of military supplies, and other such military matters.

The composition of the two councils, particularly the Senior Council, reflected at any given time the existing balance of influence within the bakufu, between the shogun and his primary vassals, and among the house daimyo. The position of great councilor (*tairō*) was less clearly defined. Presumably the name implied an advisory role over the senior councilors. But the post was not routinely filled, and its political significance is not at all clear. In the long Tokugawa history, only Ii Naosuke, who in 1858 was the last to be appointed grand councilor, used his position to affect bakufu policy. And for this he was promptly assassinated.

Aside from the councilors, several other offices reported directly to the shogun. The post of grand chamberlain, established in 1681, was an outgrowth of the office of *sobashū*, or chamberlain. The chamberlains waited on the shogun under the direction of the *rōjū*. By placing the grand chamberlain directly under the shogun, the post acquired great potential influence. When occupied by a shogun's favorite, it could be used as a means of circumventing the Senior Council. The most flagrant example of this was the case of Tanuma Okitsugu, who served under Ieharu as both senior councilor and grand chamberlain.

Also reporting to the shogun were the twenty or more masters of shogunal ceremony (*sōjaban*), who functioned as protocol officers, establishing the shogun's schedule, mediating between shogun and daimyo, and organizing the pageantry that attended the shogun's ceremonial routine. Another position concerned with shogunal ritual was that of *kōke* (master of court ceremony). This post was held in hereditary succession by the heads of certain families who had monopolized the technical details of dealing with the Kyoto court since the time of the Muromachi shogunate. They were of low rank but commanded high prestige because of their historical association with the court. They reported to the Senior Council.

Of the offices under direct shogunal command, the position of superintendent of temples and shrines (*jisha bugyō*), customarily assigned to four individuals, had as their main duties the regulation of religious orders and their landholdings. They also were responsible for maintaining law and order in the shogun's lands lying outside the Kantō. The office was frequently held jointly with that of the *sōjaban*. Two positions of particular significance outside Edo were the Kyoto deputy (Kyoto *shoshidai*) and the keeper of Osaka Castle (Osaka *jōdai*). The former was charged with overseeing the affairs of the Kyoto court and the court nobility. The latter was the senior military officer in central Japan, with special responsibility to maintain the military strength of

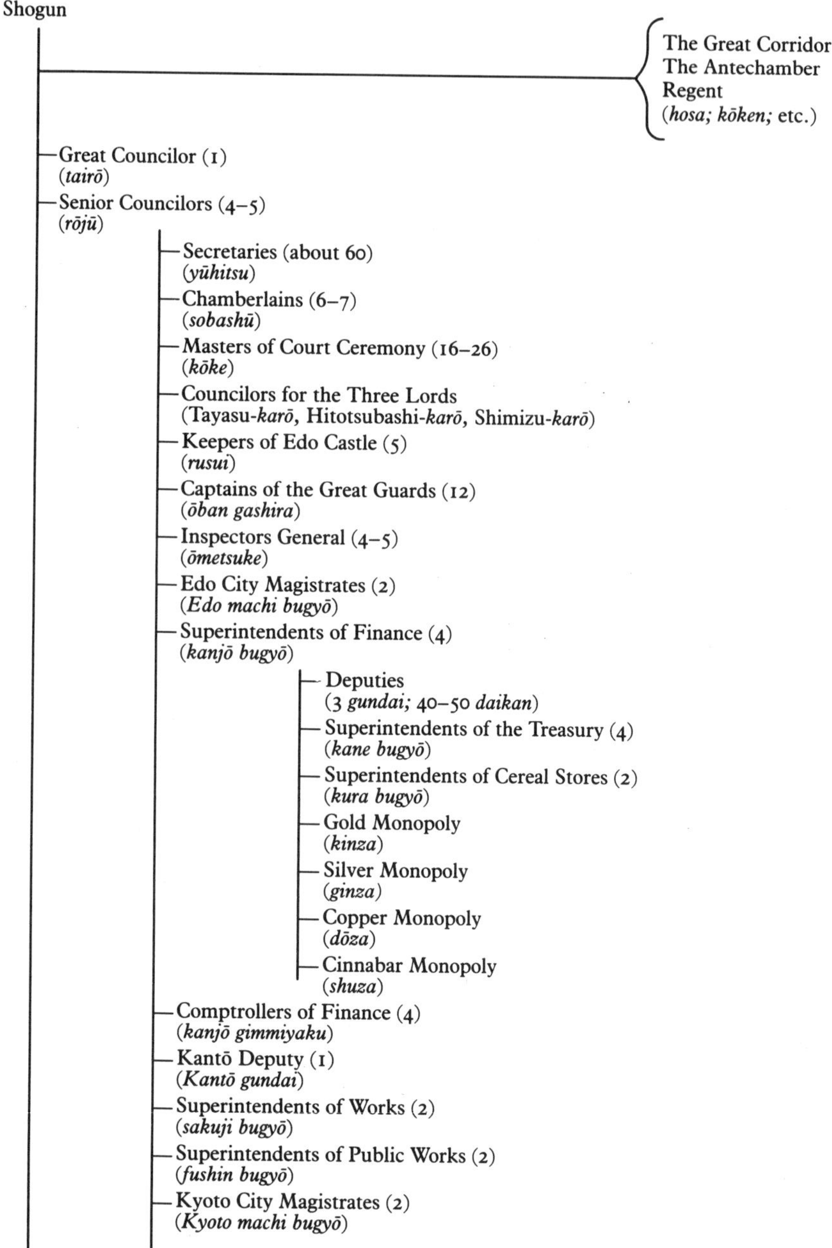

Figure 4.2 Main offices of the Tokugawa bakufu. [Source: John W. Hall, *Tanuma Okitsugu: Forerunner of Modern Japan* (Cambridge, Mass.: Harvard University Press, 1955), pp. 28–9.]

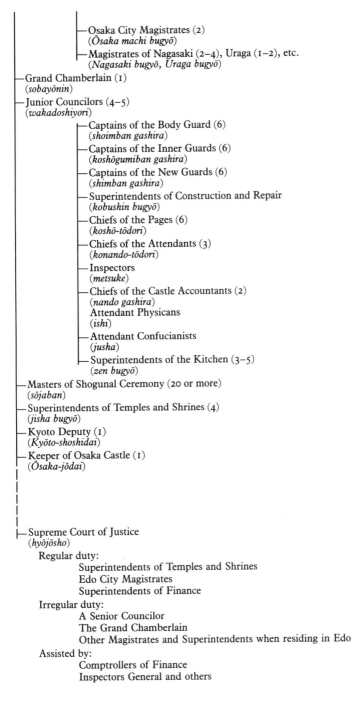

- Osaka City Magistrates (2) (*Ōsaka machi bugyō*)
- Magistrates of Nagasaki (2–4), Uraga (1–2), etc. (*Nagasaki bugyō, Uraga bugyō*)

- Grand Chamberlain (1) (*sobayōnin*)
- Junior Councilors (4–5) (*wakadoshiyori*)
  - Captains of the Body Guard (6) (*shoimban gashira*)
  - Captains of the Inner Guards (6) (*koshōgumiban gashira*)
  - Captains of the New Guards (6) (*shimban gashira*)
  - Superintendents of Construction and Repair (*kobushin bugyō*)
  - Chiefs of the Pages (6) (*koshō-tōdori*)
  - Chiefs of the Attendants (3) (*konando-tōdori*)
  - Inspectors (*metsuke*)
  - Chiefs of the Castle Accountants (2) (*nando gashira*)
  - Attendant Physicans (*ishi*)
  - Attendant Confucianists (*jusha*)
  - Superintendents of the Kitchen (3–5) (*zen bugyō*)
- Masters of Shogunal Ceremony (20 or more) (*sōjaban*)
- Superintendents of Temples and Shrines (4) (*jisha bugyō*)
- Kyoto Deputy (1) (*Kyōto-shoshidai*)
- Keeper of Osaka Castle (1) (*Ōsaka-jōdai*)
- Supreme Court of Justice (*hyōjōsho*)
  - Regular duty:
    - Superintendents of Temples and Shrines
    - Edo City Magistrates
    - Superintendents of Finance
  - Irregular duty:
    - A Senior Councilor
    - The Grand Chamberlain
    - Other Magistrates and Superintendents when residing in Edo
  - Assisted by:
    - Comptrollers of Finance
    - Inspectors General and others

Osaka Castle as the primary bakufu military presence west of the Kantō.

Edo Castle served as headquarters for the bakufu administration. Here was located the business office (*yōbeya*) close by the shogun's daytime apartments. And it was here that the two bodies of councilors attended to the business of government. Under the Senior Council some officials, such as the secretaries (*yūhitsu*), the chamberlains (*sōbashū*), and the superintendents of works (*sakuji bugyō*), saw to the maintenance of the shogun's public posture as head of state. Others, like the keepers of Edo Castle (*rusui*), the captains of the great guards (*ōban gashira*), and the inspectors general (*ōmetsuke*), were chiefly supervisory and defensive in nature. A group of officials who have not been well understood were the *metsuke* (inspectors). Described as "spies" by the early Western observers of Japan in the nineteenth century, and also as "censors" by China hands, they performed police and enforcement duties at numerous levels. Most *metsuke* served under the Junior Council and hence did not form a hierarchy of political control in concert with the inspector general.

The land base and its management

In real terms, once the necessities of military readiness had been taken care of, the most important administrative offices under the Senior Council were the superintendents of finance (*kanjō bugyō*) and the magistrates of major cities (*machi bugyō*). The former were doubly important because their authority covered both the collection of bakufu taxes and the civil administration of the villages that comprised the shogun's direct landholdings. The shogunal lands were administered much as they had been when Ieyasu was still a daimyo in the Tōkai region, that is, by a network of rural intendants (called *gundai* or *daikan*).[42] When Ieyasu moved into the Kantō, he established the office of the superintendent of the Kantō (Kantō *sōbugyō*) to oversee a number of chief intendants (*daikan gashira*). After the battle of Sekigahara, as the Tokugawa acquired more and more houseland in all parts of Japan, the intendant system was expanded, along with various makeshift arrangements for administering distant holdings. For instance, the Kyoto deputy, the keeper of Osaka Castle, and the keeper of Sumpu Castle administered the shogunal land in their vicinities. But the most commonly used expedient was to assign distant lands to

42 Kitajima, *Kenryoku kōzō*, pp. 214ff.

nearby daimyo as trust lands (*azukari dokoro*). The daimyo so designated were responsible for administering and collecting taxes on behalf of the bakufu. In the middle of the eighteenth century, between 13 and 18 percent of the *tenryō* was administered in this way. Trust arrangements were not assigned in the Kantō, but in the northern provinces they amounted to more than 387,000 *koku*.

The various temporary arrangements by which the first two shoguns managed their fiscal affairs were finally consolidated in 1642 by the creation of the office of the superintendent of finance (*kanjō gashira*).[43] The office was placed under the Senior Council to coordinate bakufu fiscal administration. At the same time, changes were made both in the type of official named to the intendancies and in their life-style. As he moved into unfamiliar Kantō territory, Ieyasu had found it expedient to appoint village samurai who had experience in village administation under the Hōjō and other eastern daimyo. Many of these officials had been able to aggrandize themselves after the Tokugawa takeover. Some had built fortified residences (*jinya*) and exercised personal, hence undesirable, command over the villages in their territories. The early practice of permitting intendants to deduct their office stipends from the annual tax payment to the bakufu was particularly open to abuse.

Corruption in rural tax collection and the lack of uniformity in the handling of rural administration prompted the bakufu to carry out reforms in this area. Gradually, administrative procedures were systematized under the Finance Office. At the same time the great rural families, like the Ina who had monopolized the posts of chief intendant, were replaced by low-ranking bannermen with stipends that averaged only 100 to 150 *koku*. Whereas in 1681 there had been as many as ninety-nine intendants, by 1734 the number had fallen to about forty-six. Thereafter, throughout the Edo era the number seldom rose above fifty. In the course of their duties *daikan* personally moved between Edo and official residences or headquarters (*daikansho*) located in the territory they administered. These headquarters were supplied with offices, prisons, and modest defenses and, of course, granaries.

Surely the most remarkable feature of the bakufu intendancy system was that so much territory could be administered by such a small number of officials. In essence some fifty low-level bannermen were assigned to administer land rated – if we subtract the trust lands from

43 Ibid., p. 347.

the overall total – at over 3.4 million *koku*. This made for an average of 70,000 *koku* per intendant, the same as a fair-sized daimyo domain. *Daikan* were given an extremely limited staff and no armed forces to speak of. Bakufu regulations carefully prescribed the authorized staff of clerks, guards, and porters at around thirty individuals for each *daikansho*. The intendant, in addition to his regular stipend, received an allowance in cash as well as maintenance allowances of bales of rice (*fuchi mai*) for the staff. But these were also too limited to serve the purpose adequately.

That so small a staff could administer so large a domain can be explained in terms of what can be called the "power content" of the *bakuhan* system. Villages in the *tenryō* were never out of range of well-armed daimyo castle headquarters, and in emergencies, intendants could call for assistance from neighboring daimyo. The relative quiescence of the rural population reflects as well the effectiveness of the mura system in which each village was taxed as a unit and in which the village headman was used as a bridge between samurai authority and farmer self-administration.

There is considerable debate over whether rural communities under the *bakuhan* system were kept as relatively tranquil as it appears they were, by the coercive power of samurai government or by the relatively benign nature of the mura system of rural administration.[44] The remarkable fact remains that in gross terms the income from the bakufu granary lands, although showing minor ups and downs, remained roughly the same throughout the last hundred years of the bakufu's existence. This can be interpreted in contradictory ways: for instance as a sign of weakness or lethargy on the part of the bakufu tax collectors, who failed to exact more taxes, or in the reverse as a sign of the debilitating oppression of samurai rule. But the mura system must surely be given credit for creating a rural environment that was not totally coercive and extractive. With the removal of the samurai class from the countryside, the mura, or village, as the basic unit of rural society and administration, defined a world that was essentially of the peasant's own making. Shogunal and daimyo authority touched this world through the village headman who no longer retained samurai status or authority.

The village as a unit of rural administration was the result of a lengthy evolution of agrarian society to free itself from the direct

44 In Western scholarship the classic controversy is between the Marxist approach, represented by E. H. Norman in his *Japan's Emergence As a Modern State*, and the more recent work of neoclassicist economic historians such as Kozo Yamamura.

control of the rural samurai.[45] Thus as the daimyo of the Sengoku era carried out their new land surveys and drew the samurai away from their fiefs, they brought into being village communities that had bargained with the daimyo to provide an agreed-upon annual tax payment in exchange for varying degrees of village self-management. Mura were composed of registered taxpaying farmers (*hyakushō*), their tenants, and dependent workers. Self-management was provided by an administrative staff composed of villagers and subject to a certain amount of village selection. Each mura had its headman (*nanushi* or *shōya*), and a villagers' representative (*hyakushō dai*). Village families had to form neighborhood groups (*goningumi*) for purposes of mutual assistance but also to serve as units of mutual responsibility and vicarious enforcement of regulations.

To say that this arrangement amounted to village self-administration and that this favored the villagers as a whole may seem too easy a judgment. Throughout the Edo era the village community remained divided between families of wealth and those of economic dependence.[46] At the start of the seventeenth century many of the villagers designated as *hyakushō* in the Taikō land surveys had been rustic samurai (*jizamurai*) before they had faced the option of joining as samurai the local daimyo in his castle town or remaining in the village and losing their samurai status. Within the village, moreover, ex-samurai were able to retain a degree of special influence, owing to the dominant role their families had once played. Such families tended to monopolize the office of headman, and most often had extensive landholdings. The kind of "extralegal" influence exerted by such wealthy villagers, however, was considered undesirable by both shogun and daimyo, so that samurai government sought to convert village headmen as much as possible into simple officeholders performing administrative functions for higher authority. It worked also to regularize rural administration.

As will be described in a later chapter, the bakufu's first noteworthy effort to reform local administration occurred after 1680 when the shogun Tsunayoshi instructed Hotta Masatoshi, at the time a member of the Senior Council, to look into the problem of *tenryō* administration. The result was the discovery of wide areas of mismanagement,

45 This subject is well covered in Chapter 10 in this volume. On the course of village evolution as a political entity, see Keiji Nagahara, with Kozo Yamamura, "Village Communities and Daimyo Power," in John Whitney Hall and Takeshi Toyoda, eds. *Japan in the Muromachi Age* (Princeton, N.J.: Princeton University Press, 1977), pp. 107–23.

46 Thomas C. Smith, "The Japanese Village in the Seventeenth Century," in Hall and Jansen, eds., *Studies*, pp. 263–82.

which led to the dismissal of some thirty-five intendants over the course of several years. Within their domains, daimyo found similar problems. There were two potential trouble spots. The first was the tendency of the enfeoffed vassals to press villagers arbitrarily, particularly over matters of taxation and labor service. The second was the possible high-handed treatment of village members by headmen and senior headmen. Both shogun and daimyo sought to convert the remnants of the local *jizamurai* system into the more prevalent stipendiary system and to bring the village headmen into strict fiscal accountability. The abolition by the bakufu of the post of *ōjoya*, or village group headmen, in 1712 is an example of this effort.

Although the intendancy system, by which the inhabitants of the shogun's granary lands were administered, appeared to be seriously understaffed, it cannot be said that there was any lack of regulatory effort. And because bakufu policies were expected to set the national standard, bakufu regulations took on special importance. Out of the flood of bakufu pronouncements, the 1643 (Kan'ei) edict carried the often-repeated prohibition against the "permanent sale of cultivated land" (*dembata eitai baibai no kinshi*). The one dating from 1649 (Keian *ofuregaki*) is of particular interest for its moralistic and condescending tone. It begins with an exhortation to rise early and work industriously. It then advises against luxurious living and prohibits the drinking of saké and tea and the smoking of tobacco. But military government was not totally restrictive. The 1649 edict contained the remarkable provision that if a farmer found the local intendant's administration unbearable, so long as his taxes were paid up, he could move to another district.[47]

Bakufu finances

The bakufu's Finance Office did more than regulate granary lands; it was charged with collecting revenue from all sources, rural as well as commercial, and with outlay. Under its authority were the central and regional granaries and treasuries. Its personnel handled the payment of stipends to housemen and some of the bannermen, the issuing of currency, and, increasingly, the setting of fiscal policy. Finance Office personnel underwent several dramatic changes during the first century of bakufu history. This was evident in its size, which went from a

47 This document can be found in English translation in David John Lu, comp., *Sources of Japanese History*, 2 vols. (New York: McGraw-Hill, 1974, vol. 1, pp. 209–10.

handful of nonspecialist bannermen to well over a hundred officials, among whom many were highly experienced in financial affairs. Specialization also was evident in the separation of the superintendants themselves into those having either financial (*katte*) or judicial (*kuji*) duties. As part of Tsunayoshi's cleanup of the bakufu finances, a separate office of financial comptrollers (*kanjō gimmiyaku*) was created in 1682 to serve as a check on the activities of the Finance Office. The comptrollers were of relatively low rank; the office was classed at five hundred *koku* and carried an office stipend of three hundred *hyō*. But because they were placed directly under the Senior Council, the comptrollers could report any negative findings directly to a higher authority. By the time of Yoshimune, the practice had come into use of giving one of the senior councilors the duty of financial oversight.[48]

An overall accounting for the finances of the Edo bakufu is not easily made. Not only were the sources of income hard to identify fully, but the items of expenditure also were not systematically recorded. For over a hundred years, it would seem, no nationwide record of income and expenditures was kept. Nor was there a clear difference between the private finances of the Tokugawa house and the bakufu's public fiscal affairs. In practice, regional separation between the Kantō and the Kansai remained strong. This situation improved somewhat after 1716 when, under the influence of the shogunal adviser Arai Hakuseki, uniform financial accounting mechanisms were adopted and eventually an annual budget was drawn up.[49]

From the start the Tokugawa bakufu suffered from certain obvious systemic problems. First, even though the shogunate assumed nationwide political and military obligations, it restricted its base of fiscal and personnel operations to the shogun's personal houseband. Second, in its basic policy, it held to the general principle that the affairs of government were properly handled as a normal function of the members of the samurai class, whose lands and stipends presumably provided them with sufficient income to perform the tasks to which they were assigned. In theory, therefore, all the bakufu had to do was to deliver to the bannermen and housemen the stipends due their rank. But it became evident that the hereditary stipends received by bannermen and housemen were not sufficient to sustain them when

48 The history of the establishment of the Finance Office in the bakufu is analyzed by Ono Mizuo in Kitajima Masamoto, ed., *Bakuhansei kokka seiritsu katei no kenkyū* (Tokyo: Yoshikawa kōbunkan, 1978), pp. 126–57.

49 Arai Hakuseki's autobiographical diary, *Oritaku shiba no ki*, was translated by Joyce Ackroyd as *Told Round a Brushwood Fire: The Autobiography of Arai Hakuseki* (Princeton, N.J.: Princeton University Press, 1979).

they were assigned to bureaucratically demanding jobs. And so a compromise was made.[50] For certain offices, special "office funds" (*yakuryō*) were added, beginning in 1655. Later, the practice of temporarily enhancing the officeholder's base stipend during his tenure, a practice known as *tashidaka*, was adopted, thereby making it possible to assign to an office an individual whose base salary was below that of the office to which he was named. These added expenditures for office and salary support were just one of many categories that required funding beyond normal expectations.

The most important source of bakufu income was, of course, granary land. This had swelled to over 4 million *koku* by the end of the seventeenth century and occasionally rose to over 4.5 million in the ensuing years. From these holdings the bakufu received between 1.4 million and 1.6 million *koku* in taxes annually. There were other sources of income, however, such as the numerous miscellaneous revenues from commercial business, export and import dues, transport taxes, and frontage taxes collected in the major cities. The bakufu also received income from the monopoly of certain commodities such as silk thread imported from China at Nagasaki. The shogun's control of the currency also yielded important revenues, first, as new coins were minted from ore produced from the shogun's mines and, after 1698, when the bakufu resorted to debasing the circulating coins. Because of the lack of documentation, it is difficult to get an overall picture of bakufu finances, but some sense of the complexity of the conditions faced by the bakufu can be gained from Furushima Toshio's Chapter 10 in this volume.[51]

The overall financial and economic health of the Edo bakufu within the *bakuhan* system should be viewed in evolutionary terms.[52] Under the early shoguns, finances were not a problem: The numerous daimyo attainders allowed the confiscation of land and goods. The high productivity of the bakufu mines fed the large stores of bullion that accumulated in Osaka, Edo, and Sumpu storehouses. At his death Ieyasu left some 1.9 million *ryō* of gold, well over the entire annual budget by 1840. This permitted a distribution of inheritance to the Owari and Kii collaterals of 30,000 *ryō* each and 15,000 *ryō* to Mito. Hidetada left to Iemitsu a 3.2 million-*ryō* reserve, permitting a distribu-

50 Kitajima, *Kenryoku kōzō*, pp. 474–9.

51 Furushima Toshio is one of the primary scholars working in this field; see his *Kinsei keizaishi no kiso katei – nengu shūdatsu to kyōdōtai* (Tokyo: Iwanami shoten, 1978). Chapter 10 in this volume reflects his findings in the larger work.

52 See the tightly reasoned survey of bakufu finances in Ono Mizuo, "Kanjōsho," in *Kokushi daijiten*, vol. 3, pp. 834–6.

tion of 32,000 *ryō* in gifts to daimyo. Under Iemitsu the bakufu confronted numerous special expenses such as the building of the Nikkō mausoleum, the giving of largess to the merchants of Edo and Kyoto when the shogun made his progress to Kyoto, and the suppression of the Shimabara Rebellion. Moreover, these were years when the bakufu could still call on the daimyo to pick up the expense of castle construction, the building of residences in Edo and Kyoto, and many other symbols of conspicuous display.

But after the third shogun died, the flow of special financial support began to move in other directions. Beginning with the great Edo fire of 1657, we find the bakufu providing loans and gifts of money to help the rebuilding of daimyo and samurai residences. Fires and periodic natural calamities, such as earthquakes and volcanic eruptions of Mt. Fuji and Mt. Asama, required costly rehabilitation. Fiscal deficits began to appear in 1678. And from this time on, maintaining solvency was a running battle. The discovery of the expedient of currency debasement was the single most useful device for balancing the bakufu budget, and it was used frequently.

Recognition of fiscal realities grew in three stages in the bakufu leadership. First came the realization that corruption was a problem and required immediate and drastic action. Second came the effort to identify special problems for specific remedial action, illustrated by Arai Hakuseki's efforts to reform bakufu policy toward foreign trade. Third, we come to the time of shogun Yoshimune, who attempted to work out an overall, comprehensive fiscal, or economic, policy for the country. He recognized that such a policy would have to include within its purview the country's growing commercial dimension.

Urban administration

From the middle of the eighteenth century a significant portion of bakufu income was derived from taxes on urban property, fees on commercial and transport activities, and other nonagricultural sources. To understand this development we must turn to the urban sector of the Edo government. The standard pattern of city administration was through the bakufu-appointed city magistrate (*machi bugyō*), who for large cities like Edo, Osaka, and Kyoto would be daimyo or bannermen of some size and importance.

The typical city under the *bakuhan* system was the castle town, like Edo, which had grown up in response to the needs of a daimyo as he organized his domains during the warfare of the sixteenth century. As the regional hegemons built fortresses of great size and drew garrison troops around them, new cities developed that became the domiciles for nearly the entire samurai class. These in turn drew large numbers of service personnel: merchants, artisans, and professional groups of all types.[53]

The bakufu set the model for urban administration, as most of the largest cities were held under its direct control. Edo, Osaka, Kyoto, Sumpu, Nagasaki, and Ōtsu, the most important of the *tenryō* cities, were each quite different in history and function, but the general pattern of administration was similiar. Bakufu administration over the nonsamurai residents was vested in the city magistrate, who maintained an office (*bugyōsho*) to which were attached a staff of clerks and enforcement officers (*yoriki, dōshin*). In both Edo and Osaka it became necessary to divide the office into two, on opposite sides of the city. And it was always customary to name two magistrates who rotated on duty on alternate months. Below the magistrates the urban population, referred to as *chōnin,* was organized much as the rural populace was, under a system of local management. The basic unit was the ward (*machi* or *chō*) headed by ward heads (*machidoshiyori*). Urban householders were required to form mutual responsibility groups (*goningumi*), as did villagers. Osaka was further divided into districts composed of several wards, and these were headed by elders (*sōdoshiyori*). Thus there were several layers of *chōnin* administrators between samurai officialdom and the city dwellers themselves.

In the formative years of the *bakuhan* system, daimyo and shogun adopted a positive attitude toward the mercantile community, offering merchants and other service groups attractive conditions in order to lure them to their castle headquarters. Although later the *chōnin* became subject to a variety of excise taxes, license fees, and compulsory loans (both forced and secured), they were never as systematically and heavily taxed as were the agriculturalists. Samurai government placed merchants under various restraints, but it also relied on the mercantile community to bridge the gap between the urban-based samurai and the rural commoners who produced food and other goods. Urbanization and the spread of money economy created conditions that enabled merchants and manufacturers to become essential to the well-being of the warrior class. But the Edo period samurai government had diffi-

53 The study of castle towns has grown in proportion to the study of daimyo domains. Chapter 11, by Nakai Nobuhiko and James L. McClain, in this volume provides a good overview of Edo period urbanization. McClain also has written a thorough survey of Kanazawa as a castle town.

culty working out institutionally a satisfactory relationship between the two segments of the society.

The first three Tokugawa shoguns articulated the shogunate's basic policies toward the commercial sector. Special service, or contract, merchants (*goyō shōnin*) – among them the houses charged with procuring precious metals and minting them into currency – were given new charters. Restrictions were placed on foreign trade to the advantage of chartered merchants who monopolized foreign imports of silk on behalf of the bakufu. The bakufu also issued generic laws and regulations (*furegaki*) that established the national structure within which the commercial economy could operate. The regulations of 1615 that dealt with such matters as the disputes between commercial litigants or problems of family inheritance were typical of the effort of the samurai government to pass on to each class the management of its own internal affairs. But the destinies of the samurai and the *chōnin* were closely linked, and when the bakufu finally woke up to the deterioration of its fiscal condition, the problems it faced were deeply embedded in the underlying economy. The financial expedients undertaken by the fifth shogun, Tsunayoshi, the shogunal adviser Arai Hakuseki, and the eighth shogun, Yoshimune, such as price fixing, currency debasement, and restraints on exports of precious metals, all reflect the effort to deal with ill-understood economic problems that were truly national in scale. Whereas military and political issues had been the primary concerns that had dictated policy choices until now, the bakufu by the time of Tsunayoshi was faced with real fiscal problems that required economically informed solutions. The debate over whether or not to carry out currency debasement discussed in Chapter 9 of this volume is an obvious case in point.

The junior councilors and military organization

The point is often made that *bakuhan* civil government was nothing more than the application to peacetime conditions of an administrative system developed by the daimyo during years of constant warfare. This should not be construed to mean that civil administration from top to bottom was handled as a sideline by officials whose normal functions were military service. During the Sengoku wars, the daimyo had obviously accentuated the military side of their houseband buildup. But the civil administration of the towns and villages within their domains was given due attention. Ieyasu's appointment, during his Okazaki years, of commissioners for civil administration is illustrative. During the years of heavy warfare, members of a daimyo's vassal band were obliged to function in both military and civil positions. When peaceful conditions were assured, these two types of service tended to become separate in practice as the qualification for office became more specialized.

As we noted, the Tokugawa houseband consisted of three major segments: the house daimyo, the bannermen, and the housemen. Whereas the senior councilors handled the affairs of the shogun's daimyo-rank vassals, the junior councilors were made responsible for carrying out functions appropriate to the other two classes of shogunal officials. These were military guard duty and service to the person of the shogun and his household. The office was occupied by four to five daimyo of minor rank.

On paper, a wartime muster of the shogun's armed forces would draw on all levels of support. Army units would be led by the senior councilors, the junior councilors, and the several daimyo. Under the command of the senior councilors were the keepers of Edo Castle, the members of the twelve great guards (*ōban*), the inspector general, and the necessary signal officers and civil engineers. Under the command of the junior councilors were ten body guard (*shoimban*) units, ten inner guard (*koshōgumiban*) groups, eight units of the new guard (*shimban*), as well as numerous specialized units trained for communication, firearms, naval warfare, and the like.

In peacetime these specialized units were expected to hold themselves in functioning order. The guard groups remained as castle guards, shogunal body guards, and military attendants when the shogun traveled outside Edo Castle. Despite the tedium of guard duty, membership in them was considered more desirable than were civil administrative positions. The more domestic of the positions under the purview of the junior council were in such services as construction and repair (*kobushin*), shogunal pages (*koshō*), shogunal attendants (*konando*), inspectors (*metsuke*), physicians (*ishi*), Confucian scholars (*jusha*), the kitchen (*zen bugyō*), women's apartments (*ōoku*), and the like. It should be kept in mind that this list of functions applied to more than just the Edo headquarters; that is, the bakufu establishment was grounded in numerous subsidiary castles, like Sumpu, Osaka, and Kyoto, and administrative positions, like the Kyoto deputy (Kyoto *shoshidai*), and each of these commands had detachments of military guards and service units assigned by Edo.

Selection for office and administrative procedures

It was frequently observed by foreign visitors to Japan in the mid-nineteenth century that the samurai government was greatly over-staffed. This was the result of carrying over into peacetime the undiminished rosters of shogun and daimyo vassal bands and attached service personnel that had grown to inflated proportions during the warfare of the last half of the sixteenth century. But the financial burden that this decision placed on the samurai government in the nineteenth century was not understood at the time. Nor should we imagine that the bureaucratic system was totally defenseless against the pressures created by the hereditary retention of stipends by so many members of an underused aristocracy.[54]

The samurai's practice of enrolling in the service rosters of the daimyo and shogun was relatively open and fluid when war was being waged. Assignment to office or to military service unit most frequently was tied to battlefield performance, and rewards for courage or loyal service were easily paid in the currency of captured fief land. But once military action had ended, the basis of assignment and promotion in rank or office had to be systematized and ultimately institutionalized. Criticism has been directed toward the hereditary nature of samurai officeholding, especially that toward the end of the Tokugawa regime. It is true that the samurai families appeared to remain, by hereditary right, on the bakufu and daimyo rolls. But what about the holding of office? Appointment to office throughout the *bakuhan* society rested on the concept of family status (*mibun* or *kakaku*). The status of a given house could be expressed in terms of military or bureaucratic rank and in size of income measured in *koku* of rice. Thus what any house inherited was rank and not office.[55]

Positions within the bureaucracy were graded according to the occupant's rank and salary. For any given office, there were obviously many qualified individuals. And for each samurai of a given status there were numerous positions for which he was qualified. Accordingly, the matching of status to office rested on the basic philosophy

54 The application of these principles of status inheritance is clearly brought out in the case of a daimyo domain such as the Bizen *han*. See Hall, "The Ikeda House and Its Retainers in Bizen," pp. 87–8.

55 Recruitment procedures were well developed in both the bakufu and the *han*. For an example of the latter, see John Whitney Hall, "The Nature of Traditional Society: Japan," in Robert E. Ward and Dankwart A. Rustow, eds., *Political Modernization in Japan and Turkey* (Princeton, N.J.: Princeton University Press, 1964), pp. 14–41.

behind the assignment to office and the requirements of the office. Because it was assumed that size of income reflected the individual's stature and administrative experience, it required a person of an appropriate income to fulfill the requirements of a given position. This minimum income requirement for office was termed *yakudaka,* and for a few, such requirements were as follows: senior councilor (25,000 *koku*), chamberlain (5,000 *koku*), inspector general or Edo city magistrate (5,000 *koku*), and page (500 *koku*).

But before long, as bannermen and housemen incurred their own financial problems, the minimum income requirement became increasingly meaningless. Thus beginning in 1665, captains of the great guard were given an office expense allowance (*yakuryō*) of two thousand *hyō* (bales of rice) to take care of office costs. Eventually this practice was applied to nearly all bakufu offices. A few examples: inspector general (one thousand *ryō*), head of the Finance Office (seven hundred *ryō*), and inspector (five hundred *ryō*). A further innovation in office compensation was the practice begun by Yoshimune of offering compensatory salary increases to individuals whose basic house income was below the minimum income requirement for a given post. Called *tashidaka,* a bannerman with a two thousand-*koku* stipend, for example, could receive a temporary salary enhancement of one thousand *koku* so as to qualify for appointment to a post listed at three thousand *koku*. Although these measures were cumbersome in practice, they helped, to some degree, open up the bakufu bureaucracy to talent from below.

Within a system so strongly colored by hereditary constraints, how were the talents of potential officeholders recognized, and how were appointments made from the pool of eligibles? Here another common bureaucratic technique was relied on, namely, the use of the personnel group, or *kumi*. Samurai were enrolled in the service registers of shogun or daimyo at a given rank and assigned to a given personnel group, before being assigned to a post. As a member of a *kumi* he came under the supervision of the *kumi* head (*kumigashira*), who served as personnel officer for the group, assisted in advancing the careers of men under his supervision, and preparing and presenting to a higher authority the petitions for promotion or transfer. The personnel group head was different from the administrative or military command superior, and this separation of the command and status systems made for a more impartial handling of bureaucratic personnel matters.

Finally, we should note that many of the positions in the bakufu bureaucracy were filled by more than one person, which reflects the common practice of multiple authority, or responsibility, and alternation of duty. In the service of both the shogun and the daimyo, especially in sensitive assignments, two or more individuals alternated in office, usually on a monthly rotation basis. This practice served to protect the political process from being dominated by any single individual, for multiple appointment meant that important policy decisions would have to be made collectively by all officials, whether or not on duty. On the other hand, duty rotation meant that minor issues were often allowed to remain undecided, in the hope that they would be handled by the next duty officer. These practices worked against rapid and decisive bureaucratic action. Just as in the practice of retaining the daimyo in a centralizable political organization, the retention of these conservative administrative practices militated against a number of "modern" tendencies in samurai government during the Edo period.

CHAPTER 5

THE *HAN*

The *han*, or daimyo domains, covered some three-quarters of the total area of the Japanese islands. They presided over most of Japan's wealth and garnered most of its taxes. Under their control came the greater part of Japan's military forces, as at least three-quarters of the samurai class were in their service. For the majority of the common people, the only form of government they knew was provided by their *han*. Its borders, seldom if ever passed, formed the edge of their known world, and its officials were the only ones they could ever expect to see. The *han* gave the majority of Japanese their roads, their bridges, their laws, and their order. When villages quarreled over water supply or rights to forage in the mountains, it was the *han* that stepped in to separate them. When crops failed, the *han* doled out rations. Should a river burst its banks, then the responsibility for relief and restoration fell to the *han*.[1]

This is not to say that those who lived in the *han* were not conscious of higher forms of authority. Above the *han* was the Tokugawa bakufu, presided over by a shogun from whom every daimyo, or *han* chief, derived his legitimacy. One step beyond that again stood the emperor and his court, powerless in fact but nevertheless the symbolic fount of all authority, even that of the bakufu itself. Yet to most people living in the *han* – the farmers, craftsmen, shopkeepers, servants, day laborers, and fishermen – shogun and emperor would have been little more than abstractions, dimly perceived and of no immediate relevance. The samurai class, being both educated and traveled to an extent denied other sections of society, would have known of these more exalted bodies – would perhaps have had some degree of personal contact with one or other of them at some time – but for most of them, too, their *han* was paramount. It was the *han* that met their needs, both material and ideological, satisfying the one with stipends and the

1 Throughout this chapter the term *han* will denote not only an area of land but also its military, administrative, and fiscal superstructure. This is in accordance with Japanese usage.

other with an opportunity to serve. The stipends may have been far from large, and the service often as much a socially acceptable counterfeit as anything of real substance, but nontheless it defined, as nothing else could, the place of this privileged and shamefully underemployed class within the community. By whatever yardstick, therefore, the *han* formed an integral part of Japanese life.

Nobody in Tokugawa Japan could have doubted the importance of the *han,* just as nobody would seriously contest it now. But such was not always the case. For more than seventy years after the *han* were abolished in 1871, they and their function in Tokugawa society were substantially ignored. During the late nineteenth and early twentieth centuries, Japanese scholars – servants themselves of strong central government – took their own preoccupations with state power and imperial loyalty with them when they studied the Edo period, only rarely looking beyond the bakufu, its individual leaders, and what their attitude toward the imperial court in Kyoto might have been. Insofar as the *han* were considered at all, it was through their association with individual daimyo – Tokugawa Mitsukuni of Mito, for example, or Hoshina Masayuki of Aizu – statesmen whose devotion to the imperial house or to Confucian morality seemed exemplary enough to warrant attention. Of the considerable role played by the *han* themselves in the social, economic, cultural, and institutional life of their time, little notice was taken.[2]

Only after World War II did attention shift significantly in the direction of *han* studies, largely through the leadership of Itō Tasaburō, a historian at the University of Tokyo. Even before the war Itō's research on a number of individual *han* – Mito, Kii, Nakamura, and Tsushima among them – had delineated a whole new field for historical research. Then, in 1956, with the publication of his *Bakuhan taisei* (The bakuhan system), he brought *han* studies to academic prominence. As the title of his book suggests, the *han* were now to be recognized as entities distinct from, and in a sense comparable to, the Tokugawa bakufu with which they shared responsibility for governing Japan. At the same time Itō Tasaburō, and the group of like-minded scholars he gathered around him – Taniguchi Sumio, Kobayashi Seiji, Kanai Madoka, and Fujino Tamotsu, among others – have between them, individually and as members of the Hanseishi kenkyūkai (Soci-

2 See, for example, the old standard works on Tokugawa history: Yoshida Tōgo, *Tokugawa seikyō kō,* 2 vols. (Tokyo: Fuzambō, 1894); Ikeda Kōen, *Tokugawa jidai shi* (Tokyo: Waseda daigaku shuppanbu, 1909); and Kurita Mototsugu, *Sōgō Nihonshi gaisetsu ge* (Tokyo: Chūbunkan, 1943).

ety for the study of *han* administrative history), managed to keep *han* studies at the forefront of Japanese historical research ever since.

To some extent, the readiness with which academic attention had moved away from the Tokugawa bakufu, the central government, and toward the *han*, which together constituted so much of Tokugawa Japan's local government, may well have reflected a postwar aversion to the old themes of prewar Japan: central power and loyalty to the emperor. To this extent it perhaps also reflected a new freedom of choice in the Japanese academic world. But it is also certain that other factors played a part – the realization, for example, of the existence in former castle towns of an immense volume of untouched documentary material, such as ledgers, diaries, memoranda, and tax records. For scholars, the temptation of these dormant riches was irresistible, particularly once the overall theoretical framework for *han* studies had been hammered out at historical conferences, notably at the 1957 meeting of the Shakai keizaishi gakkai (Society for the study of social and economic history). Also, in a variety of ways, Japanese historians were growing familiar with Western scholarship, itself becoming attuned to local history. One of the most seminal encounters took place in Okayama early in the 1950s, through the cooperative efforts of John Whitney Hall, then at the University of Michigan, and the Okayama historian Taniguchi Sumio.[3]

Over the past twenty-five years there has been little short of a *han* studies explosion, reflected in the volume of publications devoted to the subject.[4] The *han* have been restored to their rightful place in the history of the Tokugawa period. Paradoxically, however, this does not make them any easier to write about, for the overwhelming trend has been toward the dissection of individual *han*, rather than toward synthesis, and because no two *han* were precisely the same, the more minute and penetrating the dissection, the more remote the likelihood of convincing synthesis.[5] At almost any given time during the Tokugawa period there would have been as many as 260 *han* coexisting;

3 Part of the results of this collaboration are to be found in John Whitney Hall, *Government and Local Power in Japan, 500 to 1700: A Study Based on Bizen Province* (Princeton, N.J.: Princeton University Press, 1966); and Taniguchi Sumio, *Okayama hansei shi no kenkyu* (Tokyo: Hanawa shobō, 1964).

4 It would be tedious to list the major works in each genre and absolutely impossible to list them all. The eight-volume *Monogatari han shi*, and its seven-volume successor, *Dai ni ki monogatari han shi*, both edited by Kodama Kōta and Kitajima Masamoto and published by Jimbutsu ōraisha, Tokyo, in 1964–5 and 1966, respectively, contain some of the best work intended for the general reader.

5 How does one begin to encompass the experience of *han* so different in size as Sendai, which covered 1,018 villages, and Tannan, which covered a mere 23?

further, some 540 are known to have existed, however briefly.[6] It is therefore difficult to find generalizations capable of embracing the entire *han* experience. To do so would require a retreat to the barest essentials: that a *han* was a fief with a minimum productivity of ten thousand *koku* of rice per year and that it was consigned by the shogun into the custody of a vassal, who thereby merited the title of daimyo. This much can safely be said (although not without some qualification, as not every fief over ten thousand *koku* was a *han*), but not much else, and even that tells us remarkably little. Once past this basic definition, historians have usually found it necessary to divide the *han* into different groups, using for the purpose any one of a number of yardsticks.

One of these, which concentrated on the figure of the daimyo rather than on the domain itself, divided the *han* into three categories on the basis of the daimyo's political relationship to the shogun, namely, *tozama* daimyo, *fudai* daimyo, and *kamon* daimyo. The *tozama*, whose families had been substantial local magnates before the political ascendancy of Tokugawa Ieyasu in 1600, were automatically assumed to be at best neutral, and at worst hostile, to Tokugawa leadership. The *fudai*, the second category, were men who, having been Tokugawa vassals, were rewarded for their service by promotion to the status of daimyo. As the *tozama* were assumed to be either neutral or hostile, so the *fudai* were assumed automatically to be loyal and supportive. The third group, the *kamon* daimyo, sometimes linked with the *fudai*, were members of the manifold branches of the Tokugawa family, whether they bore the Tokugawa surname (as with the daimyo of Owari, Kii, and Mito) or the earlier Matsudaira surname (as with the daimyo of Takamatsu and Kuwana). Such a categorization had one clear advantage, as there was for the most part a general agreement on which daimyo fell into which category, despite a few cases of uncertainty.[7] There was also an apparent thread of logic to it, given that senior positions in the central bakufu bureaucracy were allocated to *fudai* daimyo, but never (or hardly ever) to *tozama*.

In practice, however, this classification, plausible enough in the abstract, was not necessarily a reliable determinant of enduring political complexion. The differences of 1600 do not seem to have persisted into the Tokugawa period for very long. By the early eighteenth century, as Ogyū Sorai noted in his *Seidan*, "the distinction between the

6 Fujii Sadafumi and Hayashi Rikurō, eds., *Han shi jiten* (Tokyo: Akita shoten, 1976).
7 Harold Bolitho, *Treasures Among Men: The Fudai Daimyo in Tokugawa Japan* (New Haven, Conn.: Yale University Press, 1974), p. 47, n. 7.

fudai and tozama daimyō is now merely a matter of name . . . both fudai and tozama are closely related, and, having been reared in Edo, both regard the city as their home."[8] The bakufu, for its part too, did not appear to have discriminated among *han* because of the ancestry of their respective daimyo. This was certainly the case when it offered help to daimyo in difficulties or demanded some measure of assistance from them in its turn, but even on purely formal occasions, when one might have expected due attention to be given to old comrades or their descendants, the bakufu was scrupulously impartial. Precedence at such times was invariably given to the daimyo with the largest *han*, or in the case of daimyo of equal standing, to whoever had succeeded first to his title.[9]

The *fudai–tozama* distinction, though still occasionally used, has largely been discarded as a working concept by modern historians, who have discovered that it is no longer possible to assume that the attitude of any daimyo toward national political issues owed anything to the allegiance of his ancestors; indeed, more significantly, it is no longer possible to assume that any given group of vassals would necessarily be influenced by what their daimyo thought.[10] Like any organization of human beings, the *han* were full of conflicting interests and opinions, and among them the daimyo's voice was not always decisive.

The postwar growth of *han* studies, together with the interest in social and economic history that, if it did not precipitate, then certainly accompanied it, has produced new insight into the origin and development of the *han*. Recent studies concentrate on the *han* itself, rather than the individual daimyo or his ancestry, and they take into account a whole range of phenomena that earlier approaches conspired to ignore, such as the internal social and political structure of the *han* or its size and location. Looked at historically or developmentally, the *han* can be divided into two groups: those tracing their foundation back to 1580 and earlier and those established thereafter.

Typically, in *han* formed before 1580 – that is, at a time when civil war was still very much a fact of life – few daimyo could exert more than a conditional control over their vassals. The sixteenth century was the golden age of the old-style samurai, the *jizamurai*, as they are often called: men who lived out in the countryside, on fiefs with which

8 Quoted in J. R. McEwan, *The Political Writings of Ogyū Sorai* (Cambridge, England: Cambridge University Press, 1962), pp. 75–76.

9 Bolitho, *Treasures*, chap. 3; for precedence, Hōseishi gakkai, ed., *Tokugawa kinreikō* (hereafter cited as TKRK), 11 vols. (Tokyo: Sōbunsha, 1958–61), vol. 4, p. 315.

10 For a differing view, see Conrad Totman, *Politics in the Tokugawa Bakufu, 1600–1843* (Cambridge, Mass.: Harvard University Press, 1967), chap. 8.

they had long associations and over which they exercised a substantial degree of independent control, dispensing rough and ready justice, gathering taxes, and mobilizing the inhabitants for the tasks of both war and peace. Such men presented their daimyo with a constant dilemma. He needed their support, for they and those over whom they presided accounted for a major part of his military strength, but he could seldom command it absolutely. Instead, he usually had to bargain for it, offering guarantees of one sort or another designed to strengthen the samurai's independence at the cost of his own central power. Certainly he could not afford to give offense, for once displeased the *jizamurai* were always free, in an age of civil war, to take their allegiance elsewhere. They could in fact do rather more than that, that is, gather support of their own to overthrow the daimyo, installing themselves in his stead. Some of medieval Japan's most noted families – among them the Akamatsu, once lords of three provinces, and the Ōuchi, who at their height commanded seven – were destroyed in precisely this way. It was, after all, the age of *gekokujō*, when the lesser had often been known to vanquish the greater.

Any daimyo house, to navigate these shoals into the safety of the Tokugawa period, had therefore almost inevitably been obliged to jettison many claims to authority on the way. Quite often, in such *han*, the *jizamurai* were to survive – their existence confirmed in some forty *han* as late as 1690[11] – residing in their own fiefs, taxing them, and governing them just as their ancestors had done. As a formal token of submission they might pay occasional visits to their daimyo's castle town, as the daimyo in his turn visited Edo, but their main concern was with the villages from which they derived their income.

Later daimyo, those created by the great generals of the late sixteenth century – Oda Nobunaga, Toyotomi Hideyoshi, or Tokugawa Ieyasu – or by later Tokugawa shoguns, tended to be spared these problems. For one thing, they and their men were accustomed to being moved about the country in obedience to the strategic interests of their overlord, so they had long since shrugged off much of the invisible luggage – loyalties, affections, expectations – of the past. Further, the age of *gekokujō* was over. Not only were alternative employers diminishing, but also few samurai would take up arms against a daimyo if that also meant pitting oneself against a Nobunaga, a

11 Hidemura Senzō, Kuwabata Kō, and Fujii Jōji, "Hansei no seiritsu," in vol. 10 of *Iwanami kōza Nihon rekishi* (Tokyo: Iwanami shoten, 1975), p. 66, claim thirty-eight such *han;* Fujino Tamotsu, *Daimyō: sono ryōgoku keiei* (Tokyo: Jimbutsu ōraisha, 1964), p. 61, claims forty-two.

Hideyoshi, or an Ieyasu. By the circumstances of their creation, therefore, the later daimyo were able to command bands of vassals that were much more streamlined and much more amenable to central direction, in fact – to use the terminology of most postwar scholars, for whom such things signify a shift away from feudalism – more "modern."

In contrast with their longer-established brothers, these daimyo were able to build up their *han* along completely new lines, bringing their vassals into permanent residence in the samurai quarters of the castle towns, paying them stipends, and integrating them into the political, economic, administrative, and cultural life of the *han*. For the most part, in the newer *han*, this transformation was accomplished with remarkably little ill feeling. The samurai themselves, having long since left their native villages, no longer had any traditional local authority to lose, and they were therefore often surprisingly amenable to such a move, sometimes to the point of initiating it themselves.

In 1625, after only seven years in their new *han* at Nagaoka, senior vassals of the Makino family had begun to petition for permission to surrender their fiefs (from which, as they noted, "the income can be small in some years, because parts of the domain are subject to frequent droughts or floods") and to be given stipends instead. They knew precisely what terms they wanted: "48 percent of our enfeoffment in rice, fodder for our horses, straw, and money to pay our servants."[12] This request for stipends rather than fiefs underlines another extension of the problem created by the changing relationship of the samurai to the workers of their village fiefs. Former *jizamurai*, when moved into the daimyo's castle headquarters, at first were permitted to retain certain portions of their customary powers over the workers on these lands. But increasingly, after the middle of the seventeeth century, the *han* chief absorbed the right to govern the peasantry.

At first glance, this might seem no more than a classification of *han* along purely administrative lines, with the newer *han* distinguished by their centralized and bureaucratic nature and the older ones by the lack of it. In fact, however, it correlates with a number of other important phenomena. As long as the samurai continued to reside in the villages, as they did in Tosa, Satsuma, and Echizen, then anything other than subsistence farming was discouraged. Once the samurai

12 Imaizumi Shōzō, *Nagaoka no rekishi*, 6 vols. (Sanjō: Yashima Shuppan, 1968–9), vol. 1, pp. 220–1.

were safely out of the way, however, the villagers were free to explore a range of attractive commercial activities: cash cropping, certainly, but also tax evasion, unreported land reclamation, small-scale processing, usury, and land purchases. The small minority of *han* retaining the *jizamurai* system (roughly 17 percent of all *han* at the end of the seventeeth century),[13] therefore, were on the whole among the most commercially backward parts of Tokugawa Japan. Their farmers were, at the same time, the most biddable, displaying far less overt evidence of discontent than those in other, more commercially advanced areas. On the whole they were spared the strains that all too often accompanied commercial agriculture, such as the polarization between rich and poor and between landlords and agricultural laborers, which became so much part of the late Tokugawa countryside.[14]

Another useful categorization of the *han* of the Tokugawa period is that put forward by Itō Tasaburō, who suggested that they be divided into three types, large, middling, and small.[15] As Itō saw it, large *han* were those believed capable of producing upwards of 200,000 *koku* of rice annually, that is, a matter of 26 *han* in 1614 and 20 in 1732, some 120 years later. Middling domains were those assessed at an annual productivity of from 50,000 to 200,000 *koku*, or 48 han at the beginning of the seventeenth century, and 78 in the early eighteenth. Anything else, from 50,000 *koku* down to the exiguous 10,000 *koku*, could be considered small, leaving us with 117 such *han* in 1614 and 161 in 1732.[16]

This particular taxonomy, already familiar to many through the work of Charles Perrault, is especially convincing, as it was its size, more than anything else, that determined the range of possibilities and responsibilities of any given *han*. Large *han*, wherever situated, whenever established, and whatever the original political affiliation of their daimyo, were likely to have greater military authority, more regional influence, and greater economic diversity than small ones. Their responsibilities, too, whether to larger numbers of samurai or peasants, were correspondingly more onerous. This in turn predisposed them to a rather higher degree of assertiveness than would have been the case with smaller *han*, just as it gave them a greater propensity for faction squabbles, for the stakes were so much higher. Small *han*, by contrast, had little control

13 Kanai Madoka, *Hansei* (Tokyo: Shibundō, 1962), p. 42.
14 Thomas C. Smith, *The Agrarian Origins of Modern Japan* (Stanford, Calif.: Stanford University Press, 1959), chaps. 11, 12.
15 Kanai, *Hansei*, p. 33.
16 Daimyo numbers have been calculated from Tōkyō daigaku shiryō hensanjo, ed., *Tokushi biyō* (Tokyo: Kōdansha, 1966), pp. 475–94.

over their destiny. Lacking economic flexibility, they had none of the recuperative powers of their larger neighbors and were far more at the mercy of events; without a significant force of samurai, too, there were obvious limits to their political independence or effectiveness.

In the following examination of the *han*, although I have kept such classifications in mind, I have elected to follow none of them. Instead, despite the acknowledged difficulty of producing persuasive generalizations, I have tried to do just that. In the attempt I have been forced to pass over many of the elements that made one *han* different from another, and I can therefore legitimately be accused of leaching out much of the colorful variety from a subject that is nothing if not varied. What I have tried to do, however, has been to focus on those issues with which all *han* were concerned to a greater or lesser degree – their relationship with the central government, their internal economic and political health – in the hope that the picture I present, if not exhaustive, will at least have the virtue of relative clarity.

THE *HAN* AND CENTRAL CONTROL, 1600–1651

No consideration of the *han* can hope to avoid the issue of their relations with the Edo bakufu. True, many *han* were already in existence well before the bakufu was established in 1603; for that matter, almost all of them, in one form or another, were to survive its fall, lingering on uneasily into the Meiji world. Yet ultimately the role of the *han* was defined by the bakufu, for it was the Tokugawa government that confirmed their existence and prescribed the extent of their responsibilities and the limits of their jurisdiction. Certainly they could not have existed in the form they did without the framework that the bakufu provided. Once that was taken away, they did not linger very long.

This interdependence was recognized right from the beginning of the Tokugawa period, for there is every indication that Tokugawa Ieyasu, the founder of the dynasty, was committed to the *han* as an institution. Of course, this did not prevent him from dealing severely with individual daimyo. Accordingly, immediately after his victory at Sekigahara in 1600, he set out to make sure that those who had fought against him were given cause to regret their poor judgment. Eighty-eight daimyo – among them some of Japan's more powerful provincial families, like the Ukita of Bizen, the Chōsogabe of Tosa, the Konishi, and the Masuda – were destroyed. Others lost large tracts of land, the Mōri of Hiroshima being reduced to two of the eight provinces they had once held and the Uesugi of Aizu losing three-quarters of their vast northeastern holdings. The Satake, too, were reduced from over half a million *koku* to a domain at Akita half that size.[17] But none of this could have been considered unusually severe. It was standard treatment for vanquished opponents, and nobody going into battle at Sekigahara in 1600 would have done so in ignorance of the likely consequences of defeat.

Certainly there was no reason to believe that these summary punishments threatened the institution of the *han* itself, whether in principle or practice. Without daimyo cooperation and the resources of their *han*, there would have been no Tokugawa victory at Sekigahara, so all who had assisted the victor could look forward with confidence to a reward. This, too, was part of Sengoku convention. Nor were they disappointed. Yamanouchi Kazutoyo, for example, who had declared for the Tokugawa side on the eve of Sekigahara, was given the old Chōsogabe domain on the Pacific coast of Shikoku, an area three times the size of his former holdings. Kuroda Nagamasa, too, was given a *han* at Fukuoka more than double the size of the one he left. More than that, however, a whole host of new *han* were created and placed in the care of Tokugawa vassals, sixty-eight of whom became daimyo in the two years immediately after Sekigahara, bringing with them into the Japanese political arena a whole new set of names: the Ii, the Sakai, the Mizuno, and the multitudinous branches of the Matsudaira family.[18] Without exception, the *han* of these new daimyo were considerably smaller than those they replaced, and they were, moreover, so distributed as to make it plain that they had a watching brief over less obviously dependable neighbors. But they were *han*, for all that, and as the deliberate creations of the country's single most important political figure, it would have been safe to conclude that the *han* institution itself had a secure future in the government of Japan.

What needed to be defined was the terms on which they would participate, and there could be no doubt of the Tokugawa intention on the score. It was intended that the bakufu would be paramount, and its first move in this campaign was to demand tokens of submission. Some of these were purely practical: to fund a spate of castle building by obliging the *han* to provide men, money, and materials toward the construction of a series of fortifications, among them the Nijō Castle in Kyoto, the bakufu's own fortress in Edo, and provincial castles in

17 Fujino Tamotsu, (*Shintei*) *Bakuhan taisei shi no kenkyū* (Tokyo: Yoshikawa kōbunkan, 1975), app., pp. 36–8.

18 Ibid., app. pp. 46–4.

places like Hikone, Sumpu, Nagoya, Kameyama, and Takada. Other tokens of submission were more symbolic but nonetheless impressive for that, like the obligation imposed on *han* leaders to surrender their own names and acquire new ones – the Matsudaira surname, for example, originally the name of the Tokugawa house, or, in the case of given names, a character from the name of the shogun himself.

As time went on, particularly after the Tokugawa victory in the Osaka campaigns of 1614 and 1615, the bakufu grew increasingly assertive in its relations with the *han*. In 1617, for the first time, the principle was established that all *han* would be distributed by the shogun, as head of the bakufu. In that year every daimyo received a document signed by the shogun, or bearing his vermilion seal, in which the extent of his *han* – the number and location of the villages of which it was composed, together with an estimate of their productive capacity – was formally defined. In some cases this was no more than reasonable, as many of these *han* had been conferred on their daimyo by the Tokugawa in the first place. Others, however, like the pre-1580 *han*, had evolved independently and owed nothing to Tokugawa favor. The daimyo of these domains, therefore, as they received their certificates must have done so with mixed feelings – mixed because, although the bakufu was offering them a formal guarantee of support, it was also, obliquely, suggesting an alarming possibility, namely, that at some future date the guarantee might be withdrawn, and their *han* with it. The importance of this development is obvious. It effectively altered the entire basis on which many Japanese daimyo had until now kept their domains, substituting for right by prior possession and inheritance something much more conditional, namely, right by bakufu recognition.

Two years earlier, in 1615, the daimyo had already been given warning of a new attitude. In the summer of that year, Konchiin Suden, the Zen priest who customarily assisted Tokugawa Ieyasu in religious and foreign policy matters, had read to the assembled daimyo, gathered together for the purpose in Fushimi Castle, a document designed to set the tone for all future relations between their *han* and the Edo government. This was the Buke shohatto, the Laws governing military houses. In its way it was an ostentatiously traditional document, larded with quotations from the Confucian classics, from the *Shoku Nihongi,* and from earlier Japanese legal codes like the Kemmu shikimoku, and it was certainly far more modest in tone than were later versions, which proved both lengthier and far more explicitly ambitious. Nevertheless, this first set of instructions served notice to all *han* that they were to surrender their independence in certain vital areas. That is, they were expressly forbidden to admit within their borders any criminals or traitors – fugitives, in other words, from the bakufu, as both crime and treason would be defined in Edo. It also prohibited new fortifications, or surreptitious repairs to old ones, and demanded that daimyo receive official permission before arranging marriages for members of their families.[19]

To some extent, of course, these instructions would have come as no surprise. Indeed, just a month earlier the Ikkoku ichijō-rei had restricted the *han* to no more than one fortification. Further, the daimyo of Uwajima, Nobeoka, Ushiku, and Odawara had already lost their *han*, the first two for harboring criminals and the others for having contracted unauthorized marriages.[20] Such concerns, being purely negative and defensive, were well within the Sengoku tradition. Yet the Buke shohatto also seemed to foreshadow something new. Its thirteenth and final clause urged the daimyo to appoint none but capable men as *han* administrators, thereby sounding a note to which the granting of formal certificates of enfeoffment two years later was to add resonance. The Tokugawa bakufu was claiming for itself ultimate responsibility in *han* internal affairs. If the *han* were not well governed, was the warning, then they could be forfeited.

The second version of the Buke shohatto, which appeared under the aegis of Tokugawa Iemitsu, the third shogun, in 1635, was to define beyond all ambiguity the new relationship between the *han* and the central government. The thirteen clauses of the original were now expanded to twenty-one.[21] Not all were immediately relevant to the distribution of power and authority between the *han* and the bakufu. Some indeed touched on matters of rather tangential concern (as had the 1615 version), expressing as they did support for filial piety, hostility to Christianity, or eagerness to define just who may or may not wear certain sorts of clothes or ride in palanquins. The kernel of the 1635 version, however, made quite explicit the basis on which the Tokugawa bakufu expected its relationships with the *han* to proceed. Henceforth, in addition to the previous prohibitions, daimyo were to be forbidden a variety of activities once theirs by right.

They could not interfere with highways traversing their domains, nor could they install barriers or create new embargoes. Officially designated post towns, together with lands belonging to religious insti-

19 TKRK, vol. 1, pp. 61–2. 20 Fujino, *Bakuhan*, pp. 39, 42.
21 TKRK, vol. 1, pp. 63–5.

tutions, were also removed from their immediate control. The legal authority of the *han*, too, was inhibited as never before, as they were now enjoined to "follow the laws of Edo in all things" and were ordered to leave criminal matters to the adjudication of bakufu officials and were forbidden to settle disputes among themselves. This latter prohibition was reinforced later that same year by the creation of a tribunal, the *hyōjōshō*, in which these and other matters could be settled. In two other areas, too, the bakufu was now prepared to extend its authority. An instruction issued to the southwestern *han* in 1609, to the effect that they were not to build large ships, was now made universal, with a blanket prohibition on the construction of any vessel with a capacity of more than five hundred *koku*. Similarly, the informal visits of several daimyo to Edo on a regular basis since 1600 was now – according to the text of the 1635 Buke shohatto – to be applied to all, with instructions that they were to alternate their visits, changing guard, as it were, in the fourth month of each year. Although the text did not make it clear, this applied initially only to *tozama* daimyo,[22] but by 1642 all apparently came to be included in what is now known as the *sankin kōtai* system, under which they were obliged to alternate a year of residence in their *han* with a similar period in attendance on the shogun in Edo. There were a few exceptions – the daimyo of Tsushima, whose domain was the most distant from Edo, was required to come only at three-year intervals, whereas those with domains in the Kantō – and therefore closest to Edo – worked on a six-month schedule. The daimyo of Mito, too, and any daimyo holding bakufu office, was expected to spend all his time in Edo.[23]

Quite clearly this was an ambitious program of central control, but it should be emphasized that like any other laws, the Buke shohatto, no matter what its aspirations, needed enforcement to be effective, and it was precisely on this point that the Tokugawa bakufu seemed to mean what it said. Administrative practice in the first half of the seventeenth century was to serve warning to the *han*, beyond all possibility of doubt, that the Tokugawa bakufu meant to control them. Obviously an efficient inspection system was needed, so in 1633 the bakufu, although already in receipt of confidential reports, created a group of more than thirty inspectors and charged them with monitoring those developments in the *han* most likely to be of interest to the

22 Asao Naohiro, "Shogun seiji no kenryoku kōzō," in *Iwanami kōza Nihon rekishi*, vol. 10 (Tokyo: Iwanami shoten, 1975), p. 20.
23 Fujino, *Daimyō*, pp. 93–4.

government in Edo.[24] To supplement the inspectors' activities, the daimyo were required, in 1644[25] to submit detailed maps – *kuniezu* – of their *han* to the bakufu; they were of more symbolic than practical value, perhaps, but important nonetheless.

On the basis of its intelligence, whether from formal or informal sources, the bakufu was in a position to enforce its will over the *han*, and daimyo soon came to learn that if they ignored it, they did so at their peril. After 1615, in fact, their tenure of their *han* suddenly became insecure, conditional on good behavior or, more significantly, bakufu pleasure. Over the next thirty-five years, a total of ninety-five daimyo lost their *han* or substantial parts of them. Some of them, moreover, had been Tokugawa allies in the past. Fukushima Masanori, having assisted in the victory at Sekigahara, was deprived of his vast holdings at Hiroshima nineteen years later and was packed off to retirement in the Shinano mountains, with a modest competence of 45,000 *koku*, all his power and prestige gone. Three years later, the young Mogami Yoshitoshi, whose *han* in the northeast was one of the six largest and whose father, Iechika, had been one of Tokugawa Ieyasu's closest confidants, suffered the same fate. He was given a pittance of 10,000 *koku* (itself reduced by half ten years later) at Ōmi, some three hundred miles away from his old domain. Others, equally important, were to disappear in their turn – the Katō of Kumamoto in 1632, the Horio in 1633, the Gamō finally in 1634, the Kyōgoku in 1637, the Terazawa in 1638, and the Ikoma two years later.

Outright confiscation was not the only way in which the bakufu was to assert its ultimate authority over the *han*. Over the same thirty-five-year period in which 95 *han* were confiscated, there would be a total of 250 *han* transfers, in which daimyo, their families, and their vassals (not to mention their vassals' families) were shifted from one part of the country to another in obedience to the bakufu's perceived needs. It was now apparent that if this continued, no *han* could ever be regarded as being in the permanent possession of any specific daimyo family. Never in the history of Japan had so much violence been done to local autonomy.

This was not all, for the years after the fall of Osaka in 1615 were to produce fresh demands on the *han*, demands on such a scale and so elaborately conceived as to be literally beyond the experience of any of

24 For an outline of the duties of this inspectorate, see TKRK, pp. 326–7.

25 Kitajima Masamoto, *Edo bakufu no kenryoku kōzō* (Tokyo: Iwanami shoten, 1964), p. 326.

those called upon to shoulder them. One of these was the introduction of a formal military levy, the *gun'yaku* system, which prescribed just what degree of military support each domain was expected to provide to the central government. There had been earlier intimations, in 1605 and again in 1615, but in 1633 the levy was extended to all *han* with 100,000 or fewer *koku* and – by unspoken implication – to all larger domains as well.[26] Under these scales, the daimyo of, say, a 200,000-*koku han* had to be prepared to contribute 349 horsemen, 700 musketeers, 150 bowmen, 300 pikemen, and 60 standard bearers.[27]

In a sense, impositions of this sort, even if not on this scale, were only to be expected. The daimyo were, after all, military leaders and might have been assumed to wish to maintain as many combat-ready troops as possible. They would not, however, have found other impositions quite so palatable. As we have already noted, they were obliged to contribute to the building or repair of castles, some in domains other than their own, and two in particular – Edo and Osaka – that belonged to no *han* but to the bakufu itself. Edo Castle, the residence of the Tokugawa shogun and the seat of their government, was built entirely from the resources of the Japanese daimyo, almost all of whom contributed to the project at one time or another, sixty-eight of them in one single year, 1629.[28] The same applied to the fortress at Osaka which, having been destroyed by Tokugawa forces in 1615, was thereafter rebuilt between 1620 and 1630 on a far greater scale than before, at the expense of sixty-four daimyo.[29] Thereafter it served as the focal point of bakufu power in western Japan.

The construction of such magnificent edifices passed far beyond the strategic needs of either the nation or the Tokugawa house. So lavishly were they built, and so imposing the final result, that they might more properly be regarded as statements of symbolic authority by which the leaders of each *han* government had been forced to recognize the supremacy of Edo. Certainly such was the intention of other forms of *han* tribute. The elaborate mausoleum erected at Nikkō to house part of the remains of Tokugawa Ieyasu and to enshrine his memory was built at *han* expense, and it was expected that the daimyo themselves would pay homage there from time to time. They did so first in 1617,

26 TKRK, vol. 1, pp. 89–90; Fujino, *Daimyō*, p. 111; Asao, "Shōgun seiji," p. 13; Takagi Shōsaku, "Edo bakufu no seiritsu," in *Iwanami kōza Nihon rekishi*, vol. 9 (Tokyo: Iwanami shoten, 1975), p. 144.

27 Yamagata-ken, ed., *Yamagata-ken shi* (*Shiryō-hen*), (Yamagata: Gannandō, 1961), pp. 375–8.

28 Murai Masuo, *Edo-jō* (Tokyo: Chūō kōronsha, 1964), pp. 58–59.

29 Kodama Kōta, *Genroku jidai*, vol. 16 of *Nihon no rekishi* (Tokyo: Chūō kōronsha, 1967), p. 249.

joining a variety of notables – two lion dancers, a man wearing a goblin mask, thirty-eight children dressed as monkeys – in a procession that, paying tribute to Tokugawa rule, can have done little for their self-esteem.[30] Naturally, too, it was expected that *han* forces would accompany, at their own expense, the shogun on such state occasions as formal visits to the ancestral tombs, whether at Nikkō or closer to hand at the Tōeizan in Ueno or, later, the Zōjōji at Mita. When Tokugawa Hidetada, the second shogun, went down to Kyoto in 1617, he did so in the company of "innumerable daimyo."[31] So too did Iemitsu, the third shogun, seventeen years later, escorted by 307,000 men (the largest force ever assembled in Japan to that date, according to one authority),[32] most of whom were provided by the *han*.

There were other important areas, too, in which well-established regional prerogatives were to be eroded during this period, none more striking than in the matter of foreign contact. Spiritual contact, in the form of Christianity which had gained a substantial foothold in southwestern Japan, was prohibited "in all provinces and places" with great finality, by the 1635 Buke shohatto. More tangible contacts also virtually disappeared. Foreign trade, once enjoyed by many southwestern *han* and eyed enviously by others less advantageously sited (Sendai, for instance), was closed down in several stages. By 1641 most of it had gone, and what remained was either restricted to Nagasaki, under tight bakufu supervision or, in the case of the Korean trade, conducted through Tsushima with official permission.[33]

In all of this the motive was to restrict *han* independence, to intimidate them by constant threats to their tenure, to sap their financial vigor through repeated impositions, to keep them dancing abject attendance on Tokugawa shogun both living and dead, and to curtail their intellectual, commercial, and diplomatic freedom. But that was not all. *Han* autonomy was further compromised by the hostage system, introduced in 1622.[34] Under this system the daimyo and their chief retainers all were obliged to send close relatives – wives, children, and even mothers on occasion – into permanent residence in Edo, where they could serve as surety for continued good behavior. By 1647 two

30 *Tokugawa jikki*, vols. 38–47 of Kuroita Katsumi, ed., *Shintei zōho kokushi taikei*, 2nd ed. (Tokyo: Yoshikawa kōbunkan, 1964–6), vol. 39, pp. 124–5.

31 Ibid., vol. 39, p. 132. 32 Asao, "Shogun seiji," p. 13.

33 Hidemura et al., "Hansei no seiritsu," p. 74.

34 Opinions seem to vary on the date. Takagi, "Edo bakufu," p. 151, sets it at 1622; Kanai, *Hansei*, p. 28, mentions 1634 in this context; Fujino, *Daimyō*, p. 93, also refers to 1634, but only in relation to *fudai* daimyo.

senior councilors of one large *han* were between them maintaining eight children as hostages in Edo for precisely this purpose.[35]

Of course, much of this was not new; the principles underlying many Tokugawa control mechanisms were already in common use well before 1600. The hostage system, for example, was a familiar phenomenon during the Sengoku era: Much of Tokugawa Ieyasu's own childhood and adolescence had been spent as a hostage, and he had later delivered his wife and firstborn son to Oda Nobunaga in the same capacity. Others, in their turn, had begun to send hostages to Edo long before it was compulsory: Tōdō Takatora as early as 1596, even before Hideyoshi was dead; Maeda Toshinaga and Hori Hideharu before the battle of Sekigahara; and a whole host of people afterwards, including the most powerful daimyo – Date, Nabeshima, Hosokawa, Mōri, and Shimazu.[36] Nor had the Tokugawa invented the twin control devices of fief confiscation and transfer; both Nobunaga and Hideyoshi had employed these on occasion, just as they had called upon daimyo for assistance with their own castles at Azuchi and Fushimi.[37]

Equally, Nobunaga and Hideyoshi had led the way in interfering in the internal workings of the daimyo domains, compelling the destruction of superfluous military fortifications, prohibiting private marriage alliances, and, in Hideyoshi's case, establishing a *gun'yaku* scale of sorts. Hideyoshi had also moved to control *han* external relations, ordering the expulsion of Christian priests in 1587 (although he relaxed this from time to time) and, nine years later, the crucifixion of twenty-six missionaries and converts. The elements of symbolic subjugation – oaths of allegiance, daimyo attendance at state occasions, grants of names, and so on – were also in common use before 1600.[38]

Yet, if the outlines of Tokugawa policy bore the impress of many Sengoku hands (and not just those of its two greatest generals), it must also be recognized that the Tokugawa employed that policy on a totally unprecedented scale. They controlled far more of the country than had either Nobunaga or Hideyoshi; they controlled it for an infinitely longer period; and they enforced that control far more rigorously and consistently. Effectively they had been given an opportunity to develop all of these well-known devices into a coherent system of daimyo control. Through the combined efforts of the first three shoguns in

35 TKRK, vol. 4, p. 393. 36 Kanai, *Hansei*, p. 28; Fujino, *Daimyō*, p. 92.

37 Fujino, *Daimyō*, p. 101; Mary Elizabeth Berry, *Hideyoshi* (Cambridge, Mass.: Harvard University Press, 1982), p. 131.

38 For a full account of Hideyoshi's policies, see Berry, *Hideyoshi*, *passim*.

particular – Ieyasu, Hidetada, and Iemitsu – the first half-century of Tokugawa rule created a Japan of a very new kind. It is quite clear that in the years between the victory at Sekigahara in 1600 and 1651, the year in which the third shogun died, the traditional independence of the daimyo and their *han* had been severely compromised. This is not to say that it had disappeared entirely. Domain governments were free at any time to interfere in the personal lives of the inhabitants of their *han,* certainly to whatever extent was necessary to preserve the peace, and even beyond that. They could prevent people of all classes from marrying whomever they wished, leaving their villages, traveling outside the domain, eating certain kinds of food, wearing certain kinds of clothes, and holding certain sorts of entertainment at weddings, funerals, and New Year. They could also determine whether or not their people should be free to watch performances by traveling players. But such discretionary power was discretionary only up to a point. It was now circumscribed as never before, for the daimyo and his government were no longer absolute masters of their own house. The events of the first fifty years of Tokugawa rule had made this plain, first by defining the limits of daimyo authority and then by making examples of anyone unwise enough to exceed those limits.

Equally important, it had also been made clear to the daimyo that in some areas they were to have no discretionary powers at all. Their governments could no longer use domain income exclusively for their own needs, could no longer determine their own military requirements, could no longer conduct independent relations with neighbors or the world outside, and – given the exigencies of the *sankin kōtai* system – could no longer be masters of their own movements. There had been, in this first half-century of Tokugawa rule, a complete shift in the basis on which daimyo held their domains. They could be disenfeoffed or moved at the discretion of the bakufu, for a variety of reasons – some valid, others not – but all of them beyond recourse or argument. There was no court of appeal against bakufu decisions, save the emperor, access to whom had already been blocked. So they were now dependent on the bakufu's approval, and many would have come to see themselves simply as custodians of their domains, as civil servants liable to be promoted, demoted, transferred, or dismissed according to the requirements of the government in Edo. Certainly this would have been reinforced to a certain extent by habits engendered by both the *sankin kōtai* and hostage systems, which had radically changed the orientation of samurai leaders.

Edo had become the center of the nation. Five out of every six incumbent daimyo in 1690 had been born there,[39] and all of them could look forward to spending at least half of their working lives there. Edo, where their families lived, was now their home, as Ogyū Sorai was to observe, not the *han* of which they were titular leaders.[40] Within a matter of two generations, therefore, an entire provincial aristocracy had been uprooted. A period of residence in Edo might have represented exile to the first generation of seventeenth-century daimyo, but to their grandsons it was a return home, a feeling no doubt encouraged by Edo's rapid growth as a cultural, commercial, and entertainment center. To many eighteenth-century daimyo, indeed, there seemed little reason to leave it. Sakai Tadazane, daimyo of Shōnai *han*, was so little enamored of his remote domain on the Japan Sea coast that in 1707 his senior vassals had to beg him to come home. Sakai Tadayori, his immediate successor, was apparently no better. He provided his Edo residence with a noh stage, after which, as his family chronicles note rather forlornly, "he did not visit his domain for a long time."[41]

THE *HAN* AND CENTRAL CONTROL AFTER 1651

At the death of Tokugawa Iemitsu in 1651, anybody involved in *han* government, looking back over the developments of the past fifty years, might have been excused a certain pessimism. They had surrendered during that time a great many powers to Edo and seemed likely to be called upon to surrender many more. Regional autonomy, one of the most abiding features of Japanese history, appeared to be all but at an end. Yet, among all the pessimism and despite all the inroads into local prerogatives, there were grounds for optimism, for not all of the developments of the first fifty years of Tokugawa rule had been negative. In many respects, indeed, the *han* had gained from the Tokugawa peace. True, their average size was to fall, from 93,000 *koku* early in the seventeenth century to slightly more than 65,000 *koku* in the eighteenth,[42] but overall their numbers increased. In 1614 there had been only 192 *han*, but there were 229 fifty years later, 241 in 1688 and, by 1720, 262, a number that thereafter remained largely unaltered.[43] Obviously the bakufu entertained no implacable malice toward the *han*,

39 Calculated from information contained in Kanai Madoka, ed., *Dokai kōshūki* (Tokyo: Jimbutsu ōraisha, 1967).
40 See McEwan, *The Political Writings of Ogyū Sorai.*
41 Tsuruoka shiyakusho, ed., *Tsuruoka-shi shi* (Tsuruoka: Tsuruoka-shi, 1962), pp. 323–42.
42 Calculated from Tōkyō daigaku, ed., *Tokushi biyō*, pp. 475–94.
43 Kanai, ed., *Dokai kōshūki*, pp. 46–47.

nor did it wish to increase its own holdings at their expense. Had it done so, it would have confiscated more and distributed less. Certainly it would not have been at such pains to create new *han*.

In many important respects, indeed, the centuries of Tokugawa rule provided the *han* with far more security than they had ever known. To begin with, the Tokugawa peace had freed them from their major Sengoku fear: each other. Alessandro Valignano, who had had occasion to observe Sengoku politics closely during no fewer than three visits to Japan in the late sixteenth century, noted that "none of the lords (or very few of them) are secure in their domains."[44] Now, under the Tokugawa bakufu, if the *han* were restrained as never before, they were also protected. For more than 250 years no *han* took up arms against another. There were disputes among them, of course, but these went to the bakufu for arbitration, and even the smallest *han* could expect protection. Obi *han*, locked in a border dispute with its giant neighbor Satsuma early in the seventeenth century, was able to take its case to the bakufu and win. A scant forty years earlier no *han* of 57,000 *koku* would ever have dared contest anything, let alone so vital a subject as boundaries, with an opponent more than ten times its size.[45]

Tokugawa rule had effectively released all *han* from the need for constant vigilance against each other. Equally, it had done much to enhance their internal stability by making it clear that it would countenance no usurpers from among the *han* vassals. The right to govern each *han* was entrusted to a particular individual as daimyo, and to nobody else, and this right was determined almost entirely by hereditary succession.

This new security enabled the emergence of a new kind of *han*. Sengoku strategy had dictated that they be compact geographical units, to minimize the dangers attending scattered frontiers, extended supply lines, and stretched communications. In the Tokugawa period, however, such considerations no longer applied, and certain *han* were therefore able to take advantage of the positive aspects of fragmentation and diversification. This did not have much significance for *han* like Sendai, of which only 20,000 out of its total of 612,000 *koku* were held elsewhere.[46] For smaller *han*, however, it was often of great significance: In the early eighteenth century, some 20 percent of the Nakatsu domain, in north Kyushu, was held in Hiroshima, a hundred miles

44 Michael Cooper, *They Came to Japan: An Anthology of European Reports on Japan, 1543–1640* (London: Thames and Hudson, 1965), p. 46.
45 Fujii and Hayashi, eds., *Han shi jiten*, p. 521.
46 Takahashi Tomio, *Miyagi-ken no rekishi* (Tokyo: Yamakawa shuppansha, 1969), pp. 124–5.

away. Later in the same century, Sakura *han*, northeast of Edo, held 40 percent of its fief in Dewa, on the other side of Honshu. At one time, too, only 50 percent of Odawara *han* was in the area of the castle town. The remainder was distributed over eleven different counties in six different provinces.[47] Not one of these *tobichi*, as such fragments were called, could have been defended in a civil war, but that – thanks to the Tokugawa bakufu – was no longer an important consideration. What was more significant was that *han* were able to diversify their economic bases in this way, winning access to new kinds of agricultural products or to areas of higher productivity, and insuring themselves to some extent against local crop failure and famine.

Under the Tokugawa, then, the *han* were protected to a degree unimaginable to their Sengoku predecessors. They were also given considerable assistance, for the relationship between the *han* and the bakufu was by no means completely one-sided, with the former giving while the latter took. Justifiably or not, the bakufu believed itself to carry ultimate responsibility for the well-being of the realm, and if from time to time this necessitated making demands of the *han*, it also obliged the bakufu in its turn to respond to their appeals. In such cases, bakufu assistance could take the form of gifts, like the distribution of rice during a famine in the Echigo area in 1676 or subsidies like that announced in 1720, when *han* under 200,000 *koku* (and there would have been some 180 of these) were invited to apply for help with flood control projects.[48]

By far the most common type of assistance, however, took the form of loans, usually repayable over a fixed period of time. Unavailable under normal circumstances, when *han* customarily made use of the great business houses in Kyoto, Edo, and Osaka, these loans were reserved for the emergencies of which Tokugawa Japan seemed able to produce an inordinate number. Fires, floods, typhoons, earthquakes, and volcanic eruptions all were frequent visitors to the *han* of Tokugawa Japan, but whenever a crop was ruined, a castle damaged, or an Edo mansion destroyed, the bakufu could be relied on for aid. In the overwhelming calamities, too, there was no doubt that help would be given. When a plague of grasshoppers devastated crops in western Japan in 1732, loans were immediately made available to the afflicted *han* on a fixed scale – from twenty thousand gold pieces to *han* with

47 Kodama and Kitajima, eds., *Monogatari han shi*, vol. 2, p. 390; *Dai ni ki monogatari han shi*, vol. 7, p. 415; Kimura Motoi and Sugimoto Toshio, eds., *Fudai hansei no tenkai to Meiji ishin* (Tokyo: Bungadō ginkō kenkyūsha, 1963), pp. 29–32.

48 *Yamagata-ken shi (Shiryō-hen)*, vol. 6, pp. 267–8.

300,000 *koku* and over, down to a basic two thousand gold pieces for the smallest *han*.[49] Similar loans were made available in 1784 and the 1830s, during the other great famines of the Tokugawa period.[50] Being loans, such sums were of course repayable – over a ten-year period in the case of those in 1732 – but there are examples of far more indulgent terms: Kokura *han* did not get around to discharging a debt contracted in 1635 until sixty-five years later.[51]

None of this consideration would have been possible had the Tokugawa bakufu been determined to augment its own powers at *han* expense. Had this been the case, one might have anticipated that one of the three great famines would provide the bakufu with the necessary pretext to step in and assume emergency powers that it could thereafter forget to relinquish. That it showed no sign of doing so, at least not until faced with the crisis of the mid-nineteenth century, seems to argue that – as far as the bakufu was concerned – the *han* were there to stay.

Indeed, the bakufu could not have governed without them. Their cooperation was essential, for example, to national defense. The port of Nagasaki, where almost all of Tokugawa Japan's defense and diplomacy was concentrated, depended for its protection not on Tokugawa resources but on those of neighboring *han*, several of which were charged with permanent responsibility for its safety. Hokkaido, too, was an area where the bakufu could not have functioned without the cooperation of *han* like Tsugaru, just across the straits, which was ordered to dispatch three thousand men there during the Russian scare of 1789, or Shōnai, which sent three hundred men to patrol the area during another scare twenty years later.[52] It was also expected that every coastal *han* would take charge of local coast-guard duties, an obligation that gave Nagaoka, for example, a watching brief over nearby Sado Island.[53]

That these responsibilities were observed is indicated by an incident in 1644, when a foreign vessel, presumably Chinese, blundered into Karatsu bay and was sunk by a combined fleet provided by five adjacent *han*.[54] The *han* were also needed to keep the peace, for the bakufu itself had neither the men nor the mobility to deal with any serious insurrection. Certainly the Shimabara Rebellion of 1637–8,

49 *Tokugawa jikki*, vol. 45, p. 611. 50 Ibid., vol. 47, pp. 745–63; vol. 49, p. 282.

51 Kita-Kyūshū, ed., *Buzen sōsho*, 22 vols. (Kita- Kyūshū, 1962–7), vol. 12, p. 51.

52 Furuta Ryōichi hakase kanreki kinen-kai, ed., *Tōhoku shi no shin kenkyū* (Sendai, 1963), p. 288; *Tsuruoka-shi shi*, p. 371.

53 Imaizumi, *Nagaoka no rekishi*, vol. 2, pp. 238–40.

54 Karatsu-shi shi hensan iinkai, ed., *Karatsu-shi shi* (Karatsu, Fukuoka, 1962), p. 570.

which was by far the most serious incident to confront the bakufu before the mid-nineteenth century, could not have been suppressed by Tokugawa forces alone. At the time these numbered no more than 20,000, and it took a force of 125,000 men, provided in the main by the *han* of western Japan, to settle the matter.[55] Similarly, on those occasions when the bakufu ordered the confiscation of a *han*, it relied on the forces of those adjacent to make sure that there was no likelihood of resistance, no matter on how small a scale. Peasant uprisings, too, usually needed *han* cooperation before they could be put down.

In addition to these military obligations, every *han* had an important administrative function. In fact, the *bakuhan* system was firmly based on the full cooperation of these two levels of government. Indeed, it would have been impossible for the bakufu, with its machinery concentrated in Edo, to have governed a country with such a formidable topography as Japan. It was the *han* that provided the tax collectors, magistrates, policemen, and clerks needed for government within their own borders. Further, the bakufu's own landholdings, amounting to 4 million *koku* and scattered over forty-seven provinces, would have been totally ungovernable without regular assistance from nearby *han*. This was obviously the case whenever peasant rebellions broke out.

The bakufu simply did not have – and never seemed anxious to acquire – the number of administrators necessary to govern its own domain. There were of course several coherent and well-defined areas[56] where the bakufu kept its own administrators – Nagasaki, Sado, Kōfu, and Hita among them – but so much bakufu land was strewn around the country in smaller pockets that it was often easier to rely on local *han* administrators, assigning bakufu land to their charge as trust lands (*azukarichi*). A total of twenty-six *han* were to help the bakufu in this capacity, providing caretaker services for what were, in some cases, quite large tracts of land. Aizu bore the heaviest burden, for in addition to its own domain of 230,000 *koku* it also presided over a further 880,000 *koku* of bakufu territory in adjacent parts of Mutsu, Echigo, and Shimotsuke provinces. Others, too, were obliged to carry fairly heavy loads – Nakatsu *han* in north Kyushu, for example, with a domain of 80,000 *koku*, administered almost twice as much bakufu

55 Asao, "Shōgun seiji," pp. 21, 31.
56 In fact, as many as forty-two of them; see Chihōshi kenkyū kyōgikai, ed., *Chihōshi kenkyū hikkei* (Tokyo: Iwanami shoten, 1961), pp. 144–5.

land in the same province, gathering its taxes, settling its disputes, and dealing with its criminals.[57]

Clearly, it would have required an immense upheaval to replace the *han* with a totally centralized form of government directed from Edo. Equally clearly, at least after a certain time, the Tokugawa bakufu, though standing to gain most from such a development, appeared to lose interest in the prospect. The death of Tokugawa Iemitsu, the third shogun, in 1651, virtually marked the end of any consistent assault on *han* prerogatives and responsibilities. Thereafter, Tokugawa authority began to deteriorate and, despite sporadic attempts to revive it, never regained its original impetus.

One by one, the original control mechanisms were allowed to run down. The *sankin kōtai* system continued, certainly, but without the underpinning of the hostage system, which was abandoned in 1665 in ostensible commemoration of the fiftieth anniversary of Tokugawa Ieyasu's death.[58] Impositions, too, slackened. Demands for assistance with castle building slowed to a halt by the mid-seventeenth century, to be replaced by much more modest calls for help with river work, canal construction, guard duty, and repairs to the Imperial Palace in Kyoto. True, such demands could occasionally be crippling: Sendai being pressed into providing 6,200 laborers for work on the Koishikawa canal in Edo in 1660, for example, and Satsuma laying out more than 300,000 gold pieces in flood control work in Ise, Mino, and Owari, more than four hundred miles to the east, in 1754–5. But overall, the period after 1651 showed nothing as constant or as debilitating as the preceding fifty years.[59] Rather, the bakufu itself came increasingly to shoulder the burden it had once imposed on the *han*, paying, for example, for work on the Ōi River in 1722,[60] a project from which it would never derive any benefit.

The Tokugawa bakufu's inspection scheme, too, lost its early vigor, with surprise visits from parties of *junkenshi*, charged with ferreting out any misgovernment, giving way to formal and perfunctory tours, all announced well ahead of time (even down to the details of their itinerary), all asking predictable questions, and all – inspectors and

57 For general information on *azukarichi*, see ibid., p. 146; Shindō Mitsuyuki, "Hansei kaikaku no kenkyū; – jōkamachi shōgyō no kiki o tsūjite mita Nakatsu han hōken kōzō no hōkai katei," *Keizai-gaku kenkyū* 21 (1955): 94–5.

58 Kanai, *Hansei*, p. 29; TKRK, vol. 4, p. 302, states that it was discontinued in 1670.

59 Kitajima Masamoto, ed., *Oie sōdō* (Tokyo: Jimbutsu ōraisha, 1965), p. 149; Fujino, *Daimyō*, pp. 107ff; Yoshizumi Mieko, "Tetsudai bushin ichiran-hyō" *Gakushūin daigaku bungaku-bu kenkyū nempō* 15 (1968): *passim*.

60 Tsuji Tatsuya, *Tokugawa Yoshimune* (Tokyo: Yoshikawa kōbunkan, 1958), p. 69.

inspected alike – hoping earnestly that they might be spared the necessity of presenting a critical report.[61] The *kuniezu,* detailed domain maps demanded of the daimyo in 1644, were required only once more, in 1697.[62]

As a result of this neglect, *han* were able to develop in ways of which the bakufu was to remain ignorant. Land reclamation, which doubled the area of cultivated land in Japan during the Tokugawa period, gave almost every *han* an income considerably in excess of its formal enfeoffment, but this was allowed to escape official notice. Had the bakufu been so inclined, this vast increase could have served as a pretext for a number of legitimate initiatives: It could have increased its own domain by confiscating reclaimed land, for example, or created new *han,* or at the very least it could have incorporated these new areas into the formal enfeoffment of each particular *han* and so provided a more realistic basis for future impositions and military levies. But land reclamation received little formal recognition. Only once, when the Mizuno were transferred from Fukuyama, did the bakufu initiate a new survey and bring hidden productivity out into the open. This done, the bakufu claimed the newly developed land for itself and left what remained to the Mizuno's successors.[63]

There is no doubt that as the flow of information to the bakufu dried up, so did daimyo become much more secure in the possession of their *han.* Bakufu displeasure, formerly enough to shake the largest *han,* was no longer quite such a problem, simply because Edo officialdom no longer knew what it ought to be displeased about. Further, such displeasure as it may have felt came to be expressed with far more diffidence than had once been the case. After 1651 daimyo came to be treated with notable forbearance, receiving, in the main, the lightest of reproofs for offenses that would have cost their fathers and grandfathers dearly. Open dissension among one's vassals, a misdemeanor that had cost at least seven daimyo their fiefs in the first fifty years of the Tokugawa period, was now usually punished with a reprimand, or at most a brief period of house arrest; only the really spectacular cases attracted anything more.

Signs of mental instability, or gross misgovernment, which had once invited bakufu displeasure, continued to do so to some extent, but clearly the definition had changed. The astonishing affair of Matsudaira Sadashige, daimyo of Kuwana, is a case in point. Discovering in 1710

61 Bolitho, *Treasures,* pp. 31–3. 62 Kitajima, *Edo bakufu,* p. 326.

63 Fukuyama-shi shi hensankai, ed., *Fukuyama-shi shi,* 3 vols. (Fukuyama-shi, 1963–7), vol. 2, p. 394.

that one of his officials had been cheating him, the daimyo proceeded to carry out a stupefying number of executions – the guilty man, of course, but also eight of his sons (the youngest only two years old), his grandson (also two years old), his two brothers, ten of his nephews, his octogenarian mother, and several officials. A large number of other officials were also banished or dismissed from their posts. So sensational a loss of control – foreshadowed twenty years earlier by the perceptive compilers of the *Dokai kōshūki,* who had warned of his "quick temper and hotheadedness" and his "severity with his vassals" – would never have been tolerated by the earlier Tokugawa shogun, but by 1710 it was considered to warrant no more than a transfer from one *han* to another.[64]

In 1651, the bakufu offered more evidence of its newfound solicitude for the daimyo, by permitting them the privilege of deathbed adoption. Over the preceding fifty years, forty-one daimyo families had forfeited both *han* and status for failing to produce a convincing heir, an omission that proved them incapable of providing the military and administrative continuity expected of them. Now, after 1651, moribund – or even dead – daimyo, after having had their seals affixed to a petition, could obtain the bakufu's consent to the speedy adoption of a successor and so assure a measure of stability. As a result, the next two centuries of Tokugawa rule could produce only twenty-five attainders under this heading; the bakufu had abandoned its main pretext for confiscation.[65]

It is not surprising, therefore, that with deathbed adoptions, maladministration, and misbehavior freely countenanced after 1651, disenfeoffments should have tailed away so dramatically. Between 1616 and 1651, there had been a total of 95 attainders, an average of just under 3 cases per year. The remainder of the Tokugawa period, from 1652 to 1867, presents a marked contrast, only 118 instances over more than two hundred years, or fewer than 1 a year. Indeed, if one were to exclude the rule of Tokugawa Tsunayoshi, whose incumbency as shogun from 1680 to 1709 produced an extraordinarily large number of disenfeoffments,[66] the total for the remainder of the Tokugawa period would fall to 74, or around 1 every three years.

This new tolerance also lowered the rate of fief transfers, which had been such a feature of the first half-century of Tokugawa rule. Such movements came virtually to an end after 1651, and only a tiny minor-

64 Kondō Moku and Hiraoka Jun, eds., *Kuwana-shi shi,* 2 vols. (Kuwana: Kuwana-shi kyōiku iinkai, 1959), vol. 1, pp. 183ff; Kanai, ed., *Dokai kōshūki, p. 258.*

65 Fujino, *Bakuhan,* app. pp. 41–5.

66 Forty-four, to be precise. Ibid.

ity of daimyo were ever moved thereafter. There were some exceptions: The Shirakawa domain changed hands eight times during the Tokugawa period, and the Yamagata domain twelve, and the Ogyū branch of the Matsudaira family were relocated no fewer than eleven times between 1638 and 1764. But the overall statistics leave no room for doubt that here, too, daimyo had much less to fear after 1651 than they had earlier. Between 1616 and 1651 there were 205 fief transfers, at an average rate of something close to 6 per year. The succeeding 215 years could produce only 306, an average of 1.4 per year, a decline of around 80 percent.[67]

This development, although one that might have been anticipated of a government now well established after an initial period of uncertainty, did not win total approval. Ogyū Sorai, writing in his *Seidan* early in the eighteenth century, thought it patently obvious that "daimyō should be deprived of all their lands when the administration of their households is bad, or if there are disturbances in their fiefs,"[68] while several bakufu leaders – Tokugawa Tsunayoshi, Tanuma Okitsugu, and Mizuno Tadakuni among them – seemed willing to revive some of the old severity.[69] Yet it is possible to see why the bakufu, seemingly on the very threshold of creating a new and far stronger kind of central government for Japan, should have called a halt. It owed its foundation to *han* cooperation. Further, it owed its continued existence to shogunal forbearance; certainly, with its own domain of four million *koku* (over six million including *hatamoto* fiefs), it was far more powerful than even the strongest *han*, but it did not have absolute predominance. Any combination of *han* – as the nineteenth century was to reveal – could muster the resources to topple it, so the bakufu was forced, even from the beginning, to placate and cosset them wherever possible.

The apparent ease with which the first three shoguns could dictate disenfeoffments and fief transfers was deceptive in this respect, for whenever they invoked their power, as they well knew, they risked offending all daimyo, who saw, behind the threat to others, a threat to themselves also. No attainder was ever carried out without some possibility of rebellion – vassals threatening to defy the order, to barricade themselves inside their castles, and the like – which was why nearby

67 Ibid. 68 McEwan, *The Political Writings of Ogyū Sorai*, pp. 76–77.

69 Harold Bolitho, "The Dog Shogun," in Wang Gungwu, ed., *Self and Biography* (Sydney: Sydney University Press, 1975); Harold Bolitho, "The Tempō Crisis" in Marius B. Jansen, ed., *The Nineteenth Century*, vol. 5 of *The Cambridge History of Japan* (Cambridge, England: Cambridge University Press, 1989); see also Bolitho, *Treasures*, pp. 169–79, 190–8; 209–22.

han were always asked to help enforce such decrees. But even more serious was the danger – muted, but there nevertheless – of resistance on a wider scale, in which several *han* might conceivably join forces and come to the aid of one of their number. This fear was clearly uppermost in Iemitsu's mind when, in 1632, having ordered the attainder of Katō Tadahiro (an event that left Tadahiro's neighbor, Hosokawa Tadaoki, "dumbfounded"), the shogun felt constrained to offer a personal explanation to five of Japan's most powerful daimyo – Date Masamune, Maeda Toshitsune, Shimazu Iehisa, Satake Yoshinobu, and Uesugi Sadakatsu.[70]

Other factors also worked to guarantee the *han* a large measure of security against bakufu encroachment. The hereditary principle, for example – important enough at any time in Japanese history – was particularly respected in the Tokugawa period, when it provided the underpinning for the entire social and political fabric. From the emperor down to the humblest farmer, all Japanese were held to have inherited a particular function in society, one that Nature – having allocated their positions – had decreed. The will of Heaven was therefore not to be tampered with unless absolutely necessary, especially not by shoguns who were themselves beneficiaries of the same process. Another explanation may be found in the composition of the bakufu, for its chief administrative and decision-making functions were in the hands of officials who, daimyo themselves, were already convinced both of the desirability of hereditary succession and of the need for *han* to be administered in an atmosphere of stability and security, free from outside interference. Only an extraordinary political figure, a shogun like Hidetada, Iemitsu, or Tsunayoshi or a senior councillor of the caliber of Tanuma Okitsugu or Mizuno Tadakuni, could overrule these men in the interests of the central government.[71]

This is not to say that after 1651 the *han* were entirely free from bakufu intrusion. Disputes among *han* continued to be settled by the bakufu in Edo, for its position as the nation's legal arbiter never changed; their laws, too, in conformity with the 1635 Buke shohatto, were in the main modeled on those of the bakufu. Most *han*, even old-established ones, simply found it more convenient to copy Edo laws than to formulate their own, and as society – and the legislation needed to control it – grew more complex, so this tendency increased.[72] This was no more than reasonable, for bakufu laws, for the

70 Asao, "Shōgun seiji," p. 9. 71 Bolitho, *Treasures,* chap. 5.
72 Harafuji Hiroshi, "Kaga han kahō no seikaku," *Kanazawa daigaku hō-bungaku-bu ronshū* (Hōkei hen, 5), 1958. Reprinted in Harafuji Hiroshi, *Bakufu to hampō* (Tokyo: Sōbunsha, 1980).

most part, did no more than reflect the common concerns of the ruling class: concern about Christianity, about fires, about the insubordination of the lower orders, about declining samurai morale, and the lamentable habit common to all classes of eating, drinking, and dressing above their station. Such laws could therefore be adopted by any *han* and displayed on its signboards without doing any violence to existing attitudes. Equally, the bakufu provided services recognizably essential to the nation's commercial health: keeping the major highways in order, standardizing the distance between their milestones, and providing a series of uniform weights and measures. Further, its residual powers, even if seldom used, were available on occasion, and any *han* flouting them ran a risk. It was always open to the bakufu to intervene in domain affairs, here cautioning a daimyo about his behavior, there suggesting a possible candidate for adoption or a consort for his daughter or, as happened in Shōnai in 1811, forcing the retirement of several senior vassals.[73]

Nevertheless, *han* were known to ignore bakufu instructions if they believed their interests required them to do so. Thanks to the decline in disenfeoffments and fief transfers, those interests had been allowed to become concentrated on specific fiefs, and daimyo and vassals alike, anticipating perpetual tenure, accordingly identified their own interests with those of the area assigned to them. Understandably, therefore, they could not be expected to welcome instructions from outside, especially if those instructions seemed to run counter to local interests.

Even in the best of times there was a latent conflict between the *han* and the bakufu, with each able to claim a mandate of a kind – the bakufu on the one hand pledged to govern Japan in the general interest, and the *han* on the other committed primarily to their own prosperity. Usually this conflict stayed hidden well below the surface of Tokugawa life, but on occasion an emergency could thrust the two competing mandates into sharp relief. When this happened, the *han* usually had the upper hand, simply because the bakufu had neither the strength nor the will to compel total obedience.

Most commonly, these clashes took place during famines, or indeed shortages of any kind, when the bakufu, in the interest of Japan as a whole, was obliged to order that supplies be sent where they were most needed. Yet obviously, in an atmosphere of shortage, few *han* had the confidence to part with anything they might subsequently need. Reports of poor harvests in 1660 in Mikawa, Tōtōmi, and Ise prompted a

73 *Tsuruoka-shi shi*, pp. 355; 371–4.

fairly typical reaction elsewhere, with both Aizu and Fukuyama immediately forbidding the export of any cereals, the former noting that although "it does not seem as though our farmers will starve, it is quite likely that next year will be very difficult."[74] Reports of drought in the Kantō and elsewhere eight years later were enough to spur the Aizu authorities into another embargo of foodstuffs, this time a comprehensive one – not merely rice, wheat, and barley but also soy beans, red beans, millet, buckwheat, cowpeas, sesame seed oil, and even radishes.[75] Every subsequent famine produced comparable reactions from those domains fortunate enough to have been spared: Obama banning the export of cereals and pulse in the mid-eighteenth century, and Shōnai during the great Tempō famine of the 1830s.[76] In such circumstances, every *han* was really obliged to give priority to its own needs, no matter how great the crisis elsewhere, and nothing the bakufu could do was likely to change that.

If the *han* could put their own interests first in even the severest of national emergencies, as they did all too readily, then there was little to inhibit a similar approach to lesser issues. The bakufu's attempts to control the nation's commercial life, successful to some extent in the seventeenth century, were to evoke little sympathy from the *han* as the Tokugawa period moved on and as they too had come to depend on commerce to meet mounting expenses. Economic development had compelled them all to make the most of such resources as they had or else fall behind, so they were hardly likely to obey bakufu directives that, no matter how honestly inspired, were likely to work to their disadvantage.

A 1730 order to the *han* to stop selling their rice in Osaka until further notice, for example, was issued with the best possible motives: There was a glut there, which was making the price artificially low, and so damaging both the morale and the living standards of the entire samurai class, almost all of whom had to sell their rice stipends to live. Effectively, however, the *han*, having priorities of their own, ignored the command, sending their rice to Osaka as they had always done. Circumstances hardly permitted them to do anything else. Such clashes persisted throughout the eighteenth century, with the bakufu's orders being greeted by *han* noncooperation, and by the nineteenth

74 *Fukuyama-shi shi*, vol. 2, p. 690; Aizu–Wakamatsu-shi shuppan iinkai, ed., *Aizu–Wakamatsu-shi* (Aizu–Wakamatsu: Aizu–Wakamatsu-shi, 1967), vo. 9, p. 41.

75 *Aizu Wakamatsu-shi*, pp. 74–75.

76 Fukui-ken, ed., *Fukui-ken shi*, 5 vols. (Tokyo: Sanshūsha, 1921), vol. 2, pt. 2, p. 92; *Tsuruoka-shi shi*, p. 389.

century, as the economic crisis of Tokugawa Japan sharpened, this blossomed into open defiance and competition.[77] Given the chronic financial difficulties that were to overwhelm *han* and bakufu alike, one could hardly have expected anything else.

HAN FINANCES

Traditionally, the *han* derived the bulk of their income – in many cases up to 80 percent and more[78] – from their land tax, calculated as a certain proportion (usually 40 to 50 percent, but sometimes as much as 70 percent)[79] of the estimated annual production of any given piece of land. It applied to rice paddies, of course, but also to the dry fields used to produce almost everything else, from the "miscellaneous cereals" like wheat, barley, and buckwheat, to more overtly commercial crops, like cotton, which was replacing hemp as the popular clothing material, or tobacco, whose production, initially prohibited, was legalized after 1667. Housing sites were also usually subject to land tax, except in newly created castle towns where the authorities had offered tax exemptions in an effort to attract population.[80] There was naturally a great deal of regional variation in methods of tax collection, but on the whole much of the tax on paddy fields was collected in kind, whereas that on dry fields was often, and on housing sites presumably invariably, collected in cash.[81]

There were other, lesser, taxes, known collectively as *komononari*. These had nothing to do with cultivated land but encompassed almost every other kind of economic activity – fishing, seaweed gathering, mining, timber cutting, charcoal burning, bamboo cutting, rush gathering, exploiting hot springs, and whatever other opportunities were offered by *han* natural resources. Nor did those engaged in the manufacturing and service industries escape. The net was cast wide, to include not only the more prosperous members of the community – the local associations of wholesalers, the saké brewers and the pawnbrokers, and others of the kind – but also those involved in more modest activities, like the makers of bean curd, the hairdressers, the thatchers, and the laundrymen, all of whom were obliged to pay a registration fee (*myōgakin*) or a percentage of their turnover (*unjōkin*)

77 Tsuda Hideo, "Kansei kaikaku," in *Iwanami kōza Nihon rekishi*, vol. 12 (Tokyo: Iwanami shoten, 1963), p. 257; see also Chapter 9 in this volume, and Bolitho, "The Tempō Crisis."

78 Hiroshima *han* is a case in point. See Aono Shunsui, *Daimyō to ryōmin* (Tokyo: Kyōikusha, 1983), p. 72.

79 See Suwa *han*, for example, in Fujii and Hayashi, eds. *Han shi jiten*, p. 246.

80 Aono, *Daimyō*, p. 182.

81 Fujino, *Daimyō*, pp. 32–3.

or, not uncommonly, both.[82] Such a daunting list, however, suggests a far greater importance for these miscellaneous taxes than they actually warranted. True, they tended to increase as economic activity grew more diverse, but they were never a significant element in *han* finances. In Hiroshima *han* in 1719, as against a land-tax revenue amounting to almost 80 percent of the total income, these miscellaneous taxes produced only a meager 1.5 percent.[83] The same might be said of the corvée, from which *han* originally mobilized men for service as porters, carters, messengers, and palanquin bearers in the post towns, or as laborers for road building, land reclamation, flood control, and repairs to and maintenance of the daimyo's castle. Such demands, even when commuted into payment in cash or kind, had no more than a marginal impact on *han* income.[84]

These all were traditional forms of revenue. Local rulers had been levying land taxes, miscellaneous taxes, and corvée ever since the beginning of Japanese history and continued to do so free from any interference by the central government. The trouble was that as traditional taxes, they failed to keep abreast of changing circumstances, and the *han* were to pay dearly for it. The formal distinction between wet and dry field agriculture is a case in point. The latter had never been as highly regarded as the former, for rice was the prestige cereal, credited with all sorts of benign properties, mystical, as when offered to the gods (for no other grain would do), and tonic, as when pressed on the sick as a restorative. Land capable of growing this wondrous crop, therefore, was far more highly regarded than was any dry field and so carried a substantially heavier tax burden. Its taxes, too, as we have seen, were largely collected in kind – that is, as bales of rice – unlike that on dry fields, for which a vulgar cash settlement was considered appropriate. Because the precise sum levied on dry fields was based on a notional estimate, rather than on any realistic calculation involving crop types and market prices, the taxes they paid were not always related to the returns they brought their cultivators.

Administrators, at least initially, did not readily grasp the fact that a light sandy soil, totally unsuited to wet-rice production, might nevertheless produce a crop of tobacco, for example, capable of fetching a high price at Osaka or Edo. Yet, increasingly, such was the case. The rapid growth and diversification of the economy saw more and more people moving away from subsistence farming and producing crops

82 For Kaga, see ibid., pp. 3–5; for Hikone, see Nakamura Naokatsu, ed., *Hikone-shi shi*, 3 vols. (Hikone-shi: Hikone shiyakusho, 1960), vol. 1, pp. 607–9.

83 Aono, *Daimyō*, p. 72.

84 Fujino, *Daimyō*, pp. 115–17.

for sale – tobacco and cotton, of course, but also indigo, madder, rapeseed, and vegetables. In some areas, particularly in central Japan, commercial agriculture had become the predominant mode by the eighteenth century: Over 60 percent of the arable land of the provinces of Settsu and Kawachi was given over to cotton production, which had proved so lucrative that farmers were even planting it in their paddies.[85] Agriculture, by becoming more varied, had also grown more profitable, but the *han* (and the bakufu too, for that matter) seemed unable to take advantage of it.

It is tempting to ascribe such administrative lacunae to ignorance, inertia, or even to some impermeable precommercial innocence, and indeed all of these elements may have played a part in the initial failure of the *han* to react constructively to changes in economic life. But there was another important element involved as well. For all their authority over the common people – who were, after all, dragooned into *goningumi,* or joint responsibility groups, in which all were held hostage for the good behavior of their fellows, and therefore theoretically totally responsive to direction – very few *han* administrations were strong enough to do as they pleased. This was particularly so in matters of taxation. Any intensification of taxes, whether in their rate, their incidence, or even their administration, was likely to be opposed. The first stage of such opposition took the form of argument, in which one of two lines might be pressed. One approach was to label any variation from former practice a departure from precedent and therefore, by definition, a breach of faith. The other was to draw attention to nearby *han* where things were done differently, and rather better. Given the complicated map of Tokugawa Japan, where *han,* portions of *han,* and fragments of bakufu land lay cheek by jowl, it was never difficult to point to some neighbor who, under a different administration, was receiving more favorable treatment. Because precedent was so valued and because there was so much local variation, either of these gambits could be effective.[86]

If they should fail, then farmers could turn to more emphatic measures. They could, for example, desert their farms en masse, as they did in Shōnai in 1632, when large numbers trooped across the *han* border into Akita rather than submit to a new (and presumably more accurate) land survey, or as 3,000 farmers from Takatō *han* did in 1654 in protest against administrative "tyranny."[87] The next, and graver, step was an

85 Ōtsuka shigakkai, ed., (*Shimpan*) *Kyōdo shi jiten* (Tokyo: Asakura shoten, 1969), p. 611.
86 Aono, *Daimyō,* p. 219, cites some examples from the Hiroshima area.
87 *Tsuruoka-shi shi,* p. 265; Fujii and Hayashi, eds., *Han shi jiten,* p. 247.

intimidatory show of solidarity, like that displayed by the 300,000 peasants who jammed into Hiroshima in 1718 to protest against a new (and once again presumably more accurate) survey of their lands, or the 20,000 farmers in Karatsu who joined together to protest the imposition of a new tax on low-lying land, as well as the fact that their normal taxes were now being measured out with a far larger measure than usual, and a heaped one, at that.[88] Such incidents, increasingly spilling over into violence, were frequent enough in the seventeenth century, but their rate more than doubled in the eighteenth – upwards of a thousand cases between 1715 and 1815, as against fewer than five hundred over the period 1615 to 1715.[89] In almost every case, new taxation initiatives on the part of the authorities, *han* or bakufu, according to location, was at the root of the trouble. The more efficiently these governments tried to tap the traditional sources of income, the more resistance they encountered, and the more effective that resistance was.

Of course, in all but the very largest demonstrations, the *han* had the military force needed to restore order. They often did so and frequently none too gently; it was not unknown for protest leaders to be beheaded for their pains, as a warning to future malcontents.[90] But nevertheless, the relationship between *han* officals and peasants was a particularly delicate one. Any dispute, if mishandled, could well bring about such turmoil that the bakufu would be compelled to intervene, in which case the daimyo and his officials might not go unscathed. Kōriki Takanaga lost his domain at Shimabara and Yashiro Tadataka his at Hōjō in precisely such circumstances.[91]

Peasant protest was possible because the bakufu had recognized as early as 1603 that peasants, no matter where they lived, had certain rights, among them the right to formal complaint and the right to desert their fields and move elsewhere, if necessary.[92] Subsequently, after experiencing difficulties of its own in this regard, the bakufu was to regret its magnanimity, but the principle still remained. Once confronted by a determined peasant opposition, *han* often found it politic to compromise, even to back down, rather than risk a prolonged, costly, embarrassing, and potentially damaging dispute. The fact was that *han* needed their peasants and needed them, moreover, to be reasonably healthy and moderately content. Few daimyo would have

88 Aono, *Daimyō*, p. 220; *Karatsu-shi shi*, pp. 592–3.

89 Aoki Kōji, *Hyakushō ikki no nenji-teki kenkyū* (Tokyo: Shinseisha, 1966), p. 17.

90 One of the earliest examples from the Tokugawa period is the beheading in 1608 of twelve Chōshū peasant leaders. Minegishi Kentarō, "Seiritsu-ki han keizai no kōzō," in Furushima Toshio, ed., *Nihon keizai shi taikei* (Tokyo: Tōkyō daigaku shuppan-kai, 1965), vol. 3, p. 222.

91 Fujii and Hayashi, eds., *Han shi jiten*, pp. 489, 158.

92 TKRK, vol. 5, p. 150.

disagreed with Ikeda Mitsumasa of Okayama *han*, who in 1655 spoke of his concern that "the peasants should be robust and devote themselves to their agriculture."[93] Twenty-odd years later, officials in Fukuyama *han* were warning of exhaustion among the peasantry and urging that they be allowed adequate opportunity for relaxation.[94]

The traditional framework really offered the *han* only one way of augmenting their income without unduly provoking their peasants, and this was land reclamation. If they could increase the area under cultivation and make sure that it all paid taxes at the appropriate rate, then to that extent *han* revenues would rise. The prospect was undeniably attractive, whether achieved by the *han* itself – perhaps using corvée labor – or else by local entrepreneurs working with official knowledge and permission. Many *han*, availing themselves of the opportunity, were able to expand their productive capacity by 30 percent and more: The area of cultivated land in Tsugaru *han* doubled during the seventeenth century, and in both Shōnai, farther down the Japan Sea coast, and Fukuyama, over on the Inland Sea, it increased by at least a third.[95] Between 1600 and 1720, in fact, the area of cultivated land in Japan grew by a colossal 82 percent.[96] But reclamation could not be extended indefinitely, particularly not within the limits of contemporary technology, and by the early eighteenth century those limits appeared to have been reached. The next 150 years could produce an increase of no more than 3 percent.[97] In any case, few *han* would have had a completely free hand with their reclamation; undoubtedly much of it was carried on surreptitiously by peasants who, having cleared or drained small plots for themselves, strenuously resisted the visits of any inspectors who might have discovered them.[98]

It was in the eighteenth century, when reclamation was almost at an end, that many *han* administrators became aware of a new problem. Not only was it now virtually impossible for them to increase returns from traditional sources, but more disturbing still, their revenues were actually shrinking.[99] There were several reasons for this. In part it came about through the concentration of samurai in castle towns, a phenomenon observable in much of Japan by the late seventeenth

93 Quoted in Aono *Daimyō* p. 17. 94 Ibid., p. 99.
95 Miyazaki Michio, *Aomori-ken no rekishi* (Tokyo: Yamakawa shuppansha, 1970), pp. 149–50; *Tsuruoka-shi shi*, p. 296; Aono, *Daimyō*, p. 80.
96 Aono, *Daimyō*, p. 79. 97 Ibid.
98 Miura Toshiaki, "Hamamatsu-han ryōiki no keisei to shukueki joseikin," *Chihō-shi kenkyū* 79 (1966): 85.
99 For some examples, see *Fukuyama-shi shi*, p. 496; Nagaoka shiyakusho, ed., *Nagaoka-shi shi* (Nagaoka: Nagaoka shiyakusho, 1931), p. 109; Taniguchi Sumio, *Okayama han* (Tokyo: Yoshikawa kōbunkan, 1964), pp. 145–6.

century. No matter how greatly this had contributed to the stability and coherence of *han* governments, it had robbed them of their commanding position in the countryside. Village affairs were now left almost completely in the care of the headmen, themselves farmers and therefore subject to precisely the same pressures as their fellows were. Consequently they reacted to their freedom by underreporting yields, by neglecting to register freshly cultivated land, and by concealing the extent of rural commerce.

There were other contributing factors as well. In provinces like Settsu and Kawachi, the transformation of highly taxed rice paddies into more modestly taxed cotton fields inevitably led to reduced revenues. So too did a steady drift of farming population away from the villages and into country towns, castle towns, and the great urban centers of Edo and Osaka.[100] For that matter, agriculture was notoriously unpredictable during the Tokugawa period, and most *han* found themselves compelled to reduce or suspend normal taxation from time to time to help their farmers cope with disasters of one sort or another. In the northeast, where crop failures were common, unseasonable cold was usually the problem; elsewhere the agricultural cycle could be shattered by anything from floods, typhoons, and mud slides to earthquakes and volcanic eruptions. Whatever the cause, every *han* sooner or later had to recognize genuine hardship and make some sort of allowance for it. Even Nagaoka, after three successive years of flooding in the 1680s, was forced to acknowledge the gravity of the situation to the extent of subsidizing rice sales, providing shelter for the homeless, and suspending, albeit temporarily, the torture of those who had defaulted on their taxes.[101]

Naturally, declining incomes made the *han* far more sensitive to their expenses, and these were substantial. Despite the Tokugawa peace, in which no armies took the field between 1638 and 1864, every *han* was compelled to maintain a standing army. The bakufu's *gun'yaku* requirements would admit of nothing else. Paradoxically, it had been far less costly for daimyo to maintain armies in the Sengoku period, when fighting was more or less constant, than it proved to be in the tranquillity of the Tokugawa period.

In the sixteenth century, samurai had been mobilized only when necessary and supported themselves by farming the rest of the time. Whenever they did fight, they were subject to the full rigors of mili-

100 Susan B. Hanley and Kozo Yamamura, *Economic and Demographic Change in Preindustrial Japan, 1600–1868* (Princeton, N.J.: Princeton University Press, 1977), pp. 103–14.
101 Imaizumi, *Nagaoka no rekishi*, vol. 2, pp. 122–3.

tary Darwinism: Only the fittest survived. Under the Tokugawa, however, the situation was totally different; the majority of samurai no longer farmed but lived permanently on the payroll, whether in castle towns or in Edo (where some *han* were known to keep as many as 30 to 40 percent of their samurai stationed permanently).[102] Further, because none of them ever fought, old samurai tended to fade away rather than die, never so enfeebled as to be unable to draw their stipends at twice-yearly intervals. Yet, no matter how crushing the samurai incubus, no *han* could do much about it. Ōgaki actually succeeded in ridding itself of 150 samurai in 1680, after having received special permission from the bakufu, and in the late eighteenth century, Yonezawa, attempting a gentler approach, suggested hopefully that the second and third sons of its samurai families might like to find alternate employment as farmers,[103] but these were the exceptions rather than the rule.

Even by the bakufu's 1649 standardization of *gun'yaku* obligations,[104] which called upon even the smallest *han* to maintain a force of 235 men, Tokugawa Japan would have been spectacularly well endowed with samurai. But the fact was that although the bakufu had established a minimum figure for each *han,* it had deliberately refrained from setting a maximum. In the coda to its 1649 instructions, it had effectively left open the way for *han* to employ as many samurai as they wished, so long as they all were "loyal." It was not uncommon, therefore, for *han* of comparable endowment to differ wildly from one another in samurai numbers. Yonezawa, Takada, and Kōriyama all had much the same assessed productivity – roughly 150,000 *koku* – but although the last two had no more than two thousand samurai each, Yonezawa maintained four times that number.[105] More than anything else, such discrepancies were due to differing histories. Both Takada and Kōriyama owed their creation to Tokugawa patronage in the seventeenth century, and they were therefore able to employ just as many men as required, and no more. Yonezawa, by contrast, had come into being by a different route. It was in the hands of the Uesugi, a family prominent in eastern Japan since the fourteenth century. They had survived to enter the seventeenth century with both lands and

102 *Fukuyama-shi shi,* pp. 469–70; Kimura and Sugimoto, eds., *Fudai hansei,* pp. 26–7.

103 Ōgaki shiyakusho, ed., *Ōgaki-shi shi,* 3 vols. (Ōgaki, 1930), vol. 1, pp. 415–17; Tsuda, "Kansei kaikaku," p. 278.

104 TKRK, vol. 1, pp. 90–2.

105 Hanseishi kenkyūkai, ed., *Hansei seiritsushi no sōgō kenkyū – Yonezawa han* (Tokyo: Yoshikawa kōbunkan, 1963), p. 369.

military machine largely intact but, on being deprived of half of the former in 1664, still found themselves prevented by old ties of loyalty and obligation (and perhaps by fear of repercussions) from shedding anything like half their vassals. Many other *han* – Chōshū among them – were similarly placed.

It was all an immense burden. *Han* did what they could with their samurai, training and educating many of them for useful employment as civil servants of one sort of another – magistrates, censors, schoolmasters, secretaries, gamekeepers, policemen, foresters, bailiffs – and appointing those left over to sonorous and virtually meaningless military positions – guards, lancers, captains of the colors, and buglers (or at least blowers of conch shells).

A glance at the administrative structure of any *han* shows a bewildering range of posts: about 150 of them in Sakura *han* and almost as many in Owari.[106] Yet it was all so much window dressing. There was simply not enough business to engage the services of such a vast number of samurai – probably as many as 350,000 in the service of the various *han* – all of the time. Even with rotation and rostering there was not enough useful work to go around, so few could ever hope for more than temporary employment. Their status, nevertheless, remained constant, and so did their right to a basic salary. They served merely as a standing army (perhaps lounging army would be more apt a description), kept waiting for whatever emergency should arise. Ironically, that emergency did not eventuate for over two hundred years, and when it did, it found them lamentably unprepared.

The other major drain on *han* finances was a by-product of the *sankin kōtai* system, under which daimyo were required to take up residence in Edo every alternate year. No part of this ritual was ever done cheaply. It was unthinkable, for example, that a daimyo should sidle unobtrusively into Edo. Instead, he made it his business to set out on his journey with as splendid an escort as possible. The daimyo *gyōretsu*, or procession, numbering as many as a thousand men with spears and pennants, was one of the most splendid sights Tokugawa Japan had to offer. It was also one of the most costly, for it was no easy matter to move large numbers of men across Japan. In the case of the more distant *han*, like Karatsu in north Kyushu, for example, when the journey needed more than thirty overnight stops, the outlay for

106 Kimura and Sugimoto, *Fudai hansei*, p. 21; Hayashi Tōichi, *Owari han no kōhōshi no kenkyū* (Tokyo: Nippon gakujutsu shinkōkai, 1962), pp. 153–6.

food and shelter en route was enormous. Every other year Saga *han*, Karatsu's near neighbor, customarily spent 20 percent of that year's income on the journey alone.[107]

Nor did the cost diminish once the daimyo and his retinue had reached Edo. "Above all, we must economize when we are in Edo," warned the senior vassals of the daimyo of Karatsu in 1782, and not without reason.[108] Virtually everything the daimyo and his vassals needed for their stay in Edo, from food and fuel to paper and ink, had to be bought there at Edo prices, almost always higher than those current at home. There were, too, unremitting temptations to spend – familiar enough to any urban society, but particularly intense in a city where samurai from all over Japan competed with one another in keeping up appearances. Each daimyo, too, no matter how frugal by personal inclination, was caught up in the same contest and was obliged to live in a manner befitting his eminence, real or pretended.

All of them therefore maintained mansions of some elegance, often set in notable gardens, traces of which are still to be seen in Tokyo: the Kōrakuen for example, once the property of Mito *han*, or the Rikugien, which belonged to the Yanagisawa of Kōriyama. It was customary for *han* to have more than one such residence. The chief one, known as the *kami-yashiki,* functioned as a permanent legation, where a staff of officials attended to the *han*'s Edo business and where the daimyo was housed during his *sankin kōtai* stays. A secondary residence, or *naka-yashiki,* accommodated the daimyo's heir apparent but also provided shelter for the daimyo whenever necessary, as, for example, on the many occasions when the official residence had been either destroyed by fire or was being rebuilt in readiness for the next. It was common, too, for *han* to have yet another residence, this time a *shimo-yashiki,* or holiday house, in some distant quarter of the city, to which the daimyo and his family could repair during the worst of the summer heat. As reported in the *Edo zusetsu* of 1799, there were 265 official residences and another 734 secondary residences and holiday houses scattered around the city.[109]

Compared with such massive outlays, the normal run of expenses back in the *han* seems rather meager. It was expected, and indeed often explicitly stated, that the *han* themselves were to be administered

107 *Karatsu-shi shi,* p. 617; Sasaki Junnosuke, *Daimyō to hyakushō,* vol. 15 of *Chūō kōron Nihon no rekishi* (Tokyo: Chūō kōronsha, 1966), p. 156.
108 Matsuyoshi Sadao, *Kanemochi daimyō bimbō daimyō* (Tokyo: Jimbutsu ōraisha, 1964), p. 69.
109 Cited in Fujino, *Daimyō,* p. 95.

as conservatively as possible, eschewing all expenses not absolutely necessary to their primary function of feeding the samurai and maintaining the system. Typically, budgets began and ended with the needs of the samurai class (stipends and education) and their obligations (*han* defense and alternate attendance). The needs of the remaining 90 percent of *han* population figure only occasionally and grudgingly in *han* ledgers, and then only in times of crisis. Under normal circumstances they were left to fend for themselves, their lives, customs, and amusements frequently the subject of *han* regulation, but never its object. All they gained in return for their taxes was the attempted perpetuation of conditions under which their future contributions to *han* finances might be maximized.

In any case, no *han* could really have afforded to do anything more for its common people. As it was, with revenues stagnant or declining and enormous commitments in Edo and to their samurai, it was more and more difficult for the *han* to balance their budgets. It is hardly necessary to go through the dispiriting roll call of those *han* that tottered through the eighteenth and early nineteenth centuries (and even part of the seventeenth century) poised precariously on the knife-edge between indigence and bankruptcy. It was a state common to them all, to a greater or lesser degree, and their responses to it were broadly similar. The instinctive reaction to the crisis, when it first appeared, was for *han* governments to accuse the common people of living above their station and to call upon them to spend less and surrender more. Next came internal economy drives, initially for fixed periods (five years being the favored figure), but sooner or later these periods became consecutive; one such initiative launched by Kanazawa *han* in 1779 was still in force twenty years later.[110] At such times not even the daimyo's own household expenses escaped scrutiny, a fact that was sometimes known to drive needy daimyo into the welcoming arms of the pawnbrokers. It was in precisely such circumstances that Sakai Tadazane of Shōnai came to pledge two family heirlooms – a noted tea bowl and a painting – for a thousand gold pieces. His successor, Tadayori, beset by similar difficulties, did the same with his wife's hair ornaments, originally part of her dowry.[111]

Overwhelmingly, however, *han* governments confronted the financial crisis with the help of moneylenders, usually the great merchant houses of Osaka and Kyoto – the Kōnoike (who had thirty-one indebted *han* on their books by the end of the seventeenth century),[112]

110 Ibid., p. 207. 111 *Tsuruoka-shi shi*, pp. 326, 336. 112 Fujino, *Daimyō*, p. 163.

the Sumitomo, the Masuya, and others – but gradually coming to rely on local merchants as well.

The borrowing had in fact begun very early, particularly in the case of *han* like Sendai, Chōshū, Satsuma, Saga, and Tosa, all of which were compelled to contribute heavily to the bakufu's castle-building projects at the beginning of the seventeenth century.[113] By the end of that century, however, and long after the heaviest of bakufu impositions had been met, every *han* had gone into debt. Few of them ever emerged, for the interest on those debts (usually from 5 to 7 percent per annum)[114] was to prove beyond the resources of all but the very richest of *han*. Tosa, by 1688, was spending 34 percent of its budget repaying loans; Hiroshima, across the Inland Sea, unable to meet even the interest on its debt, owed the Kōnoike house a sum that in 1745 had grown precisely ten-fold since 1719; for Okayama, by 1829, payments to moneylenders had come to represent the largest single item in its annual budget.[115] The *han* had thus built such a superstructure of debt for themselves that only the most draconian measures – the unilateral repudiation of all debts, for example[116] – could set them free. Budget deficits and chronic debts were as much a part of *han* life as they are of our own, and no matter how much contemporaries deplored them, it is certain that they, like ourselves, also learned to live with them, at least until the cataclysmic events of the mid-nineteenth century.

There were just two other avenues open to *han* wishing to enhance their finances. In most cases, neither of them proved to be anything more than a mild palliative, leaving the superstructure of *han* debts largely untouched. Both of them, however, were of some political significance. In following one of them, *han* governments found themselves at odds with local residents; in following the other, they were to erode their relations with their own samurai. Nevertheless, given the circumstances in which they found themselves, the *han* had little alternative but to pursue them both.

The first was essentially a reaction to the commercial development of the Tokugawa period, in which the medieval ideal of individual self-sufficiency crumbled under the pressures of commercial farming and specialized manufacture. It was not long before the *han* governments responded to the change, with mercantilist policies that encouraged local products with protection inside the domain (to stop money from

113 Ibid., p. 200; Sasaki, *Daimyō*, pp. 132–3. 114 Fujino, *Daimyō*, p. 164.
115 Hirao Michio, *Tosa han* (Tokyo: Yoshikawa kōbunkan, 1965), pp. 33–34; Aono, *Daimyō*, p. 73; Taniguchi, *Okayama hansei*, p. 160.
116 Bolitho, "The Tempō Crisis," pp. 32–3.

leaving the *han*) and outside with purposeful marketing (to bring money into the *han*). This attention proved a mixed blessing to local producers, however.

Those who benefited by protection – the ink makers of Aizu, for example, freed from competition by a ban on imported ink in 1791 – could not have been more pleased.[117] Such was not the case, though, with producers of more highly prized commodities. As the indigo growers of Tokushima, the madder growers of Yonezawa, the lacquer makers of Aizu, the potters of Saga, and countless other farmers and craftsmen were to discover, few *han* could resist trying to siphon away the profits. The experience of the Karatsu paper-mulberry growers in this regard is fairly typical. With their crop subject to compulsory acquisition orders by the *han* and with severe punishment threatened for anyone attempting to evade such orders, they were obliged to sell what they grew to none but authorized buyers, and at a third of the price obtainable outside the domain.[118] The *han*, having bought cheaply, intended to sell dear elsewhere and to pocket the proceeds. Indeed, quite often in such cases, local producers were to be paid in *hansatsu*, *han* paper currency, worth virtually nothing outside the *han* borders and little more inside. It was a tidy scheme, but it did not often work. Inevitably there was resistance. The Karatsu case is no less typical in this respect, for its paper-mulberry farmers rioted in 1771, as did cotton farmers in Fukuyama in 1752, Matsuyama tea growers in 1741, Oka tobacco growers in 1811, and innumerable other farmers and craftsmen and manufacturers at various times during the Tokugawa period.[119] So fierce were these protests, and so determined and inventive local producers in evading official directives, that few *han* managed to recoup their finances as easily as they had originally hoped. Nevertheless, illusion though it may have been, it was virtually the last one that most *han* had, and they therefore clung to it all the more tenaciously.

The remaining possibility for *han* intent on relieving financial pressures was yet another form of borrowing. This time, however, rather than from the great merchant houses, which always had to be appeased in some way, loans were levied from a captive source – the samurai themselves. Such inroads into samurai salaries began quite early in the Tokugawa period: as early as 1623 in Chōshū, 1639 in Hiroshima, the 1650s in Fukuyama, and the 1670s in

117 *Aizu–Wakamatsu-shi*, vol. 9, p. 238. 118 *Karatsu-shi shi*, p. 621.

119 Ibid., p. 593; *Fukuyama-shi shi*, p. 537; Aono, *Daimyō*, p. 187; Kishida Tsutomu, "Kyūshū no bunjinga," in Mikami Tsugio, ed., *Kyūshū no ega to tōgei* (Tokyo: Heibonsha, 1975), p. 246.

Nagaoka.[120] Initially samurai were called upon only intermittently to give back part of their salaries, usually in reponse to some immediate need, as in the case of Nagaoka, where a special levy was made to pay for a wedding in the daimyo's family.[121] But once the first step had been taken and the principle established that samurai could be expected to surrender part of their stipends in the general interest, then it was much easier the next time there was an emergency.

Ultimately, forced loans from samurai became a constant feature of *han* life. In Shōnai *han* between 1690 and 1797 there were just nine years in which all samurai received their full stipends; the rest of the time anybody with more than two hundred *koku* was obliged to part with a percentage of it (usually 7 percent). In 1741, nobody received any salary at all; instead they were given a daily ration of rice and a small amount of copper cash, just enough to see them through the immediate crisis and no more. Nor was their experience unusual; at Hikone, reduced stipends were so much a matter of course that samurai had to be notified when they were to be paid in full. In Matsushiro *han*, full stipends were granted only once in 138 years.[122]

In all of this the samurai were to prove themselves far more tractable than the peasants were. Such security as they had depended entirely on their *han*, so they could be relied on to make whatever sacrifices were necessary, even if it meant "temporary" salary reductions that were never made good or "loans" that were never repaid. For all of them, the alternative – dismissal and the total loss of salary and status – was generally far less attractive than genteel poverty. Nevertheless, their cooperation was far from enthusiastic, and all *han* were to pay for these exactions in two ways. First, poverty produced a samurai class far too poorly equipped and demoralized to meet even the smallest emergency. Second, in the context of *han* political life, hardship forced samurai of all ranks to take a far keener interest in *han* affairs than they might otherwise have done and so ultimately helped bring about a revolution in government.

HAN POLITICS

It is not to be thought that the samurai had been totally tamed by the conditions of life in Tokugawa Japan. True, many of them had been

120 Fujino, *Daimyō*, p. 210; Aono, *Daimyō*, p. 74; *Fukuyama-shi shi*, p. 5, Imaizumi, *Nagaoka no rekishi*, vol. 1, p. 118.

121 *Nagaoka-shi shi*, p. 114.

122 *Tsuruoka-shi shi*, pp. 322, 339; *Hikone-shi shi*, vol. 1, pp. 624–5; Fujino, Daimyō, p. 214.

removed from their old country estates and brought into residence in the new castle towns, but this in itself did not necessarily mean subjection. Certainly they were now under constant scrutiny, utterly reliant on their salaries, and virtually denied alternative employment. They were infinitely more dependent than they had ever been; yet they were far from quiescent. Paradoxically, the establishment of the Tokugawa peace had created circumstances that not only enabled samurai to question their daimyo's prerogative but, on occasion, compelled them to do so and so made inevitable a degree of political ferment.

In theory, of course, no challenge to daimyo authority should have been possible. In accepting each daimyo's submission, the Tokugawa government guaranteed its support to every one of them in turn. Their legal right to govern their *han* was therefore unassailable. So, too, was a certain moral obligation, for Heaven had selected each one of them for precisely that position. As Uesugi Harunori, daimyo of Yonezawa, expressed it in a piece of calligraphy written on his accession in 1767, this obligation was clear: "Father and Mother of the People," the inscription read, followed by a poem, "Inheriting the command of this domain, I must never forget that I am father and mother to my people."[123] There were also practical considerations, as the daimyo, it was thought, were the custodians of secret traditions enabling them to rule far more effectively than ordinary men could. Such, at least, was believed of the daimyo of Saga, alleged in *Hagakure* to have had a number of secret books entrusted to him on his accession.[124] For all of these reasons, it was the clear duty of the samurai to obey their daimyo, even, for some favored samurai in the early seventeenth century, to follow him to the grave in token of their loyalty, devotion, and obedience.

Yet in practice there were difficulties. The daimyo of Tokugawa Japan, no less than their Sengoku predecessors, walked a tightrope – nearer to the ground, perhaps, and slightly slacker, but still needing to be traversed with the utmost care. Many realized how volatile their vassals could be, sometimes feeling impelled to warn them, as did the daimyo of Shōnai in 1648, against "factious, conspiratorial, or obstructive behavior" or, as did the young daimyo of Aizu forty years later, demanding of his senior vassals a special oath of loyalty, signed in

123 Naramoto Tatsuya, Hosokawa Morisada, and Murakami Genzō, eds., *Edo daimyō hyakke*, vol. 22 of *Taiyō bekkan* (Tokyo: Heibonsha, 1978), p. 162.

124 Naramoto Tatsuya, ed., *Hagakure*, vol. 17 of *Nihon no meicho* (Tokyo: Chūō kōronsha, 1969), pp. 54–5.

blood.[125] Paradoxically, these difficulties were directly traceable to bakufu policies. By compelling daimyo to spend at least half of their working lives in Edo under the *sankin kōtai* system, for example, the bakufu had effectively obliged them to leave the larger part of normal decision making in the hands of those senior vassals permanently resident in the *han*. Daimyo therefore were only intermittently in contact with *han* affairs and even when in residence were inevitably tempted to leave decisions to those who were better informed.

Still more serious was the Tokugawa government's commitment to the principle of hereditary succession. This virtually guaranteed the appointment of the fit and unfit alike. Not even the demonstrably infirm, the palpably dull-witted or the openly uninterested were disqualified. A confidential appraisal of daimyo in the late seventeenth century was able to call attention to those who could never have survived in an earlier period: Matsuura Masashi, "who has made friends of every merchant and priest in Edo with a liking for *kemari*";[126] Itami Katsumasa, "devoted to beautiful women and boys"; Date Munezumi, "totally obsessed with sex, spending all day in his bedchamber while feigning indisposition"; and Hoshina Masayoshi, "ignorant and totally lacking in ability."[127] By the eighteenth century, Arai Hakuseki was able to use the term "daimyo's sons" as a derisive epithet, a judgment confirmed 150 years later by Ernest Satow, who met too many daimyo to have any great opinion of them.[128] Not uncommonly, too, the bakufu was prepared to confirm any legitimate heir as daimyo, no matter how young he might be – even indeed before he could walk. Of the 163 daimyo in 1691 for whom such information is available, a total of 85, or more than half, appear to have become daimyo before reaching the age of twenty.[129]

The regular absence of all daimyo from their *han*, combined with the Tokugawa government's almost total support for hereditary succession, was enough to create a power vacuum in many *han*, but not for long. Inevitably it was filled, sometimes by relatives or, increasingly, by senior vassals. By 1691 it was obviously accepted that this was likely; the same confidential report that spoke so freely of

125 *Yamagata-ken shi (shiryō-hen)*, vol. 5, p. 352; *Aizu Wakamatsu-shi shi*, vol. 9, pp. 106–7.
126 *Kemari*, one of Japan's traditional sports was a football game in which a number of players cooperated in keeping a deerskin ball in the air for as long as possible.
127 Kanai, ed., *Dokai kōshūki*, pp. 701, 616, 478, 578.
128 Miyazaki Michio, ed., *Teihon "Oritaku shiba no ki" shakugi* (Tokyo: Shibundō, 1964), p. 575; Sir Ernest Satow, *A Diplomat in Japan* (Oxford, England: Oxford University Press, 1968), p. 37.
129 Calculated from Kanai, ed., *Dokai kōshūki*.

daimyo shortcomings made this clear: "Leaving the government of one's people to senior vassals has both good and bad features," it warned. "It is good when the vassal puts loyalty first and follows the right path selflessly and unswervingly. But if the vassal is deceitful and harbors mischievous designs while counterfeiting loyalty . . . and uses his authority selfishly and unjustly, then that house will surely fall."[130]

Equally, other pressures made sure that vassals were not merely able to supplant their daimyo in all but name but indeed were obliged to. Political power by itself was perhaps not such a prize, offering at the most a massage for the ego, marginally better living conditions, and agreeable opportunities for the exercise of patronage. But the alternative, as far as samurai were concerned, could be disastrous. If a daimyo, selected by no process more discriminating than the accident of birth, were to attempt to rule his *han* personally, then who could say what havoc he might let loose? He might be led by flatterers to overturn the traditional samurai hierarchy; he might prove spendthrift; or he might bankrupt the *han* or even, by attracting Tokugawa displeasure, put his own tenure at risk, and with it that of all his samurai as well.

The dangers inherent in daimyo autocracy were just too great to allow samurai, dependent as they were on their *han* and its well-being, the luxury of meek obedience. Naturally, they preferred their daimyo to be ciphers, like the well-loved Makino Tadataka, who became daimyo of Nagaoka at the age of seventeen. Although he died the following year and would therefore have had neither the years nor the time to do very much, his reputation is nevertheless that of a model ruler: "He was careful not to neglect military matters," the chronicles say, "and was concerned always for the common people. He instructed his government that old ways should be reformed and abuses corrected, that honest men should be promoted and corrupt officials dismissed. . . . He knew how to teach his people through the impartial use of severity and mercy. Conditions improved immediately, and hardships were thankfully forgotten."[131] Such a daimyo was no trouble to anyone and therefore was always appreciated. Even those marginally more active could be controlled with a minimum of effort and within the political conventions; the only evidence of struggle would then be confined to ripples on the surface – resignations, dismissals, appointments, and muted complaints – the last sometimes embodied in appeals to the

130 Ibid., pp. 587–8. 131 Imaizumi, *Nagaoka no rekishi,* vol. 1, pp. 82–3.

daimyo's good sense and better nature or, should these prove unsuccessful, in an occasional case of remonstratory suicide.[132]

The encomium for the young Makino Tadataka, dead in his nineteenth year, contrasts vividly with the reputations of determined reformers like Mizuno Tadatoki, whose policies in Okazaki *han* so outraged his senior vassals that they placed him under house arrest and forced him to retire.[133] This was playing the game hard, but given what was at stake, it could scarcely have been otherwise. Throughout the Tokugawa period, indeed, a constant succession of *oiesōdō*, spectacular public disputes, was to mark those occasions when daimyo and samurai came into conflict over policy issues or, alternatively, when samurai and samurai came into conflict over the daimyo. Some of the more celebrated of these disputes offer enough drama – father against son (Miyazu *han*), brother against brother (Tokuno *han*), uncle against nephew (Sendai *han*), daimyo against vassals (Yonezawa *han*), vassals against daimyo (Kokura *han*), and vassal against vassal (Suwa *han*), all punctuated with arrests, suicides, executions, assassinations, poison plots, and mass walkouts – to satisfy the most jaded kabuki audience.

Some, indeed, did just that. The famous Sendai incident, heavily fictionalized, first appeared on the stage forty years after it erupted and thereafter provided the framework for some thirty different plays.[134] It is not too difficult to see why. The situation – a power vacuum in the *han* brought on by the enforced retirement of the daimyo, and his replacement by his two-year-old son – was pure kabuki. So were the leading characters in the struggle that soon exploded, a wicked uncle, an even more wicked greatuncle, and a number of unscrupulous vassals, all of them whipping up conspiracies, murder plots, and formal letters of complaint to the government in Edo. The denouement, a meeting of opponents at an inquiry held in the residence of a senior bakufu politician, added a touch of Grand Guignol, as swords were drawn and four men were cut down, two dying instantly and the others receiving mortal wounds.[135]

Such disputes were not without their risks. With tempers running high, violence was not uncommon. But there were more serious hazards still. Once one of these incidents became public, it then invited bakufu intervention, and this could sometimes take an unpalatable

132 For an example of a complaint, see *Tsuruoka-shi shi*, pp. 323–4; for a remonstratory suicide, see *Karatsu-shi shi*, p. 607.

133 Kitajima Masamoto, "Meikun no higeki," in Itō Tasaburō, ed., *Kokumin seikatsu shi kenkyū*, vol. 1 of *Seikatsu to seiji* (Tokyo: Yoshikawa Kōbunkan, 1957).

134 Kitajima, ed., *Oiesōdō*, pp. 173–4. 135 Ibid., p. 168.

form, as Edo did not usually approve of troublemakers, and execution or exile was not uncommon. Still more serious, the bakufu could interpret such events as proof of a *han*'s inability to govern itself and issue a confiscation order. This was precisely the way in which the Mogami of Yamagata, the Hiraoka of Tokuno, the Matsudaira of Echigo, and the Kyōgoku of Miyazu came to lose their domains, and how Morioka and Kōriyama *han* both came to be split in two. That samurai were prepared to take such risks indicates just how seriously they viewed their political role. No matter how great the possible perils of action, the probable penalties of inaction were often greater still.

Some degree of conflict is inevitable in politics. Without it, indeed, what we know as politics would cease to exist. But it must be acknowledged that certain aspects of *han* government, by their very secrecy and inefficiency, tended to invite disagreement among the overwhelming majority of samurai, who being ineligible for high office, were not privy to the reasoning of those who were. No *han* could prevent its vassals questioning its policies, although many felt obliged to try from time to time, as did Nakatsu, which in 1738 forbade its samurai even to discuss any of the new domain laws.[136] Nearly a hundred years earlier Ikeda Mitsumasa of Okayama had put the position still more bluntly, warning that "anyone who interferes in any government business whatsoever is not a samurai; he is a malefactor, even if he is our vassal."[137] Given the rules governing selection for *han* office throughout most of the Tokugawa period, a certain measure of discontent was unavoidable, for as with the positions of emperor, shogun, and daimyo, those of senior officials in the *han* had also largely come to be filled by reason of birth. In the wars of the Sengoku period it was usually the case that no man could hold for very long an office he was incapable of filling successfully, but here too, the Tokugawa peace had intervened.

By the middle of the seventeenth century, or even earlier, the samurai hierarchy in most *han* had been stabilized. The head of each samurai family had been allotted a stipend (whether or not he always received it all) that served as an index of his status in the *han*, and this in turn determined his eligibility for positions in the *han* military and administrative hierarchy. The fine calibration to be seen among the samurai of Sakura *han* can serve as a fairly typical example of the

136 Kuroya Naofusa, *Nakatsu-han shi* (Tokyo: Hekiun-so, 1940), p. 322.
137 Taniguchi, *Okayama han*, p. 55.

system here: Of the 152 different kinds of official position, the most important advisory posts were limited to the heads of seven families, none of which had a stipend of less than 250 *koku*. To be eligible for the office of censor, a stipend of between 70 and 120 *koku* was needed; to be a secretary, it took an income of between thirty and fifty bales of rice per year; and to work as an assistant accountant, fourteen to sixteen bales.[138]

Of course, many of these 152 positions were of little consequence, demanding neither particular skill nor particular energy for their performance. In an age of peace it mattered as little who was captain of the colors (anyone with from 150 to 500 *koku*) as it did who was chosen to beat drums and gongs (anyone with 3 *koku* and ten bales). Neither was likely to be called upon for anything other than ceremonial duties. But it mattered very much who filled the key advisory and administrative posts, for here was where the important decisions had to be made. Sakura *han*, by allowing seven men to monopolize these positions, was effectively turning its back on the talents and energies of the other two thousand-odd members of its vassal band. It was hardly alone, however. All *han* did so, even the larger ones. Saga drew on the heads of eighteen samurai families when filling its most important positions, and Owari fifty. The largest *han* found their top advisers and administrators from among as many as eighty families, but given the total pool of samurai (roughly thirty thousand in the case of Sendai), we may doubt that even they had so much as begun to exploit the reservoir of samurai talent.[139]

There is no doubt that in the long run the *han* suffered by filling demanding positions with those who were eligible rather than suitable, for senior vassal families were subject to precisely the same genetic limitations as were their daimyo. There was just no guarantee that any group of seven men (or even seventy) could produce enough inspired (or even competent) officials to oversee the increasingly complex business of *han* government. Indeed, the members of such families were prepared to admit as much, preferring to base their authority on grounds other than mere talent: "Although it is desirable that senior councilors be capable and mature," one of them was to observe, "nevertheless men like ourselves, who come from lines of hereditary senior councilors, must themselves become senior council-

138 Kimura and Sugimoto, *Fudai hansei*, pp. 21–3.

139 Fujino Tamotsu, "Hansei kakuritsu-ki no shomondai – seihoku Kyūshū sho han (Hirado, Ōmura, Saga kaku han o chūshin to shite)," in *Shakai keizai shigaku* 24 (1958): 259; Kodama and Kitajima, eds., *Monogatari han shi*, vol. 4, p. 132, vol. 2, pp. 68–69.

ors, even should they be young and untalented. . . . Those families that have traditionally held the office of senior councilor are familiar with the domain laws and so pass on their knowledge to their children and grandchildren. They can also note down memoranda and bequeath them to their children, so that no matter how many generations pass, our ancient laws will be maintained."[140] This was a recipe for conservatism, and on the whole the record of *han* governments during the Tokugawa period does no more than confirm a general impression of stagnation.

It was not impossible for daimyo to interfere with this charmed circle of hereditary advisors, and many did so, sometimes by introducing a system of temporary salaries, or *tashidaka*, by which men might be promoted to positions for which they were otherwise ineligible, or sometimes by showering rewards on favorites. Mizuno Katsusada of Fukuyama did this in the mid-seventeenth century, raising Inekuma Saemon from a stipend of one hundred *koku* to something fifteen times that amount, thereby giving him a status equivalent to that of senior councilor. Such favorites always encountered the implacable hostility of the hereditary councilor class, and their appearance was usually the signal for an outbreak of tension within the domain. The very least such men could expect would be charges of corruption (for how could an outsider be promoted if not dishonestly?) or selfishness (for why would he wish to be if not for his own benefit?) Occasionally, as in the case of Inekuma Saemon, it ended in suicide on the death of the daimyo protector.[141]

In the last resort, the grip of hereditary senior councilors could be loosened only by a crisis grave enough to warrant extraordinary measures. Even then it was not easy. An immediate emergency, like a flood or famine or a particularly severe financial crisis, might confer temporary authority on an outsider with special skills, who would set about rebuilding the dikes, or take charge of famine relief, or slash expenditures, but once the crisis itself had dissipated, then so too would the hierarchical hiccup it had occasioned. Such at least was the case through the seventeenth and much of the eighteenth centuries.

When the chronic financial problems of *han* governments began to bite, however, this situation changed, for reduced salaries, though they affected all samurai, particularly hurt the poorest among them. Not unnaturally, they began to lash out. In some cases, like the mass desertion of samurai from Kokura in 1814 after yet another salary

140 Imaizumi, *Nagaoka no rekishi*, vol. 1, p. 172. 141 *Fukuyama-shi shi*, p. 53.

reduction, their target was the *han* itself. In others it was the daimyo, one of whom, the daimyo of Oka *han*, was taken publicly to task for his personal extravagance in 1812, by one of his lower samurai, a poet and painter called Tanomura Chikuden. More generally, however, the discontent of the poorer samurai found its target among their richer and more prominent fellows, the members of the traditional councilor class. Increasingly it was seen as inequitable that there should be so great a discrepancy between the salaries of these *baka karō*, or "idiot councilors," as they came to be called, and their lesser brethren.[142] That discrepancy was certainly glaring enough. In Nakatsu, 78.2 percent of all expenditure on salaries went to a mere 15.5 percent of samurai.[143] More important, in the context of *han* government, it seemed increasingly unwise to leave policy in the hands of men who in the course of two hundred years had shown themselves incapable of adapting to changing circumstances.

The nineteenth century, therefore, ushered in a revolution – sometimes only half-formed and imperfectly articulated, but a revolution nevertheless – in the governments of many *han*. The situation was too grave to be ignored, for to the standard economic worries was added a frightening confluence of new concerns: concern with mounting unrest in the countryside, where the peasantry was rioting on an unprecedented scale; concern with a growing alien interest in Japan's corner of the Pacific; concern therefore that *han* and bakufu alike would need to spend far more in their defense than ever before – money, moreover, that none of them had; concern that with a flagging government in Edo the nation might once more be plunged into turmoil; and concern too, paradoxically, that if the Tokugawa bakufu were to restore its authority it would be at *han* expense.[144] A crisis of such magnitude could not be solved by half-measures. When it was finally confronted, in the last three decades of Tokugawa rule, it was by a new kind of samurai administrator, one caring little for hereditary privilege, as he had climbed from the lower rungs of the samurai ladder, and caring still less for the conventions of *han* government, of which (as neither his father nor grandfather was capable of instructing him) he was mercifully ignorant. The revolution in government such men brought to their *han* in the nineteenth century – characterized by new commercial initiatives, by the creation of peasant militia, by the rationalization of samurai stipends, by independent diplomatic activ-

142 Kishida, "Kyūshū no bunjinga," p. 246; Andō Hideo, ed., *Chiritsubo–Kawai Tsugunosuke nikki*, vol. 257 of *Tōyō Bunko* (Tokyo: Heibonsha, 1974), p. 304.

143 Shindō, "Hansei kaikaku," pp. 117–19.

144 Bolitho, "The Tempō Crisis."

ity, by participation in an internecine race for arms – was perhaps a natural reaction to Japan's problems. Natural or not, however, it ultimately destroyed the bakufu and with it, after three short years, the *han* themselves.

BIBLIOGRAPHY

Ackroyd, Joyce, trans., *Told Round a Brushwood Fire: The Autobiography of Arai Hakuseki.* Princeton, N. J.: Princeton University Press, 1979.

Abe Yukihiro 阿部征寛. *Mōko shūrai.* 蒙古襲来. Tokyo: Kyōikusha 教育社, 1980.

Aida Nirō 相田二郎. *Mōko shūrai no kenkyū.* 蒙古襲来の研究. Tokyo: Yoshikawa kōbunkan 吉川弘文館, 1971.

Aizu-Wakamatsu-shi shuppan iinkai 会津若松史出版委員会, ed. *Aizu-Wakamatsu-shi* 会津若松史. Aizu-Wakamatsu: Aizu-Wakamatsu-shi 会津若松市, 1967.

Amino Yoshihiko 網野善彦. "Kamakura makki no shomujun" 鎌倉末期の諸矛盾. In Rekishigaku kenkyūkai and Nihonshi kenkyūkai 歴史学研究会・日本史研究会, comp. *Kōza Nihonshi* 講座日本史, vol. 3. Tokyo: Tōkyō daigaku shuppankai 東京大学出版会, 1970.

Amino Yoshihiko 網野善彦. "Kamakura bakufu no kaizoku kin'atsu ni tsuite – Kamakura makki no kaijō keigo o chūshin ni" 鎌倉幕府の海賊禁圧について－鎌倉末期の海上警護を中心に. *Nihon rekishi* 日本歴史, no. 229 (April 1973): 1–20.

Amino Yoshihiko 網野善彦. *Mōko shūrai* 蒙古襲来. Vol. 10 of *Nihon no rekishi* 日本の歴史. Tokyo: Shōgakkan 小学館, 1974.

Amino Yoshihiko 網野善彦. "Zōshushi kōjiyaku no seiritsu ni tsuite – Muromachi bakufu sakayayaku no zentei" 造酒司麹役の成立について－室町幕府酒屋役の前提. In Takeuchi Rizō hakase koki kinenkai 竹内理三博士古希記念会, comp. *Zoku shōensei to buke shakai* 続荘園制と武家社会. Tokyo: Yoshikawa kōbunkan 吉川弘文館, 1978.

Andō Hideo 安藤英男, ed. *Chiritsubo: Kawai Tsugunosuke nikki* 塵壺：河井継之助日記. Vol. 257 of *Tōyō bunko* 東洋文庫. Tokyo: Heibonsha 平凡社, 1974.

Aoki Kōji 青木虹二, *Hyakushō ikki sōgō nempyō* 百姓一揆総合年表. Tokyo: San'ichi shobō 三一書房, 1971.

Aono Shunsui 青野春水. *Daimyō to ryōmin* 大名と領民. Tokyo: Kyōikusha 教育社, 1983.

Arakawa Hidetoshi 荒川秀俊. "Bun'ei no eki no owari o tsugeta no wa taifū dewa nai" 文永の役の終りを告げたのは台風ではない. *Nihon rekishi* 日本歴史.

Arnesen, Peter. *The Medieval Japanese Daimyo: The Ōuchi Family's Rule in Suō and Nagato*: New Haven, Conn.: Yale University Press, 1979.

Arnesen, Peter. "The Provincial Vassals of the Muromachi Bakufu." In Jeffrey P. Mass and William B. Hauser, eds. *The Bakufu in Japanese History*. Stanford, Calif.: Stanford University Press, 1985.

Ashida Koreto 蘆田伊人. *Goryōchi-shikō* 御料地史考. Tokyo: Teishitsu Rinyakyoku 帝室林野局, 1937.

Asao Naohiro 朝尾直弘. "shōgun seiji no kenryoku kōzō" 将軍政治の権力構造. In *Iwanami kōza Nihon rekishi* 岩波講座日本歴史. Vol. 10. Tokyo: Iwanami shoten 岩波書店, 1975.

Asao, Naohiro, with Marius B. Jansen. "Shogun and Tennō." In John W. Hall, Keiji Nagahara, and Kozo Yamamura, eds. *Japan Before Tokugawa: Political Consolidation and Economic Growth, 1500–1650*. Princeton, N. J.: Princeton University Press, 1981.

Berry, Mary Elizabeth. *Hideyoshi*. Cambridge, Mass.: Harvard University Press, 1982.

Bolitho, Harold. *Treasures Among Men: The Fudai Daimyo in Tokugawa Japan*. New Haven, Conn.: Yale University Press, 1974.

Bolitho, Harold. "The Dog Shogun." In Wang Gungwu, ed. *Self and Biography*. Sydney: Sydney University Press, 1975.

Bolitho, Harold. "The Tempō Crisis." In Marius B. Jansen, ed. *The Nineteenth Century*. Vol. 5 of *The Cambridge History of Japan*. Cambridge, England: Cambridge University Press, 1989.

Boot, Willem Jan. "The Deification of Tokugawa Ieyasu." *Japan Foundation Newsletter*, Vol. xiv, No. 5, February 1987.

Chihōshi kenkyū kyōgikai 地方史研究協議会, *Chihōshi kenkyū hikkei* 地方史研究必携. Tokyo: Iwanami shoten 岩波書店, 1961.

Collcutt, Martin. *Five Mountains: The Rinzai Zen Monastic Institution in Medieval Japan*. Cambridge, Mass.: Harvard University Press, 1981.

Cooper, Michael, ed. *They Came to Japan: An Anthology of European Reports on Japan, 1543–1640*. Berkeley and Los Angeles: University of California Press, 1965.

Dai Nihon shiryō 大日本史料, vol. 9. Tokyo: Tōkyō teikoku daigaku 東京帝国大学, 1909.

Elison, George. *Deus Destroyed: The Image of Christianity in Early Modern Japan*. Cambridge, Mass.: Harvard University Press, 1973.

Elison, George, and Bardwell L. Smith, eds. *Warlords, Artists, & Commoners: Japan in the Sixteenth Century*. Honolulu: University of Hawaii Press, 1981.

Endō Iwao 遠藤巌. "Nambokuchō nairan no naka de" 南北朝内乱のなかで. In Kobayashi Seiji 小林清治 and Ōishi Naomasa 大石直正, eds. *Chūsei Ōu no sekai* 中世奥羽の世界. Tokyo: Tōkyō daigaku shuppankai 東京大学出版会, 1978.

Farris, William W. *Heavenly Warriors: The Evolution of Japan's Military, 500–1300*. Cambridge, Mass.: Harvard University Press, 1993.

Friday, Karl E. *Hired Swords: The Rise of Private Warriors in Early Japan*. Stanford, Calif.: Stanford University Press, 1992.

Fujii Sadafumi 藤井貞文 and Hayashi Rikurō 林陸朗, eds. *Han shi jiten* 藩史辞典. Tokyo: Akita shoten 秋田書店, 1976.

Fujiki, Toyohiko, with Elison, George. "The Political Posture of Oda Nobunaga." In John Whitney Hall, Keiji Nagahara, and Kozo Yamamura, eds. *Japan Before Tokugawa: Political Consolidation and Economic Growth, 1500–1650*. Princeton, N. J.: Princeton University Press, 1981.

Fujino Tamotsu 藤野保. "Hansei kakuritsu-ki no shomondai – seihoku Kyūshū sho han (Hirado, Ōmura, Saga kaku han o chūshin to shite)" 藩制確立期の諸問題 - 西北九州諸藩 (平戸, 大村, 佐賀各藩を中心として). *Shakai keizai shigaku* 社会経済史学 24 (1958): 111–42.

Fujino Tamotsu 藤野保. *Daimyō: sono ryōgoku keiei* 大名：その領国経営. Tokyo: Jimbutsu ōraisha 人物往来社, 1964.

Fujino Tamotsu 藤野保. *Bakuhan taisei shi no kenkyū* 幕藩体制史の研究. Tokyo: Yoshikawa kōbunkan 吉川弘文館, 1961; rev. ed. 1975.

Fujino Tamotsu 藤野保. *Bakusei to hansei* 幕制と藩制. Tokyo: Yoshikawa kōbunkan 吉川弘文館, 1979.

Fukui-ken 福井県, ed. *Fukui-ken shi* 福井県史. 5 vols. Tokyo: Sanshūsha 三秀舎, 1920–2.

Fukuda Toyohiko 福田豊彦. "Muromachi bakufu no hōkōshū" 室町幕府の奉公衆. *Nihon rekishi* 日本歴史, no. 274 (March 1971): 46–65.

Fukuda Toyohiko 福田豊彦. "Muromachi bakufu no hōkōshū no kenkyū – sono jin'in kōsei to chiikiteki bumpu" 室町幕府の奉公衆の研究 - その人員構成と地域的分布. *Hokkaidō musashi joshi tanki daigaku kiyō* 北海道武蔵女子短期大学紀要, no. 3 (March 1971): 1–52.

Fukuyama-shi shi hensankai 福山市史編纂会, ed. *Fukuyama-shi shi* 福山市史. 3 vols. Fukuyama-shi, 1963–7.

Furushima Toshio 古島敏雄. *Kinsei keizaishi no kiso katei – nengu shūdatsu to kyōdōtai* 近世経済史の基礎過程 - 年貢収奪と共同体. Tokyo: Iwanami shoten 岩波書店, 1978.

Furuta Ryōichi hakase kanreki kinen-kai 古田良一博士還暦記念会, ed. *Tōhoku shi no shin kenkyū* 東北史の新研究. Sendai: Bunri tosho shuppansha 文理図書出版社, 1955.

Gay, Suzanne. "Muromachi Bakufu Rule in Kyoto: Administration and Judicial Aspects." In Jeffrey P. Mass and William B. Hauser, eds. *The Bakufu in Japanese History*. Stanford, Calif.: Stanford University Press, 1985.

Goble, Andrew. "The Hōjō and Consultative Government." In Jeffrey P. Mass, ed. *Court and Bakufu in Japan: Essays in Kamakura History*. New Haven, Conn.: Yale University Press, 1982.

Gomi Katsuo 五味克夫. "Nitta-gū shitsuin Michinori gushoan sonota" 新田宮執印道教具書案その他. *Nihon rekishi* 日本歴史, no. 310 (March 1974): 13–26.

Gotō Norihiko 後藤紀彦. "Tanaka bon seifu – bunrui o kokoromita kuge shinsei no koshahon" 田中本政府 - 分類を試みた公家新制の古写本. *Nempō, chūseishi kenkyū*, 年報, 中世史研究, no. 5 (May 1980): 73–86.

Grossberg, Kenneth A. "Bakufu and Bugyonin: The Size of the House

Bureaucracy in Muromachi Japan." *Journal of Asian Studies* 35 (August 1976): 651–4.

Grossberg, Kenneth A. *Japan's Renaissance: The Politics of the Muromachi Bakufu*. Cambridge, Mass.: Harvard University Press, 1981.

Grossberg, Kenneth A. ed., and Kanamoto, Nobuhisa, trans. *The Laws of the Muromachi Bakufu: Kemmu Shikimoku (1336) and the Muromachi Tsuikahō*. Tokyo: *Monumenta Nipponica* and Sophia University, 1981.

Gunsho ruijū 群書類従, vol. 4. Tokyo: Keizai zasshisha 経済雑誌社, 1898.

Gyobutsubon, Mōko shūrai ekotoba (fukusei) 御物本・蒙古襲来絵詞 (複製). Fukuoka: Fukuokashi kyōiku iinkai 福岡市教育委員会, 1975.

Haga Norihiko 羽下徳彦. "Muromachi bakufu samurai dokoro kō" 室町幕府侍所考. In Ogawa Makoto 小川信, ed. *Muromachi seiken* 室町政権. Vol. 5 of *Ronshū Nihon rekishi* 論集日本歴史. Tokyo: Yūshōdō 雄松堂, 1975.

Hall, John Whitney. *Tanuma Okitsugu: Forerunner of Modern Japan*. Cambridge, Mass.: Harvard University Press, 1955.

Hall, John Whitney. "The Nature of Traditional Society: Japan." In Robert E. Ward and Dankwort A. Rustow, eds. *Political Modernization in Japan and Turkey*. Princeton, N. J.: Princeton University Press, 1964.

Hall, John Whitney. *Government and Local Power in Japan, 500–1700: A Study Based on Bizen Province*. Princeton, N. J.: Princeton University Press, 1966.

Hall, John Whitney. "The Ikeda House and Its Retainers in Bizen." In John W. Hall and Marius B. Jansen, eds. *Studies in the Institutional History of Early Modern Japan*. Princeton, N. J.: Princeton University Press, 1968.

Hall, John Whitney. "Kyoto As Historical Background." In John W. Hall and Jeffrey P. Mass, eds. *Medieval Japan: Essays in Institutional History*. New Haven, Conn.: Yale University Press, 1974.

Hall, John Whitney, and Toyoda Takashi, eds. *Japan in the Muromachi Age*. Berkeley and Los Angeles: University of California Press, 1977.

Hanley, Susan B., and Kozo Yamamura, *Economic and Demographic Change in Preindustrial Japan, 1600–1868*. Princeton, N. J.: Princeton University Press, 1977.

Hanseishi kenkyūkai 藩政史研究会, ed. *Hansei seiritsushi no sōgō kenkyū – Yonezawa han* 藩制成立史の総合研究 – 米沢藩. Tokyo: Yoshikawa kōbunkan 吉川弘文館, 1963.

Harafuji Hiroshi 服藤弘司. "Kaga han kahō no seikaku" 加賀藩家法の性格. *Kanazawa daigaku hō-bungakubu ronshū* 金沢大学法文学部論集 (*Hōkei hen* 法経編 5), 1958. Reprinted in Harafuji Hiroshi 服藤弘司. *Bakufu to hampō* 幕府と藩法. Tokyo: Sōbunsha 創文社, 1980.

Harrington, Lorraine F. "Social Control and the Significance of Akutō." In Jeffrey P. Mass, ed. *Court and Bakufu in Japan: Essays in Kamakura History*. New Haven, Conn.: Yale University Press, 1982.

Harrington, Lorraine F. "Regional Outposts of Muromachi Bakufu Rule: The Kantō and Kyūshū." In Jeffrey P. Mass and William B. Hauser, eds. *The Bakufu in Japanese History*. Stanford, Calif.: Stanford University Press,

1985.

Hashimoto Yoshihiko 橋本義彦. *Heian kizoku shakai no kenkyū* 平安貴族社会の研究. Tokyo: Yoshikawa kōbunkan 吉川弘文館, 1976.

Hatada Takashi 旗田巍. *Genkō – Mōko teikoku no naibu jijō* 元寇 – 蒙古帝国の内部事情. Tokyo: Chūō kōronsha 中央公論社, 1965.

Hauser, William B. "Osaka Castle and Tokugawa Authority in Western Japan." In Jeffrey P. Mass and William B. Hauser, eds. *The Bakufu in Japanese History*. Stanford, Calif.: Stanford University Press, 1985.

Hayashi Tōichi 林董一. *Owari han kōhōshi no kenkyū* 尾張藩公法史の研究. Tokyo: Nihon gakujutsu shinkōkai 日本学術振興会, 1962.

Heiji monogatari emaki, Mōko shūrai ekotoba 平氏物語絵巻, 蒙古襲来絵詞. Vol. 9 of *Nihon emakimono zenshū* 日本絵巻物全集. Tokyo: Kadokawa shoten 角川書店, 1964.

Hidemura Senzō 秀村選三, *Kuwabata Kō* 桑波田興, and Fujii Jōji 藤井譲治. "Hansei no seiritsu" 藩制の成立. In *Iwanami kōza Nihon rekishi* 岩波講座日本歴史. Vol. 10. Tokyo: Iwanami shoten 岩波書店, 1975.

Hiraizumi Kiyoshi 平泉澄. "Nihon chūkō" 日本中興. In Kemmu chūkō roppyakunen kinenkai 建武中興六百年記念会, comp. *Kemmu chūkō* 建武中興. Tokyo: Kemmu chūkō roppyakunen kinenkai 建武中興六百年記念会, 1934.

Hirao Michio 平尾道雄. *Tosa han* 土佐藩. Tokyo: Yoshikawa kōbunkan 吉川弘文館, 1965.

Hori, Kyotsu. "The Economic and Political Effects of the Mongol Wars." In John Whitney Hall and Jeffrey P. Mass, eds. *Medieval Japan: Essays in Institutional History*. New Haven, Conn.: Yale University Press, 1974.

Hōseishi gakkai 法制史学会, ed. *Tokugawa kinreikō* 徳川禁令考, 11 vols. Tokyo: Sōbunsha 創文社, 1959–61.

"Ichiki monjo" 一木文書. In *Ichikawa shishi, kodai-chūsei shiryō* 市川市史, 古代・中世史の研究. Ichikawa: Ichikawa shi 市川市, 1973.

Iida Hisao 飯田久夫. "heishi to Kyūshū" 平氏と九州. In Takeuchi Rizō hakase kanreki kinenkai 竹内理三博士還暦記念会, comp. *Shōensei to buke shakai* 荘園制と武家社会. Tokyo: Yoshikawa kōbunkan 吉川弘文館, 1969.

Iikura Harutake 飯倉晴武. "Ōnin no ran ikō ni okeru Muromachi bakufu no seisaku" 応仁の乱以降における室町幕府の政策. *Nihonshi kenkyū* 日本史研究, no. 139–40 (March 1974): 140–55.

Ikeuchi Hiroshi 池内宏. *Genkō no shinkenkyū* 元寇の新研究. 2 vols. Tokyo: Tōyō bunko 東洋文庫, 1931.

Ikeda Kōen 池田晃淵. *Tokugawa jidai shi* 徳川時代史. Tokyo: Waseda daigaku shuppan-bu 早稲田大学出版部, 1909.

Imaizumi Shōzō 今泉省三. *Nagaoka no rekishi* 長岡の歴史. 6 vols. Sanjō: Nojima shuppan 野島出版, 1968–72.

Imatani Akira 今谷明. *Sengokuki no Muromachi bakufu no seikaku* 戦国期の室町幕府の性格, vol. 12. Tokyo: Kadokawa shoten 角川書店, 1975.

Imatani Akira 今谷明. "Kōki Muromachi bakufu no kenryoku kōzo – tokuni sono senseika ni tsuite" 後期室町幕府の権力構造 – 特にその専制化について.

In Nihonshi kenkyūkai shiryō kenkyū bukai 日本史研究会史料研究部会, ed. *Chūsei Nihon no rekishi zō* 中世日本の歴史像. Tokyo: Sōgensha 創元社, 1978.

Ishii Masatoshi 石井正敏. "Bun'ei hachinen rainichi no Kōraishi ni tsuite – Sanbetsushō no Nihon tsūkō shiryō no shōkai" 文永八年来日の高麗使について – 三別抄の日本通交史料の紹介. *Tōkyō daigaku shiryō hensanjo hō* 東京大学史料編纂所報, no. 12 (March 1978): 1–7.

Ishii Ryosuke 石井良助. *Taika no kaishin to Kamakura bakufu no seiritsu* 大化の改新と鎌倉幕府の成立. Tokyo: Sōbunsha 創文社, 1958.

Ishii Susumu 石井進. "Takezaki Suenaga ekotoba no seiritsu" 竹崎季長絵詞の成立. *Nihon rekishi* 日本歴史, no. 273 (1971): 12–32.

Ishii Susumu 石井進 et al., eds. *Chūsei seiji shakai shisō zō* 中世政治社会思想像. Vol. 21 of *Nihon shisō taikei* 日本思想大系. Tokyo: Iwanami shoten 岩波書店, 1972.

Ishii Susumu 石井進. "Shimotsuki sōdō oboegaki" 霜月騒動おぼえ書き. In *Kanagawa-ken shi dayori, shiryō hen* 神奈川縣史だより, 資料編, vol. 2. Yokohama: Kanagawa ken 神奈川県, 1973.

Ishimoda Shō 石母田正. "Heishi seiken no sōkan shiki setchi" 平氏政権の総官職設置. *Rekishi hyōron* 歴史評論, no. 107 (July 1959): 7–14.

Ishimoda Shō 石母田正. "Kamakura bakufu ikkoku jitō shiki no seiritsu" 鎌倉幕府一国地頭職の成立. In Satō Shin'ichi 佐藤進一, and Ishimoda Shō 石母田正, eds. *Chūsei no hō to kokka* 中世の法と国家. Tokyo: Tōkyō daigaku shuppankai 東京大学出版会, 1960.

Itō Kiyoshi 伊藤喜良. "Muromachi ki no kokka to Tōgoku" 室町期の国家と東国. *Rekishigaku kenkyū* 歴史学研究, special issue (October 1979): 63–72.

Itō Tasaburō 伊東多三郎. "Bakuhan taisei ron" 幕藩体制論. In *Shin Nihonshi kōza* 新日本史講座. Tokyo: Chūō kōronsha 中央公論社, 1947.

Jansen, Marius B. *China in the Tokugawa World*. Cambridge, Mass.: Harvard University Press, 1992.

Kanai Madoka 金井圓. *Hansei* 藩政. Tokyo: Shibundō 至文堂, 1962.

Kanai Madoka 金井圓, ed. *Dokai Kōshūki* 土芥寇讎記. Tokyo: Jimbutsu ōraisha 人物往来社, 1976.

Kanzaki Akitsoshi 神崎彰利. *Kenchi* 検地. Tokyo: Kyōikusha 教育社, 1983.

Karatsu-shi shi hensan iinkai 唐津市史編纂委員会, ed. *Karatsu-shi* 唐津市. Karatsu, Fukuoka, 1962.

Kasai Sachiko 笠井幸子. Ōshū heiran to tōgoku bushidan" 奥州兵乱と東国武士団 *Rekishi kyōiku* 歴史教育 16 (1968): 27–40.

Kasamatsu Hiroshi 笠松宏至. *Nihon chūsei-hō shiron* 日本中世法史論. Tokyo: Tōkyō daigaku shuppankai 東京大学出版会, 1977.

Kasamatsu Hiroshi 笠松宏至, Satō Shin'ichi 佐藤慎一, and Momose Kesao 百瀬今朝男, eds. *Chūsei seiji shakai shisō* 中世政治社会思想. Vol. 22 of *Nihon shisō taikei* 日本思想大系. Tokyo: Iwanami shoten 岩波書店, 1981.

Katsumata Shizuo, with Collcutt, Martin. "The Development of Sengoku Law." In John Whitney Hall, Keiji Nagahara, and Kozo Yamamura, eds. *Japan Before Tokugawa: Political Consolidation and Economic Growth, 1500–*

1650. Princeton, N. J.: Princeton University Press, 1981.

Kawai Masaharu 河合正治. *Ashikaga Yoshimasa* 足利義政. Tokyo: Shimizu shoin 清水書院, 1972.

Kawazoe Hiroshi 川副博. "Einin san'nen ki kōshō" 永仁三年記考証. *Shichō* 史潮 50 (January 1953): 33–52.

Kawazoe Shōji 川添昭二. "Chinzei kanrei kō" 鎮西管領考. *Nihon rekishi* 日本歴史, nos. 205 and 206 (June and July 1965): 2–14 and 29–53.

Kawazoe Shōji 川添昭二. *Chūkai, Genkō bōrui hennen shiryō - ikoku keigo banyaku shiryō no kenkyū* 注解元寇防塁編年史料 - 異国警護番役史料の研究. Fukuoka: Fukuokashi kyōiku iinkai 福岡市教育委員会, 1971.

Kawazoe Shōji 川添昭二. *Gen no shūrai* 元の襲来. Tokyo: Popurasha ポプラ社, 1975.

Kawazoe Shōji 川添昭二. *Mōko shūrai kenkyū shiron* 蒙古襲来研究史論. Tokyo: Yūzankaku 雄山閣, 1977.

Kimura Motoi 木村礎 and Sugimoto Toshio 杉本敏夫, eds. *Fudai hansei no tenkai to Meiji ishin* 譜代藩政の展開と明治維新. Tokyo: Bungadō ginkō kenkyūsha 文雅堂銀行研究社, 1963.

Kishida Hiroshi 岸田裕之. "Shugo Akamatsu-shi no Harima no kuni shihai no hatten to kokuga" 守護赤松氏の播磨国支配の発展と国衙. *Shigaku kenkyū* 史学研究, nos. 104 and 105 (1968).

Kishida Tsutomu 岸田勉. Kyūshū no bunjinga" 九州の文人画. In Mikami Tsugio 三上次男, ed. *Kyūshū no kaiga to tōgei* 九州の絵画と陶芸. Tokyo: Heibonsha 平凡社, 1975.

Kitajima Masamoto 北島正元. "'Meikun' no higeki" 「名君」の悲劇. In Itō Tasaburō 伊東多三郎, ed. *Kokumin seikatsu shi kenkyū* 国民生活史研究. Vol. 1 of *Seikatsu to seiji* 生活と政治. Tokyo: Yoshikawa kōbunkan 吉川弘文館, 1957.

Kitajima Masamoto 北島正元. *Edo bakufu no kenryoku kōzō* 江戸幕府の権力構造. Tokyo: Iwanami shoten 岩波書店, 1964.

Kitajima Masamoto 北島正元, ed. *Oie sōdō* 御家騒動. Tokyo: Jimbutsu ōraisha 人物往来社, 1965.

Kitajima Masamoto 北島正元. *Edo bakufu* 江戸幕府. Vol. 16 of *Nihon no rekishi* 日本の歴史. Tokyo: Shōgakkan 小学館, 1975.

Kitajima Masamoto 北島正元, ed. *Bakuhansei kokka seiritsu katei no kenkyū* 幕藩制国家成立過程の研究. Tokyo: Yoshikawa kōbunkan 吉川弘文館, 1978.

Kobayashi Seiji 小林清治, and Ōishi Naomasa 大石直正, comps. *Chūsei Ōu no sekai* 中世奥羽の世界. Tokyo: Tōkyō daigaku shuppankai 東京大学出版会, 1978.

Kodama Kōta 児玉幸多 and Kitajima Masamoto 北島正元, eds. *Monogatari han shi* 物語藩史. 8 vols. Tokyo: Jimbutsu ōraisha 人物往来社, 1964–5.

Kodama Kōta 児玉幸多 and Kitajima Masamoto 北島正元, eds. *(Dai ni ki) Monogatari han shi* 第2期物語藩史. Tokyo: Jimbutsu ōraisha 人物往来社, 1966.

Kodama Kōta 児玉幸多. *Genroku jidai* 元禄時代. Vol. 16 of *Nihon no rekishi* 日

本の歴史. Tokyo: Chūō kōronsha 中央公論社, 1967.

Koizumi Yoshiaki 小泉宜右. *Akutō* 悪党. Tokyo: Kyōikusha 教育社, 1981.

Koji ruien 古事類苑, vol. 44. Tokyo: Yoshikawa kōbunkan 吉川弘文館, 1969.

Kokan Shiren 虎関師錬, "Genkō shakusho" 元亨釈書. In Kuroita Katsumi 黒板勝美, ed. *Shintei zōho kokushi taikei* 新訂増補国史大系, vol. 31. Tokyo: Yoshikawa kōbunkan 吉川弘文館, 1930.

Kokushi daijiten henshū iinkai 国史大辞典編集委員会, comp. *Kokushi daijiten* 国史大辞典. Tokyo: Yoshikawa kōbunkan 吉川弘文館, 1979–.

Kondō Moku 近藤杢 and Hiraoka Jun 平岡潤, eds. *Kuwana-shi shi* 桑名市史. 3 vols. Kuwana: Kuwana-shi kyōiku iinkai 桑名市教育委員会, 1959–65.

Kurita Mototsugu 栗田元次. *Sōgō Nihonshi gaisetsu, ge* 総合日本史概説・下. Tokyo: Chūbunkan 中文館, 1943.

Kuroita Katsumi 黒板勝美, ed. *Tokugawa jikki* 徳川実記. Vols. 38–47 of *Shintei zōho Kokushi taikei* 新訂増補国史大系. Tokyo: Yoshikawa kōbunkan 吉川弘文館, 1964–6.

Kuroya Naofusa 黒屋直房. *Nakatsu-han shi* 中津藩史. Tokyo: Hekiun-so 碧雲荘, 1940.

Kuwata Tadachika 桑田忠親. *Tokugawa Ieyasu, sono tegami to ningen* 徳川家康－その手紙と人間. Tokyo: Shin jimbutsu ōraisha 新人物往来社, 1971.

Kyōto daigaku bungakubu kokushi kenkyūshitsu 京都大学文学部国史研究室, ed. *Hirado Matsuura ke shiryō* 平戸松浦家資料. Kyoto, 1951.

Kuroda Toshio 黒田俊雄. "Mōko shūrai" 蒙古襲来. In *Nihon no rekishi* 日本の歴史, Vol. 8. Tokyo: Chūō kōronsha 中央公論社, 1965.

Kuwayama Kōnen 桑山浩然. "Muromachi bakufu no sōsōki ni okeru shoryō ni tsuite" 室町幕府の草創期における所領について. *Chūsei no mado* 中世の窓 12 (April 1963); 4–27.

Kuwayama Kōnen 桑山浩然. "Muromachi bakufu keizai kikō no ichi kōsatsu, nōsen kata kubō mikura no kinō to seiritsu" 室町幕府経済機構の一考察－納銭方・公方御倉の機能と成立. *Shigaku zasshi* 史学雑誌 73 (September 1964): 9–17.

Kuwayama Kōnen 桑山浩然. "Muromachi bakufu keizai no kōzō" 室町幕府経済の構造. In *Nihon keizaishi taikei* 日本経済史大系, vol. 2. Tokyo: Tōkyō daigaku shuppankai 東京大学出版会, 1965.

Kuwayama Kōnen 桑山浩然. *Muromachi bakufu hikitsuke shiryō shūsei* 室町幕府引付史料集成, vol. 1. Tokyo: Kondō shuppansha 近藤出版社, 1980.

Lu, David John, comp. *Sources of Japanese History*. 2 vols. New York: McGraw-Hill, 1974.

McCullough, Helen Craig. trans. *The Taiheiki: A Chronicle of Medieval Japan*. New York: Columbia University Press, 1959.

McCullough, Helen Craig. *Yoshitsune: A Fifteenth Century Japanese Chronicle*. Tokyo: University of Tokyo Press, 1966.

McCullough, William H. "Shōkyūki: An Account of the Shōkyū War of 1221." *Monumenta Nipponica* 19 (1964): 163–215.

McCullough, William H. "The *Azuma kagami* Account of the Shōkyū War."

Monumenta Nipponica 23 (1968): 102–55.

McEwan, J. R. *The Political Writings of Ogyū Sorai*. Cambridge, England: Cambridge University Press, 1962.

Mass, Jeffrey P. "The Emergence of the Kamakura Bakufu." In John Whitney Hall and Jeffrey P. Mass, eds. *Medieval Japan: Essays in Institutional History*. New Haven, Conn.: Yale University Press, 1974.

Mass, Jeffrey P. "Jitō Land Possession in the Thirteenth Century." In John Whitney Hall and Jeffrey P. Mass, eds. *Medieval Japan: Essays in Institutional History*. New Haven, Conn.: Yale University Press, 1974.

Mass, Jeffrey P. *Warrior Government in Early Medieval Japan*. New Haven, Conn.: Yale University Press, 1974.

Mass, Jeffrey P. *The Kamakura Bakufu: A Study in Documents*. Stanford, Calif.: Stanford University Press, 1976.

Mass, Jeffrey P. "The Origins of Kamakura Justice." *Journal of Japanese Studies* 3 (Summer 1977): 299–322.

Mass, Jeffrey P. *The Development of Kamakura Rule, 1180–1250: A History with Documents*. Stanford, Calif.: Stanford University Press, 1979.

Mass, Jeffrey P. "Translation and pre-1600 History." *Journal of Japanese Studies* 6 (Winter 1980): 61–88.

Mass, Jeffrey P, ed. *Court and Bakufu in Japan: Essays in Kamakura History*. New Haven, Conn.: Yale University Press, 1982.

Mass, Jeffrey P. "The Early Bakufu and Feudalism." In Jeffrey P. Mass, ed. *Court and Bakufu in Japan: Essays in Kamakura History*. New Haven, Conn.: Yale University Press, 1982.

Mass, Jeffrey P. "Patterns of Provincial Inheritance in Late Heian Japan." *Journal of Japanese Studies* 9 (Winter 1983): 67–95.

Mass, Jeffrey P. "What Can We Not Know About the Kamakura Bakufu." In Jeffrey P. Mass and William B. Hauser, eds. *The Bakufu in Japanese History*. Stanford, Calif.: Stanford University Press, 1985.

Mass, Jeffrey P. *Lordship and Inheritance in Early Medieval Japan: A study of the Kamakura Sōryō System*. Forthcoming.

Mass, Jeffrey P, and Hauser, William B., eds. *The Bakufu in Japanese History*. Stanford, Calif.: Stanford University Press, 1985.

Matsuyoshi Sadao 松好貞夫. *Kanemochi daimyō bimbō daimyō* 金持大名貧乏大名. Tokyo: Jimbutsu ōraisha 人物往来社, 1964.

Minegishi Kentarō 峯岸賢太郎. "Seiritsu-ki han keizai no kōzo" 成立期藩経済の構造. In Furushima Toshio 古島敏雄, ed. *Nihon keizaishi taikei* 日本経済史大系. Vol. 3. Tokyo: Tōkyō daigaku shuppankai 東京大学出版会, 1965.

Mitobe Masao 水戸部正男. *Kuge shinsei no kenkyū* 公家新制の研究. Tokyo: Sōbunsha 創文社, 1961.

Miura Hiroyuki 三浦周行. *Hōseishi no kenkyū* 法制史の研究. Tokyo: Iwanami shoten 岩波書店, 1919.

Miura Hiroyuki 三浦周行. *Nihonshi no kenkyū* 日本史の研究, vols. 1 and 2. Tokyo: Iwanami shoten 岩波書店, 1930, reprinted in 1981.

Miura Toshiaki 三浦俊明. "Hamamatsu-han ryōiki no keisei to shukueki josei-kin" 浜松藩領域の形成と宿駅助成金. *Chihōshi kenkyū* 地方史研究 79 (1966): 1–29.

Miyagawa Mitsuru 宮川満, with Kiley, Cornelius J. "From Shōen to Chigyō: Proprietary Lordship and the Structure of Local Power." In John Whitney Hall and Toyoda Takeshi, eds. *Japan in the Muromachi Age*. Berkeley and Los Angeles: University of California Press, 1977.

Miyazaki Michio 宮崎道生, ed. *Teihon "Oritaku shiba no ki" shakugi*. 定本折たく柴の記釈義. Tokyo: Shibundō 至文堂, 1964.

Miyazaki Michio 宮崎道生. *Aomori-ken no rekishi* 青森県の歴史. Tokyo: Yamakawa shuppansha 山川出版社, 1970.

Mōko shūrai ekotoba 蒙古襲来絵詞. Vol. 14 of *Nihon emaki taisei* 日本絵巻大成. Tokyo: Chūō kōronsha 中央公論社, 1978.

Mori Katsumi hakase koki kinen kai 森克己博士古希記念会, ed. *Taigai kankei to seiji bunka* 対外関係と政治文化. Vol. 2 of *Shigaku ronshū* 史学論集. Tokyo: Yoshikawa kōbunkan 吉川弘文館, 1974.

Morisue Yumiko 森末由美子. "Muromachi bakufu goryōsho ni kansuru ichi kōsatsu" 室町幕府御料所に関する一考察. In Ogawa Makoto 小川信, ed. *Muromachi seiken* 室町政権. Vol. 5 of *Ronshū Nihon rekishi* 論集日本歴史. Tokyo: Yūshōdō 雄松堂, 1975.

Morris, Ivan. *The Nobility of Failure*. New York: Holt, Rinehart and Winston, 1975.

Murai Masuo 村井益男. *Edo-jō* 江戸城. Tokyo: Chūō kōronsha 中央公論社, 1964.

Murai Shōsuke 村井章介. "Mōko shūrai to Chinzei tandai no seiritsu" 蒙古襲来と鎮西探題の成立. *Shigaku zasshi* 87 (April 1978): 1–43.

Nagahara Keiji 永原慶二. "Zen-kindai no tennō" 前近代の天皇 *Rekishigaku kenkyū* 歴史学研究, no. 467 (April 1979): 37–45.

Nagahara Keiji 永原慶二, and Kishi Shōzō 貴志正造, eds. *Azuma kagami* 吾妻鏡. 6 vols. Tokyo: Jimbutsu ōraisha 人物往来社, 1976–77.

Nagahara, Keiji, with Kozo Yamamura. 'Village Communities and Daimyo Power." In John W. Hall and Takeshi Toyoda, eds. *Japan in the Muromachi Age*. Berkeley and Los Angeles: University of California Press, 1977.

Nagahara, Keiji, with Kozo Yamamura. "The Sengoku Daimyo and the Kandaka System." In John W. Hall, Keiji Nagahara, and Kozo Yamamura, eds. *Japan Before Tokugawa: Political Consolidation and Economic Growth, 1500–1650*. Princeton, N. J.: Princeton University Press, 1981.

Nagaoka shiyakusho 長岡市役所, ed. *Nagaoka-shi shi* 長岡市史. Nagaoka: Nagaoka shiyakusho 長岡市役所, 1931.

Nakamura Kichiji 中村吉治. *Nihon hōkensei saihenseishi* 日本封建制再編成史. Tokyo: Mikasa shobō 三笠書房, 1940.

Nakamura Naokatsu 中村直勝. *Nihon shin bunka shi, Yoshino jidai* 日本新文化史吉野時代. Tokyo: Nihon dentsū shuppanbu 日本電通出版部, 1942.

Nakamura Naokatsu 中村直勝, ed. *Hikone-shi shi* 彦根市史. 3 vols. Hikone-shi:

Hikone shiyakusho 彦根市役所, 1960–4.

Nakamura Naokatsu 中村直勝. *Nanchō no kenkyū* 南朝の研究. Vol. 3 of *Nakamura Naokatsu chosaku shū* 中村直勝著作集. Kyoto: Tankōsha 淡交社, 1978.

Nakamura Naokatsu 中村直勝. *Shōen no kenkyū* 荘園の研究. Kyoto: Tankōsha 淡交社, 1978.

Naramoto Tatsuya 奈良本辰也, ed. *Hagakure* 葉隠. Vol. 17 of *Nihon no meicho* 日本の名著. Tokyo: Chūō kōronsha 中央公論社, 1969.

Naramoto Tatsuya 奈良本辰也, Hosokawa Morisada 細川護貞, and Murakami Genzō 村上元三, eds. *Edo daimyō hyakke* 江戸大名百家. Vol. 22 of *Taiyō bekkan* 太陽別巻. Tokyo: Heibonsha 平凡社, 1978.

Nitta Hideharu 新田英治. "Kamakura kōki no seiji katei" 鎌倉後期の政治過程. In *Iwanami kōza Nihon rekishi* 岩波講座日本歴史, vol. 6. Tokyo: Iwanami shoten 岩波書店, 1975.

Norman, E. H. "Japan's Emergence As a Modern State." In John W. Dower, ed. *Origins of the Modern Japanese State: Selected Writings of E. H. Norman*. New York: Random House, 1975.

Ōae Ryō 大饗亮. "Jitō shiki o meguru shomondai" 地頭職をめぐる諸問題. *Hōkei gakkai zasshi* 法経学会雑誌 13 (1964): 26–32.

Ōgaki shiyakusho 大垣市役所, ed. *Ōgaki-shi shi* 大垣市史. 3 vols. Ōgaki, 1930.

Ogawa Makoto 小川信. *Ashikaga ichimon shugo hatten shi no kenkyū* 足利一門守護発展史の研究. Tokyo: Yoshikawa kōbunkan 吉川弘文館, 1980.

Okuno Takahiro 奥野高廣 Kōshitsu gokeizai shi no kenkyū 皇室御経済史の研究. Tokyo: Unebi shobō 畝傍書房, 1942.

Okutomi Takayuki 奥富敬之. *Kamakura Hōjōshi no kisoteki kenkyū* 鎌倉北条氏の基礎的研究. Tokyo: Yoshikawa kōbunkan 吉川弘文館, 1980.

Ōtsuka shigakkai 大塚史学会, ed. (*Shimpan*) *Kyōdoshi jiten* (新版) 郷土史辞典. Tokyo: Asakura shoten 朝倉書店, 1969.

Reischauer, Edwin O. "Japanese Feudalism." In Rushton Coulborn, ed. *Feudalism in History*. Princton, N. J.: Princeton University Press, 1956.

Ryō Susumu 龍肅. *Kamakura jidai, ge: Kyoto – kizoku seiji dōkō to kōbu no kōshō* 鎌倉時代, 下：京都－貴族政治の動向と公武の交渉. Tokyo: Shunjūsha 春秋社, 1957.

Sansom, George B. *A History of Japan to 1334*. Stanford, Calif.: Stanford University Press, 1958.

Sasagawa Taneo 笹川種男, comp. *Shiryō taisei* 史料大成. Tokyo: Naigai shoseki 内外書籍, 1937.

Sasaki Junnosuke 佐々木潤之介. *Daimyō to hyakushō* 大名と百姓. Vol. 15 of *Nihon no rekishi* 日本の歴史. Tokyo: Chūō kōronsha 中央公論社, 1966.

Sasaki Junnosuke 佐々木潤之介. "Bakuhansei kokka ron" 幕藩制国家論. In Hara Hidesaburō 原秀三郎 et al., comps. *Kinsei* 近世. Vol. 3 of *Taikei Nihon kokka shi* 大系日本国家史. Tokyo: Tōkyō daigaku shuppankai 東京大学出版会, 1975.

Sasaki, Junnosuke, with Ronald P. Toby. "The Changing Rationale of Daimyo

Control in the Emergence of the Bakuhan State." In John W. Hall, Keiji Nagahara, and Kozo Yamamura, eds. *Japan Before Tokugawa: Political Consolidation and Economic Growth, 1500–1650*. Princeton, N. J.: Princeton University Press, 1981.

Satō Shin'ichi 佐藤進一. *Kamakura bakufu soshō seido no kenkyū* 鎌倉幕府訴訟制度の研究. Tokyo: Meguro shoten 目黒書店, 1946.

Satō Shin'ichi 佐藤進一. "Bakufu ron" 幕府論. In *Shin Nihon shi kōza* 新日本史講座. Tokyo: Chūō kōronsha 中央公論社, 1949.

Satō Shin'ichi 佐藤進一. "Kamakura bakufu seiji no senseika ni tsuite" 鎌倉幕府政治の専制化について. In Takeuchi Rizō 竹内理三, ed. *Nihon hōkensei seiritsu no kenkyū* 日本封建制成立の研究. Tokyo: Yoshikawa kōbunkan 吉川弘文館, 1955.

Satō Shin'ichi 佐藤進一. "Muromachi bakufu kaisōki no kansei taikei" 室町幕府開創期の官制体系. In Satō Shin'ichi 佐藤進一, and Ishimoda Shō 石母田正, eds. *Chūsei no hō to kokka* 中世の法と国家. Tokyo: Tōkyō daigaku shuppankai 東京大学出版会, 1960.

Satō Shin'ichi 佐藤進一. "Muromachi bakufu ron" 室町幕府論. In *Iwanami kōza Nihon rekishi* 岩波講座日本歴史, vol. 7. Tokyo: Iwanami shoten 岩波書店, 1963.

Satō Shin'ichi 佐藤進一. *Zōho Kamakura bakufu shugo seido no kenkyū* 増補鎌倉幕府守護制度の研究. Tokyo: Tōkyō daigaku shuppankai 東京大学出版会, 1971.

Satow, Sir Ernest. *A Diplomat in Japan*. Oxford, England: Oxford University Press, 1968.

Seno Seiichirō 瀬野清一郎. *Kamakura bakufu saikyojō shū* 鎌倉幕府裁許状集. 2 vols. Tokyo: Yoshikawa kōbunkan 吉川弘文館, 1970.

Seno Seiichirō 瀬野清一郎. *Chinzei gokenin no kenkyū* 鎮西御家人の研究. Tokyo: Yoshikawa kōbunkan 吉川弘文館, 1975.

Shibata Akimasa 柴田顯正, ed. *Tokugawa Ieyasu to sono shūi* 徳川家康と其周圍. 3 vols. Okazaki-shi: Okazaki shiyakusho 岡崎市役所, 1926.

Shihōshō 司法省. *Tokugawa kinrei kō* 徳川禁令考. 6 vols. Tokyo: Yoshikawa kōbunkan 吉川弘文館, 1931–2.

Shimada Jirō 島田次郎. "Hanzei seido no seiritsu" 半済制度の成立. In Ogawa Makoto 小川信, ed. *Muromachi seiken* 室町政権. Vol. 5 of *Ronshū Nihon rekishi* 論集日本歴史. Tokyo: Yūshōdō 雄松堂, 1975.

Shindō Mitsuyuki 新藤光行. "Hansei kaikaku no kenkyū – jōkamachi shōgyō no kiki o tsūjite mita Nakatsu han hōken kōzō no hōkai katei" 藩政改革の研究 – 城下町商業の危機を通じて見た中津藩封建構造の崩壊過程. *Keizaigaku kenkyū* 経済学研究 21:2 (1955).

Shinoda, Minoru. *The Founding of the Kamakura Shogunate*. New York: Columbia University Press, 1960.

Smith, Thomas C. *The Agrarian Origins of Modern Japan*. Stanford, Calif.: Stanford University Press, 1959.

Smith, Thomas C. "The Japanese Village in the Seventeenth Century." In

John W. Hall and Marius B. Jansen, eds. *Studies in the Institutional History of Early Modern Japan*. Princeton, N. J.: Princeton University Press, 1968.

Steenstrup, Henrik Carl Trolle. "Hōjō Shigetoki (1198–1261) and His Role in the History of Political and Ethical Ideas in Japan." Ph.D. Diss., Harvard University, 1977.

Sugiyama Hiroshi 杉山博. "Muromachi bakufu" 室町幕府. In *Nihon rekishi kōza* 日本歴史講座. Tokyo: Tōkyō daigaku shuppankai 東京大学出版会, 1957.

Sugiyama Hiroshi 杉山博. "Shugo ryōgokusei no tenkai" 守護領国制の展開. In *Iwanami kōza Nihon rekishi* 岩波講座日本歴史, vol. 7. Tokyo: Iwanami shoten 岩波書店, 1963.

Sugiyama Hiroshi 杉山博. *Dokushi sōran* 読史総覧. Tokyo: Jimbutsu ōraisha 人物往来社, 1966.

Susser, Bernard. "The Toyotomi Regime and the Daimyo." In Jeffrey P. Mass and William B. Hauser, eds. *The Bakufu in Japanese History*. Stanford, Calif.: Stanford University Press, 1985.

Taga Munehaya 多賀宗隼. *Kamakura jidai no shisō to bunka* 鎌倉時代の思想と文化. Tokyo: Meguro shoten 目黒書店, 1946.

Takagi Shōsaku 高木昭作. "Edo bakufu no seiritsu" 江戸幕府の成立. In *Iwanami kōza Nihon rekishi* 岩波講座日本歴史. Vol. 9. Tokyo: Iwanami shoten 岩波書店, 1975.

Takahashi Tomio 高橋富雄. *Miyagi-ken no rekishi* 宮城県の歴史. Tokyo: Yamakawa shuppansha 山川出版社, 1969.

Takeuchi Rizō 竹内理三, comp. *Heian ibun* 平安遺文. 15 vols. Tokyo: Tōkyōdō 東京堂, 1947–80.

Takeuchi Rizō 竹内理三, comp. *Zoku shiryō taisei* 続史料大成. 22 vols. Kyoto: Rinsen shoten 臨川書店, 1967.

Takeuchi Rizō 竹内理三, ed. *Kamakura ibun* 鎌倉遺文. 36 vols. Tokyo: Tōkyōdō 東京堂, 1971–88.

Takeuchi Rizō hakase koki kinenkai 竹内理三博士古希記念会, comp. *Zoku shōensei to buke shakai* 続荘園制と武家社会. Tokyo: Yoshikawa kōbunkan 吉川弘文館, 1978.

Tanaka Minoru 田中稔. "Jōkyū kyōgata bushi no ichi kōsatsu – rango no shin jitō buninchi o chūshin to shite" 承久京方武士の一考察 – 乱後の新地頭補人地を中心として. *Shigaku zasshi* 史学雑誌 65 (1956): 21–48.

Tanaka Minoru 田中稔. "Kamakura-dono otsukai kō" 鎌倉殿御使考. *Shirin* 史林 45 (November 1962): 1–23.

Tanaka Minoru 田中稔. "Kamakura shoki no seiji katei – kenkyū nenkan o chūshin ni shite" 鎌倉初期の政治過程 – 建久年間を中心にして. *Rekishi kyōiku* 歴史教育 11 (1963): 19–26.

Tanaka Minoru 田中稔. "Jōkyū no rango no shin jitō buninchi" 承久の乱後の新地頭補任地. *Shigaku zasshi* 史学雑誌. 79 (1970): 38–53.

Tanaka Takeo 田中健夫. *Chūsei kaigai kōshōshi no kenkyū* 中世海外交渉史の研究. Tokyo: Tōkyō daigaku shuppankai 東京大学出版会, 1959.

Tanaka, Takeo, with Sakai, Robert. "Japan's Relations with Overseas Countries." In John Whitney Hall and Toyoda Takeshi, eds. *Japan in the Muromachi Age*. Berkeley and Los Angeles: University of California Press, 1977.

Tanaka Yoshinari 田中義成. *Nambokuchō jidaishi* 南北朝時代史. Tokyo: Meiji shoin 明治書院, 1922.

Taniguchi Sumio 谷口澄夫, *Okayama han* 岡山藩, Tokyo: Yoshikawa kōbunkan 吉川弘文館, 1964.

Taniguchi Sumio 谷口澄夫. *Okayama hanseishi no kenkyū* 岡山藩政史の研究. Tokyo: Hanawa shobō 塙書房, 1964.

Toki Zenmaro 土岐善麿. *Shinshū Kyōgoku Tamekane* 新修京極為兼. Tokyo: Kadokawa shoten 角川書店, 1968.

Tōkyō daigaku shiryō hensanjo 東京大学史料編纂所, ed. *Shiryō sōran* 史料総覧, vol. 5. Tokyo: Tōkyō daigaku shuppankai 東京大学出版会, 1965.

Tōkyō daigaku shiryō hensanjo 東京大学史料編纂所, ed. *Tokushi biyō* 讀史備要. Tokyo: Naigai shoseki 1933; Kōdansha 講談社, 1966.

Totman, Conrad. *Politics in the Tokugawa Bakufu, 1600–1843*. Cambridge, Mass.: Harvard University Press, 1967.

Toyoda Takeshi 豊田武. "Genkō tōbatsu no shoseiryoku ni tsuite" 元寇討伐の諸勢力について. In Ogawa Makoto 小川信, ed. *Muromachi seiken* 室町政権. Vol. 5. of *Ronshū Nihon rekishi* 論集日本歴史. Tokyo: Yūshōdō 雄松堂, 1975.

Tsuda Hideo 津田秀夫. "Kansei kaikaku" 寛政改革. In *Iwanami kōza Nihon rekishi* 岩波講座日本歴史. Vol. 12. Tokyo: Iwanami shoten 岩波書店, 1963.

Tsuji Tatsuya 辻達也. *Tokugawa Yoshimune* 徳川吉宗. Tokyo: Yoshikawa kōbunkan 吉川弘文館, 1985.

Tsuji Tatsuya 辻達也. *Edo kaifu* 江戸開府. Vol. 4 of *Nihon no rekishi* 日本の歴史. Tokyo: Chūō kōronsha 中央公論社, 1966.

Tsukahira, Toshio Geroge. *Feudal Control in Tokugawa Japan: The Sankin Kōtai System*. Harvard East Asian Monographs, no. 20. Cambridge, Mass.: Harvard University Press, 1966.

Tsukushi Yutaka 筑紫豊. *Genkō kigen* 元寇起源. Fukuoka: Fukuoka kyōdo bunkakai 福岡郷土文化会, 1972.

Tsunoda, Ryusaku, William Theodore de Bary, and Donald Keene, comps. *Sources of the Japanese Tradition*. New York: Columbia University Press, 1958.

Tsuruoka shiyakusho 鶴岡市役所, ed. *Tsuruoka-shi shi* 鶴岡市史. Tsuruoka: Tsuruoka-shi 鶴岡市, 1962.

Uwayokote Masataka 上横手雅敬. "Renshosei no seiritsu" 連書制の成立. In *Kokushi ronshū* 国史論集, vol. 2. Kyoto: Dokushikai 読史会, 1959.

Uwayokote Masataka 上横手雅敬. "Kamakura seiken seiritsuki o meguru kingyō" 鎌倉政権成立期をめぐる近業. *Hōseishi kenkyū* 法政史研究 11 (1969): 175–81.

Varley, H. Paul. *Imperial Restoration in Medieval Japan*. New York: Columbia University Press, 1971.

Varley, H. Paul, trans. *Jinnō Shōtōki: A Chronicle of Gods and Sovereigns*. New

York: Columbia University Press, 1980.

Varley, H. Paul. "The Hōjō Family and Succession to Power." In Jeffrey P. Mass, ed. *Court and Bakufu in Japan: Essays in Kamakura History*. New Haven, Conn.: Yale University Press, 1982.

Weber, Max. *The Theory of Social and Economic Organization*. New York: Free Press, 1964.

Wintersteen, Prescott B. "The Early Muromachi Bakufu in Kyoto." In John Whitney Hall and Jeffrey P. Mass, eds. *Medieval Japan: Essays in Institutional History*. New Haven, Conn.: Yale University Press, 1974.

Wintersteen, Prescott B. "The Muromachi Shugo and Hanzei." In John Whitney Hall and Jeffrey P. Mass, eds. *Medieval Japan: Essays in Institutional History*. New Haven, Conn.: Yale University Press, 1974.

Yamada An'ei 山田安栄. *Fukuteki hen* 伏敵編. 2 vols. Tokyo: Yoshikawa kōbunkan 吉川弘文館, 1891.

Yamagata-ken 山形県, ed. *Yamagata-ken shi (Shiryō-hen)* 山形県史 (資料編). Tokyo: Gannando 巌南堂, 1961.

Yamaguchi Osamu 山口修. *Mōko shūrai* 蒙古襲来. Tokyo: Tōgensha 桃源社, 1964, 1979.

Yashiro Kuniharu 八代国治, ed. *Kokushi sōsetsu* 国史叢説. Tokyo: Yoshikawa kōbunkan 吉川弘文館, 1925.

Yasuda Motohisa 安田元久. *Nihon zenshi* 日本全史 (*chūsei* 1). Tokyo: Tōkyō daigaku shuppankai 東京大学出版会, 1958.

Yasuda Motohisa 安田元久. *Shugo to jitō* 守護と地頭. Tokyo: Shibundō 至文堂, 1964.

Yasuda Motohisa 安田元久. "Gokenin-sei seiritsu ni kansuru ichi shiron" 御家人制成立に関する一試論. *Gakushūin daigaku bungakubu kenkyū nempō* 学習院大学文学部研究年報 16 (1969): 81–110.

Yoshida Tōgo 吉田東伍. *Tokugawa seikyō kō* 徳川政教考. 2 vols. Tokyo: Fuzambō 冨山房, 1894.

Yoshizumi Mieko 善積美恵子. "Tetsudai bushin ichiran-hyō" 手伝普請一覧表. In *Gakushūin daigaku bungaku-bu kenkyū nempō* 学習院大学文学部研究年報 15 (1968): 87–119.

GLOSSARY-INDEX

Minamoto Yukiie 源行家 (?–1186), 9–10
Minatogawa, battle of 湊川の戦 (1336), xii
mines, 194
Mito domain 水戸藩, 214, 240
miuchibito 御内人 (private vassals of *tokusō*), 68–9, 71
Miura family 三浦氏, 5, 42–3
Miyoshi Yasuari 三好康有, 60
Mizuno Katsusada 水野勝貞, daimyo, 251
Mizuno Tadakuni 水野忠邦, senior councillor, and Tempō Reforms, 228–9
Mizuno Tadatoki 水野忠辰, 248
Mogami Yoshitoshi 最上義俊, daimyo, 215
monchūjo 問注所 (Board of Inquiry), 29, 31
monetary system: coinage, 179, 194–5, 197
Mongol invasions, x, 21, 43; initial Yüan overtures, 47–51; bakufu response to Yüan overtures, 53–4; invasion of 1274 and aftermath, 54–60; invasion of 1281 and aftermath, 61–6; and *kamikaze*, 55–6; land rewards following, 57, 65
Mōri house 毛利家, 172, 210
Morinaga 護良, Prince (1308–35), 89–90
Mōri Terumoto 毛利輝元, daimyo, 161, 163
Munetaka 宗尊, Prince (1242–74), 43
mura 村, *see* villages
Muromachi bakufu 室町幕府, 148; founding of, 99–105; administration organs, 127–35; attempt to control *shugo*, 116–17, 123–4; authority of, 92, 109; changes in structure, 129–30; control of provinces, 117–125; distribution of power, 117–128; economic foundation, 135–41; effectiveness of rule, 91; establish office of *kanrei*, 123; and *kanrei-yoriai* system, 125; landholdings of, 135–8; legitimization of military rule, 105–10; narrowed scope of control, 132–3; power of appointment and income, 140; and provincial administration, 109–17; and Sengoku period, 141–6; system of justice, 131–2; taxation, 138–41
Mutō (shōni) Sukeyoshi 武藤 (少弐) 資能 (1198–1281), 48
myōgakin 冥加金 (merchant license fee), 232

Nabeshima Naoshige 鍋島直茂, daimyo, 172
Nagaoka domain 長岡藩, 208, 223, 237, 244
Nagasaki 長崎, 171, 179, 196, 217, 223–4
Nagasaki Takatsuna (Enki) 長崎高綱 (円喜), 86
Nagasaki Takasuke 長崎高資, 86
Nagoe Mitsutoki 名越光時, 42
Nagoya (Owari) domain 名古屋 (尾張) 藩, 178
naidaijin 内大臣 (interior minister), 164
Nakatsu domain 中津藩, 211, 224–5, 249, 252
Nambokuchō disturbance 南北朝の動乱 (two rival courts, 1336–92), xi, 122–3
nanushi 名主 (village headman), *see shōya*
Nara 奈良, 172
Natsuka Masaie 長束正家 (?–1600), officer for Hideyoshi, 161
natural disasters, 195, 222–3, 237
nengu 年貢 (annual grain tax), 232
Nigatsu disturbance 二月の乱 (1272), 53–4
Nijō Castle 二条城, 165–6, 168, 178, 211
Nikkō 日光, 168, 195, 216–17
Nitta family 新田氏, 10
Nitta Yoshisada 新田義貞 (1301–38), 100, 103–4
Nitta Yoshishige 新田義重, 149
Northern and Southern Courts, rivalry between, 103, 121–2; *see also* Nambokuchō disturbance

Obama domain 小浜藩, 231
ōban 大番 (great guards), 198
ōban gashira 大番頭 (captains of the great guards), 198
ōbanyaku 大番役 (imperial guard service in Kyoto), 36–7
Obi domain 飫肥藩, 221
Oda Nobukatsu 織田信雄, daimyo, 155
Oda Nobunaga 織田信長 (1534–82), xiv, xv, 145–6, 154–5, 218
Odawara domain 小田原藩, 222; *see also* Hōjō of Odawara
Ōgaki domain 大垣藩, 238
Ōgimachi 正親町, Emperor (1517–93), 145–6
ōgosho 大御所 (retired shogun), 164
Ogyū Sorai 荻生徂徠, scholar, 205–6, 220, 228
Oka domain 岡藩, 243, 252
Okayama domain 岡山藩, 242
Okazaki castle 岡崎城, 152–3
Okehazama, battle of 桶狭間の戦, 153